DIAGRAPHICS

DIAGRAPHICS

Macarena San Martín

An Imprint of HarperCollinsPublishers

DIAGRAPHICS
Copyright © 2011 by Harper Design and **maomao** publications

All rights reserved. No part of this book may be used or reproduced in any manner whatsoever, without written permission except in the case of brief quotations embodied in critical articles and reviews. For information, address Harper Design, 10 East 53rd Street, New York, NY 10022.

HarperCollins books may be purchased for educational, business, or sales promotional use. For information, please write: Special Markets Department, HarperCollins*Publishers*, 10 East 53rd Street, New York, NY 10022.

First Edition:
Published by **maomao** publications in 2011
Via Laietana, 32 4th fl., of. 104
08003 Barcelona, Spain
Tel.: +34 93 268 80 88
Fax: +34 93 317 42 08
www.maomaopublications.com

maomao affirms that it possesses all the necessary rights for the publication of this material and has duly paid all royalties related to the authors' and photographers' rights. **maomao** also affirms that it has violated no property rights and has respected common law, all authors' rights and all other rights that could be relevant. Finally, **maomao** affirms that this book contains no obscene nor slanderous material.

English language edition first published in 2011 by:
Harper Design
An Imprint of HarperCollins*Publishers*,
10 East 53rd Street
New York, NY 10022
Tel.: (212) 207-7000
Fax: (212) 207-7654
harperdesign@harpercollins.com
www.harpercollins.com

Distributed throughout the world by:
HarperCollins*Publishers*
10 East 53rd Street
New York, NY 10022
Fax: (212) 207-7654

Publisher: Paco Asensio

Editorial Coordination: Anja Llorella Oriol

Editor & Texts: Macarena San Martín

Translation: Cillero & de Motta

Art Direction: Emma Termes Parera

Layout: Maira Purman

Cover Design: Maira Purman

ISBN: 978-0-06-197014-6

Library of Congress Control Number: 2010943089

Printed in Spain: Gráficas Calima, S.A.

First Printing, 2011

Introduction		6
Maps		8
Sketches and Diagrams		82
Graphs		144
Index		254

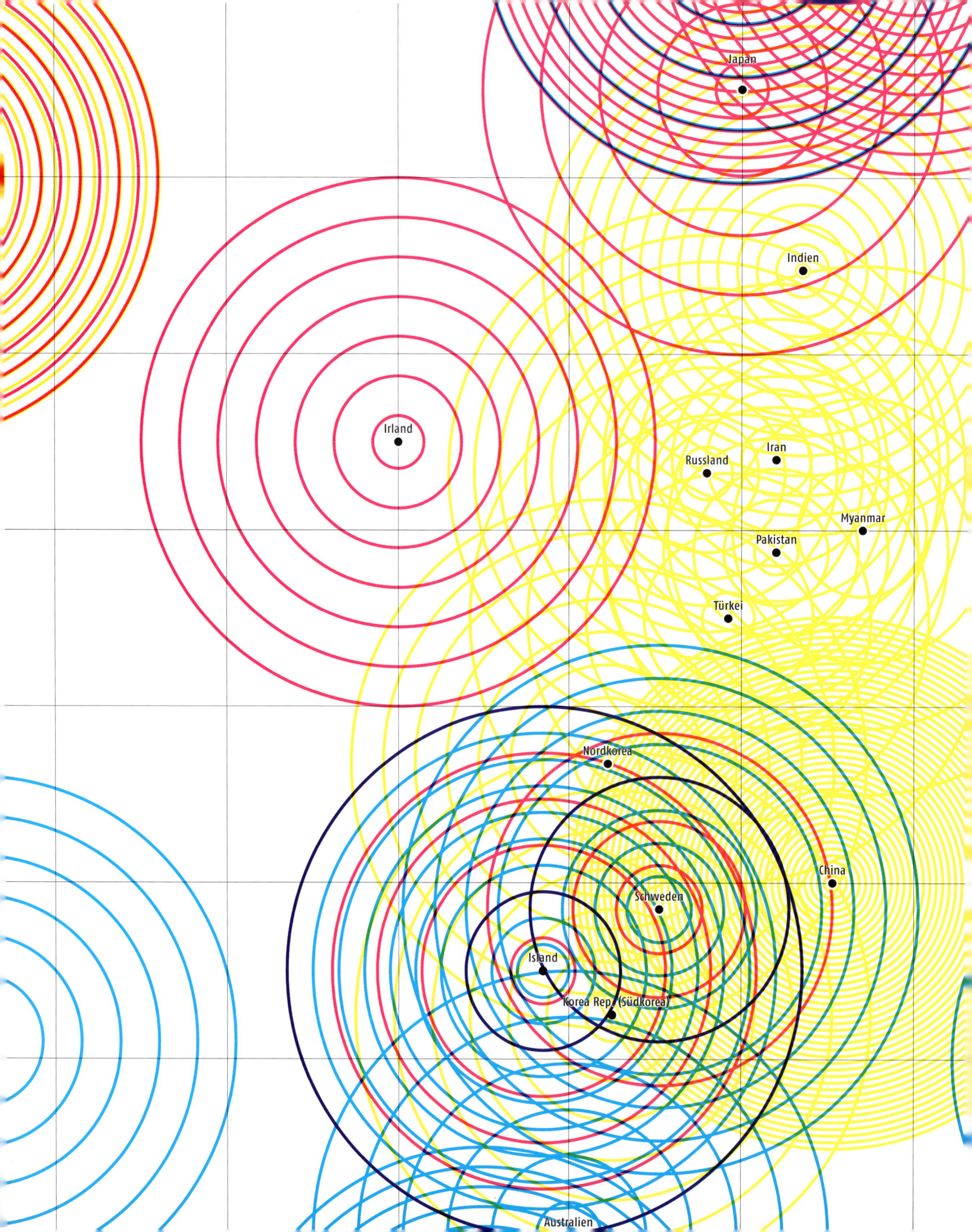

Introduction

They say a picture is worth a thousand words. A picture's power of communication is incredible: It crosses social borders and breaks language and cultural barriers. A picture has the added benefit of being much more pleasing to the eye than does a jumble of words. One of the clearest examples of this is the world map. A verbal description of the earth's countries, islands, poles, and seas would create a book similar in size to the Bible and by no means would it be as efficient as a map. This is why, in many cases, when certain information has to be transmitted, we opt for a visual representation with the aid of different resources, such as computer graphics, graphs, pictographs, and symbols.

Information design is a branch of design that focuses on clear, simple, and direct communication, optimizing all available resources. In order to be successful, it is fundamental that the designer is capable of summarizing and prioritizing the information and arranging it in a way that is aesthetically pleasing.

As information can come from any field, each situation is different; therefore so are the qualities and characteristics to be communicated, which is why there are many existing types of visual representation. *Diagraphics*, therefore, has been sorted into three groups: maps, sketches and diagrams, and graphs.

A map is a two-dimensional representation of an area made to scale, making it possible to measure distances and surface area with a certain level of accuracy. These characteristics mark the level of originality of the design. However, elements such as color as well as the volume of the image or the collage can make the difference between your run-of-the-mill school map and a designer one.

Sketches and diagrams are commonly used to present certain information where visual language is the priority and the use of words is minimized. In these instances, arrows, lines, and outlines can effectively communicate a project's message in a way that words simply can't. Sketches and diagrams transcend language barriers, making them accessible to audiences all around the world.

Given that numerical values are generally involved in graphs, whether percentages or quantities, they have acquired a mathematical connotation, even though they are not used exclusively in this area. The most common graphs are line charts, pie charts, and bar graphs, and thanks to them, it is easy to visualize, for example, the behavior between two or more variables, where they meet or the way in which opinions are divided on certain topics.

Welcome to the impressive world of information design where even a tedious financial report can be transformed into an attractive design piece.

map
n (from the Latin *mappa*, napkin, perhaps of Punic origin) **1** A representation, usually on a flat surface, of a region of the earth or heavens. **2** Something that represents with a clarity suggestive of a map.

Êtres indésirables ::
Atelier Aquarium :: www.atelieraquarium.com ::

Taking the genocides that occurred last century as a starting point, Atelier Aquarium's Simon Renaud created a story in which fictitious characters tackled imaginary situations. Since the places and deeds surrounding them really do exist, the infographics illustrating the story were executed with precision and were based on authentic historical data. The story was set down in a book printed in three colors, size 6.3 inch × 8.3 inch.

camps d'Auschwitz
1941 › 1944

Auschwitz II Birkenau
1943

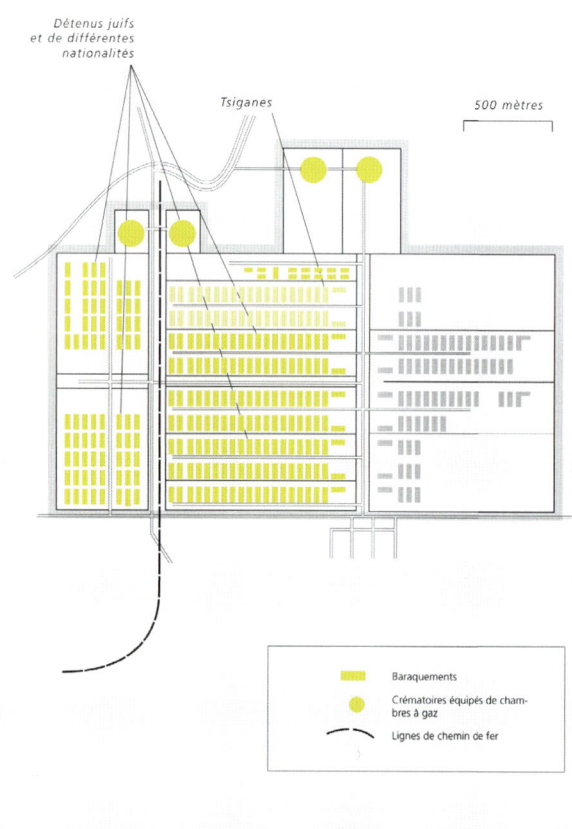

© Simon Renaud, Jérémie Nuel/Atelier Aquarium

génocides reconnus par l'ONU
1948 › 1994

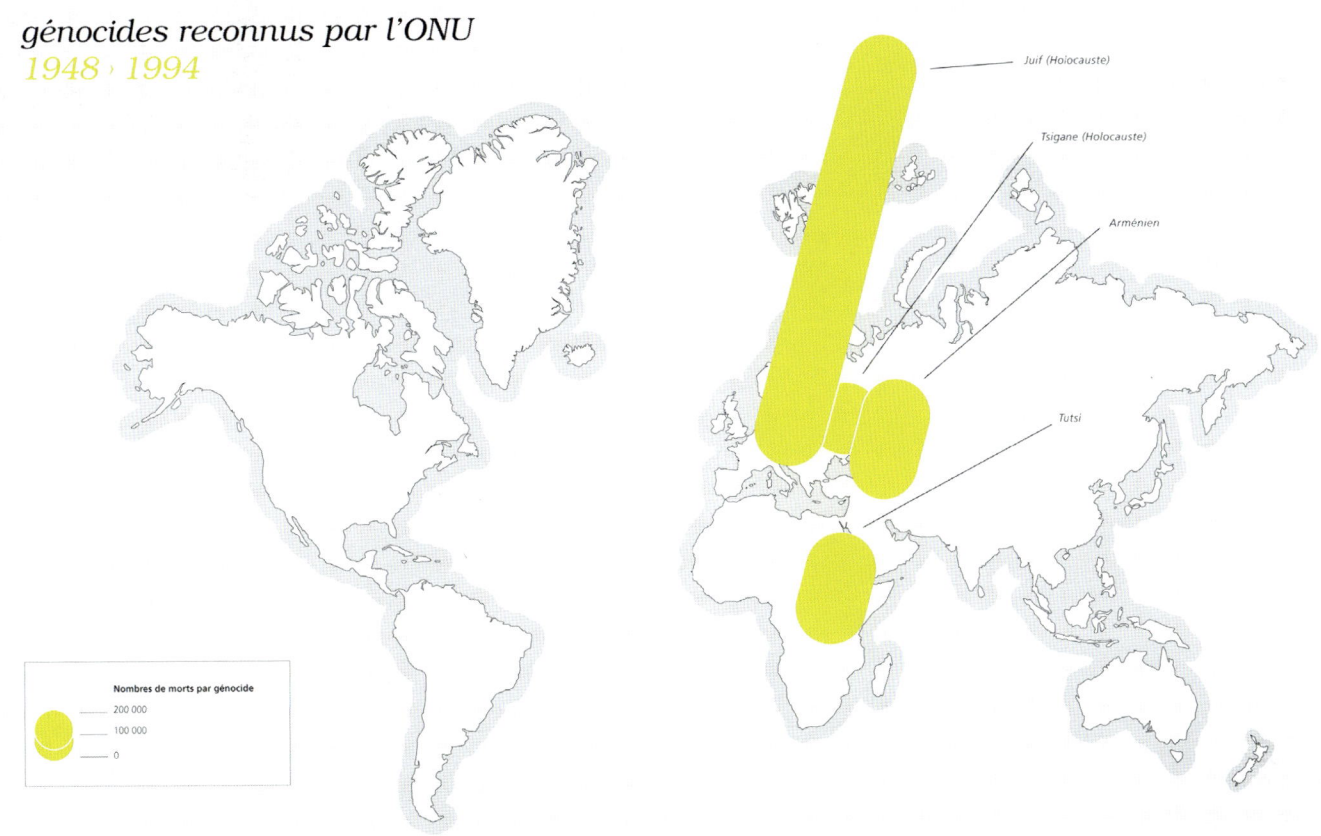

flux de déportation vers les principaux camps
1915 › 1916

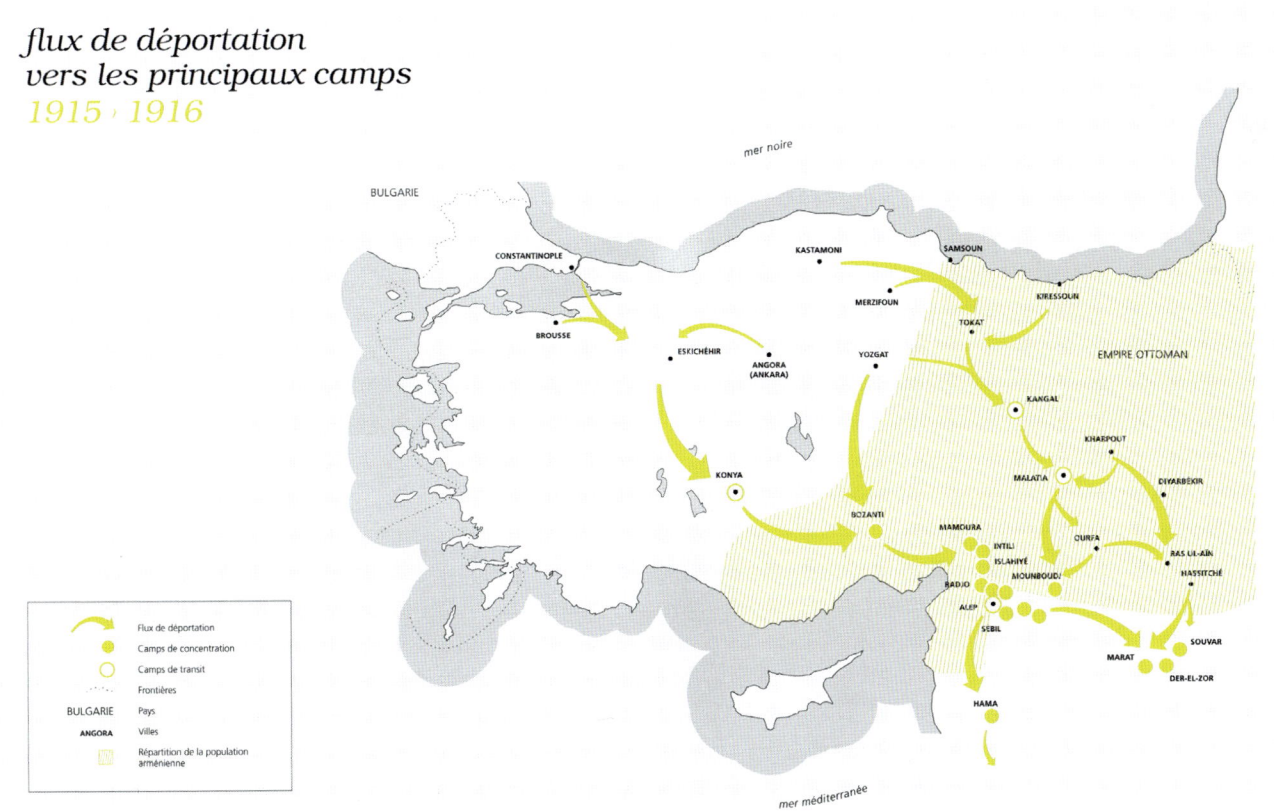

Maps II

Newer Orleans ::
Dirkje Bakker, Nelleke Wegdam/No Office :: www.no-office.nl ::

One of the many events organized after Hurricane Katrina was that of Newer Orleans in Rotterdam, in which a selection of renowned international architects presented their own individual view on the aftermath. For the brochure, this map was designed showing the paths of the hurricanes that have crossed the United States in the past hundred years, while at the same time conveying the idea of the chaos and devastation caused in New Orleans during and after the passage of Katrina.

Infact ::
Lava Amsterdam :: www.lava.nl ::

Political maps are those that show how the territory of different countries is politically divided. Infact takes this concept to the extreme and completely separates the countries of Asia. Each country is assigned a height value based on its first AIDS case/outbreak. The goal of the campaign was to "heighten" people's awareness of this disease on the continent.

Am Puls der Stadt ::
Lichtwitz – Büro für visuelle Kommunikation :: www.lichtwitz.com ::

Lichtwitz, a Viennese design studio, developed and designed the catalog and show graphics for the 2008 exhibition "Am Puls der Stadt" (Pulse of the City), which analyzed two thousand years of the Karlsplatz. The design firm created a series of maps and diagrams illustrating the events that occurred in each place on the square at various times throughout its history.

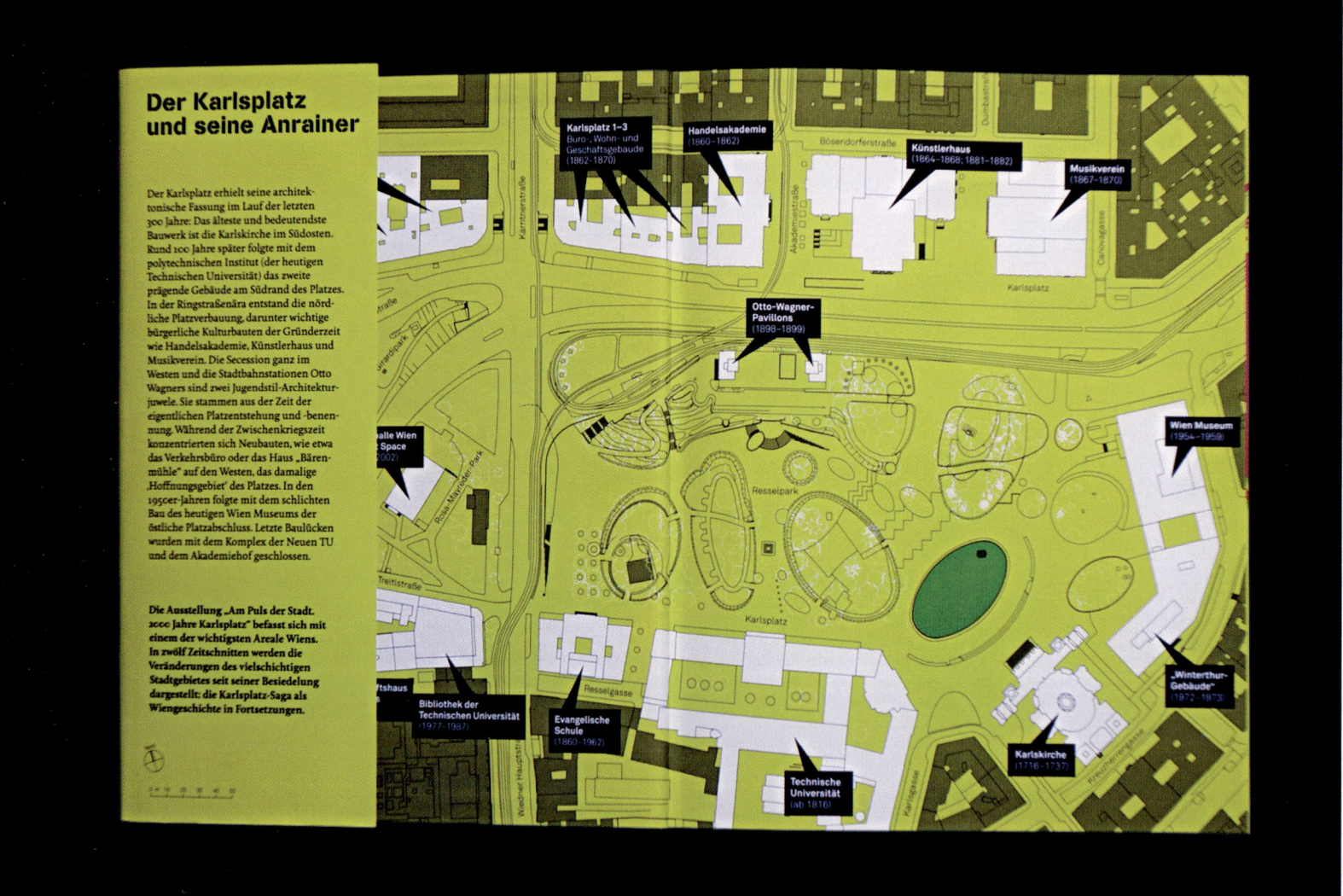

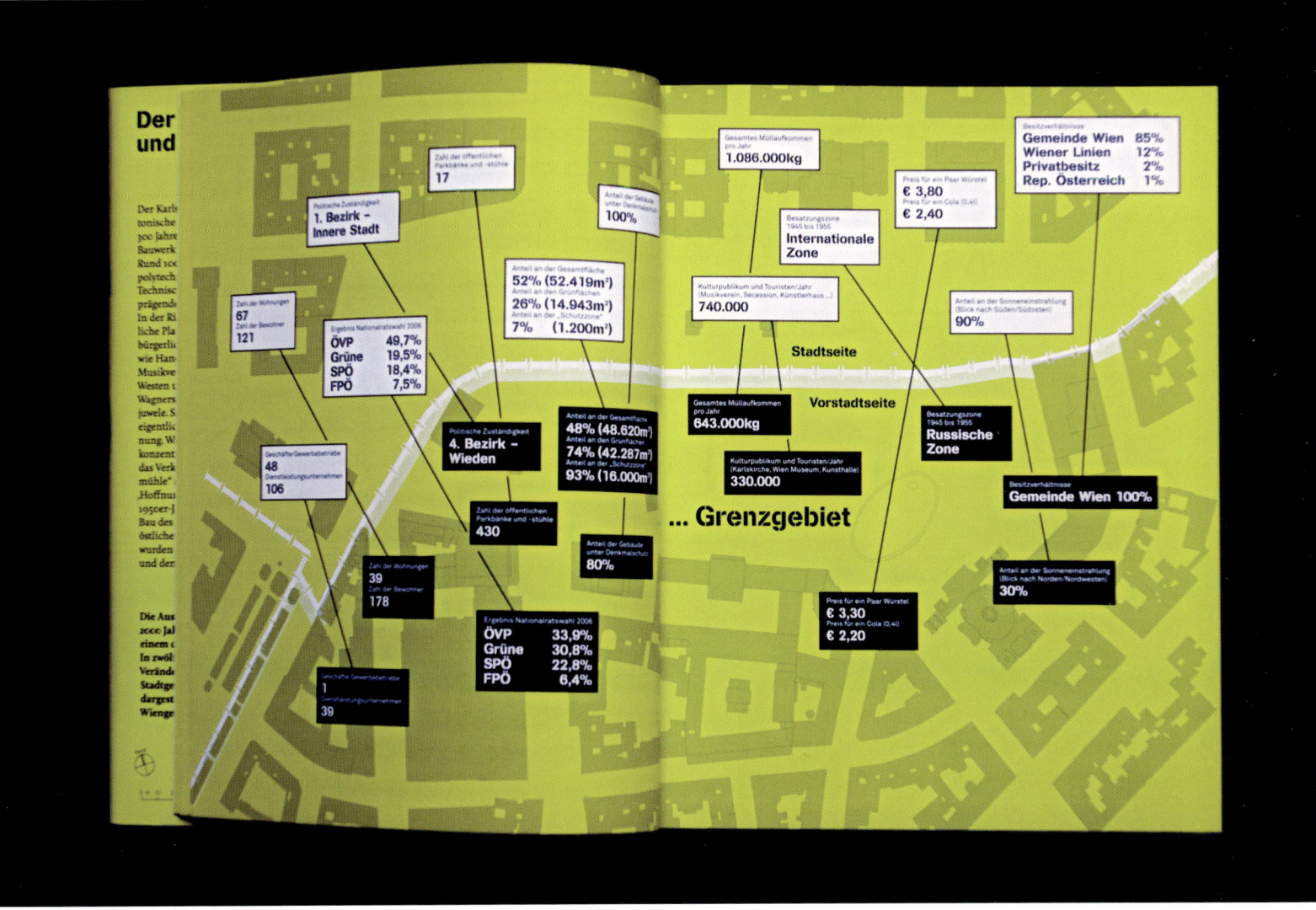

Maps 15

2003-2008 Kunsthaus Graz Annual Report ::
Lichtwitz – Büro für visuelle Kommunikation :: www.lichtwitz.com ::

This map plays with both full and empty spaces: the shapes, i.e. the continents that form the map, are white while the background has been filled in with color. The museum's information is shown in black, and is easier to read due to the contrast in colors. As an additional element, the designers incorporated the circle into the overall design.

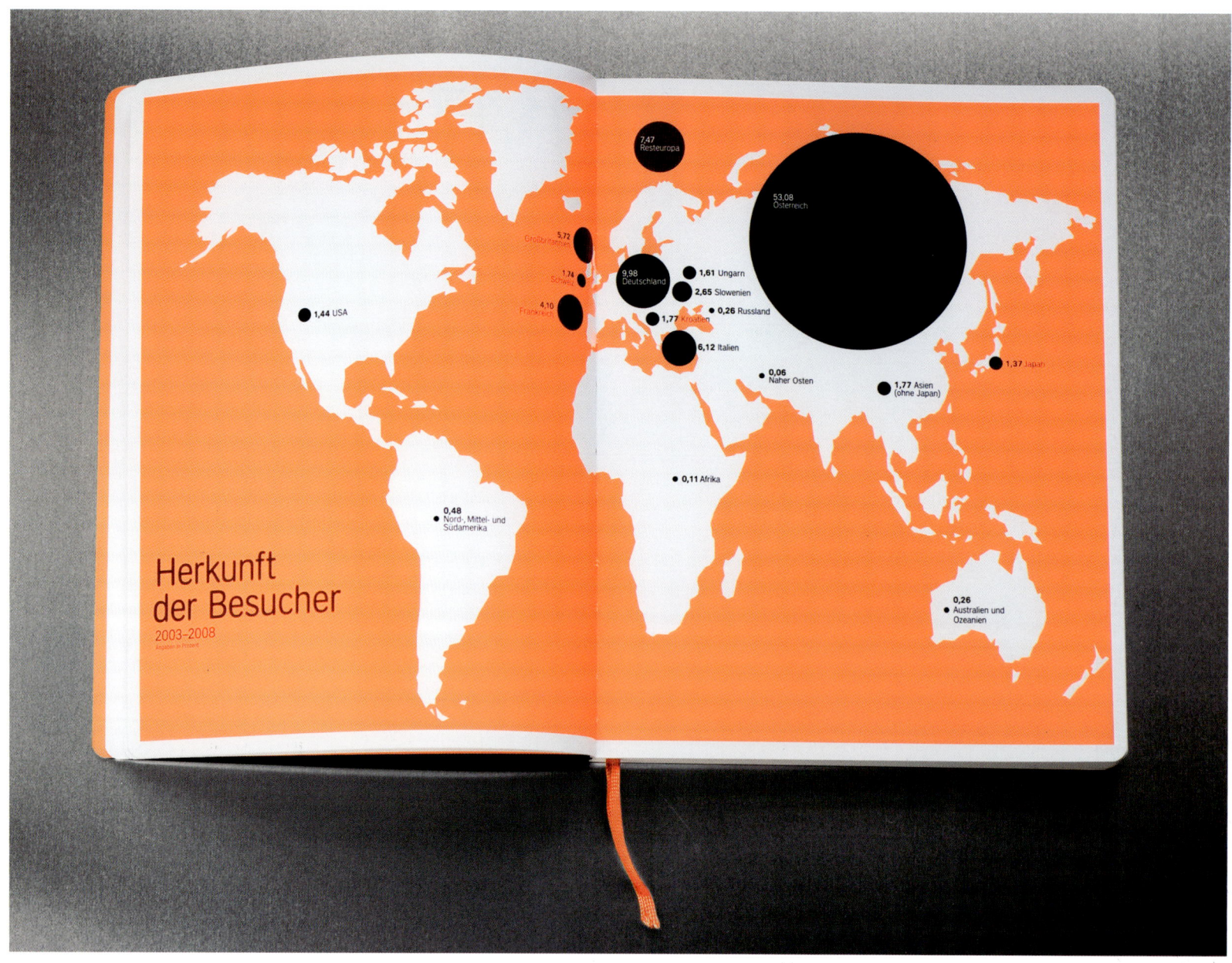

16 Maps

Maps | 7

Weltkarte ::
Apfel Zet :: www.apfelzet.de ::

Professor Reinhard Bittner is a renowned German surgeon. Apart from countless operations, he has also given more than five hundred scientific conferences both at home and abroad. This map shows some of the locations of these seminars. The most popular places—Europe and Germany in particular—have been enlarged to make the map easier to read.

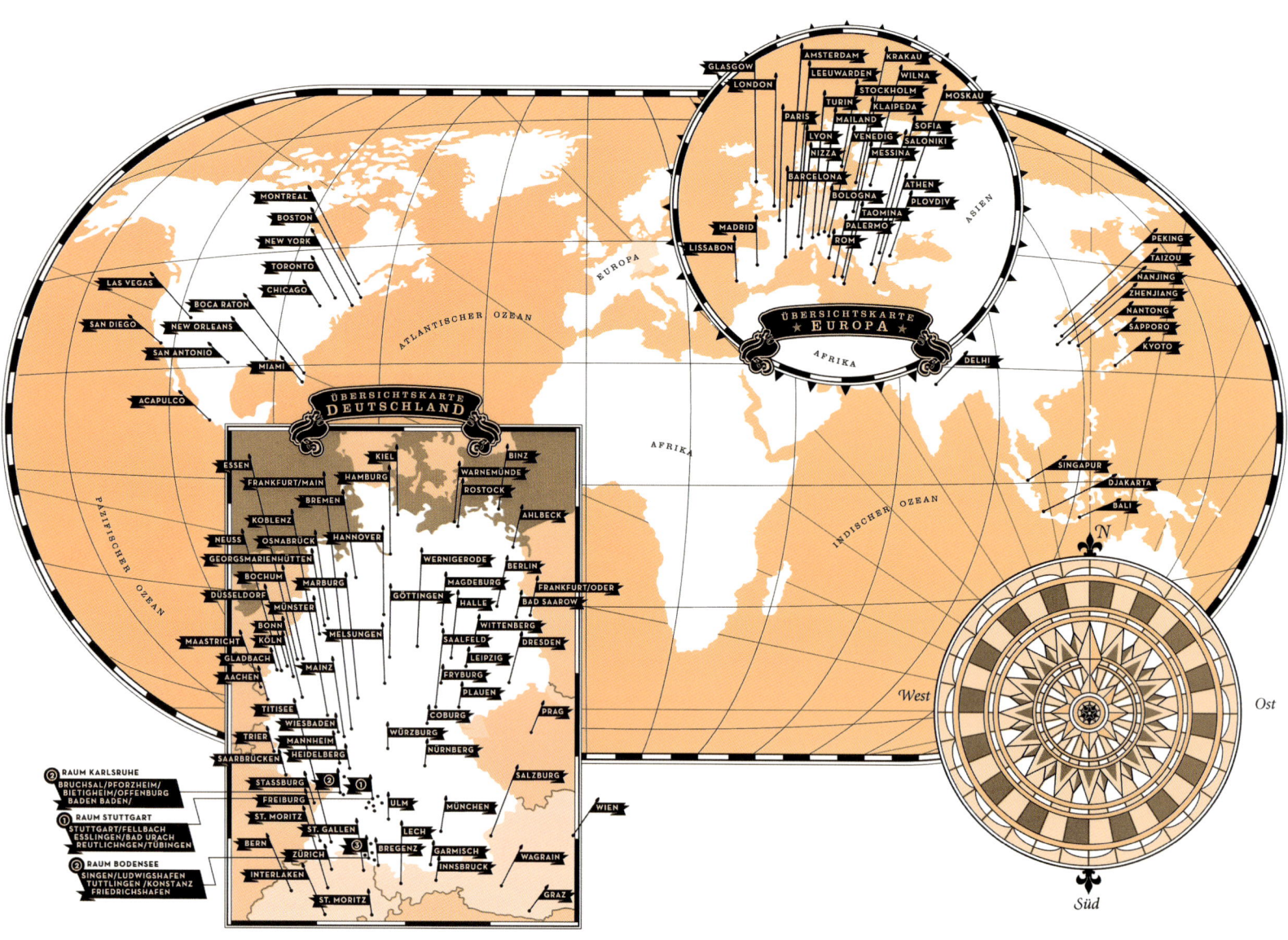

women'secret franchise book ::
Cla-se :: www.cla-se.com ::

This map forms part of the corporate book for women'secret, a brand of female underwear. The map reveals the brand's presence throughout the world at that time (through shops and franchises) and the company's plans for future growth and development. Information is differentiated from one another through the use of different colors. The map itself is gray, which allows the color to really pop and be understood quickly and easily.

Stores around the world
More than **300** stores around the world.
More than **200** corporate stores in Europe.
90 franchises, in **20** countries (with more to come...)

Projected international expansion
By the end of **2005** women'secret will have **132** franchise stores in **28** countries.
Every year **50** new stores open and **3** new countries are incorporated.
By **2010** there will be over **380** stores in **43** countries.

→ corporate stores
→ franchises
→ expansion 2005
→ future expansion

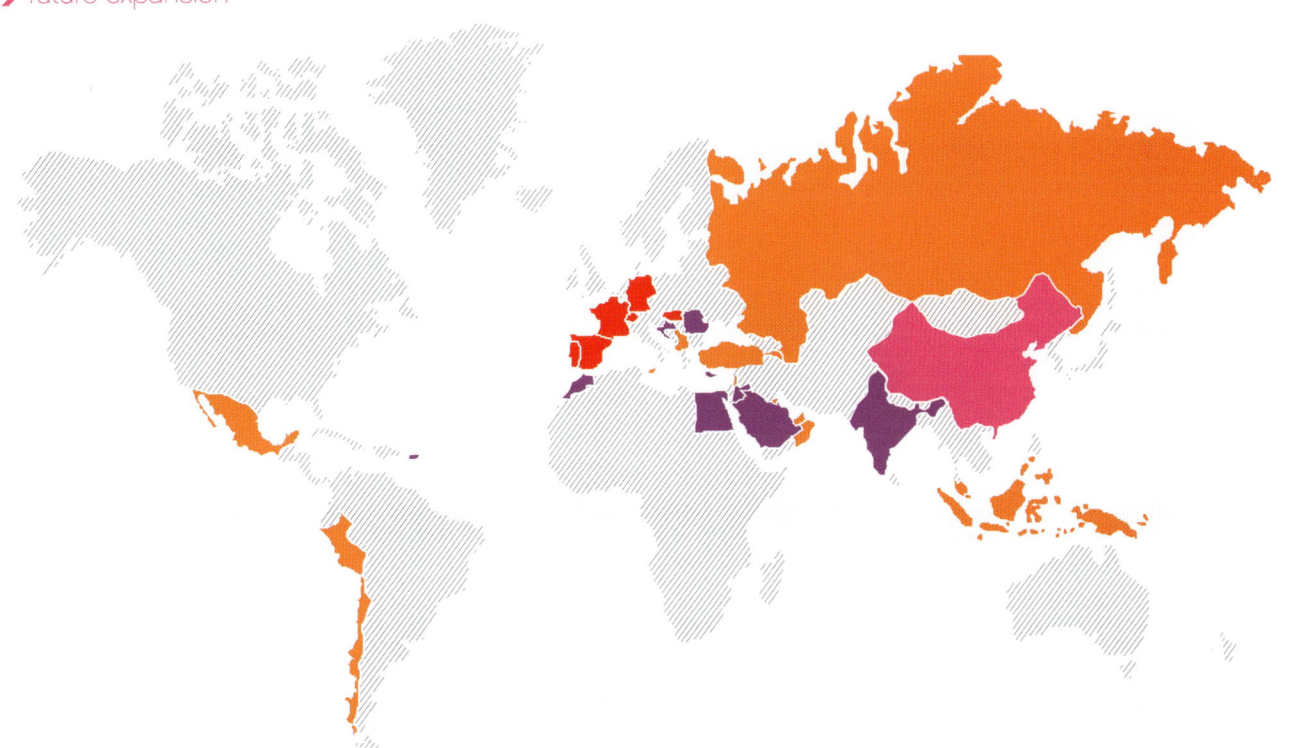

The Human's Development ::
We Ain't Plastic :: www.weaintplastic.com ::

In the twenty-first century, countries need strong human development to participate in world progress. Nevertheless, nearly 12 percent of the world's countries have inadequate education as well as poor health and living standards. This interactive map enables users to identify which developing countries are currently in need of the most aid.

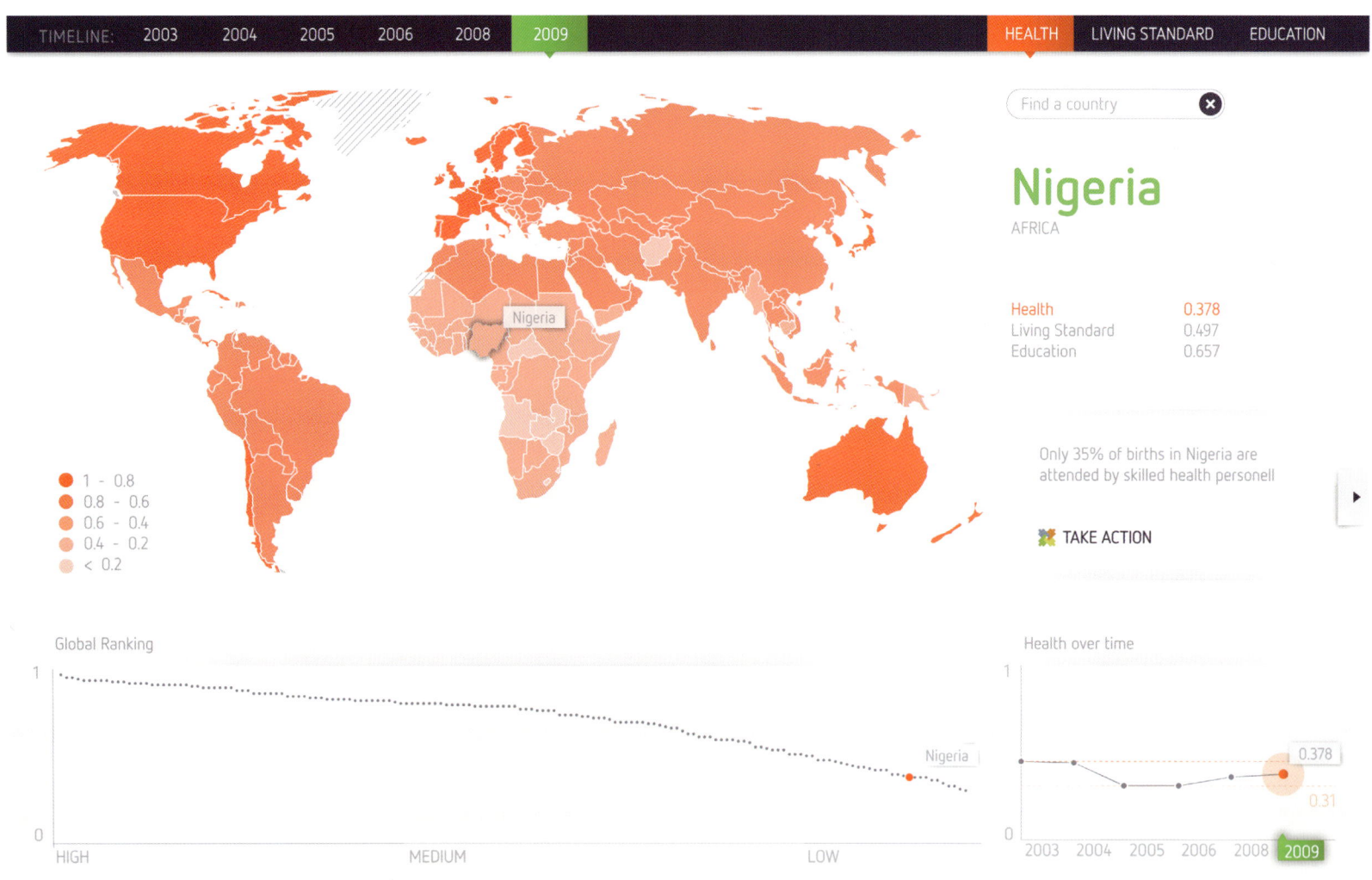

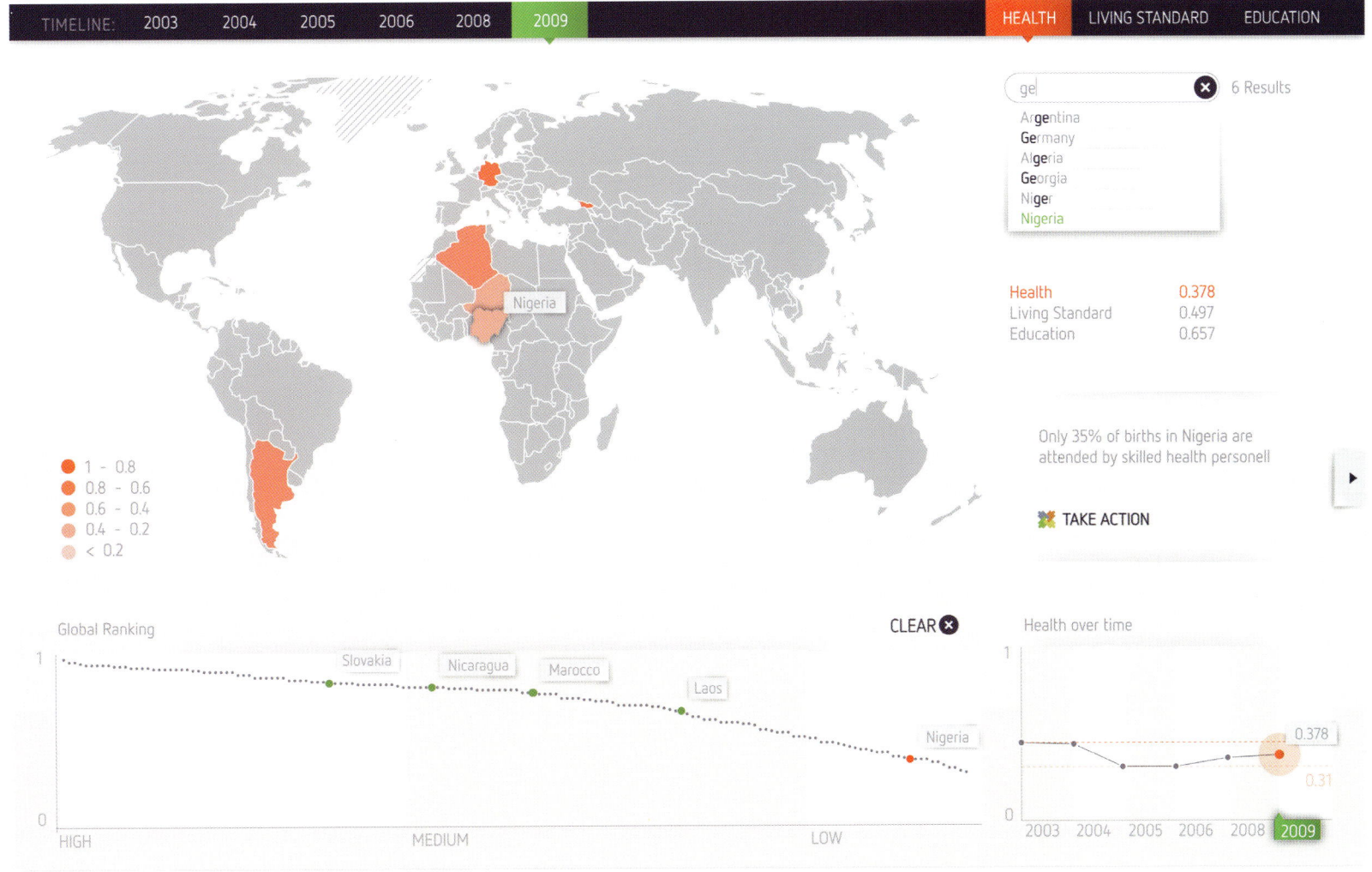

Maps 21

Northern Experiments – The Barents Urban Survey 2009 ::
Tanja Bergquist, Espen Røyseland, Øystein Rø, Ariane Spanier :: www.arianespanier.com ::

These pages form part of a book that focuses on the debate concerning the urban phenomena of key cities located near the Barents Sea (those cities in the north of Norway, Sweden, Finland, and northwestern Russia). The maps—which illustrate the chapter Survey Index—offer information on the location, area, population, and industry of the cities selected.

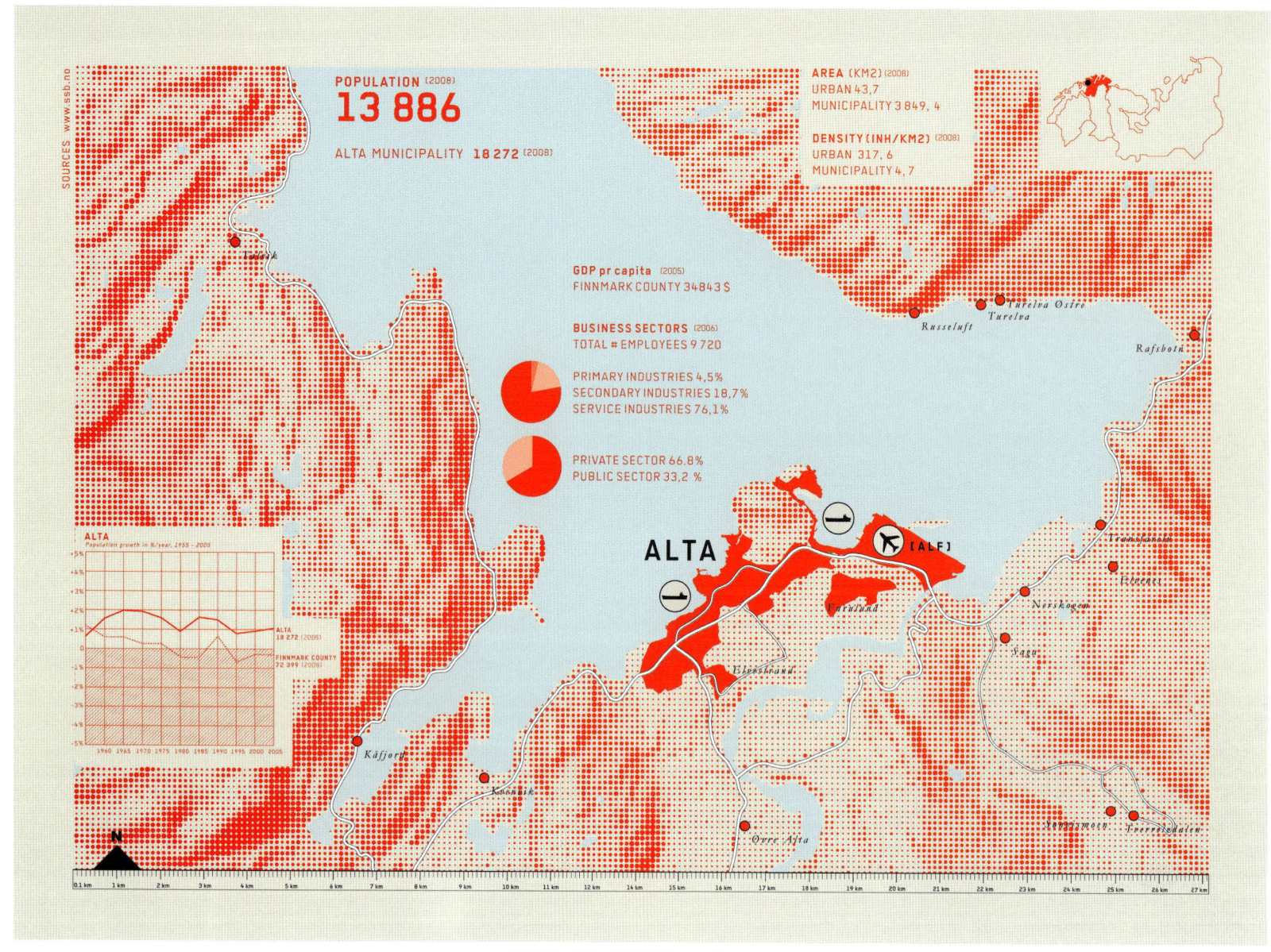

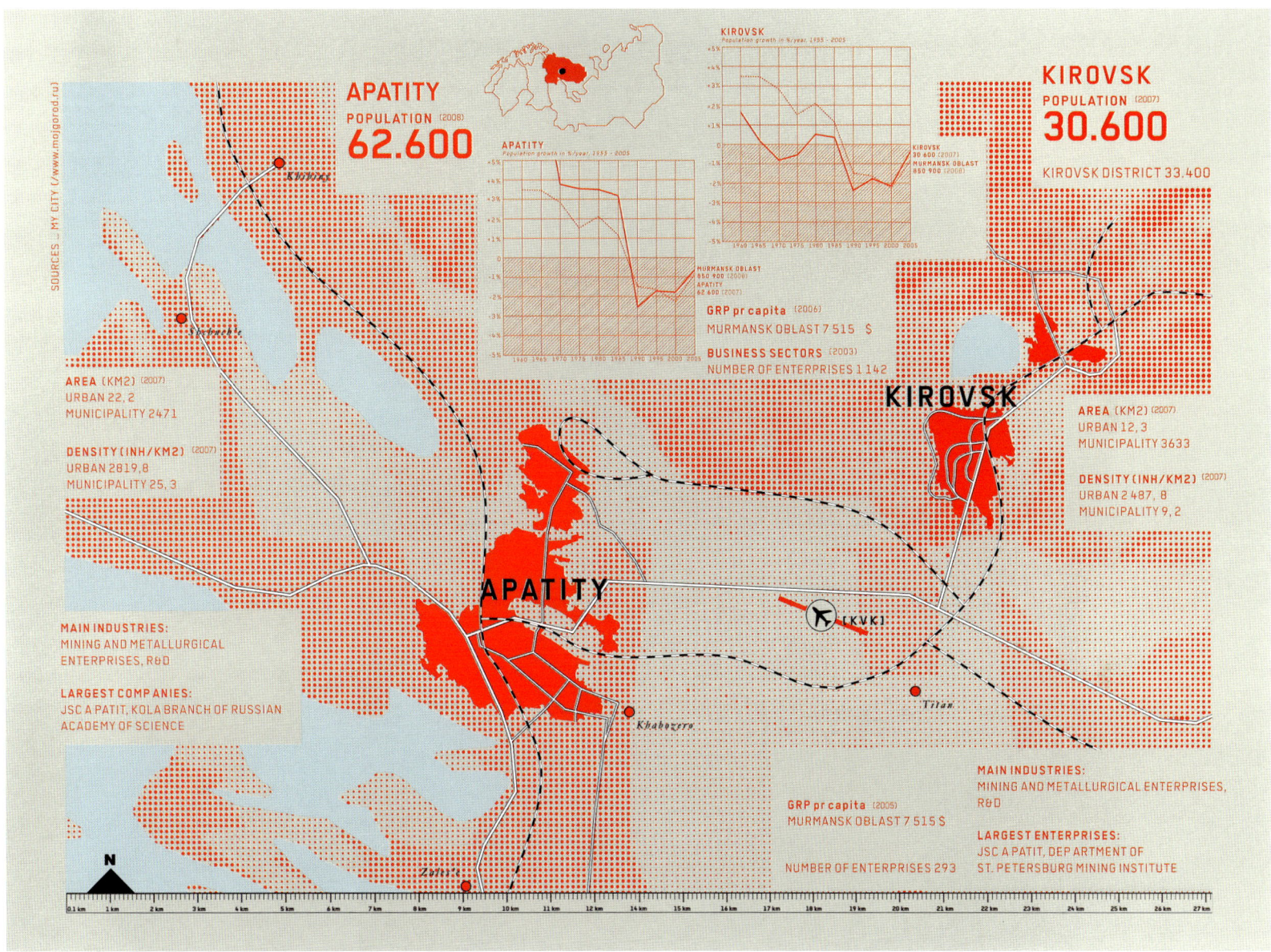

Subjective Atlas of Serbia ::
Annelys de Vet :: www.subjectiveatlasofserbia.info ::

"I do not know what personal is, what I am, who I am, what Serbia is. All the boundaries are constantly changing; everything changes from one day to another. Nationality, identity… I don't know, I don't know what that is." This statement was uttered by one of the more than thirty artists that have breathed life into this atlas, turning it into a tool to help users understand the society of modern-day Serbia.

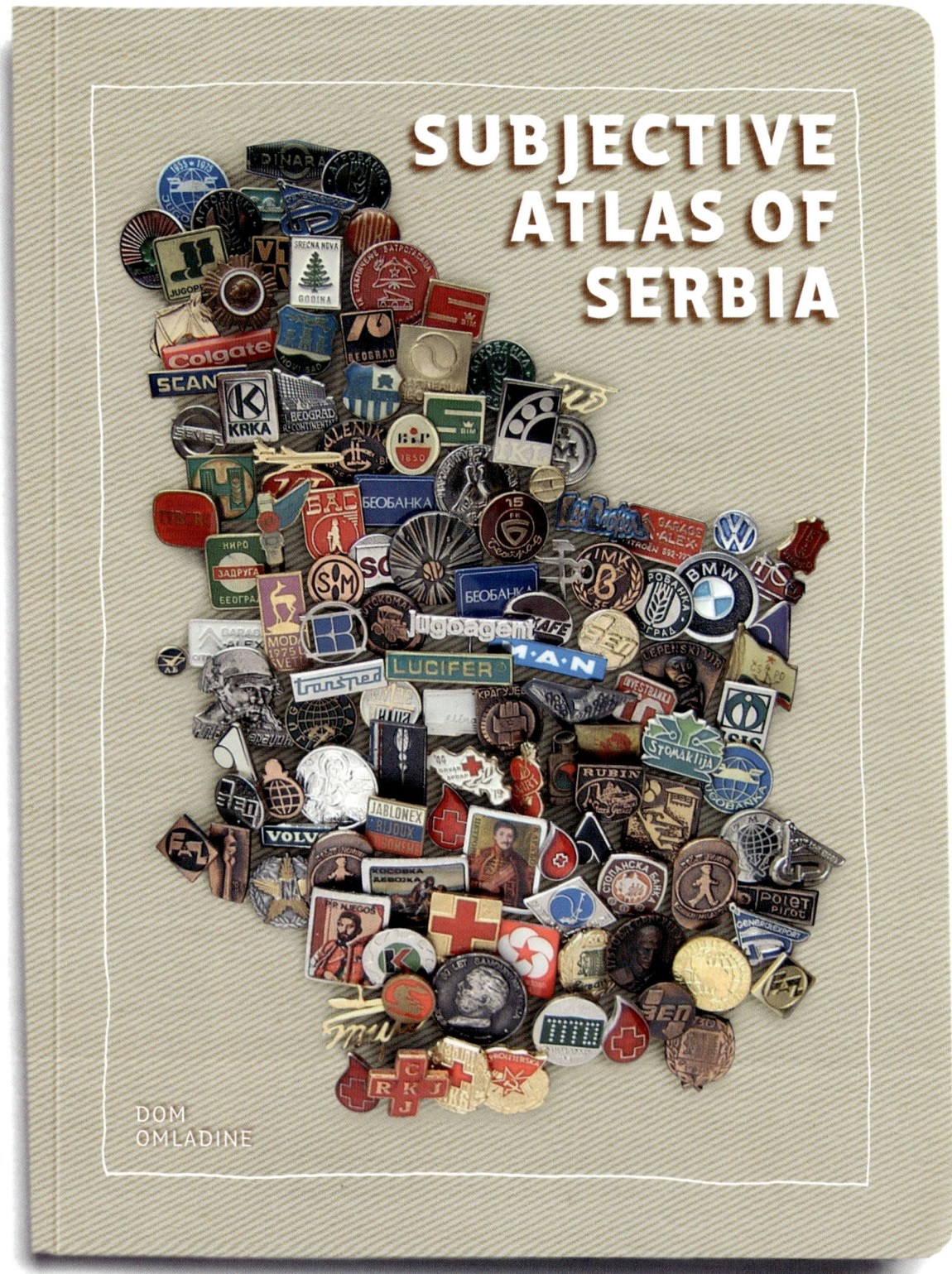

El mapa de Serbia es representado con distintos elementos y materiales, en función de lo que cada artista consideró que mejor definía a su país.

Maps 25

Gezondgids ::
Lava Amsterdam :: www.lava.nl ::

This original map was created to illustrate a report published in the magazine *Gezondgids* on the origin of fruit imported into Holland. So as not to fall into the trap of offering up an all too obvious illustration, the team from Lava Amsterdam looked for another resource that was related to the theme and decided to use a watermelon as the world, carving the map of Europe on its outer skin, which produced just the right effect.

5

FRUIT

Appels en peren vergeleken

Een appel uit de Betuwe is milieuvriendelijker dan zijn Nieuw-Zeelandse neefje. Maar bij de duurzaamheid van fruit speelt meer: hoe zit het bijvoorbeeld met de bestrijdingsmiddelen?

Het is altijd wel ergens ter wereld het seizoen voor een bepaald soort fruit, of we bootsen het seizoen na in een verwarmde kas. Het milieu betaalt een prijs voor dat ruime fruitaanbod. Zo is de teelt in kassen energieslurpend. Aardbeien telen in een kas kost 5 tot 6 keer zo veel energie als op de volle grond. Daar staat tegenover dat die Hollandse kasaardbeien wat minder bestrijdingsmiddelen bevatten dan hun zusjes uit andere Europese landen, en aanzienlijk minder dan aardbeien van buiten Europa.

Het invliegen van fruit kost veel energie. Naast aardbeien zijn het vooral de andere luxe fruitsoorten die per vliegtuig arriveren, zoals bessen, papaja's, lychees en ananas. Ze zijn te bederfelijk voor vervoer per schip. Minder kwetsbaar fruit, zoals bananen en kiwi's, komt meestal wel per schip en dat scheelt in brandstof. Maar een Hollandse appel die per vrachtwagen uit de Betuwe komt, doet het op dit punt nog beter. Het is dus maar goed dat het meestgegeten fruit in Nederland tevens het meestgeteelde is: appels.

Bestrijdingsmiddelen
Fruit kan aangetast worden door schimmels, schurft en insecten en daarom maakt de gangbare fruitteelt gebruik van bestrijdingsmiddelen (zie ook hoofdstuk 4). De biologische fruitteelt vormt de bekende uitzondering: chemische bestrijdingsmiddelen zijn daar uit den boze. Er wordt gebruikgemaakt van rassen die minder gevoelig zijn voor ziekten en plagen en bij de bestrijding worden natuurlijke vijanden als sluipwespen en lieveheersbeestjes ingezet. De groei van onkruid wordt in boomgaarden tegengegaan door het zaaien van witte klaver en gras. Overigens zijn natuurlijke bestrijdingsmiddelen, zoals kalkzwavel tegen schurft, wel toegestaan. Het marktaandeel van biologisch fruit is met 1,7% nog minimaal. Een tussenvorm is fruit geteeld volgens de normen van Milieukeur, waarbij minder kunstmest en chemische bestrijdingsmiddelen worden gebruikt. Er zijn appels, peren en aardbeien met Milieukeur verkrijgbaar.

De kans op resten bestrijdingsmiddelen is het kleinst bij fruit uit Nederland. Bij fruit uit het buitenland worden de wettelijke normen vaker overschreden, zo blijkt uit controles door de Voedsel en Waren Autoriteit (VWA). De recentste gegevens van VWA betreffen controles in 2007. Bij aardbeien geldt: hoe verder weg, des te meer bestrijdingsmiddelen. Ruim 18% van de doosjes aardbeien van buiten Europa bevatte in 2007 te veel bestrijdingsmiddelen. Bij Europese aardbeien ging het om ruim 3% en bij de Hollandse aardbeien om nog geen 2%. De Hollandse appels scoorden nog beter: in 2007 werd geen enkele overschrijding gevonden. Bij appels uit het buitenland – zowel uit Europa als daarbuiten – was bij 9 à 10% sprake van te veel resten van bestrijdingsmiddelen. Bananen en peren zijn 'schone' fruitsoorten, met geen enkele overschrijding in 2007. →

Energievriendelijk fruit
Zijn Spaanse nectarines een milieuvriendelijker keus dan Italiaanse? De Groente- en Fruitkalender van Milieu Centraal (milieucentraal.nl) geeft antwoord. Op de meloenwereldbol staan voor allerlei verse fruitsoorten de beste keuzes: de landen waaruit je het fruit het best kunt kiezen met het oog op het milieu.

NEDERLAND
Appels
Bramen
Peren
Pruimen

BELGIË
Appels
Peren

FRANKRIJK
Abrikozen
Appels
Pruimen

SPANJE
Grapefruits
Mandarijnen
Sinaasappels

ITALIË
Kiwi's
Nectarines

MAROKKO
Mandarijnen
Sinaasappels

SENEGAL
Mango's

ZUID-AFRIKA
Pruimen

Deloitte NewsMap ::
The Partners :: www.thepartners.co.uk ::

For the Deloitte world meeting in 2008, the company wanted a presentation that, besides connecting with and involving their audience, would reflect the concept of being one step ahead of the competition. To communicate this idea, The Partners developed an interactive touch screen using cutting-edge software that gathered financial information from thousands of sources in headlines. This information was then written on the map, whose circles expanded when touched.

391 **375** **173** **27** **1** **7** **6** **69**

Fortress Europe ::
LUST :: www.lust.nl ::

These maps show the number of people that flee to Europe each year in search of a better future and, instead, end up dying in refugee centers. The living conditions they have to face in such places, which are similar to prisons, are so harsh that cause of death ranges from fatal hunger strikes to suicide. The information also shows the country of origin of these ill-fated individuals.

2 Chad
Arson:2

1 Chile
Suicide:1

118 China
Accident:10
Drowned:35
Force:1
Medical:2
Murdered:3
Suffocated:58
Suicide:7
Others:2

1 Columbia
Medical:1

29 Comoros
Drowned:29

14 Congo
Frozen:1
Medical:4
Stowaway:1
Suicide:6
Others:2

2 Croatia
Suicide:2

5 Cuba
Frozen:1
Stowaway:4

175 Gambia
Drowned:108
Force:2
Frozen:1
Starvation:60
Suicide:1
Others:3

10 Georgia
Drowned:2
Frozen:4
Militarisation:2
Suicide:2

66 Ghana
Accident:1
Arson:3
Drowned:49
Force:2
Frozen:3
Medical:1
Stowaway:3
Suffocated:1
Suicide:2
Others:1

131 Guinea
Drowned:3
Force:1
Frozen:2
Missing:60
Murdered:3
Starvation:60
Suicide:1
Others:2

327 India
Drowned:309
Force:1
Frozen:1
Militarisation:2
Stowaway:2
Suffocated:4
Suicide:2
Others:4
Unknown:2

166 Iran
Arson:1
Drowned:135
Force:1
Medical:2
Murdered:1
Suicide:20
Others:5
Unknown:1

358 Iraq
Accident:5
Arson:1
Drowned:273
Force:2
Frozen:10
Medical:1
Militarisation:13
Stowaway:20
Suffocated:12
Suicide:6
Others:7
Unknown:7

5 Ivory Coast
Drowned:2
Suicide:1
Others:1
Unknown:1

60 Liberia
Drowned:54
Medical:1
Stowaway:1
Suffocated:1
Others:2
Unknown:1

22 Libya
Drowned:9
Starvation:13

2 Lithuania
Suicide:1
Others:1

113 Mali
Drowned:36
Medical:15
Starvation:52
Suicide:10

31 Mauritania
Drowned:30
Force:1

10 Moldova
Accident:3
Drowned:6
Militarisation:1

11 Mongolia
Drowned:9
Force:1
Medical:1

757 Morocco
Accident:12
Arson:6
Drowned:658
Force:7
Medical:2
Militarisation:2
Missing:4
Starvation:19
Stowaway:16
Suffocated:10
Suicide:10
Others:4
Unknown:7

49 Romania
Accident:5
Arson:1
Drowned:8
Force:3
Frozen:1
Militarisation:1
Stowaway:11
Suffocated:10
Suicide:3
Others:6

12 Russia
Drowned:1
Frozen:1
Militarisation:3
Suicide:5
Others:2

16 Rwanda
Drowned:14
Medical:1
Others:1

431 Senegal
Drowned:244
Medical:5
Missing:56
Starvation:60
Stowaway:1
Suicide:1
Others:19
Unknown:45

4 Serbia
Arson:2
Suicide:1
Others:1

10 Togo
Arson:1
Drowned:1
Force:2
Missing:1
Suicide:5

79 Tunisia
Arson:11
Drowned:51
Force:1
Medical:4
Militarisation:1
Missing:1
Stowaway:1
Suffocated:2
Suicide:3
Others:1
Unknown:3

140 Turkey
Arson:4
Drowned:89
Force:2
Frozen:1
Medical:1
Militarisation:11
Missing:7
Starvation:1
Stowaway:2
Suffocated:9
Suicide:10
Others:1
Unknown:2

2 Uganda
Frozen:1
Suicide:1

13 Ukraine
Arson:3
Drowned:1
Frozen:1
Medical:1
Suicide:6
Others:1

14 Vietnam
Accident:3
Arson:3
Drowned:1
Force:3
Suicide:3
Others:1

1 Yemen
Murdered:1

4 Zimbabwe
Drowned:1
Force:1
Medical:1
Suicide:1

1 Belarus
Suicide:1

2 Benin
Stowaway:2

5 Bolivia
Accident:5

19 Bosnia and Herzegovina
Arson:2
Medical:3
Stowaway:1
Suffocated:2
Suicide:9
Others:2

5 Bulgaria
Arson:1
Drowned:1
Force:1
Frozen:1
Suicide:1

2 Burkina Faso
Suffocated:1
Suicide:1

2 Burundi
Militarisation:2

8 Cameroon
Medical:1
Stowaway:4
Suffocated:1
Others:2

5 Dominican
Arson:1
Stowaway:2
Suicide:2

16 D.R. Congo
Arson:6
Drowned:1
Force:2
Medical:1
Stowaway:1
Suicide:4
Others:1

13 Ecuador
Accident:12
Others:1

168 Egypt
Drowned:165
Medical:1
Suicide:2

100 Eritrea
Accident:1
Arson:3
Drowned:79
Starvation:9
Suicide:4
Others:2
Unknown:2

16 Ethiopia
Drowned:1
Suicide:13
Others:2

11 F.Y.R.O.M.
Accident:0
Arson:5
Drowned:3
Medical:1
Others:1
Unknown:1

2 Gabon
Medical:1
Stowaway:1

6 Jamaica
Force:1
Medical:1
Murdered:1
Suicide:3

60 Jordan
Drowned:60

1 Kazhakstan
Suicide:1

5 Kenya
Force:1
Stowaway:1
Suicide:3

132 Kurdistan
Accident:8
Arson:4
Drowned:89
Frozen:1
Medical:2
Militarisation:3
Murdered:1
Stowaway:5
Suicide:9
Others:9
Unknown:1

1 Kyrgyzstan
Suicide:1

3 Latvia
Murdered:1
Suicide:2

14 Lebanon
Accident:11
Arson:3

2 Nepal
Drowned:1
Suicide:1

1 New Zealand
Others:1

156 Nigeria
Drowned:102
Force:4
Frozen:1
Medical:18
Stowaway:6
Suffocated:6
Suicide:13
Others:6

384 Pakistan
Drowned:346
Frozen:7
Medical:2
Militarisation:18
Stowaway:1
Suffocated:2
Suicide:3
Unknown:5

180 Palestine
Arson:1
Drowned:174
Militarisation:1
Suffocated:1
Suicide:3

2 Peru
Accident:1
Suicide:1

1 Phillipines
Suicide:1

6 Poland
Arson:2
Drowned:1
Suffocated:1
Suicide:2

14 Sierra Leone
Arson:1
Drowned:10
Force:1
Starvation:1
Others:1

2 Slovakia
Force:1
Suicide:1

353 Somalia
Accident:3
Drowned:262
Force:1
Frozen:50
Militarisation:1
Murdered:4
Starvation:26
Suicide:1
Others:4
Unknown:1

381 Sri Lanka
Drowned:338
Frozen:1
Medical:4
Missing:1
Starvation:1
Stowaway:1
Suffocated:24
Suicide:11

122 Sudan
Drowned:114
Force:1
Medical:2
Suffocated:1
Suicide:1
Others:3

2 Suriname
Arson:2

58 Syria
Drowned:53
Militarisation:1
Suicide:4

3 Tanzania
Missing:1
Stowaway:1
Others:1

42 Asia
Drowned:32
Force:3
Frozen:3
Militarisation:2
Murdered:1
Stowaway:1

1072 Africa
Drowned:682
Force:2
Medical:2
Missing:119
Starvation:182
Stowaway:19
Suffocated:3
Suicide:6
Others:32
Unknown:26

86 Maghreb
Accident:1
Drowned:73
Starvation:5
Suicide:1
Others:3
Unknown:3

562 North Africa
Arson:5
Drowned:523
Frozen:2
Militarisation:5
Stowaway:6
Suffocated:8
Others:7
Unknown:6

1327 Sub-Saharan
Drowned:1041
Force:3
Frozen:1
Medical:10
Militarisation:5
Starvation:150
Stowaway:3
Suffocated:6
Others:32
Unknown:76

128 West Africa
Drowned:126
Stowaway:2

7 Yugoslavia
Arson:2
Force:1
Medical:1
Suicide:1
Unknown:2

3314 Unknown
Accident:7
Arson:9
Drowned:2263
Force:18
Frozen:21
Medical:40
Militarisation:21
Missing:532
Murdered:2
Starvation:48
Stowaway:47
Suffocated:6
Suicide:14
Others:117
Unknown:169

FORTRESS EUROPE

OVER 13000 REFUGEE DEATHS IN 15 YEARS

Every year thousands of refugees are trying to flee to Europe in their search for safety from persecution, for economic security or just 'a better life'. Each year hundreds of them drown on the way from Africa to Italy or Spain, suffocate in sealed containers, starve in locked trucks, are blown to pieces by land mines between Turkey and Greece or freeze on their way over the mountains. And if they finally manage to arrive in "Fortress Europe" they are not at all safe. They are fenced-in, in refugee centres, some of which do not differ from a normal prison. Some of these refugees cannot deal with the misery and the inhuman conditions in which they are held and start a hunger strike or sew their eyes and mouth shut to protest against their situation. Some of them even commit suicide. Although many European states celebrate the lowest numbers of refugees in years, people still plea for stricter rules and limitations for refugees.

It is at least ironic that the origin of the name "Europe" is the legend of Europa who was abducted by the Greek God Zeus in the form of a bull. He swam with this Middle Eastern princess upon his back from a beach in Canaan to his island, Crete. This story is often referred to as 'the rape of Europa'. Nowadays, Canaan is named Lebanon, situated on the Asian continent. When we started this project it was based on a list with 11105 refugee deaths. The time it took to make the maps the list grew over 13000. History seems to continue the same way it always did.

For this map the legend is
1 person = 1 line.

Soource: UNITED for Intercultural Action

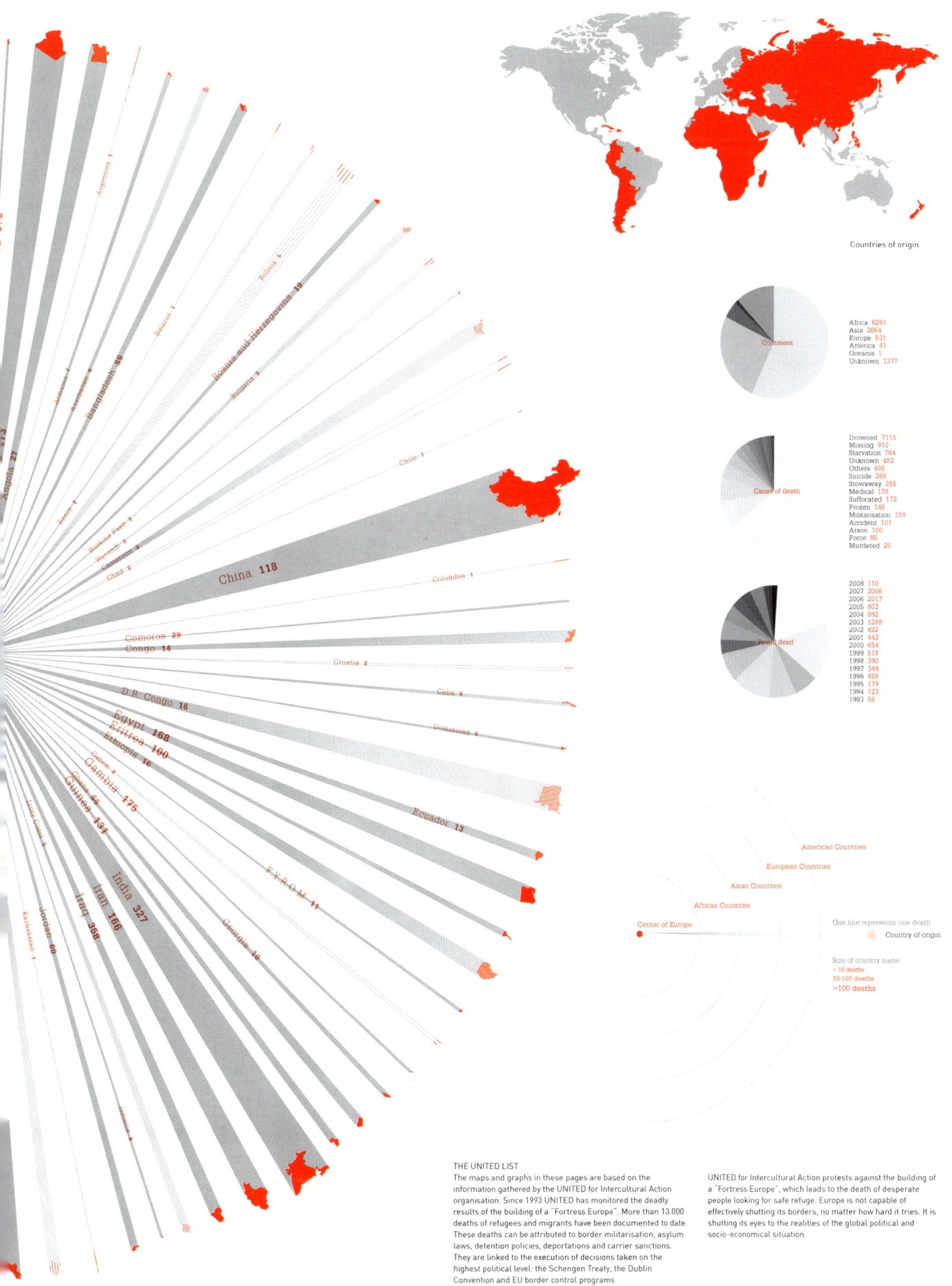

Countries of origin

Africa 6291
Asia 2864
Europe 531
America 41
Oceania 1
Unknown 1377

Continent

Drowned 7115
Missing 910
Starvation 764
Unknown 482
Others 405
Suicide 268
Stowaway 255
Medical 178
Suffocated 172
Frozen 146
Militarisation 109
Accident 101
Arson 100
Force 80
Murdered 20

Cause of death

2008 110
2007 2006
2006 2017
2005 803
2004 892
2003 1288
2002 822
2001 443
2000 654
1999 519
1998 390
1997 344
1996 459
1995 179
1994 123
1993 56

Found dead

American Countries
European Countries
Asian Countries
African Countries
Center of Europe

One line represents one death
Country of origin

Size of country name
< 10 deaths
10-100 deaths
>100 deaths

THE UNITED LIST
The maps and graphs in these pages are based on the information gathered by the UNITED for Intercultural Action organisation. Since 1993 UNITED has monitored the deadly results of the building of a "Fortress Europe". More than 13.000 deaths of refugees and migrants have been documented to date. These deaths can be attributed to border militarisation, asylum laws, detention policies, deportations and carrier sanctions. They are linked to the execution of decisions taken on the highest political level: the Schengen Treaty, the Dublin Convention and EU border control programs.

UNITED for Intercultural Action protests against the building of a "Fortress Europe", which leads to the death of desperate people looking for safe refuge. Europe is not capable of effectively shutting its borders, no matter how hard it tries. It is shutting its eyes to the realities of the global political and socio-economical situation.

Maps 31

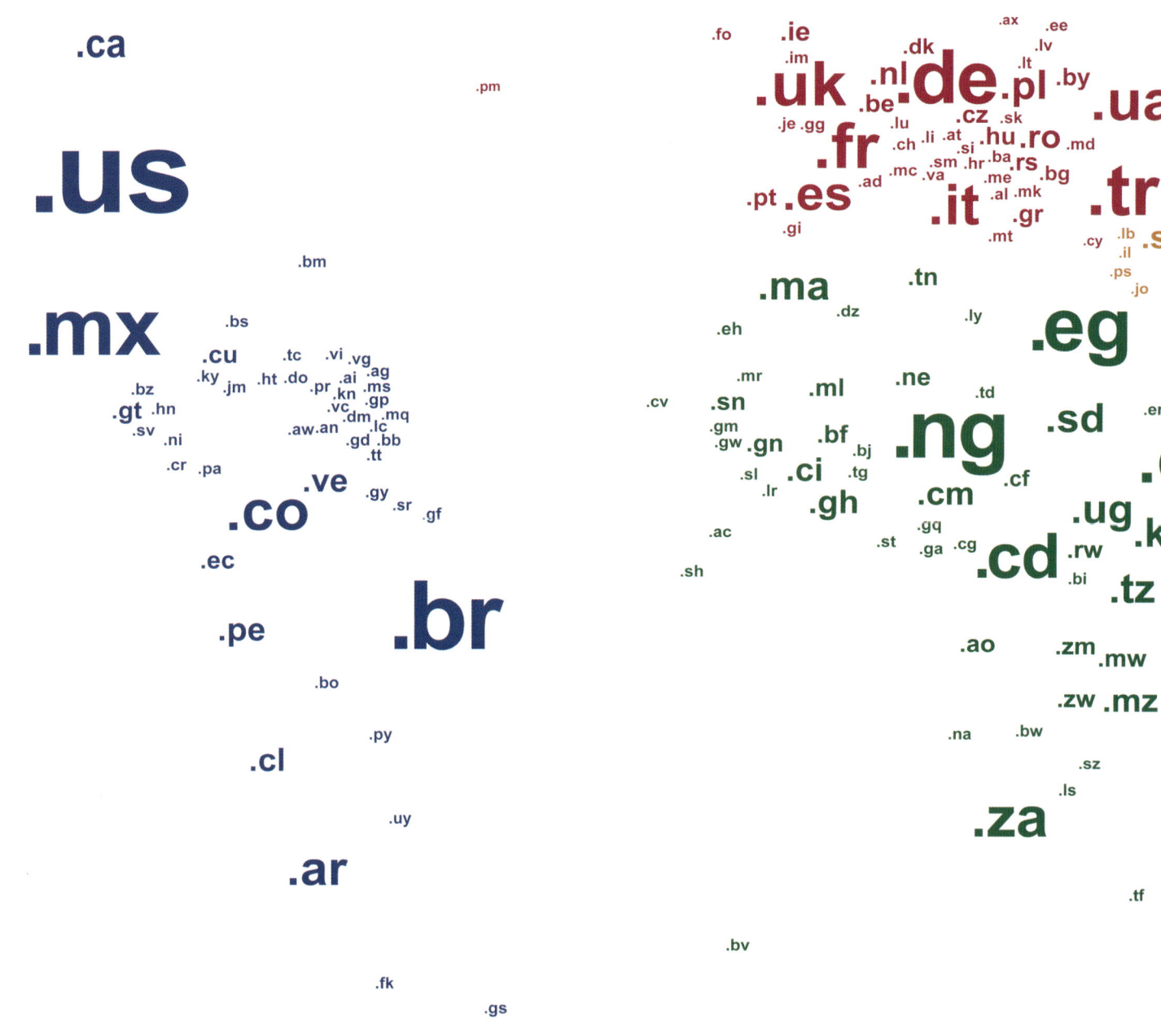

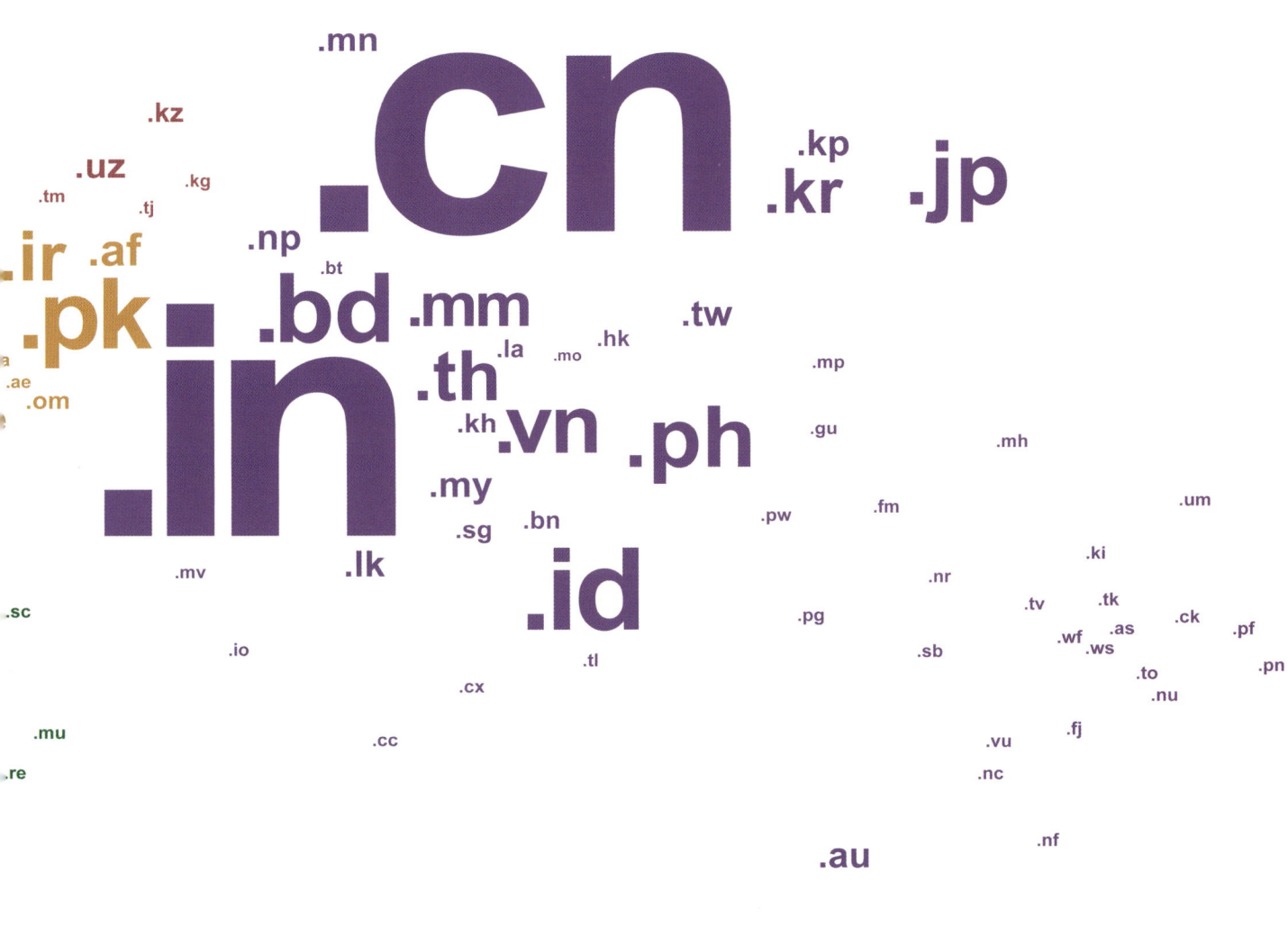

KPN telephone cards ::
Peter van den Hoogen, Erica Terpstra/Coup :: www.coup.nl ::

The introduction of the euro in Europe necessitated a graphic way to explain the new currency. These KPN telephone cards include a map on the back of the cards that show the countries that use the euro as well as the coins and notes that exist in this currency.

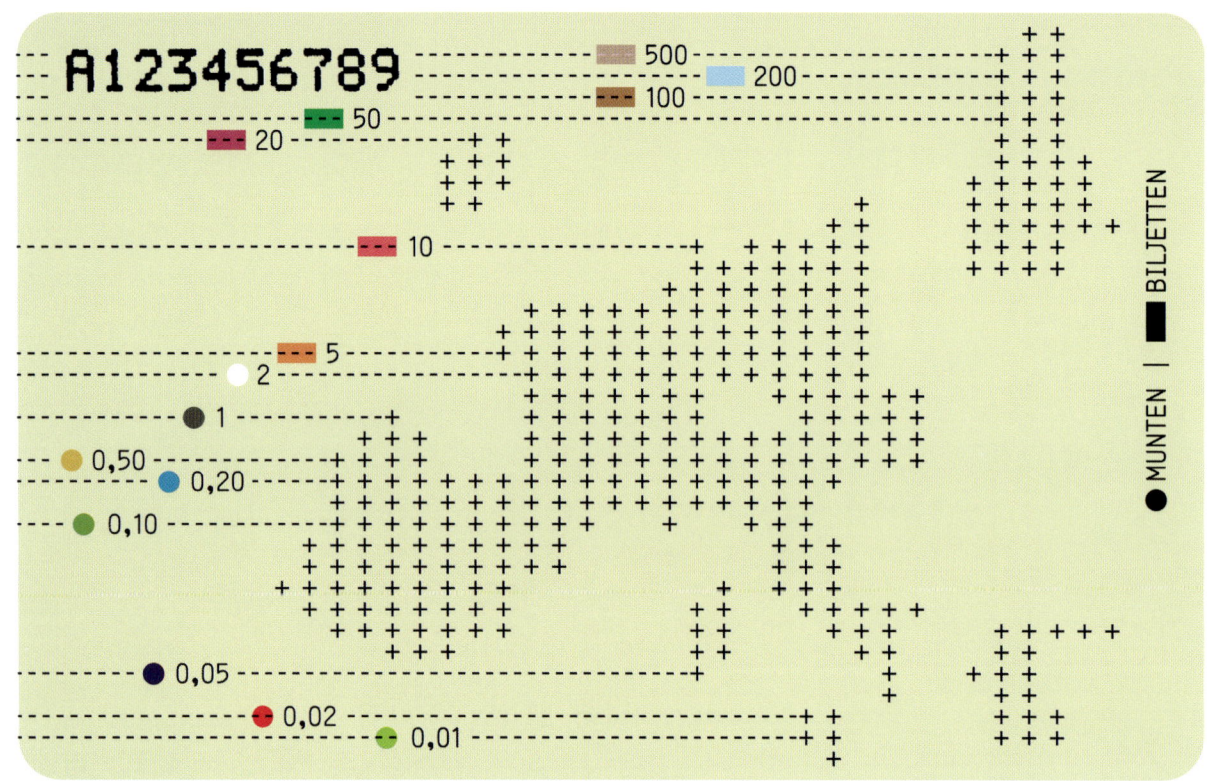

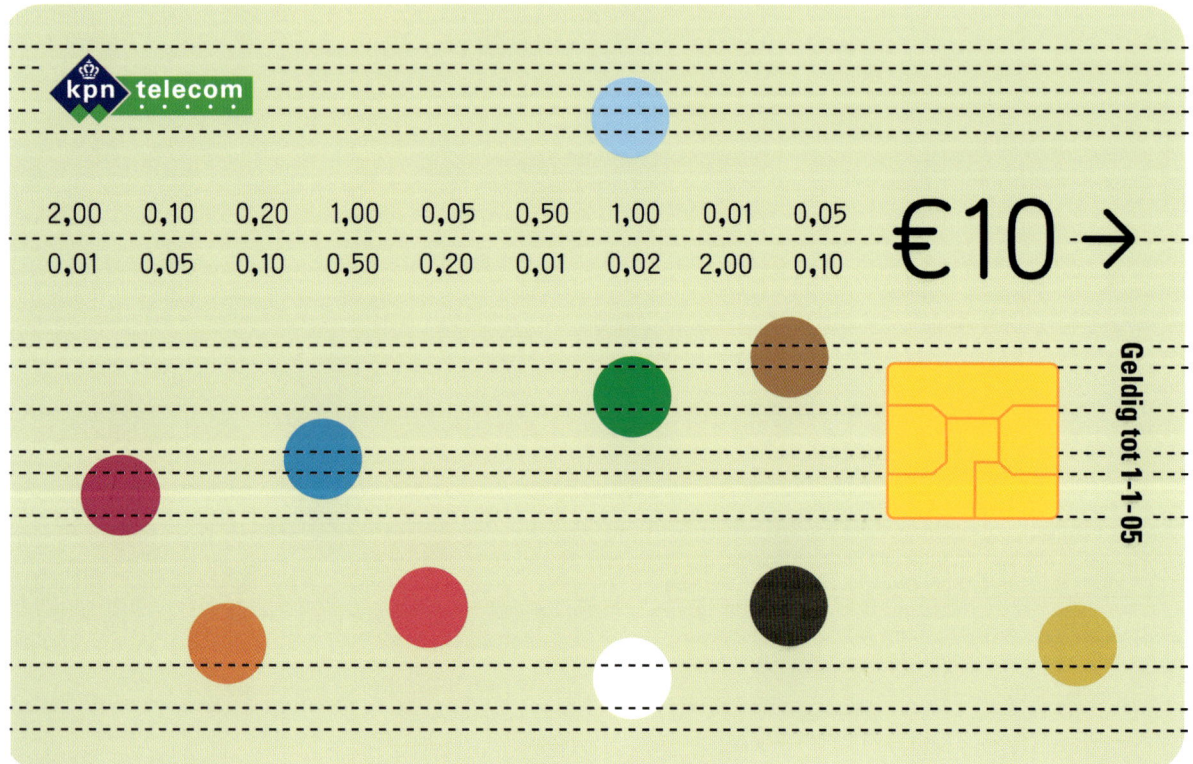

34 **Maps**

Nous étions indésirables en France ::
Atelier Aquarium :: www.atelieraquarium.com ::

With an almost square format, this book, *Nous étions indésirables en France*, tells the story of a couple of Jewish intellectuals exiled in France during the Second World War. The narrative is supported by maps that visually interpret the story's various scenes and settings.

The type of graphics and the colors chosen are a direct reference to the tools used by the French government during this time: red and blue crayons.

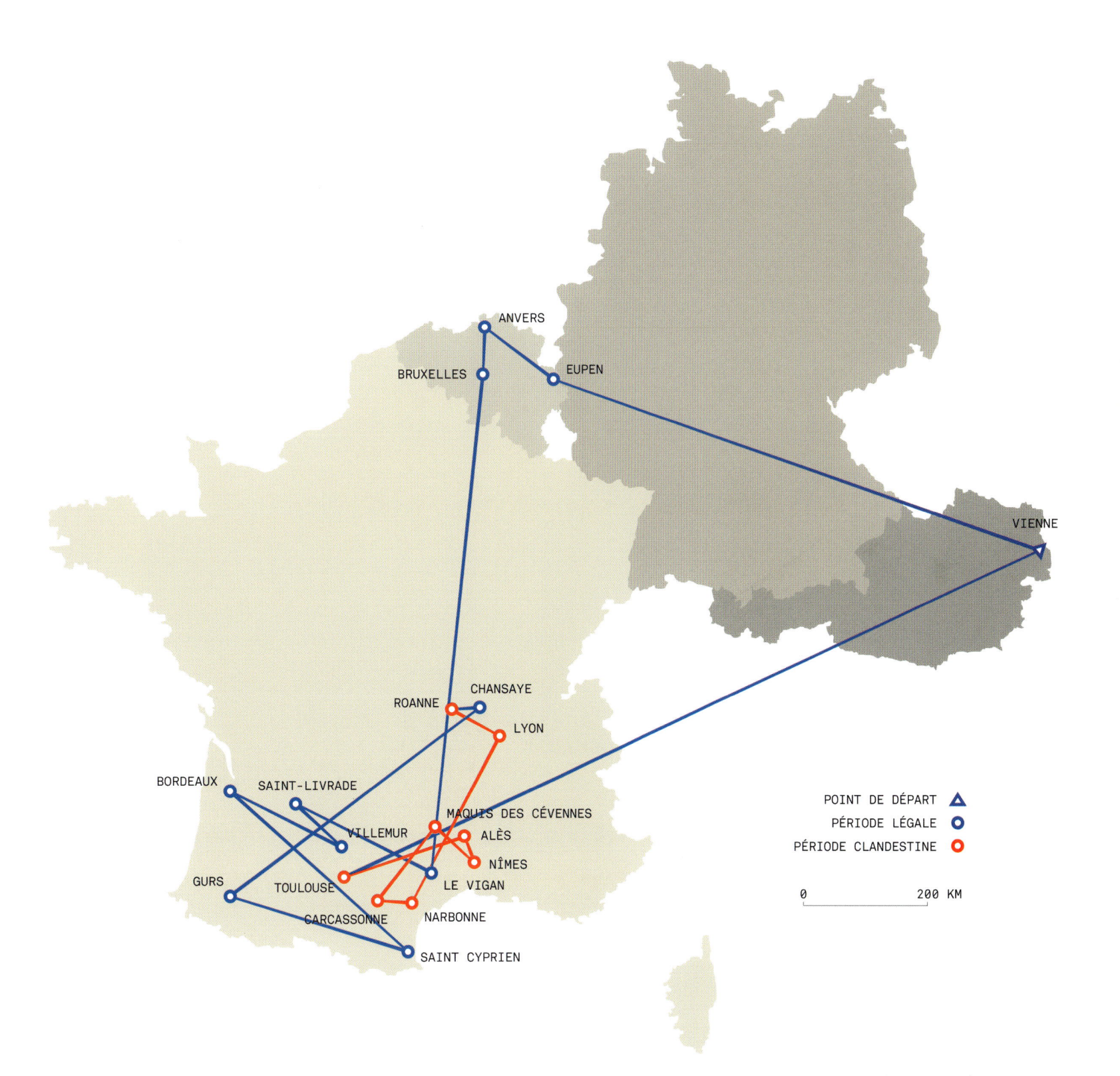

POINT DE DÉPART △
PÉRIODE LÉGALE ○
PÉRIODE CLANDESTINE ○

0   200 KM

© Simon Renaud, Jérémie Nuel/Atelier Aquarium

Subjective Atlas of Palestine ::
Annelys de Vet :: www.subjectiveatlasofpalestine.info ::

Marvellous landscapes, peaceful urban scenes, and frolicking kids: Who would associate these images with Palestine? The media too often only shows the darker side of the country and portrays the local inhabitants as the aggressor. To remedy this, Annelys de Vet invited several Palestinian artists to make their own personal map of the country. Given their emotional proximity to the topic, the result was anything but ordinary.

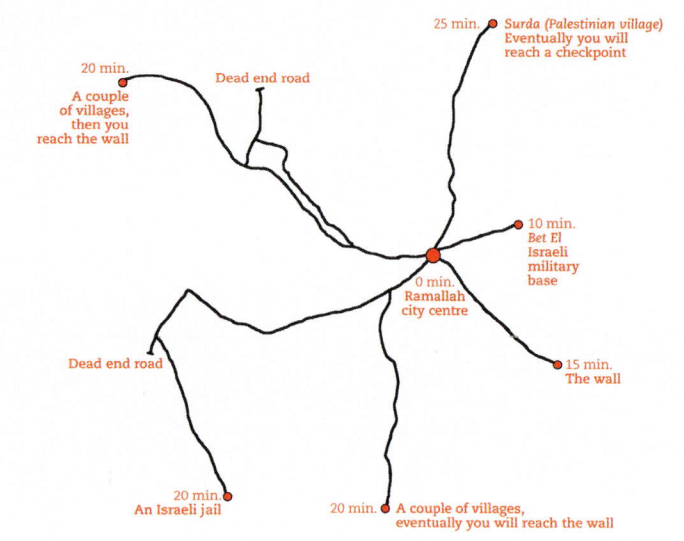

36 **Maps**

Maps 37

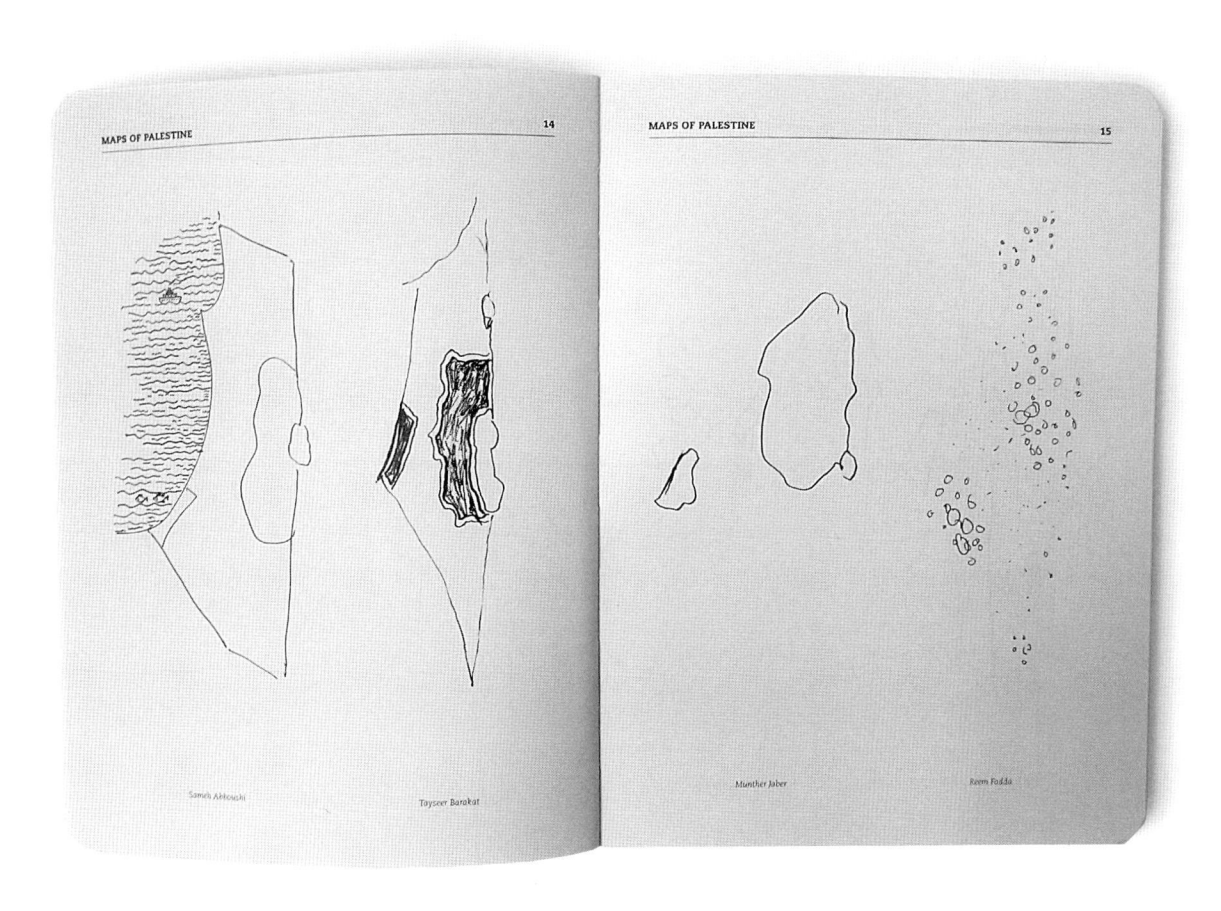

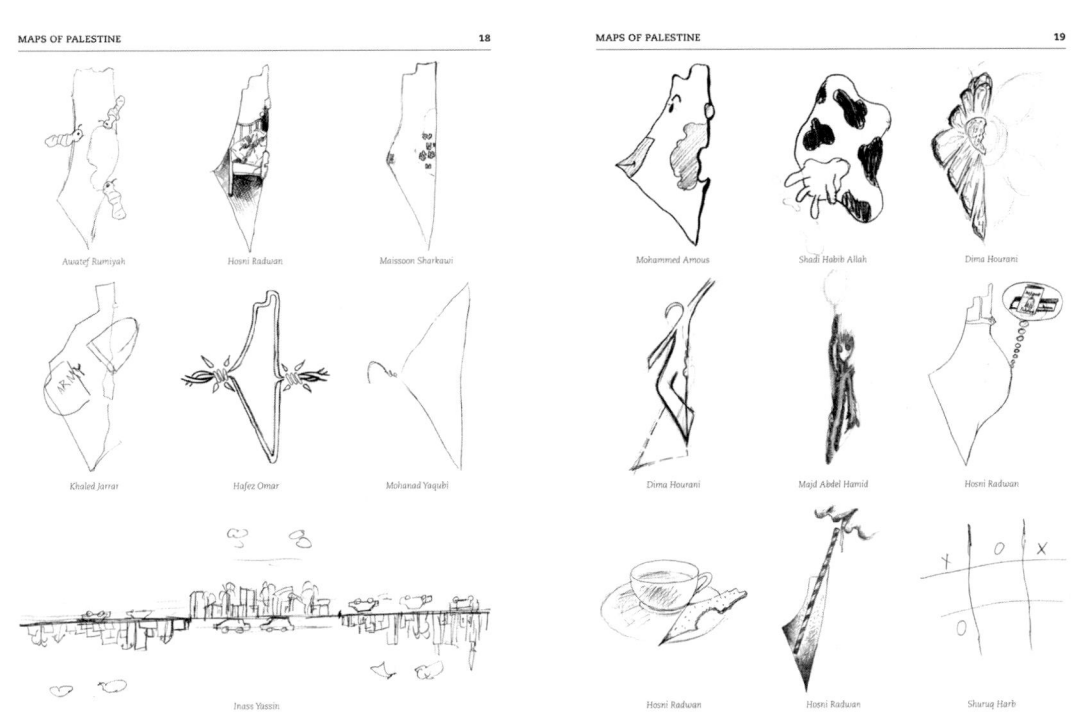

Milano Made in Design ::
Leftloft :: www.leftloft.com ::

Every year, thousands of students from all over the world converge on Milan to study design and generate creativity. This directory—presented in New York during a traveling exhibition organized by the Province of Milan and the Milan Chamber of Commerce in collaboration with the Region of Lombardy—is a compilation of all the exact information concerning the show, represented through educational maps and charts.

STUDIARE DESIGN A MILANO
STUDYING DESIGN IN MILAN

9.620 Studenti — Design students in Milan
3.843 Studenti stranieri — Foreign Students

- Politecnico di Milano — **4.000** Studenti / Students
- Accademia di Brera — **270** Studenti / Students
- Istituto Marangoni — **2.000** Studenti / Students
- Istituto Europeo di Design — **2.300** Studenti / Students
- Scuola Politecnica di Design — **200** Studenti / Students
- Nuova Accademia di Belle Arti — **500** Studenti / Students
- Domus Academy — **250** Studenti / Students

fonte/source: DESIGNfocus 2006

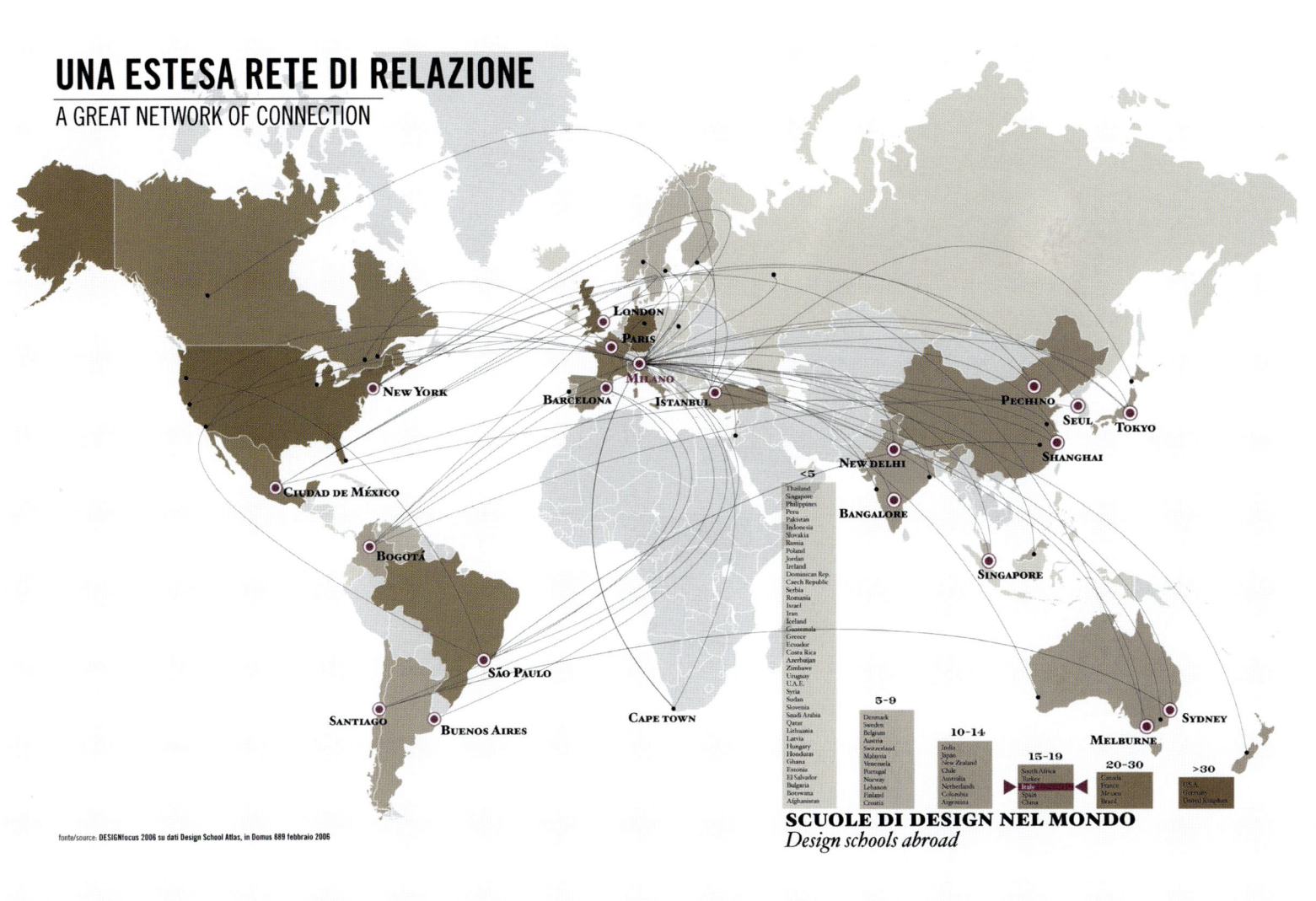

UNA ESTESA RETE DI RELAZIONE
A GREAT NETWORK OF CONNECTION

SCUOLE DI DESIGN NEL MONDO
Design schools abroad

fonte/source: DESIGNfocus 2006 su dati Design School Atlas, in Domus 889 febbraio 2006

Leftloft | Infographics Special

Greenland
18.5%

Mark – Another Architecture ::
Lesley Moore :: www.lesley-moore.nl ::

The magazine *Mark* is devoted to architecture and the exploration of its boundaries. Each week it includes an infographic on a topic of global concern. In this case, the map is formed by the name of each country together with a slab of roof, the size of which is proportional to the number of households living there without any of the minimum conditions laid down by UN-HABITAT.

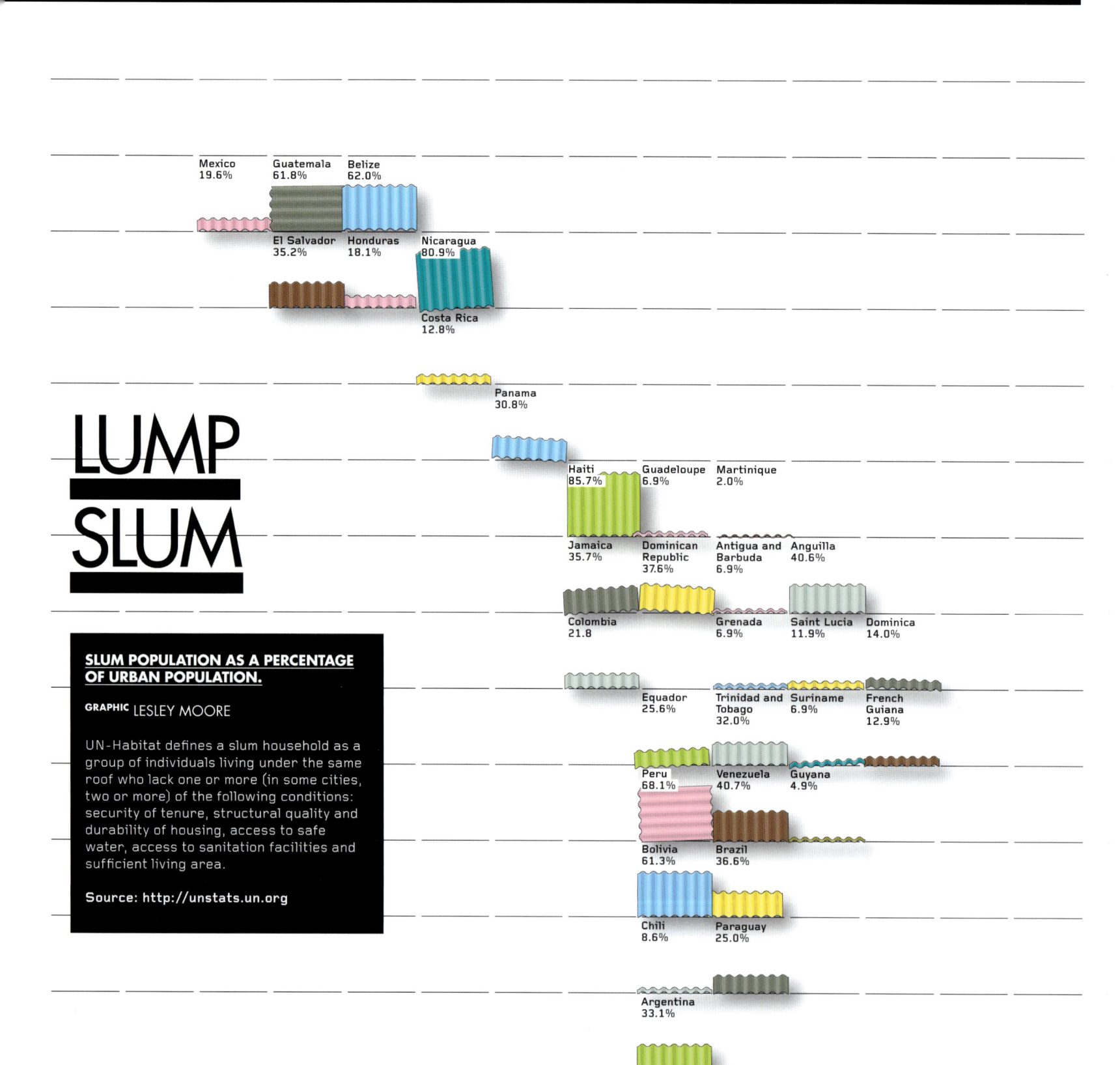

Mexico
19.6%

Guatemala
61.8%

Belize
62.0%

El Salvador
35.2%

Honduras
18.1%

Nicaragua
80.9%

Costa Rica
12.8%

Panama
30.8%

LUMP
SLUM

Haiti
85.7%

Guadeloupe
6.9%

Martinique
2.0%

Jamaica
35.7%

Dominican Republic
37.6%

Antigua and Barbuda
6.9%

Anguilla
40.6%

Colombia
21.8

Grenada
6.9%

Saint Lucia
11.9%

Dominica
14.0%

SLUM POPULATION AS A PERCENTAGE OF URBAN POPULATION.

GRAPHIC LESLEY MOORE

UN-Habitat defines a slum household as a group of individuals living under the same roof who lack one or more (in some cities, two or more) of the following conditions: security of tenure, structural quality and durability of housing, access to safe water, access to sanitation facilities and sufficient living area.

Source: http://unstats.un.org

Equador
25.6%

Trinidad and Tobago
32.0%

Suriname
6.9%

French Guiana
12.9%

Peru
68.1%

Venezuela
40.7%

Guyana
4.9%

Bolivia
61.3%

Brazil
36.6%

Chili
8.6%

Paraguay
25.0%

Argentina
33.1%

Country	%
Norway	0.0%
Finland	0.0%
Russia	0.0%
Ireland	0.0%
England	0.0%
Sweden	0.0%
Denmark	0.0%
Poland	0.0%
Belgium	0.0%
The Netherlands	0.0%
Switzerland	0.0%
Hungary	0.0%
France	0.0%
Germany	0.0%
Austria	0.0%
Bulgaria	0.0%
Portugal	0.0%
Spain	0.0%
Italy	0.0%
Croatia	0.0%
Romania	0.0%
Greece	0.0%
Turkey	17.9%
Mongolia	64.9%
Marocco	32.7%
Tunesia	3.7%
Syrian Arab Republic	10.4%
Jordan	15.7%
Iraq	56.7%
Afghanistan	98.5%
China	37.8%
Republic of Korea	37.0%
Cape Verde	69.6%
Mauritania	94.3%
Algeria	11.8%
Libyan Arab Jamahiriya	35.2%
Egypte	39.9%
Occupied Palestinian Territory	60.0%
Saudi Arabia	19.8%
Iran	44.2%
Pakistan	73.6%
Nepal	92.4%
Bhutan	44.1%
Senegal	76.4%
Mali	93.2%
Niger	96.2%
Chad	99.1%
Sudan	85.7%
Eritrea	69.9%
Yemen	65.1%
Oman	60.5%
India	55.5%
Bangladesh	84.7%
Gambia	67.0%
Guinea-Bissau	93.4%
Guinea	72.3%
Cote d'Ivoire	69.9%
Burkina Faso	76.5%
Nigeria	79.2%
Cameroon	69.9%
Sri Lanka	13.6%
Sierra Leone	95.8%
Liberia	55.7%
Ghana	69.6%
Togo	80.6%
Benin	83.6%
Ethiopia	99.4%
Somalia	97.1%
Equatorial Guinea	86.5%
Central African Republic	92.4%
Rwanda	87.9%
Uganda	93.0%
Kenya	70.7%
Myanmar	26.4%
Laos People's Democratic Republic	66.1%
Vietnam	47.4%
Gabon	66.2%
Burundi	65.3%
United Republic of Tanzania	92.1%
Thailand	2.0%
Philippines	44.1%
Congo	90.1%
Democratic Repunlic of the Congo	49.5%
Malawi	91.1%
Comoros	61.2%
Cambodia	72.2%
Angola	83.1%
Zambia	74.0%
Zimbabwe	3.4%
Madagascar	92.9%
Namibia	37.9%
Botswana	60.7%
Mozambique	94.1%
South Africa	33.2%
Lesotho	57.0%

Mark 9, August–September 2007

TOURIST TRAP

TOURISM, THE WORLD'S BIGGEST INDUSTRY, IS NOT ALWAYS A BOON FOR PHYSICAL PLANNING.

GRAPHIC **LESLEY MOORE**

Some countries have to pack in more tourists each year than the head count of their resident populations. France, for example, home to around 60 million inhabitants, welcomes 76 million tourists a year, making it the world's primary tourist destination. Spain, second in line for that honour, attracts 55 million visitors annually and has only 43 million inhabitants. The consequences for a country's physical planning are well known: traditional fishing villages become coves of concrete, and former artists' colonies in historic metropolitan neighbourhoods evolve into tourist traps that prostitute their origins. Seen in this light, the United States, with 'only' 49 million visitors a year and a population currently pushing 300 million, is an oasis of authenticity and peace. The strangest ratios, however, are found in China's special administrative region Macao (gambling capital of the East) and on island paradises like Guam (part of the Pacific region of Micronesia), whose 166,000 inhabitants share 541 km2 with over a million tourists each year. Surely those who truly admire the natural beauty of Guam should vow never to set foot in that country.

Number of tourists (x 1000)
Number of inhabitants (x1000)
Ratio of tourists to locals

Source: World Tourism Organization, www.unwto.org

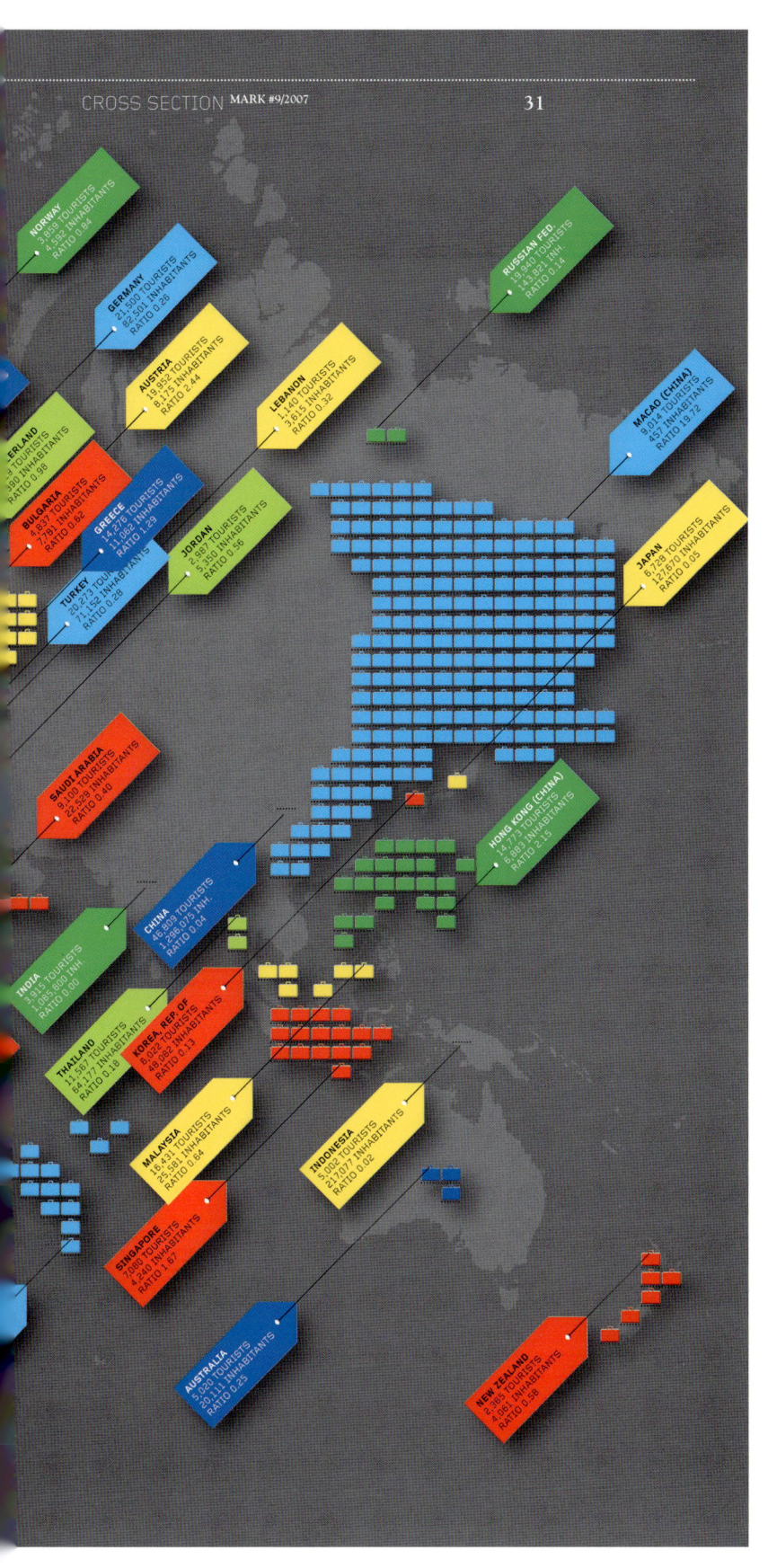

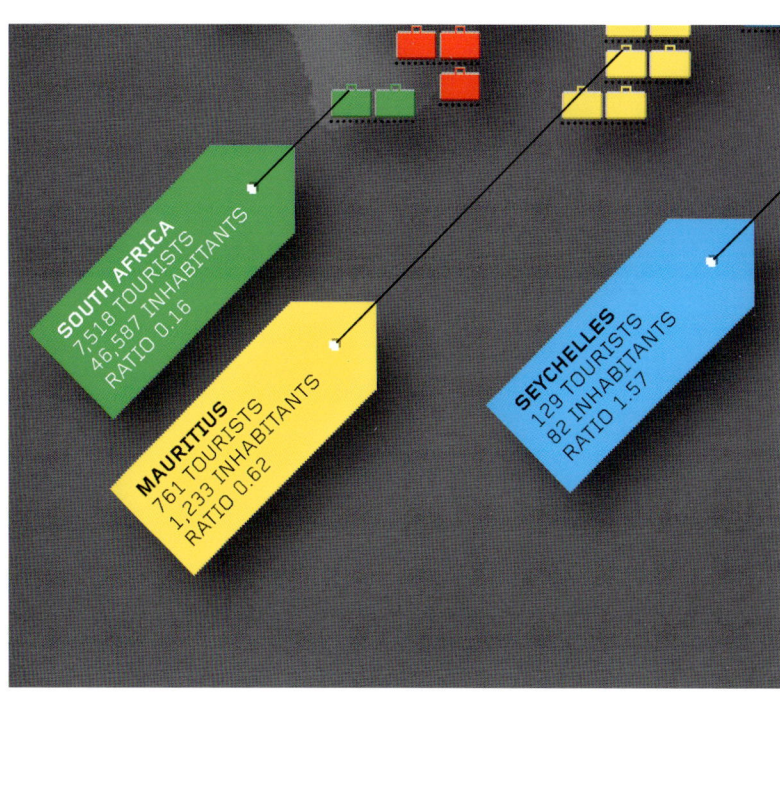

Mark 12, February–March 2008

Between Land and Sea ::
Paulus M. Dreibholz/Atelier for Typography and Graphic Design :: dreibholz.com ::

The exhibition "Between Land and Sea" brought four artists together with two things in common: residence in the United Kingdom and having the sea and its coastline as their main research topic. The exhibition was staged at a gallery on the Belgian coast. The gallery poster displayed a map that showed the sea levels near Ramsgate, the place all boats going from London to Ostend have to pass through.

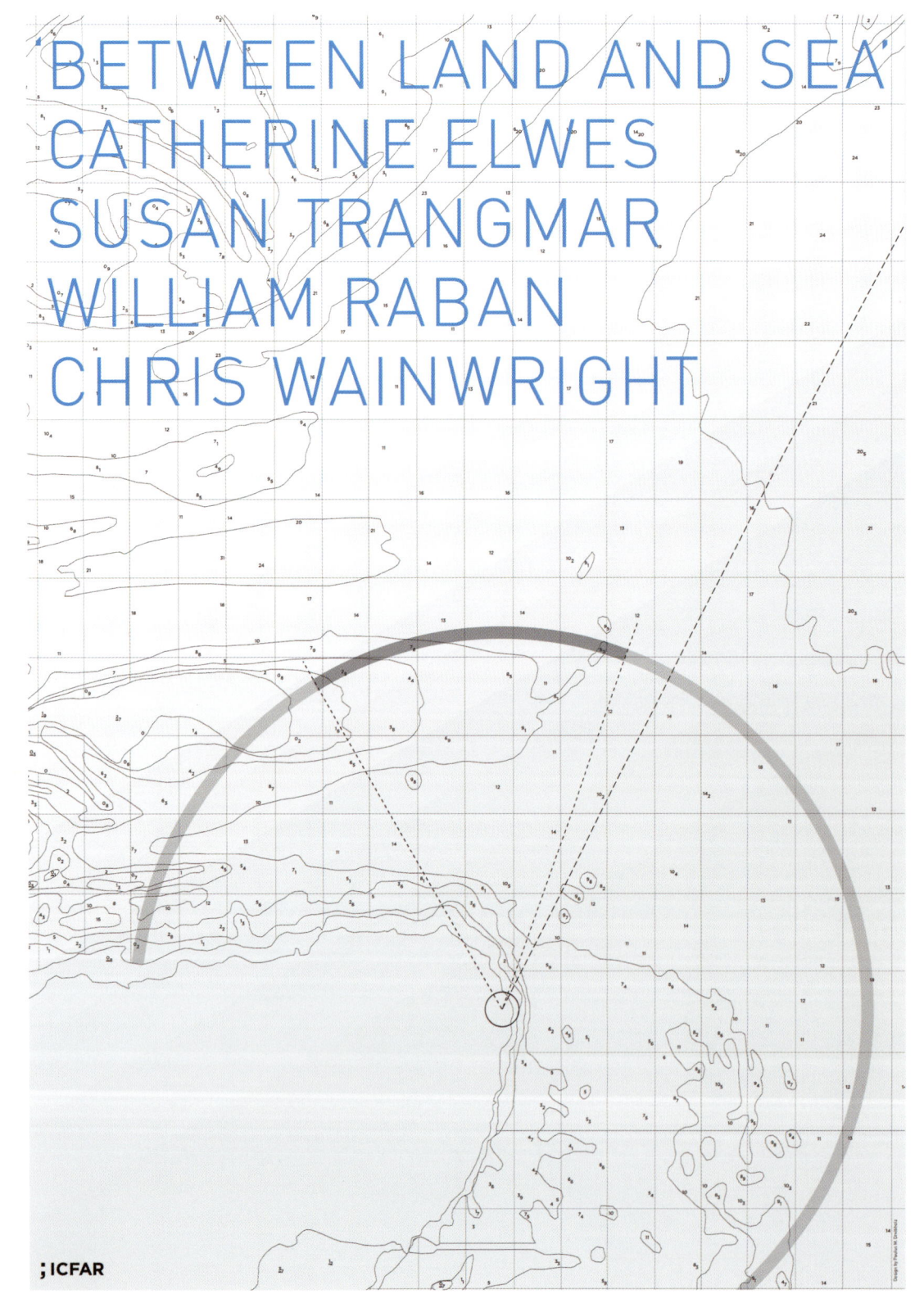

© Eva Engelbert

Shale Gas Map ::
Apfel Zet :: www.apfelzet.de ::

This image forms part of an illustrated booklet that was put together by the Berlin studio Apfel Zet for an energy company that exploits shale gas. The map indicates which areas in Europe currently have most to gain from this gas and in which countries it is extracted. The size of the gas tank illustrated on each of these maps represents the volume of extraction, allowing for easy comparison.

Stroom Travels ::
LUST :: www.lust.nl ::

This is an invitation for WorldTravels, the second town excursion in the Stroom Travels series that explores various facets of a city. LUST did not want the invitation to become a traveling tourist illustration, but part of the trip itself, and therefore they decided to design another global tour going around The Hague, which coincides with real destinations on the world map.

STROOM TRAVELS

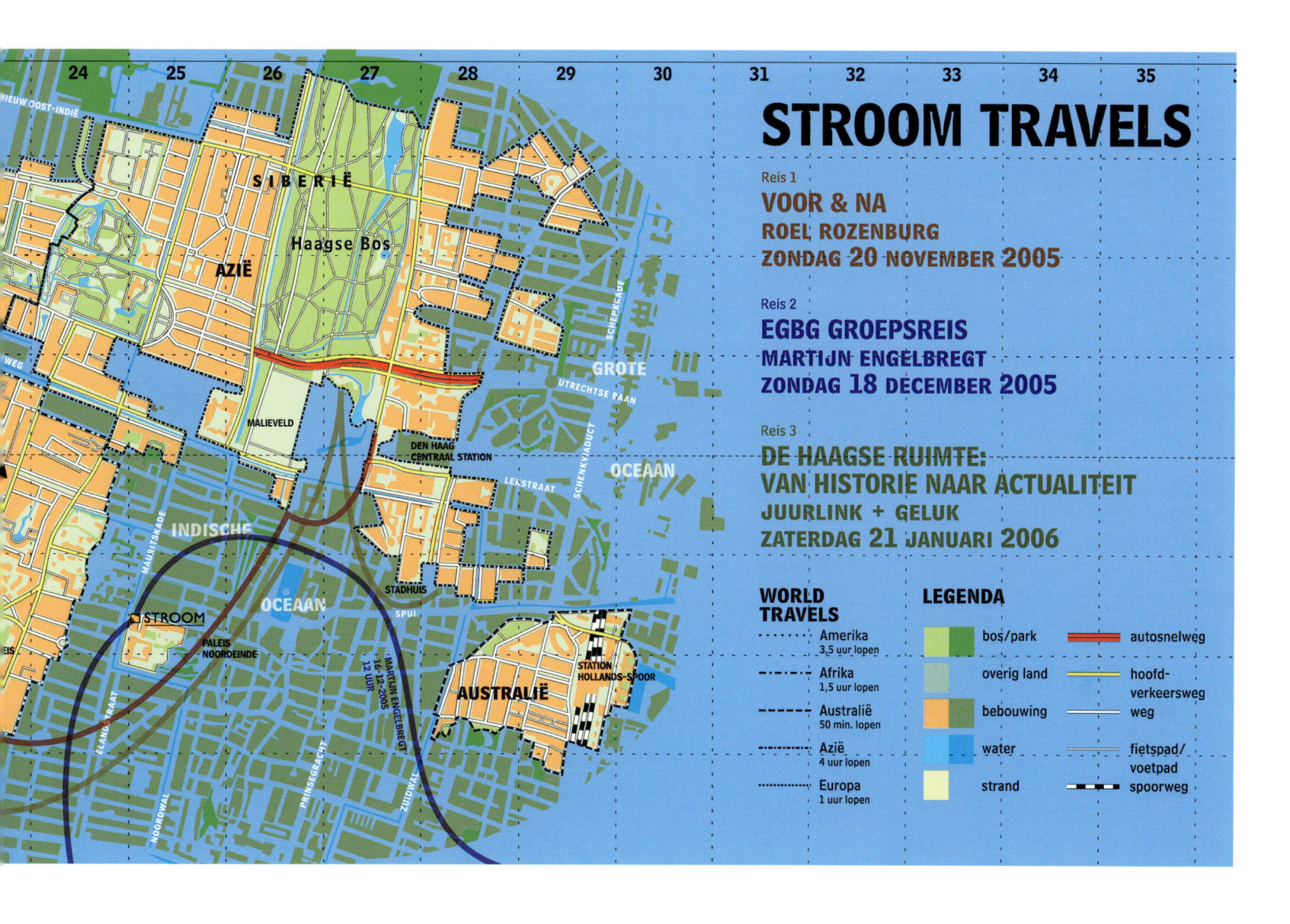

Reis 1
VOOR & NA
ROEL ROZENBURG
ZONDAG 20 NOVEMBER 2005

Reis 2
EGBG GROEPSREIS
MARTIJN ENGELBREGT
ZONDAG 18 DECEMBER 2005

Reis 3
**DE HAAGSE RUIMTE:
VAN HISTORIE NAAR ACTUALITEIT**
JUURLINK + GELUK
ZATERDAG 21 JANUARI 2006

WORLD TRAVELS

- Amerika — 3,5 uur lopen
- Afrika — 1,5 uur lopen
- Australië — 50 min. lopen
- Azië — 4 uur lopen
- Europa — 1 uur lopen

LEGENDA

- bos/park
- overig land
- bebouwing
- water
- strand
- autosnelweg
- hoofdverkeersweg
- weg
- fietspad/voetpad
- spoorweg

Maps 47

Globalize Me! ::
JUNG + WENIG :: www.jungundwenig.com ::

Using China as an example, this work shows the current impact of globalization on demographic, economic, and social development. The information needed to create it was taken from the CIA world factbook, from the University of Harvard, and statistics from the German government.

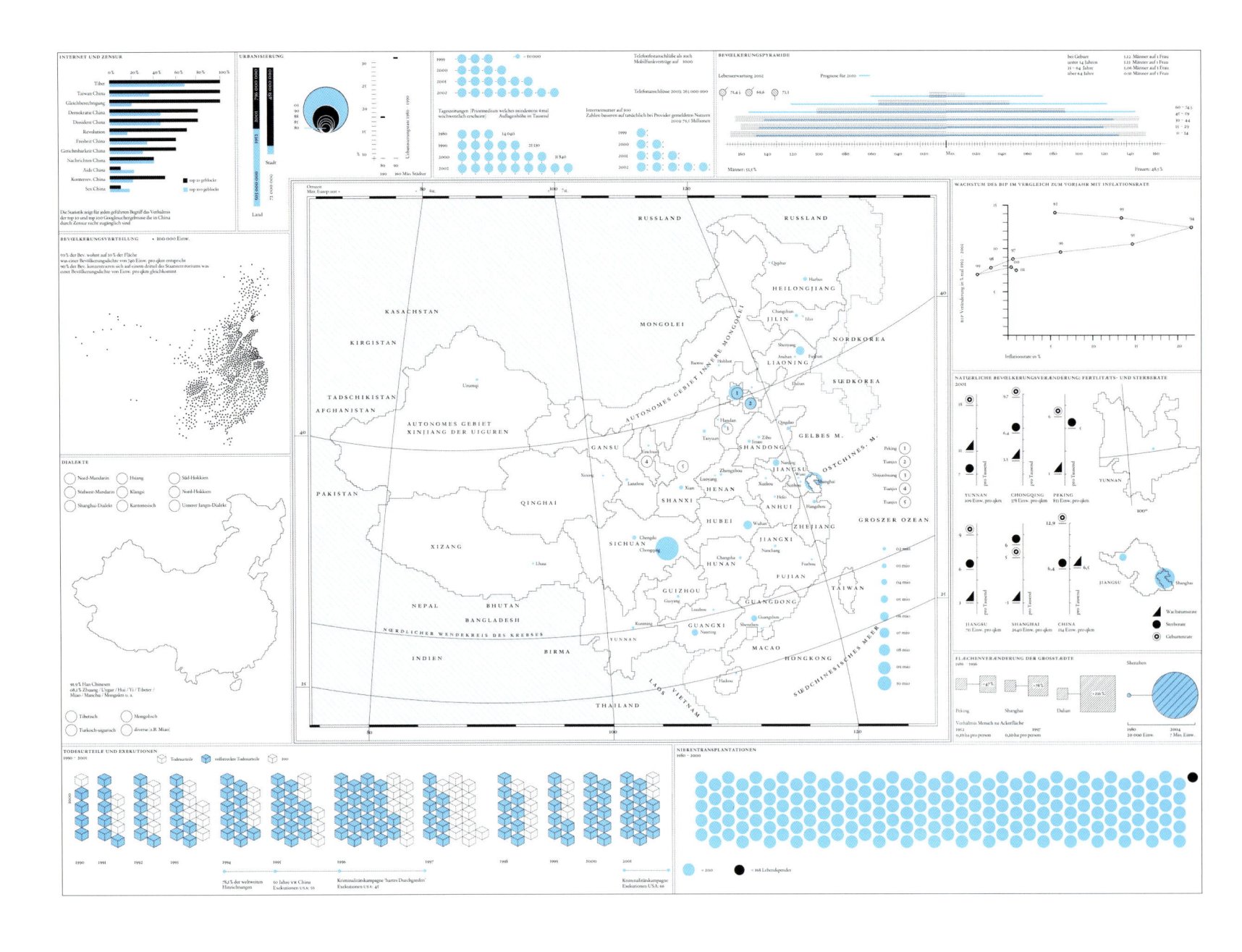

A Weird and Wonderful Guide to Amsterdam ::
Lava Amsterdam :: www.lava.nl ::

Amsterdam is one of the cities where *le cool* exists: a weekly cultural agenda and an alternative guide to the city. Each week, an illustrator, photographer, or designer is given the responsibility to produce the cover of this electronic newsletter, offering their own view of the city. Lava Amsterdam designed a cover in 2008, in which it was decided to turn the spotlight on the most remote and charming places in the city.

The tiny terrace of café **'T SMALLE** catches late sunlight on summer evenings, though you'll be lucky to catch a table. Try to dock your boat at their platform, order a 'witbier' or a chilled white wine, enjoy the beautiful view of the tree-lined canal, sit back and enjoy. EGELANTIERSGRACHT 12 (JORDAAN)

Spend a night on a houseboat: **LE MAROXIDIEN** ▶ SEE PAGE 28

Fresh air, beautiful open water... hungry yet? Set sail for the **SAN MARCO PIZZERIA**, where you can order a killer Quattro Formaggio from the comfort of your little boat. AMSTELKADE 148A (DE PIJP)

If the water is calling your inner nesting instinct, start your new life with a visit to the **HOUSEBOAT MUSEUM**. Set on a houseboat, its decoration is typical of those moored around the city, and should satisfy your curiosity enough not to bother irate floating locals by peeping inside their houses. PRINSENGRACHT, OPPOSITE 296 (JORDAAN) HOUSEBOATMUSEUM.NL

CAFÉ DE JAREN is an Amsterdam institution. With its open, airy interior and huge bank of glass windows overlooking the canals, it's a little piece of city heaven. The outside terrace is a much-coveted suntrap, and while you don't need to own a boat in order to enjoy this café, it's with a sense of joy, pride and smugness that you dock at the terrace, and order the excellent apple cake. NIEUWE DOELENSTRAAT 20-22 (CENTRUM)

Amsterdam from the water side

The canals are fake. Unlike Venice, nature didn't make Amsterdam a city of canals – it's a wide river, tamed and built on top of. Having forced nature to heel, the Dutch now flock to the canals at the merest sign of sunshine. Why? Because there is no better way to view the city than from the water. Start by renting a pedal boat, or even better, your own little motorboat. You can man the helm yourself, or rent a boat including a skipper well used to the crazy boat traffic around the city. Basic rules: keep to starboard (right), let the big boats pass first, speed limit is 18km/h. And don't end up on the huge river IJ, unless you want to get close to a freighter ship.
Two great places to get afloat:
• Boothurenamsterdam.com: KORTE PRINSENGRACHT 42 (JORDAAN) +31(0)6-21454326
• Amsterdam & Water: BINNEN VISSERSSTRAAT 5 (JORDAAN) +31(0)20-620 9335

NeoPolis Masterplan ::
The Luxury of Protest :: www.theluxuryofprotest.com ::

This map is a conceptual view of the development of a technology park located in the Ukraine, in which special care was taken to provide for the construction work to take place in phases that were ecologically sustainable. This is the first of seven brochures which, when opened, reveal each phase of the project, specifically indicating the percentage of land used at each stage, depicted with proportional black circles.

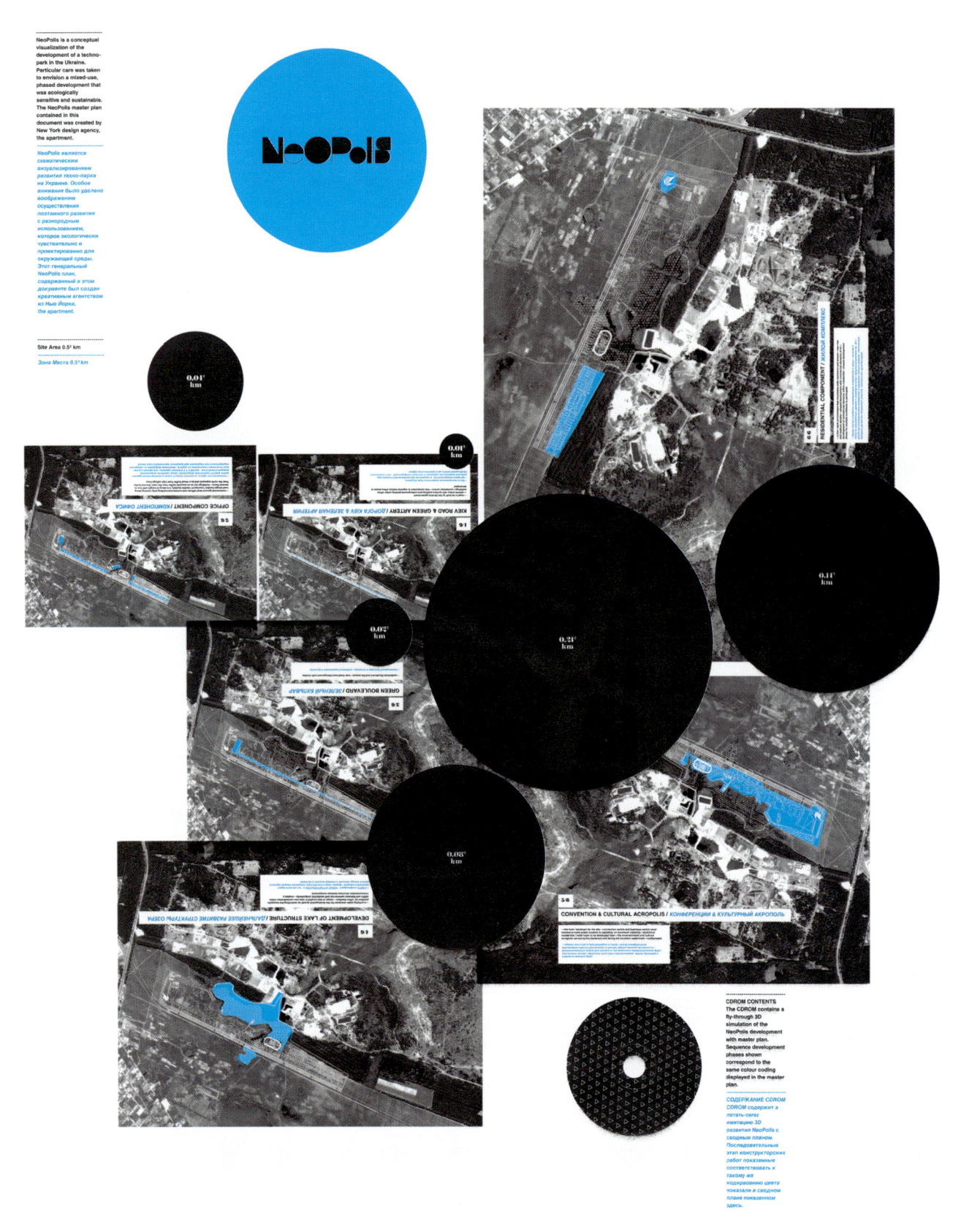

NeoPolis is a conceptual visualization of the development of a techno-park in the Ukraine. Particular care was taken to envision a mixed-use, phased development that was ecologically sensitive and sustainable. The NeoPolis master plan contained in this document was created by New York design agency, the apartment.

NeoPolis является схематически вхуализированным развитием текно-парка на Украине. Особое внимание было уделено воображению осуществления поэтапного развития с разнородным использованием, которое экологически чувствительно и проектировано для окружающей среды. Этот генеральный NeoPolis план, содержащийся в этом документе был создан креативным агентством из Нью Йорка, the apartment.

Site Area 0.5² km

Зона Места 0.5² km

CDROM CONTENTS
The CDROM contains a fly-through 3D simulation of the NeoPolis development with master plan. Sequence development phases shown correspond to the same colour coding displayed in the master plan.

СОДЕРЖАНИЕ CDROM
CDROM содержит в петаль-сечез имитацию 3D развития NeoPolis с сводным планом. Последовательные этап конструкторских работ показанные соответствовать к гамму же кодирование цвета показали в сводном плане пожаленном здесь.

50 **Maps**

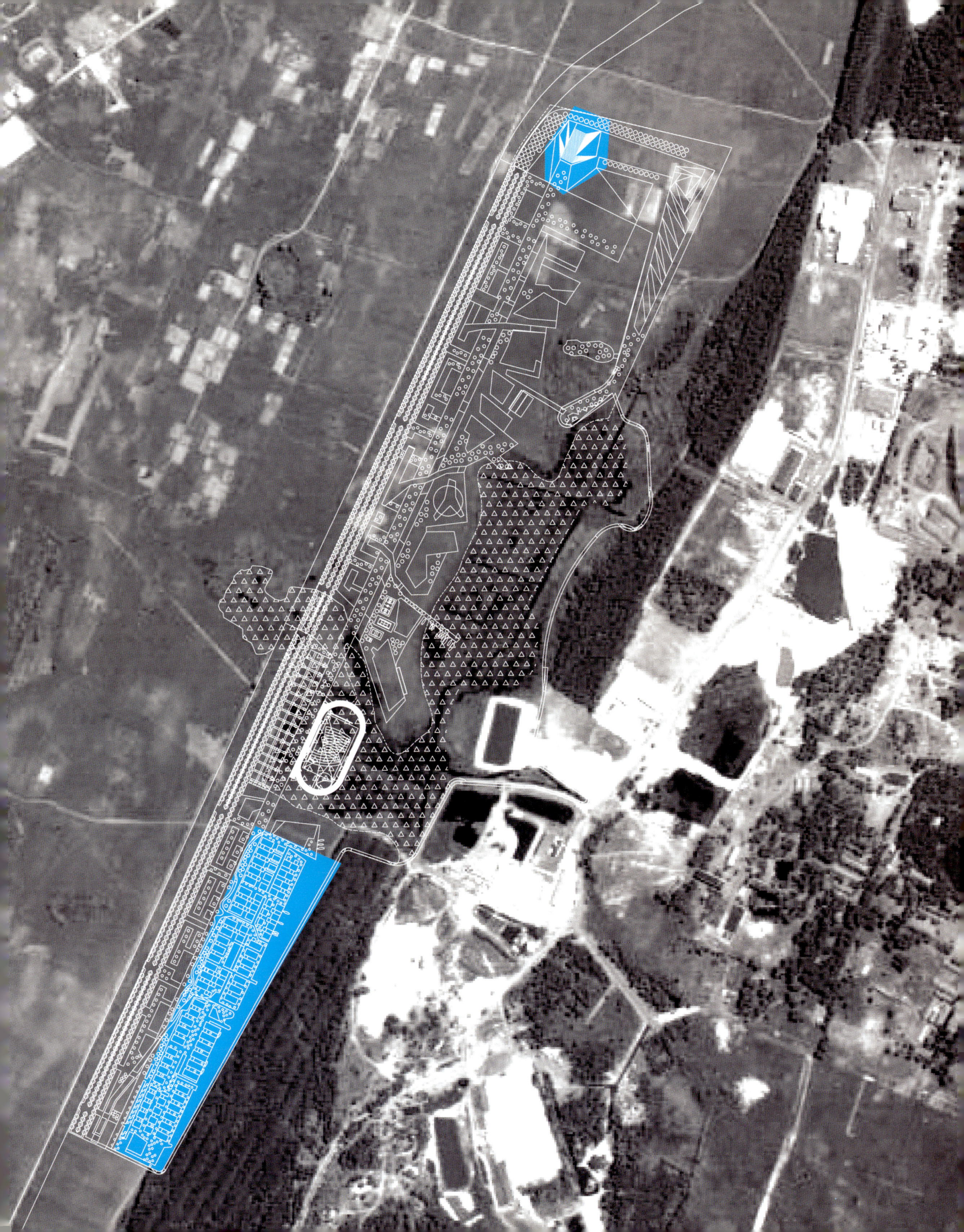

Territori. Anuari Territorial de Catalunya ::
Jordi Boix 40Gurus ::www.jordiboix40gurus.com ::

The *Anuari* (yearbook) is a book that is published every year in Catalonia as a reference tool that helps users find out more about what is happening in the community with respect to changes, projects, and territorial disputes throughout the year. All sections were labeled with symbols that act as visual reference points for a rapid interpretation of the diagram.

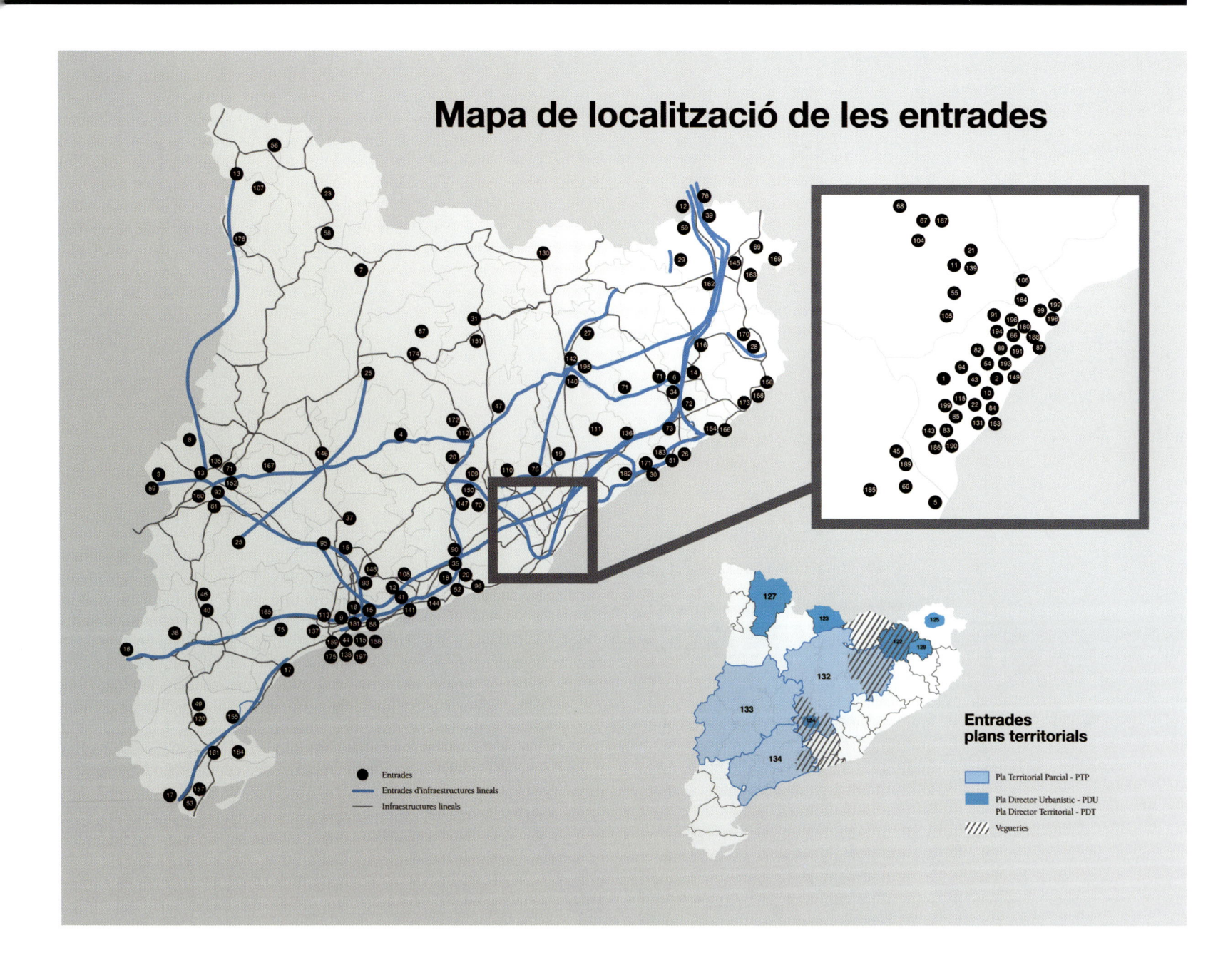

Mapa de localització de les entrades

Entrades plans territorials
- Pla Territorial Parcial - PTP
- Pla Director Urbanístic - PDU
- Pla Director Territorial - PDT
- Vegueries

Entrades
Entrades d'infraestructures lineals
Infraestructures lineals

Maps 53

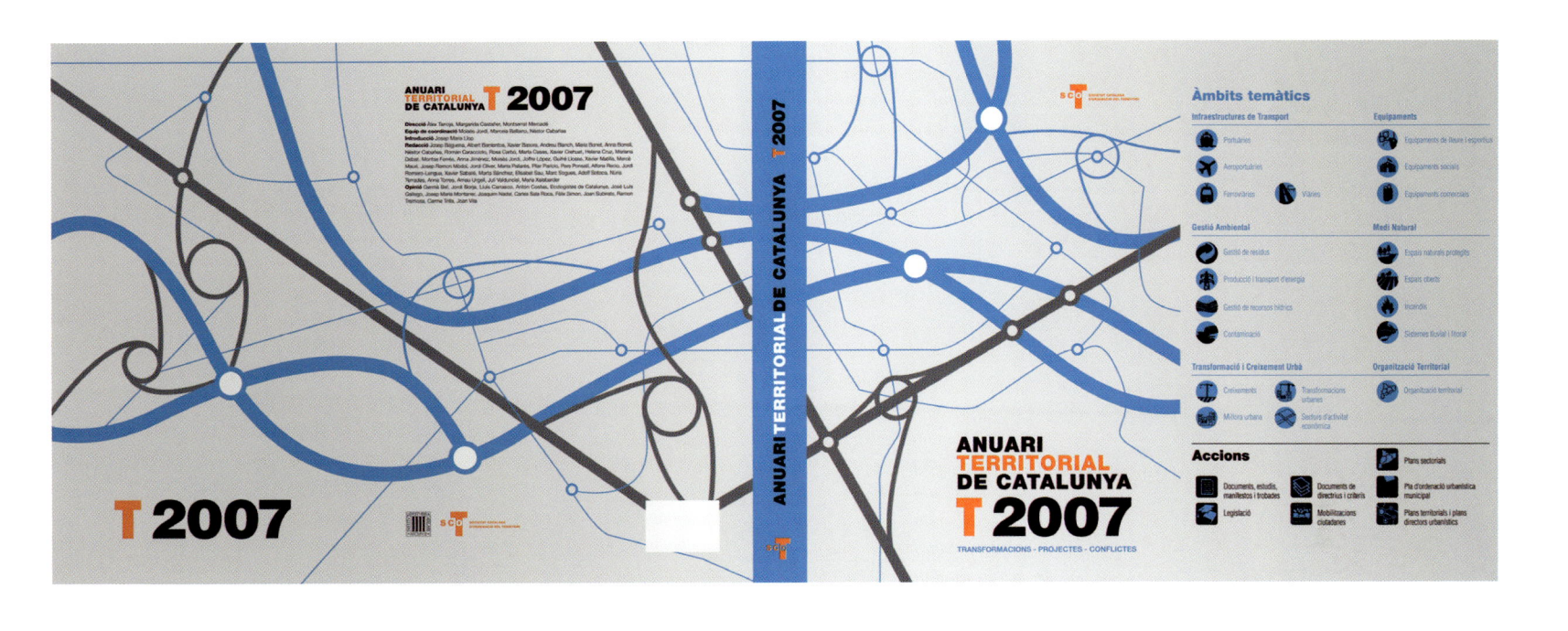

mapping:ch ::
Lorenzo Geiger :: www.lorenzogeiger.ch ::

mapping:ch is a collection of twelve maps (developed as a graduation project at the Hochschule der Künste Bern/Haute école des arts de Berne), which invite readers to travel around a statistically imaginary Swiss landscape. Using concepts such as innovation, globalization, or monotony, three key maps were developed, each one supplemented by three maps that show more specific detail.

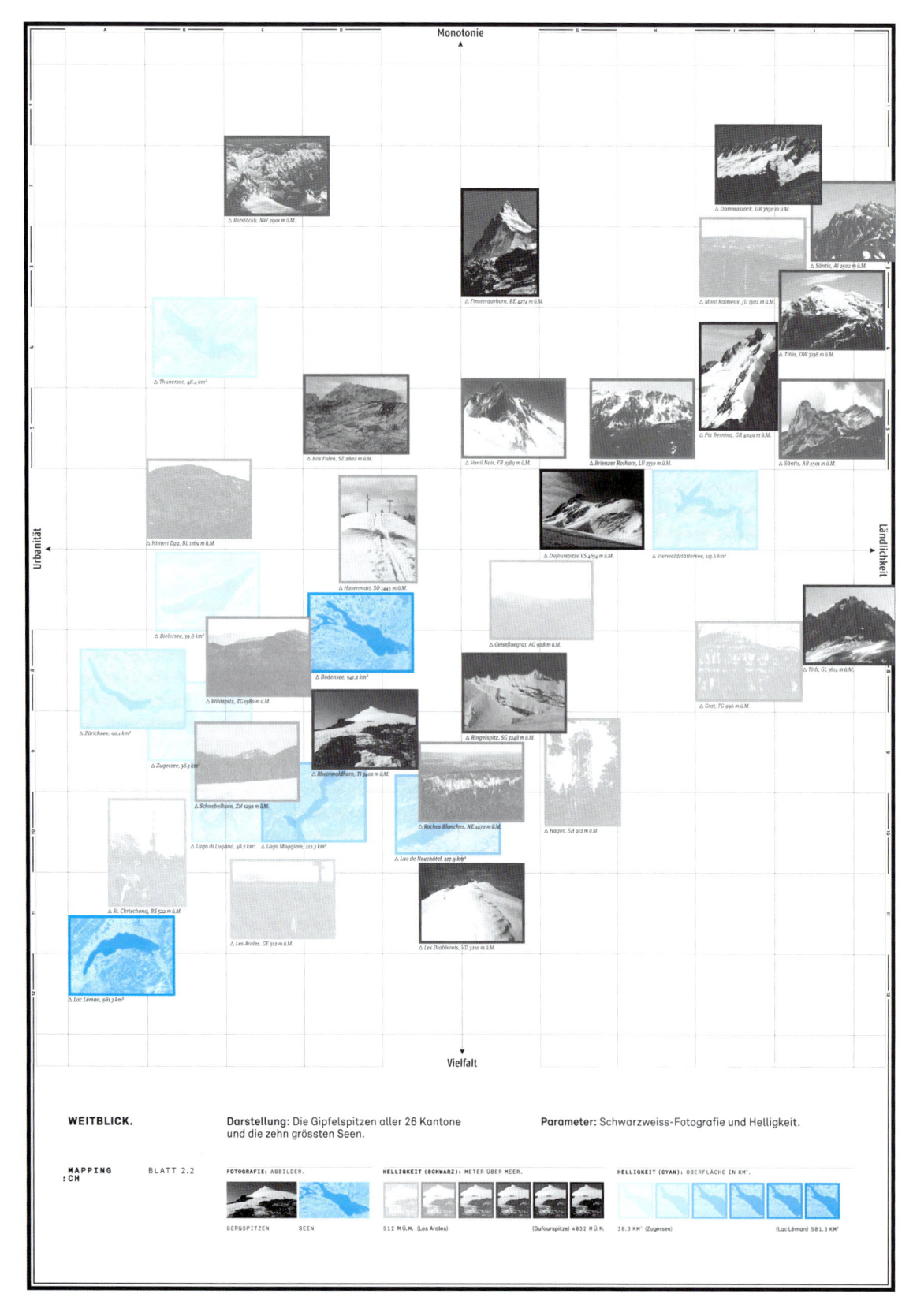

54 **Maps**

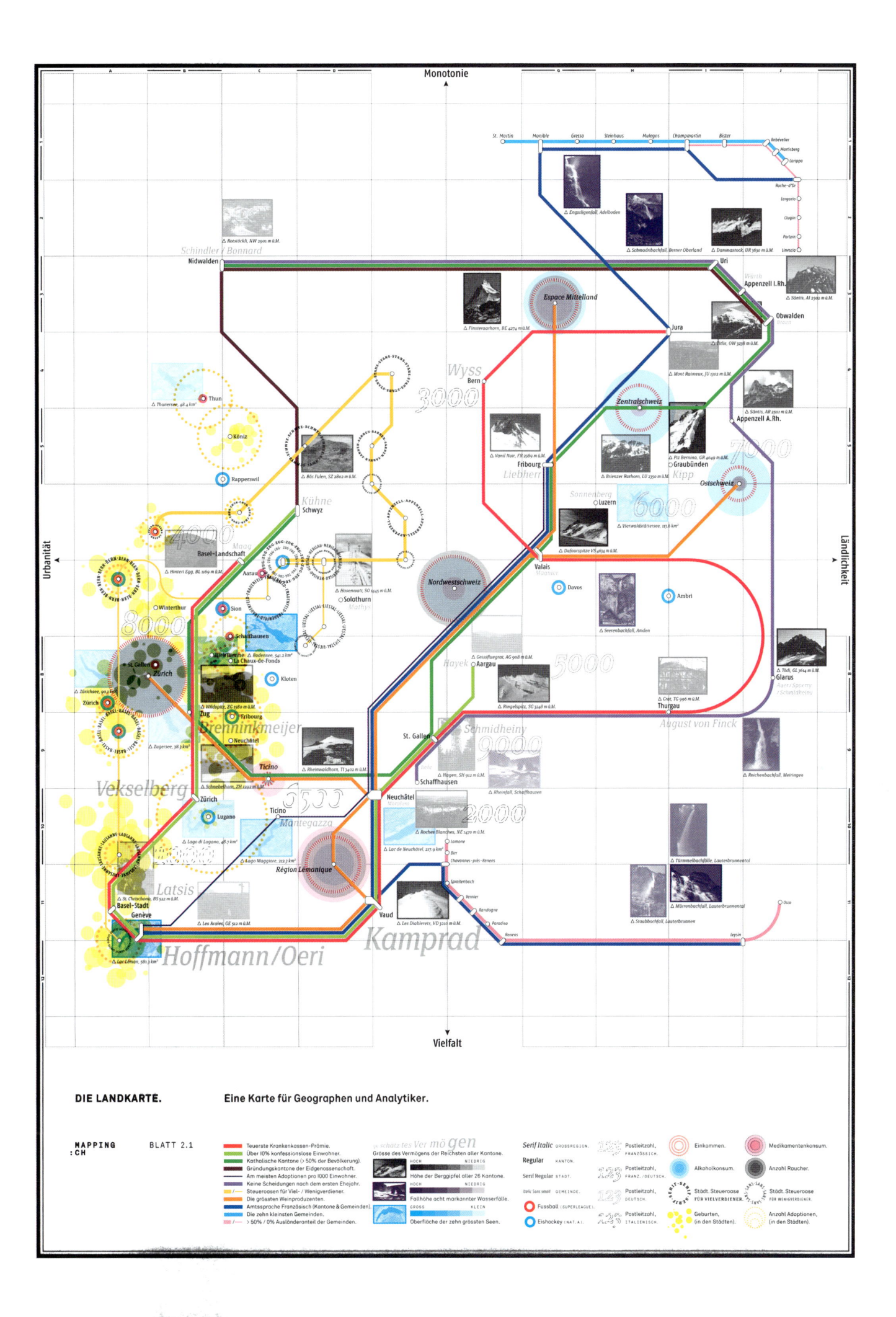

DIE LANDKARTE. Eine Karte für Geographen und Analytiker.

MAPPING :CH BLATT 2.1

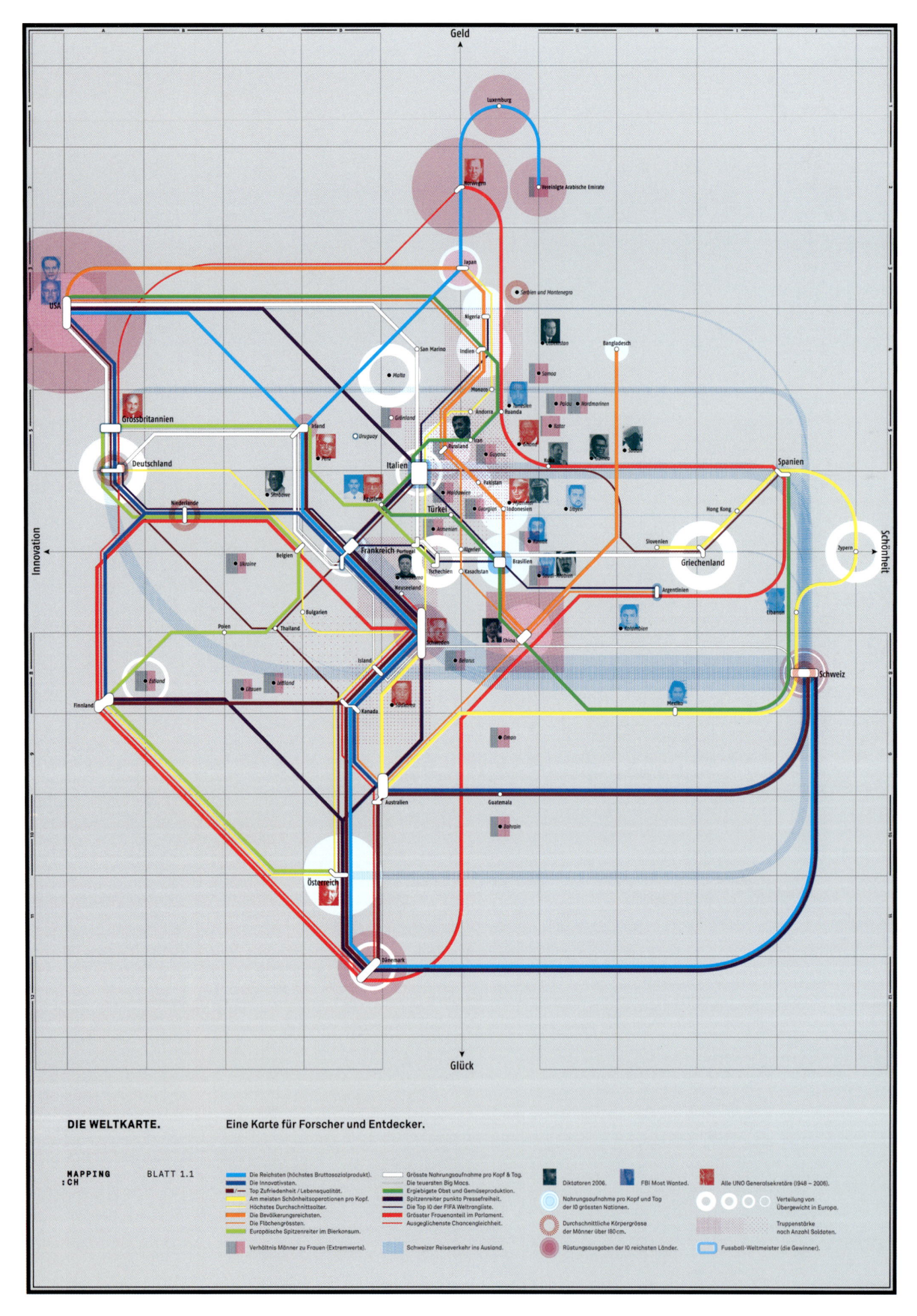

DIE WELTKARTE.
Eine Karte für Forscher und Entdecker.

MAPPING :CH BLATT 1.1

- Die Reichsten (höchstes Bruttosozialprodukt).
- Die Innovativsten.
- Top Zufriedenheit / Lebensqualität.
- Am meisten Schönheitsoperationen pro Kopf.
- Höchstes Durchschnittsalter.
- Die Flächengrössten.
- Die Bevölkerungsreichsten.
- Europäische Spitzenreiter im Bierkonsum.
- Grösste Nahrungsaufnahme pro Kopf & Tag.
- Die teuersten Big Macs.
- Ergiebigste Obst und Gemüseproduktion.
- Spitzenreiter punkto Pressefreiheit.
- Die Top 10 der FIFA Weltrangliste.
- Grösster Frauenanteil im Parlament.
- Ausgeglichenste Chancengleichheit.

- Verhältnis Männer zu Frauen (Extremwerte).
- Schweizer Reiseverkehr ins Ausland.

- Diktatoren 2006.
- FBI Most Wanted.
- Nahrungsaufnahme pro Kopf und Tag der 10 grössten Nationen.
- Durchschnittliche Körpergrösse der Männer über 180 cm.
- Rüstungsausgaben der 10 reichsten Länder.

- Alle UNO Generalsekretäre (1948 – 2006).
- Verteilung von Übergewicht in Europa.
- Truppenstärke nach Anzahl Soldaten.
- Fussball-Weltmeister (die Gewinner).

56 **Maps**

Maps 57

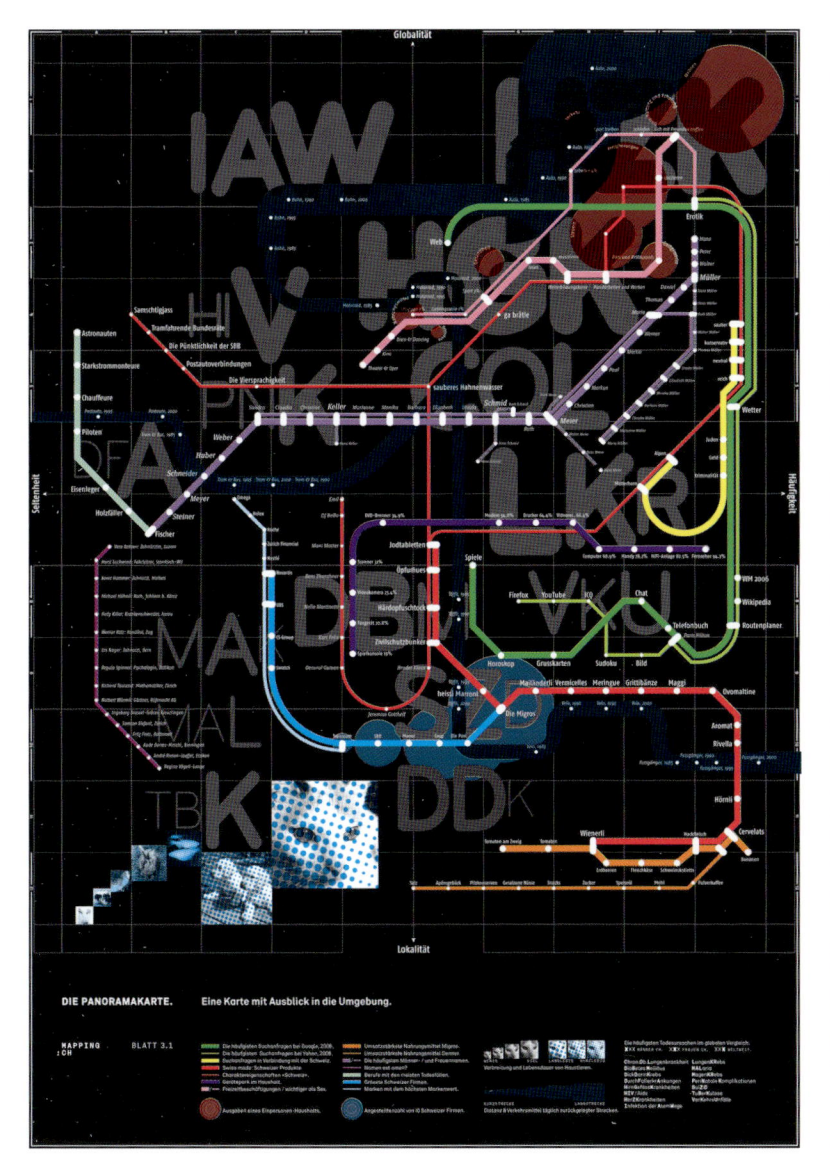

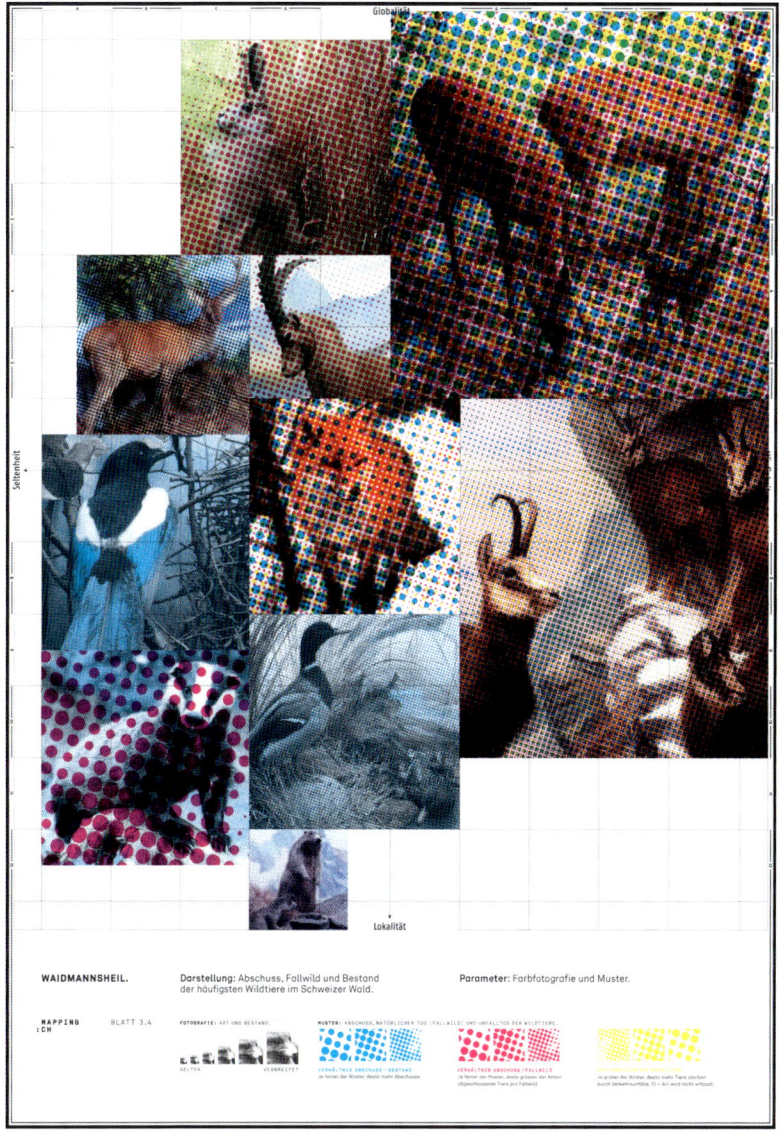

Noordzee ::
LUST :: www.lust.nl ::

Many people perceive the North Sea as being vast and empty. LUST switches this premise with Noordzee and illustrates the sea's fullness: Humans have left their marks, ships that have run aground, and cables, pipes, and traces of oil have left their own residue. Noordzee is a visual manifestation of a young inner sea that is described from twenty-one alternative points of view, producing twenty-one thematic maps. The combination of these maps reveals fascinating links and gives rise, in a geological grid, to 421 truly unique maps.

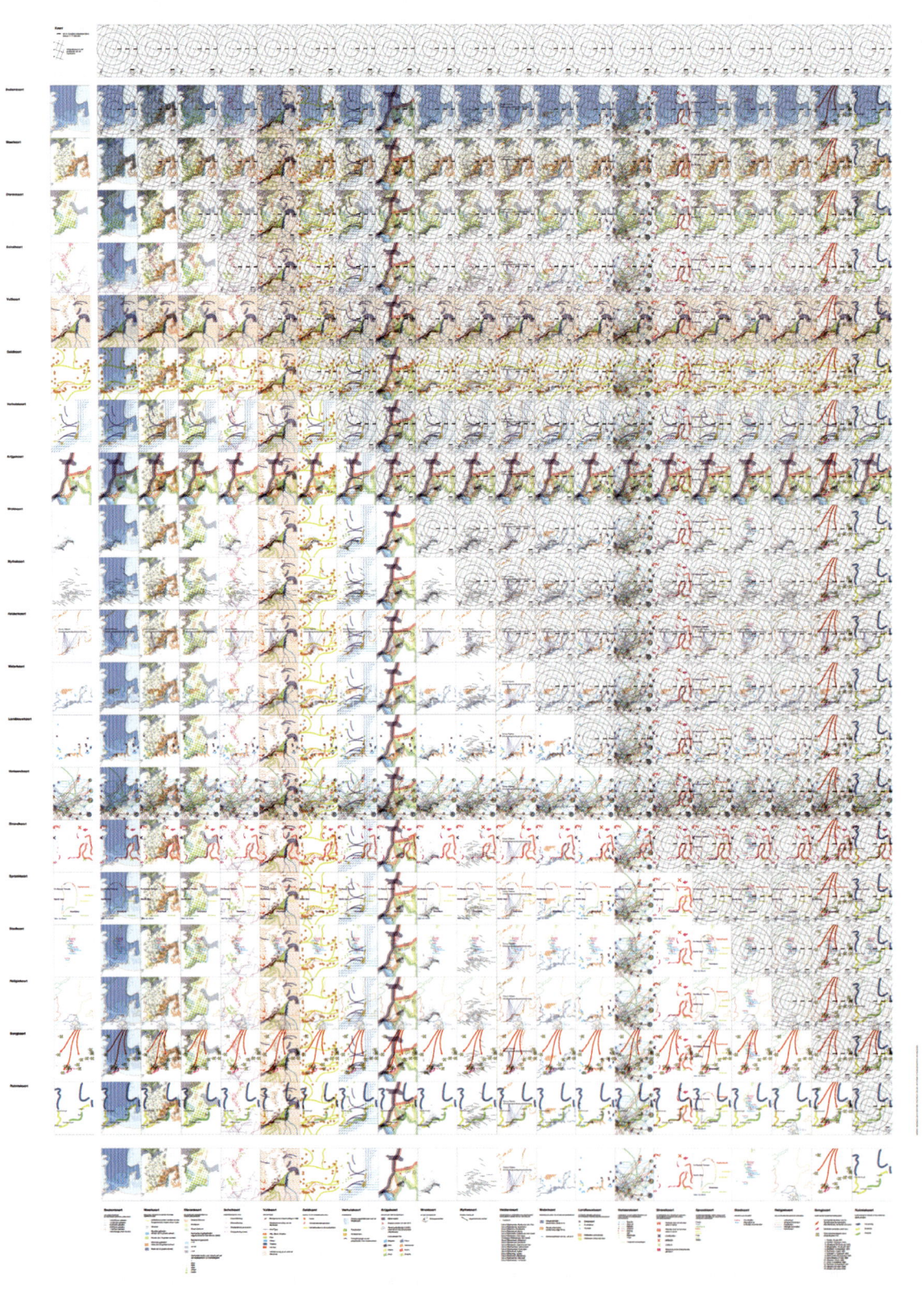

58 **Maps**

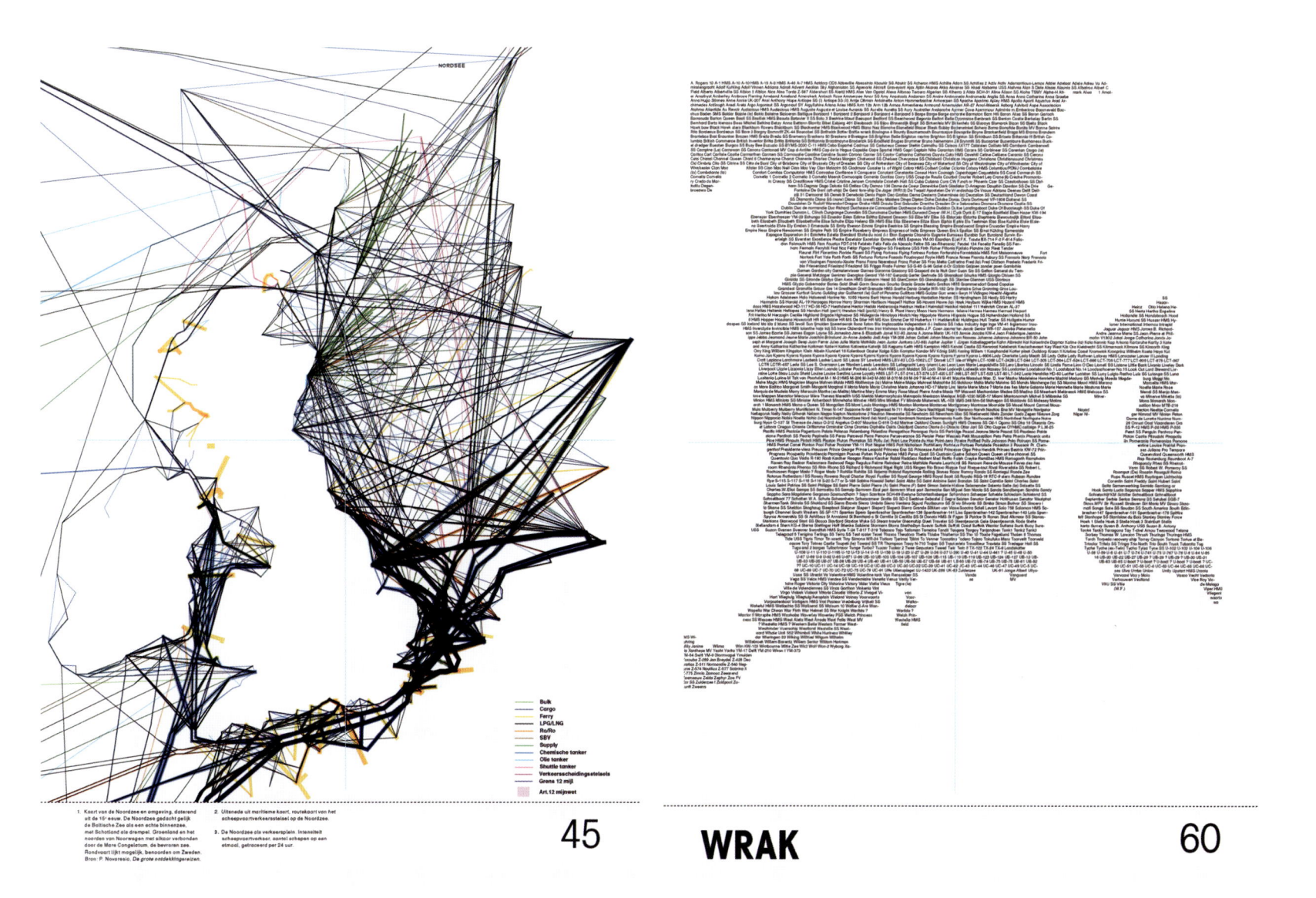

1. Kaart van de Noordzee en omgeving, daterend uit de 16e eeuw. De Noordzee gedacht gelijk de Baltische Zee als een echte binnenzee, met Schotland als drempel. Groenland en het noorden van Noorwegen met elkaar verbonden door de Mare Congelatum, de bevroren zee. Rondvaart lijkt mogelijk, benoorden om Zweden. Bron: P. Novoresio, De grote ontdekkingsreizen.

2. Uittreksel uit maritieme kaart, routekaart van het scheepvaartverkeerstelsel op de Noordzee.

3. De Noordzee als verkeersplein. Intensiteit scheepvaartverkeer, aantal schepen op een etmaal, getraceerd per 24 uur.

45 **WRAK** 60

WERELD

LAND

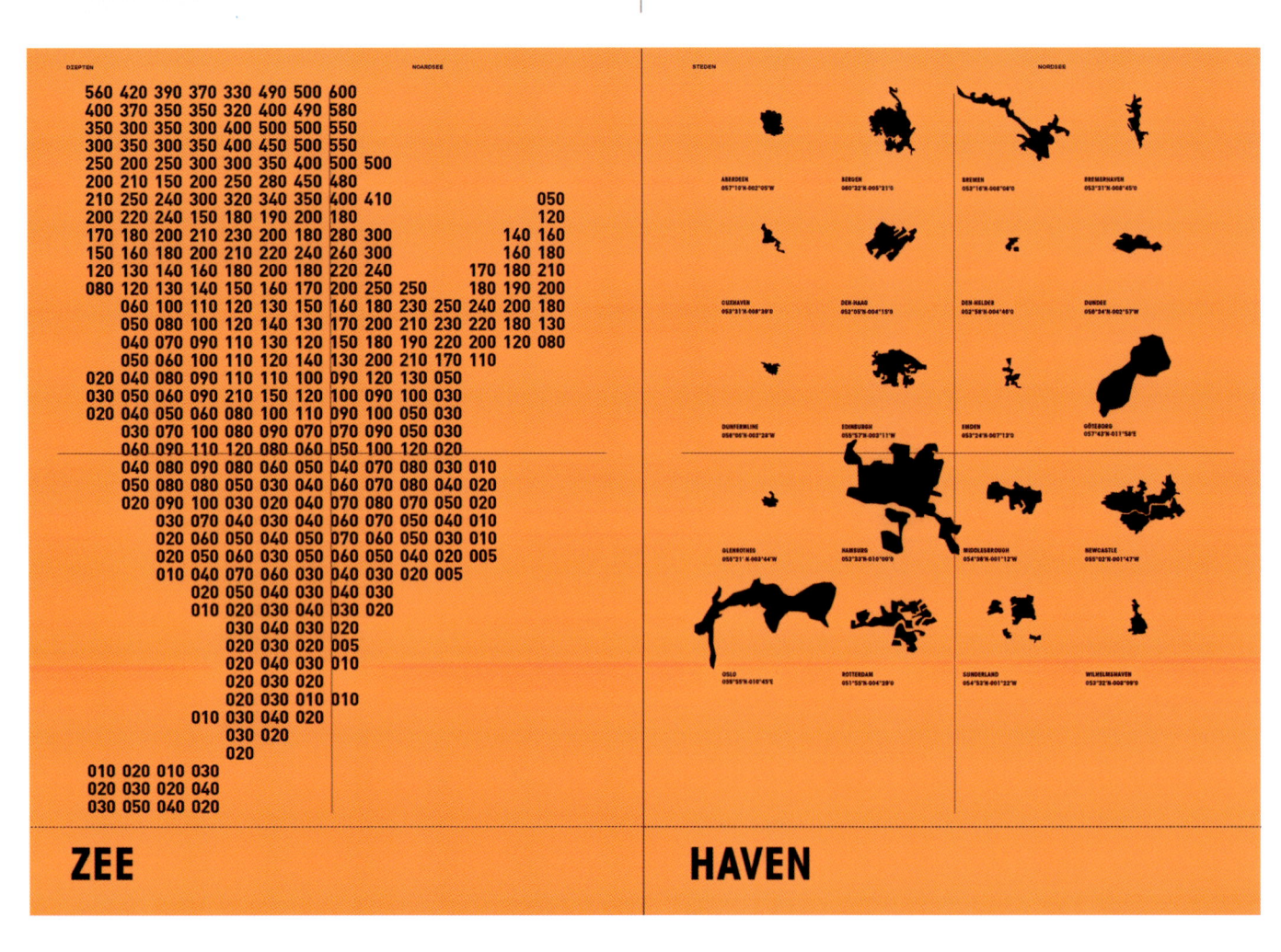

ZEE

HAVEN

NORDSEE · NORDSJÖN

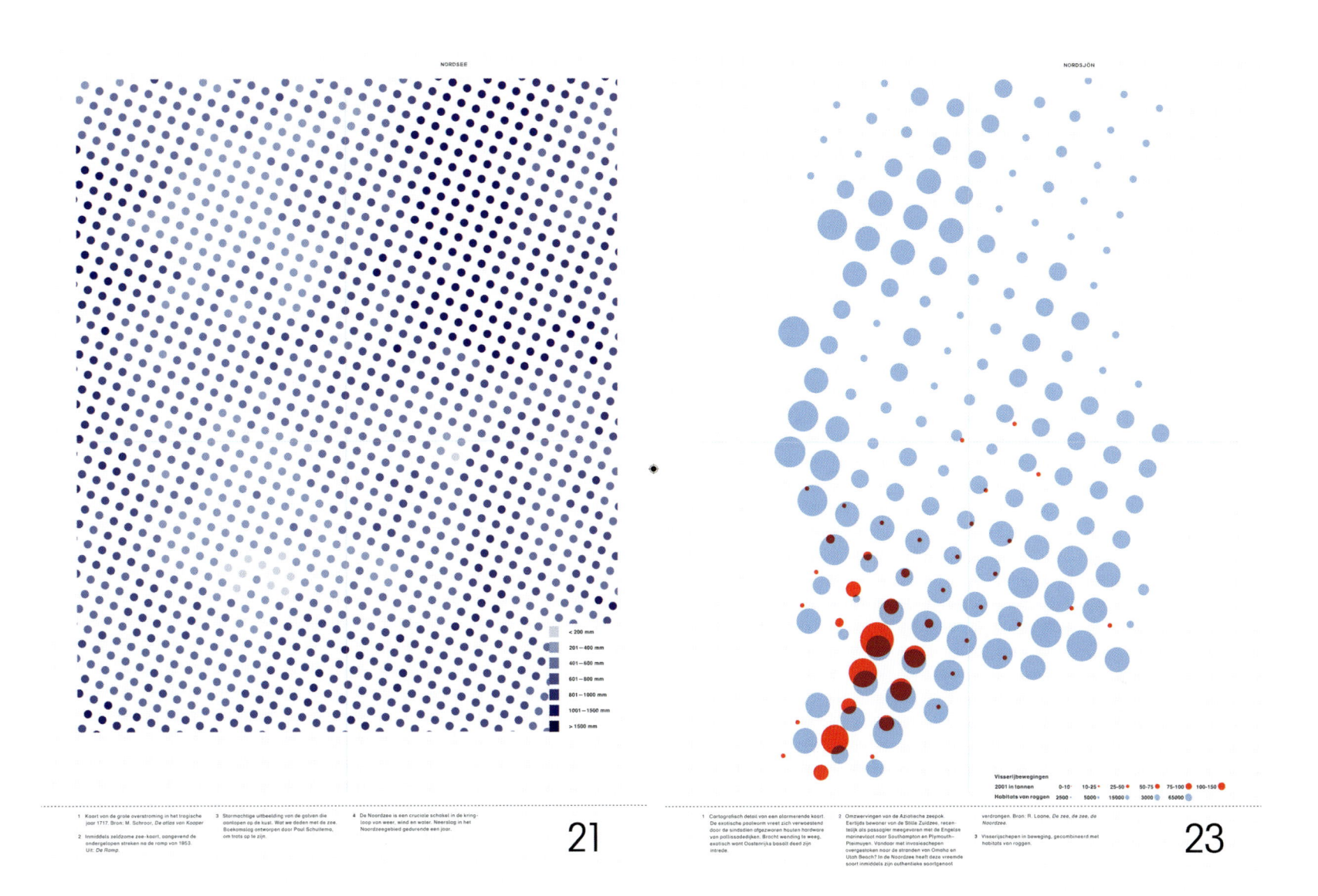

| < 200 mm |
| 201 – 400 mm |
| 401 – 600 mm |
| 601 – 800 mm |
| 801 – 1000 mm |
| 1001 – 1500 mm |
| > 1500 mm |

1 Kaart van de grote overstroming in het tragische jaar 1717. Bron: M. Schroor, *De atlas van Kooper*
2 Inmiddels zeldzame zee-kaart, aangevend de ondergelopen streken na de ramp van 1953. Uit: *De Ramp*.
3 Stormachtige uitbeelding van de golven die aanlopen op de kust. Wat we deden met de zee. Boekomslag ontworpen door Paul Schuitema, om trots op te zijn.
4 De Noordzee is een cruciale schakel in de kringloop van weer, wind en water. Neerslag in het Noordzeegebied gedurende een jaar.

21

Visserijbewegingen
2001 in tonnen   0-10 ·   10-25 ·   25-50 ●   50-75 ●   75-100 ●   100-150 ●
Habitats van roggen   3500 ·   5000 ·   15000 ○   3000 ○   65000 ○

1 Cartografisch detail of een alarmerende kaart. De exotische pokkuurn vreet zich verwoestend door de sindsdien afgezworen houten hoofdwere van polissedeidjken. Bracht wending te weeg, exotisch want Oostenrijk boodt deed zijn intrede.
2 Omzwervingen van de Azjatische zeepok. Eertijds bewoner van de Stille Zuidzee, recentelijk als passagier meegevoeren met de Engelse marinevloot naar Southampton en Plymouth-Plzenveyn. Vandaar met invasieschepen overgestoken naar de stranden van Omaha en Utah Beach? In de Noordzee heeft deze vreemde soort inmiddels zijn authentieke soortgenoot verdrongen. Bron: R. Loone, *De zee, de zee, de Noordzee*.
3 Visserijschepen in beweging, gecombineerd met habitats van roggen.

23

Maps 61

Europan 9 Norway ::
Ariane Spanier :: www.arianespanier.com ::

Europan Norway is a non-profit foundation responsible for organizing Europan, the European architectural competition, in Norway. On the occasion of the ninth edition of Europan, a catalog was designed with thin lines being the main feature on its pages. A map shows the competitors' geographical origins.

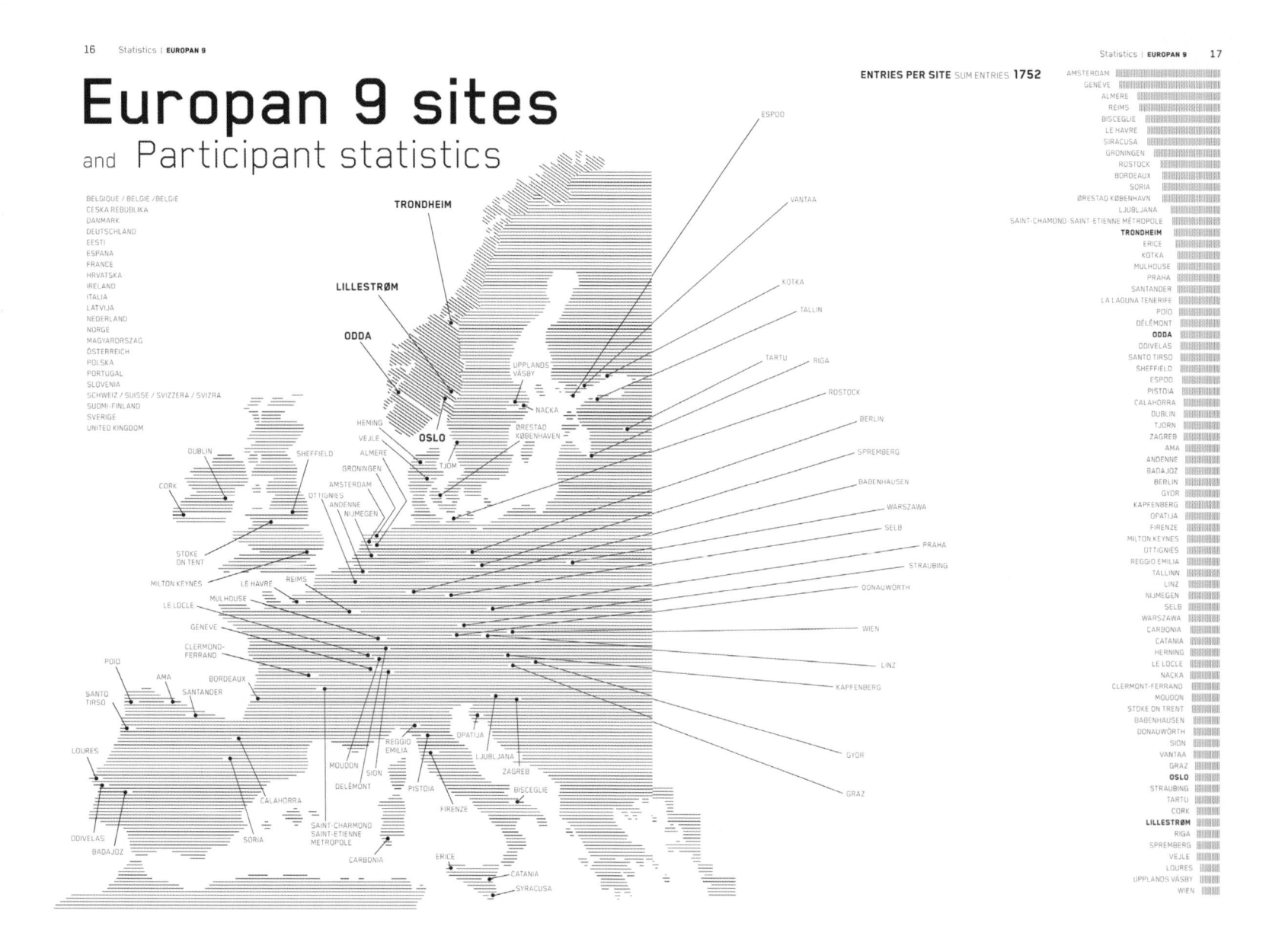

Association Nationale pour la Formation permanente du personnel Hospitalier (ANFH) ::
Atelier Chévara etc :: www.atelier-chevara.com ::

Instead of hiding those graphic elements that may occasionally go unnoticed, Atelier Chévara etc decided to transform them into monumental sculptures and turn on the spotlight. So the maps and charts become the graphic argument of the project, but in such a way that they do not hinder their basic function: namely, to display the information, which in this case is the distribution of those establishments belonging to the ANFH.

LA STRUCTURE
26 DÉLÉGATIONS RÉGIONALES : LA PROXIMITÉ

L'ANFH compte plus de **1000 administrateurs**, tous professionnels issus de la fonction publique hospitalière, qui siègent de façon paritaire dans les instances nationales et régionales.

L'ANFH regroupe **206 professionnels** de la formation sur le terrain

26 délégués régionaux
25 conseillers en dispositifs individuels
30 conseillers formation
125 conseillers en gestion de fonds

Pour 5 régions, la totalité des établissements adhère à l'ANFH (Corse, Guyane, Haute-Normandie, Océan Indien et Poitou-Charentes) et l'ensemble des agents peut bénéficier des financements viennent ensuite les régions Auvergne, Languedoc-Roussillon et Limousin ayant chacune un taux d'adhésion en termes d'agents concernés de plus de 99%.
Au total, 16 régions sur 26 ont un taux d'adhésion des établissements supérieur à 90%.

Au niveau national, 92,3% des établissements de la FPH sont adhérents à l'ANFH en 2008 ce qui recouvre 82,4% des agents.

2 306 nombre total d'établissements adhérents
762 782 nombre total d'agents

LES INSTANCES NATIONALES

■ **L'Assemblée Générale (AG)** se compose des membres du Conseil d'Administration (CA) et de six membres désignés paritairement par chacun des Conseils Régionaux de Gestion (CRG).
Réunie au moins une fois par an, elle fixe les orientations de l'ANFH et approuve les comptes annuels.

■ **Le Conseil d'Administration (CA)** se compose de vingt membres représentant les employeurs et vingt membres représentant les organisations syndicales. Il est chargé de mettre en application les décisions de l'Assemblée Générale, de gérer les fonds et de veiller au bon fonctionnement de l'association.

■ **Trois commissions** instruisent les affaires et émettent un avis avant décision du Conseil d'Administration :
• la Commission des Affaires Administratives et Financières (CAAF),
• la Commission d'Audit Interne (CAI),
• la Commission d'Études et Développement de la Formation Permanente (CEDFP).

■ **Le Bureau National (BN)** est élu chaque année au sein du Conseil d'Administration. Il est composé paritairement du Président, du Vice-président et de quatre autres membres. Il est chargé de l'exécution des décisions du conseil d'administration et en prépare les réunions.

■ **Le Comité de Gestion National (CGN)** a été créé dans le cadre de la gestion du Congé de Formation Professionnelle. Son rôle est de collecter et de gérer la cotisation des établissements et de définir les règles de prise en charge.

LES INSTANCES RÉGIONALES

Chaque délégation régionale est administrée localement par des instances paritaires :

■ **un Conseil Régional de Gestion (CRG)**, chargé de la mise en œuvre de la politique nationale et régionale,

■ **un Conseil Pédagogique Régional (CPR)**, à vocation consultative,

■ **un Comité de Gestion Régional (CGR)** qui gère les fonds destinés au financement du CFP et du bilan de compétences.

LE SIÈGE

Sur les 300 salariés que compte l'ANFH, une soixantaine travaille au siège avec pour objectifs, en application des décisions des instances nationales, de :

■ **organiser** et tenir la comptabilité de l'association,

■ **contrôler la gestion** et veiller au respect des règles de la collecte,

■ **informer les établissements** et les agents sur les droits et les dispositifs de la formation,

■ **servir de support technique, financier et informatique** aux délégations régionales,

■ **mettre au point les logiciels** destinés aux établissements,

■ **réaliser une veille sectorielle** sur l'actualité de la fonction publique hospitalière et de la formation professionnelle continue.

DES DÉLÉGATIONS RÉGIONALES

Les délégations régionales mettent en œuvre et gèrent les actions de formation définies par les instances régionales en fonction des besoins exprimés par les établissements de leur territoire. Les délégués régionaux sont en majorité originaires du secteur hospitalier.

Ils ont une expertise reconnue dans le domaine de la formation.
Pour accroître le niveau de professionnalisation des salariés de l'ANFH, la chaire de formation des adultes du CNAM a notamment mis au point début 2008 un « Certificat de compétence de conseiller en ingénierie de formation », spécialement adapté pour les conseillers des délégations régionales ANFH.

97 38 208 (Nord-Pas-de-Calais)
124 43 408 (Bretagne)
75 18 885 (Basse-Normandie)
79 29 241 (Haute-Normandie)
91 30 376 (Picardie)
183 45 635 (Pays-de-la-Loire)
125 56 004 (Île-de-France)
67 28 606 (Champagne-Ardenne)
104 34 251 (Lorraine)
141 33 344 (Centre)
92 28 080 (Poitou-Charentes)
124 29 476 (Bourgogne)
51 18 250 (Franche-Comté)
67 28 797 (Alsace)
72 16 107 (Limousin)
107 24 538 (Auvergne)
110 41 014 (Rhône)
138 40 392 (Aquitaine)
111 37 143 (Midi-Pyrénées)
87 31 944 (Languedoc-Roussillon)
87 30 930 (Alpes)
141 59 290 (PACA)

15 5 569 (Martinique)
3 1 787 (Guyane)
8 7 969 (Océan Indien)
7 3 538 (Corse)

Subjectieve Atlas van Nederland ::
Annelys de Vet :: www.annelysdevet.nl ::

For this project, more than a dozen students from Design Academy in Eindhoven drew maps of the Netherlands, showing the habits, culture, and language of its citizens. The pages of this book, designed and published by Annelys de Vet, illustrates what binds the Dutch people together.

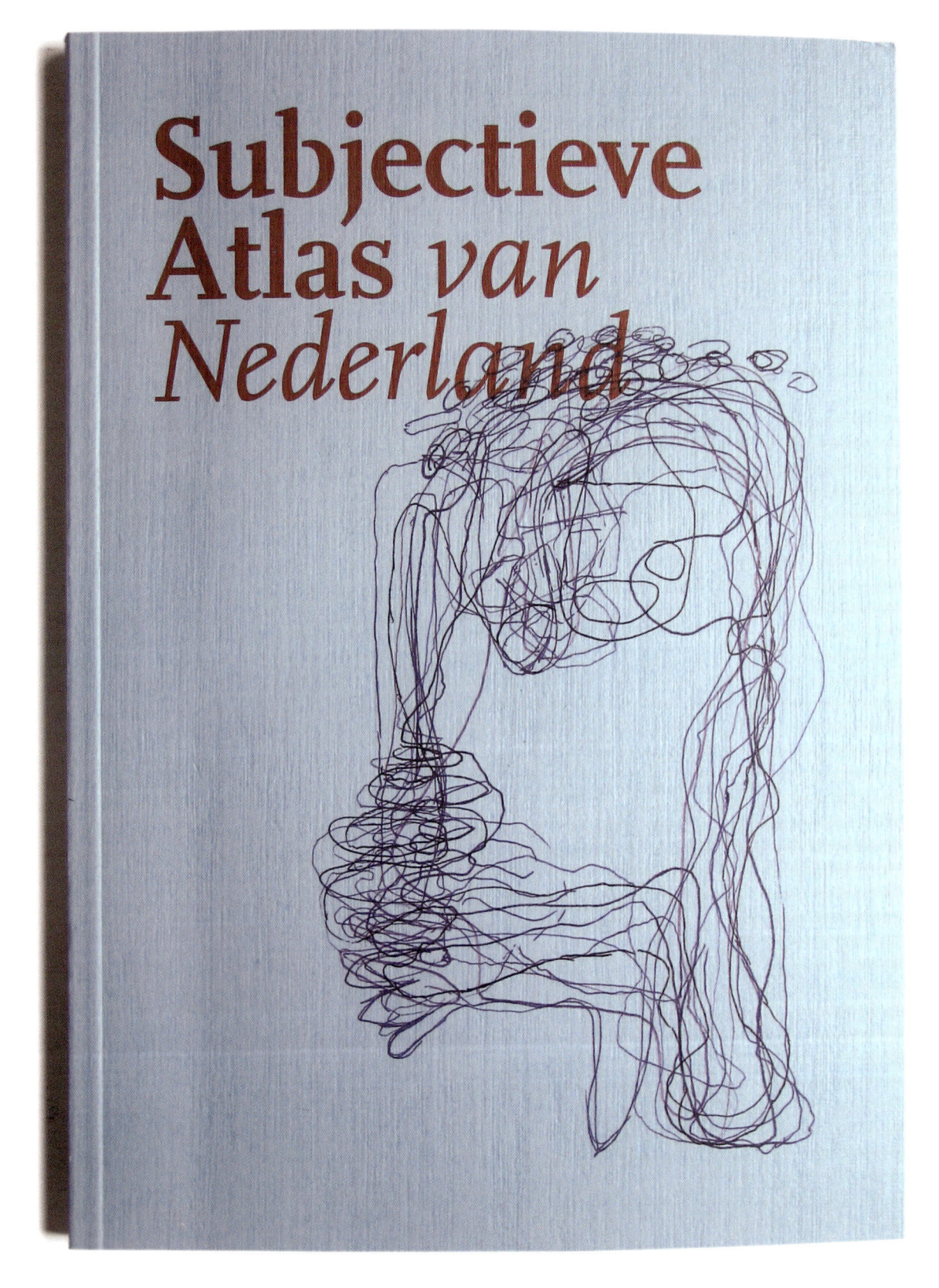

What if?, Itay Lahav

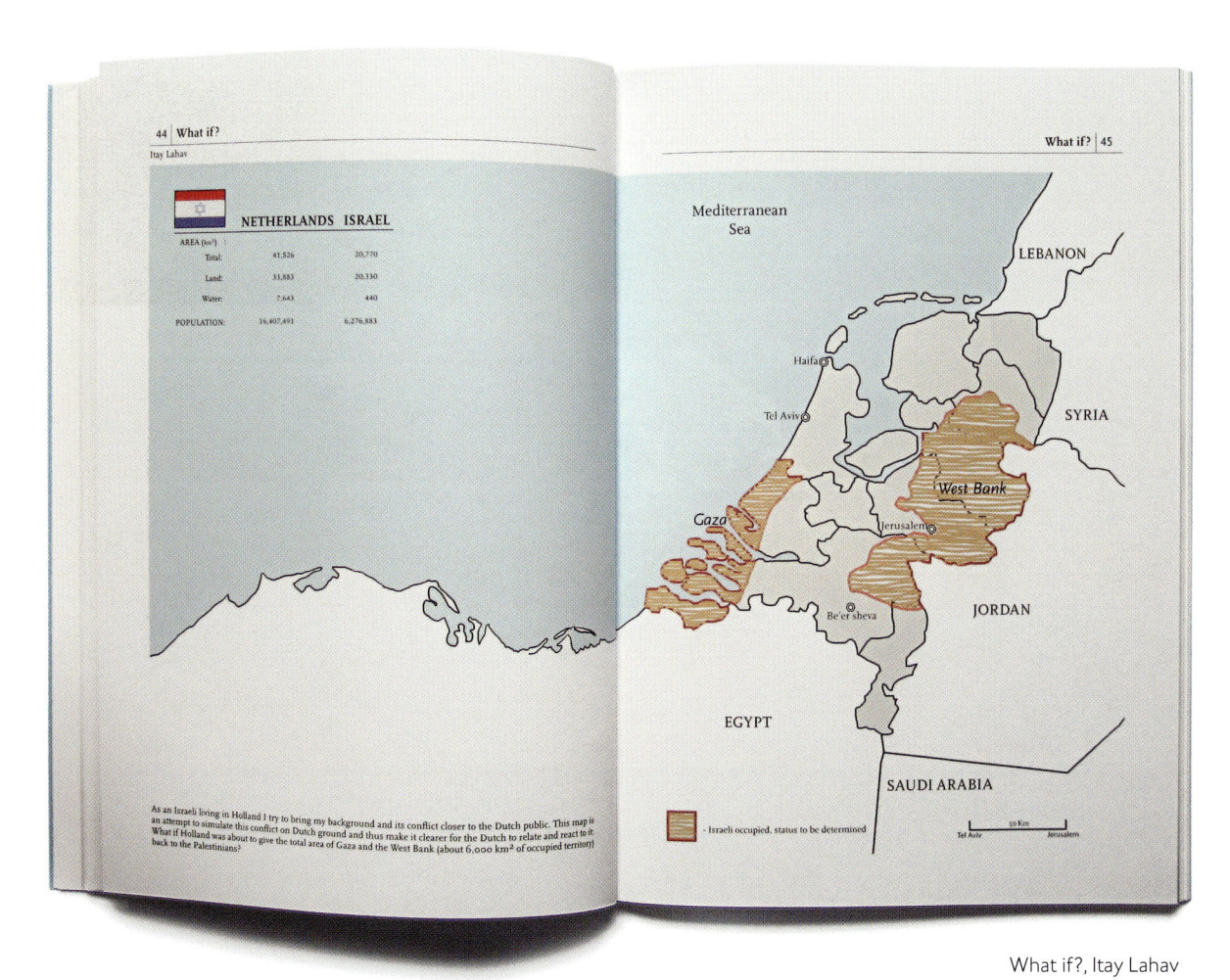

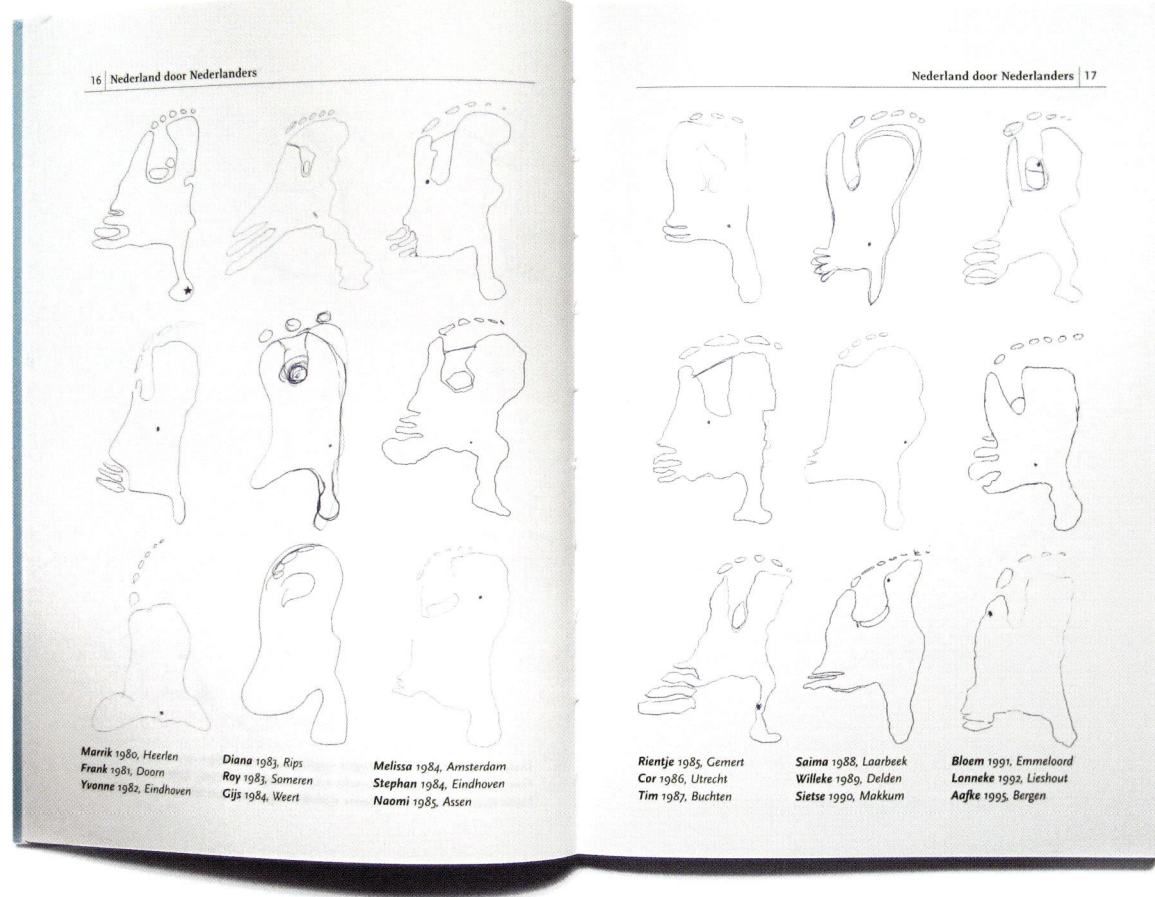

The Netherlands by the Dutch, Jeanine Essink

Maps 65

Etnia Barcelona Poster ::
Jordi Boix 40Gurus :: www.jordiboix40gurus.com ::

Etnia Barcelona is a company that manufactures designer glasses. The company wanted a new image for its brand based on the values expressed in its products, a project for which the Catalan studio Jordi Boix 40Gurus was commissioned. One of the key elements in redesigning the brand was the use of vivid color to promote a youthful, dynamic sense of energy and vision.

66 **Maps**

Never Again ::
Patrick Maun :: patrickmaun.com ::

This poster is part of a multidiscipline artistic exploration called *The Genocide Project*, which has denounced violence since 2005, representing it in various ways such as installations, videos, and photos. "Never Again" is a maxim that every country, and every single person has repeated on various occasions throughout history. Yet, genocide continues to happen with startling regularity.

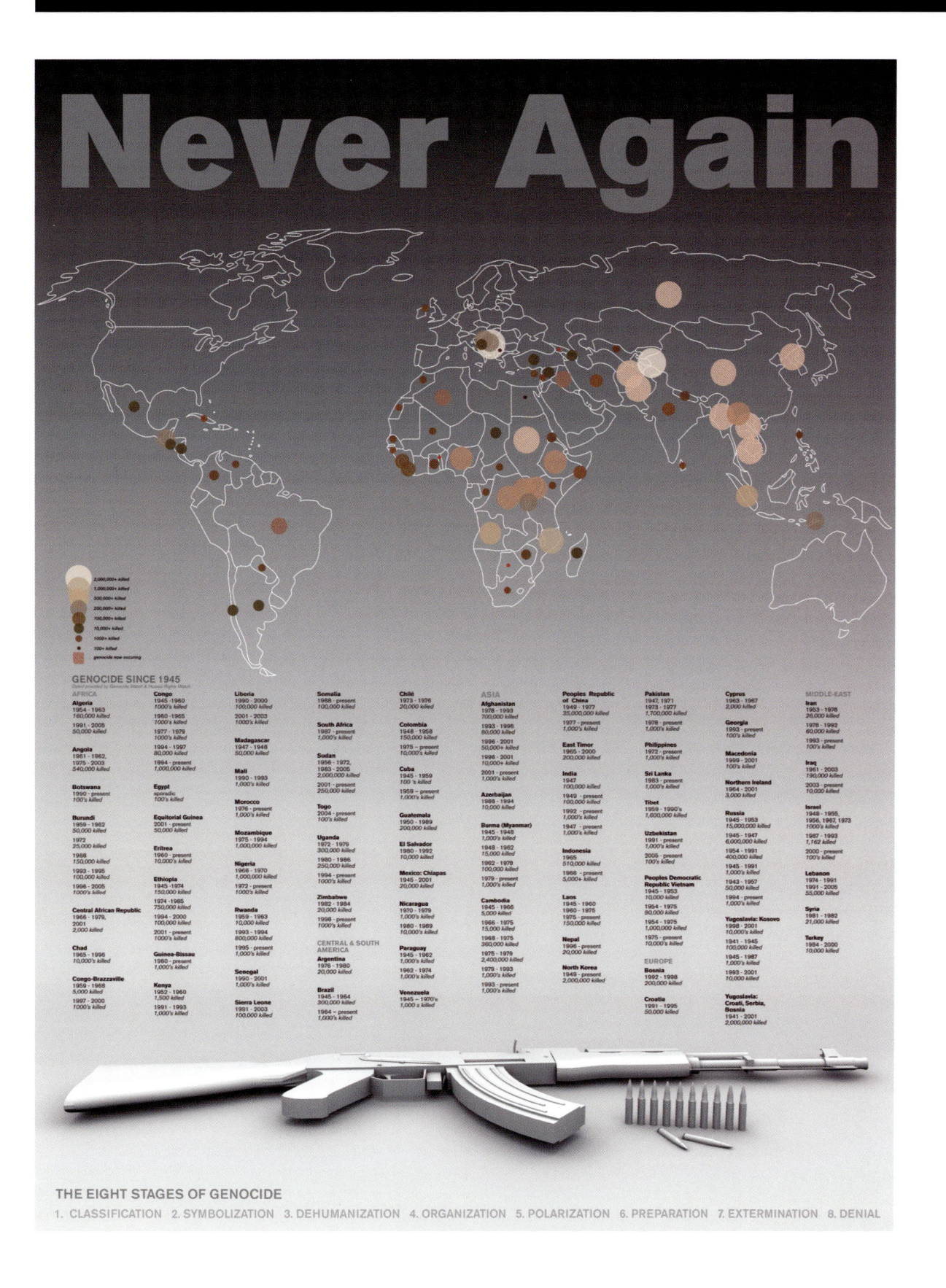

Maps 67

Parco agricolo Sud Milano ::
Leftloft :: www.leftloft.com ::

The Region of Lombardy commissioned Leftloft, an Italian studio, with the design of the identity of the nineteen projects for the re-evaluation of the agricultural park Parco Sud, with the intention of protecting farming activities and educating people to use environmental resources in a responsible way. The projects consisted of a series of explanatory posters, a brochure in CD format, signage, illustrations, infographics, and a Web site.

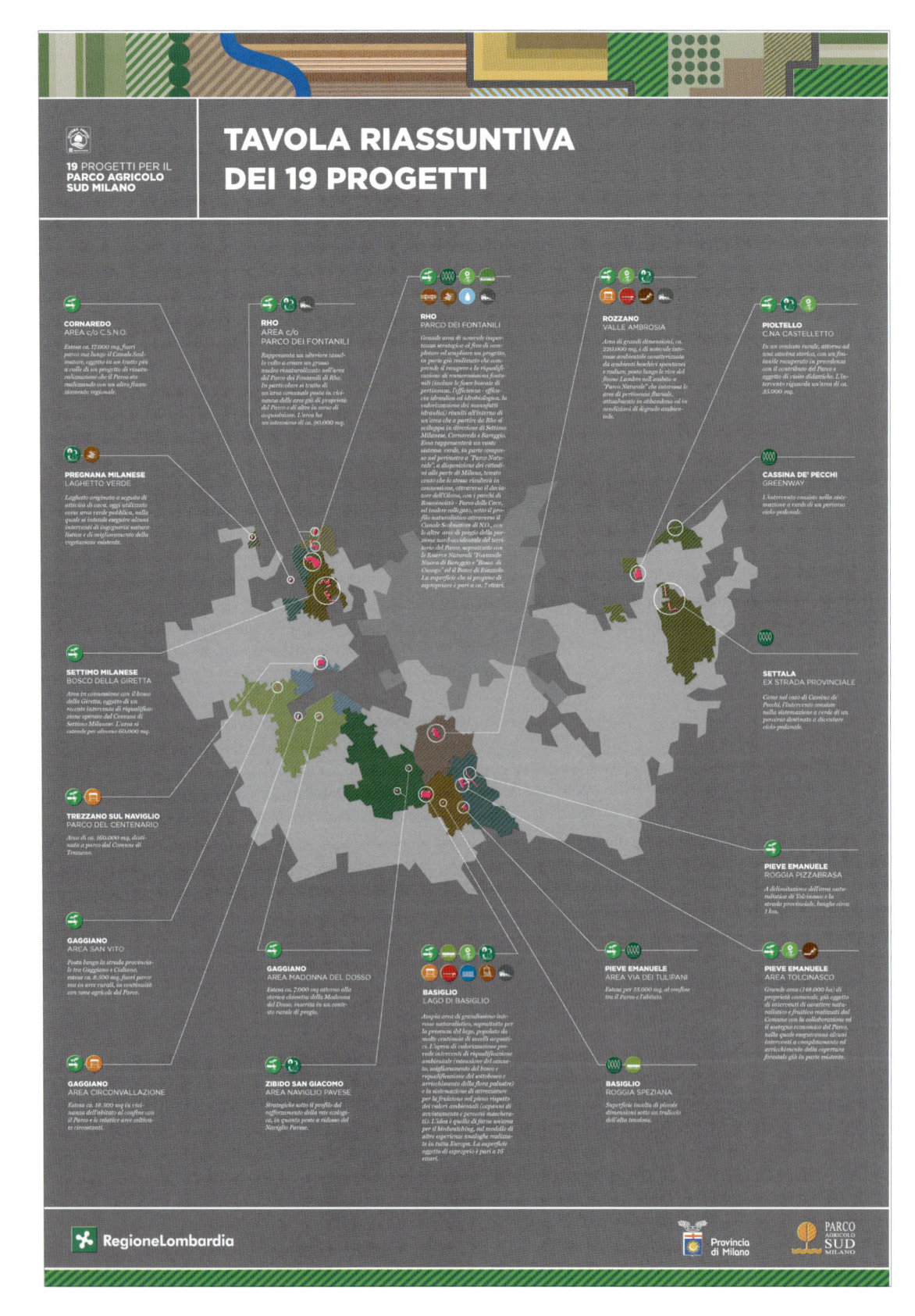

INTERVENTI DI **MIGLIORAMENTO FORESTALE**

DIREZIONE **CORNAREDO**

DIREZIONE **VIGHIGNOLO**

DI **PER**

The Hague Catered Capital ::
LUST :: www.lust.nl ::

In 2009 the Stroom Den Haag Foundation organized Foodprint, a program focusing on discovering the influence of food on the culture, form, and function of a city, with The Hague as a case study. On this occasion, LUST was invited to design a series of maps showing the impact of food consumption on the offices or catering facilities used by ministers.

CateredCapital:
- Levensmiddelenwinkels
- Restaurants
- Cateringbedrijven
- Ambassades
- Ministeries
- Verzorg/verpleeg/ziekenhuizen

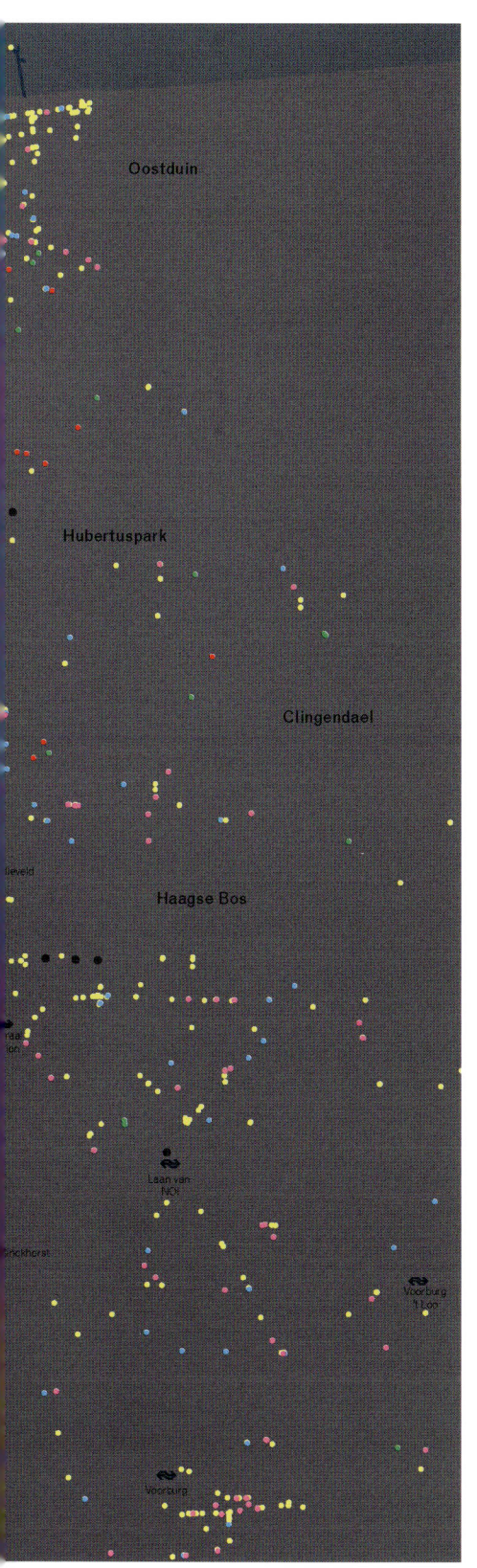

Oostduin

Hubertuspark

Clingendael

Haagse Bos

Laan van NOI

Voorburg

Voorburg

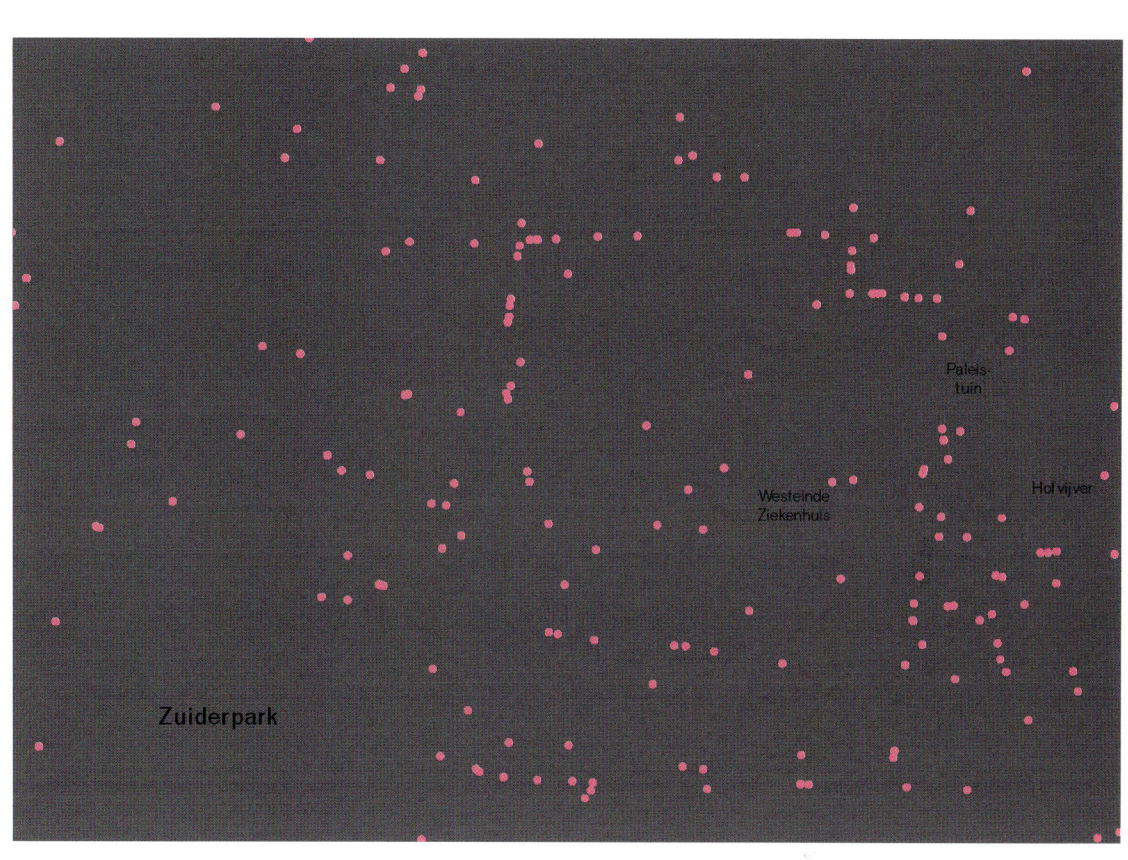

Paleis-
tuin

Westeinde
Ziekenhuis

Hof vijver

Zuiderpark

Maps 71

Get Involved Poster ::
TwoPoints.Net :: www.twopoints.net ::

The Get Involved parties staged in London are famous for their original posters, one of which was designed by TwoPoints.Net. This poster stands out because of reader participation: the poster's dots need to be aligned with the aid of a GPS in order to work out the event name and location. Each color represents a different letter and the final dot indicates the club's address.

2004 Mondriaan Foundation Annual Report ::
LUST :: www.lust.nl ::

The Mondriaan Foundation annual report provides information on the thousands of projects financed by the foundation. LUST developed a typographic system to illustrate the projects and opted for clean infographics to reflect the artistic and cultural nature of the foundation. This project won the prize for the Best Designed Annual Report in 2005.

Ondersteuning

Beeldende kunst en vormgeving

290 aanvragen
164 gehonoreerd
56,5%

De KunstKoopregeling is in deze kaart buiten beschouwing gelaten

Ondersteuning totaal € 25.766.725
Beeldende kunst en vormgeving € 8.615.263

41

Wolf Theiss Country Brochures ::
The Partners :: www.thepartners.co.uk ::

Wolf Theiss is a legal firm in central Europe that sets great stock in acquiring knowledge and understanding of the local market in each of the countries where the firm has a presence. The firm wanted to reflect company philosophy in their graphic communications, and commissioned The Partners (the same studio that had already revamped their corporate brand) to produce these brochures. Thanks to their graphics, the firm now stands out from other firms in the same sector.

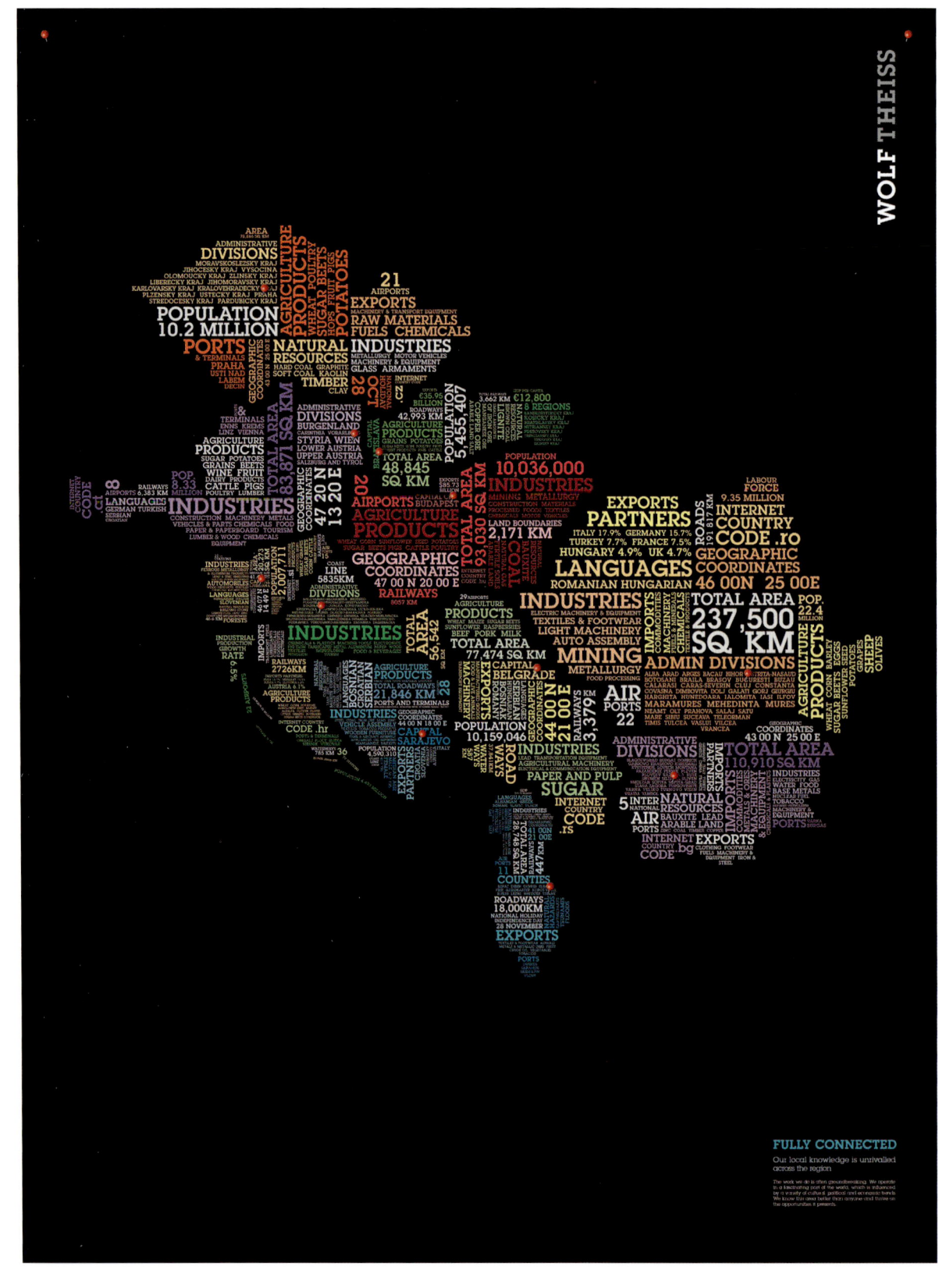

Maps 75

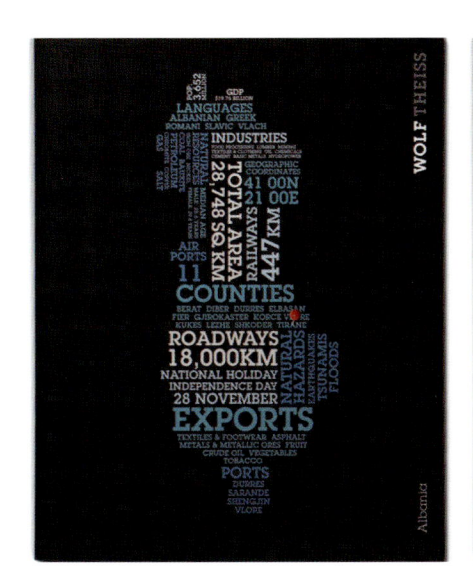

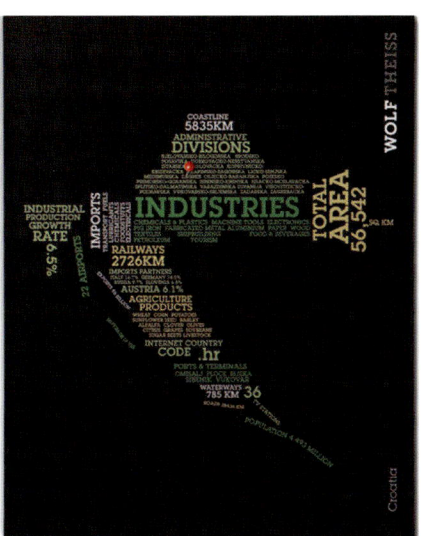

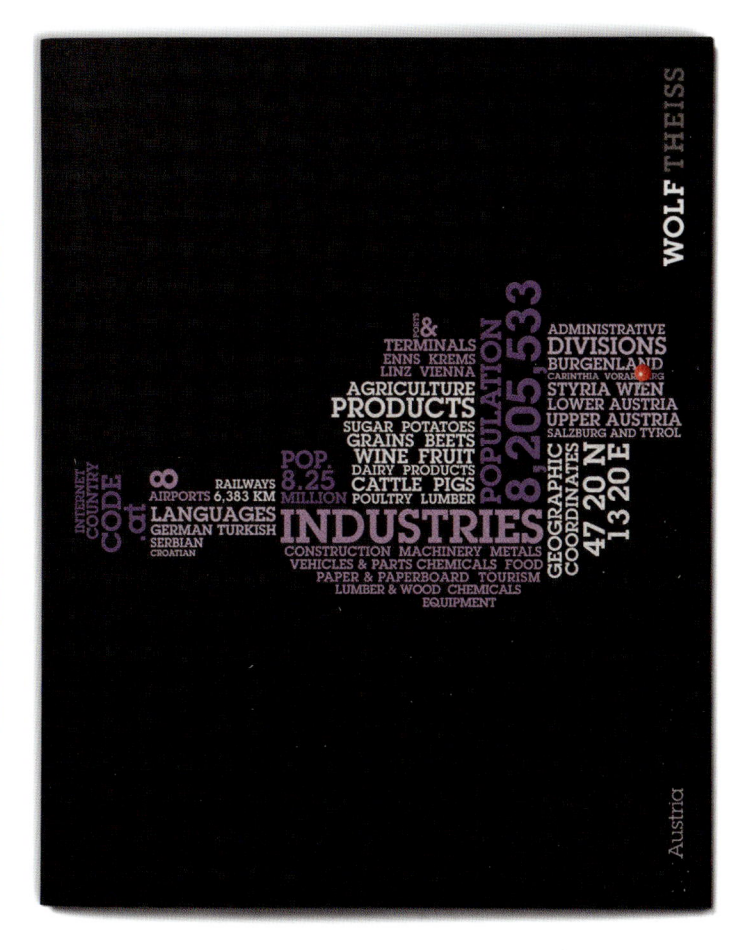

World/Spectrum/Archive ::
LUST :: www.lust.nl ::

This interesting project assesses the positive and negative connotations of the news to obtain an image of the state of the world every day. Five pieces of news are extracted from each country. This information is then analyzed, and an average of negative and positive words is determined. LUST is then able to determine what color—bright for positive news and sober for negative—should be used to print that country's headlines on that particular day. In this way, it is possible to visualize how a country changes over time.

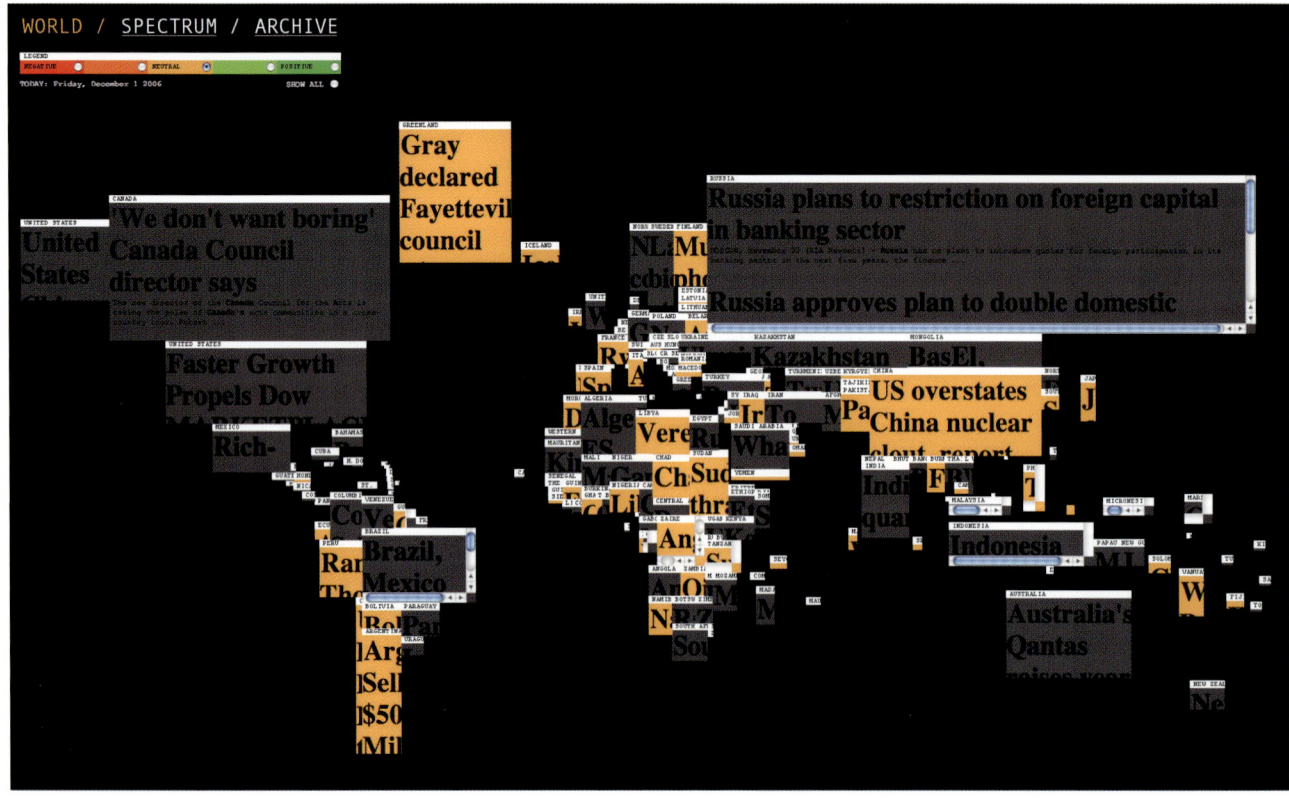

Maps 77

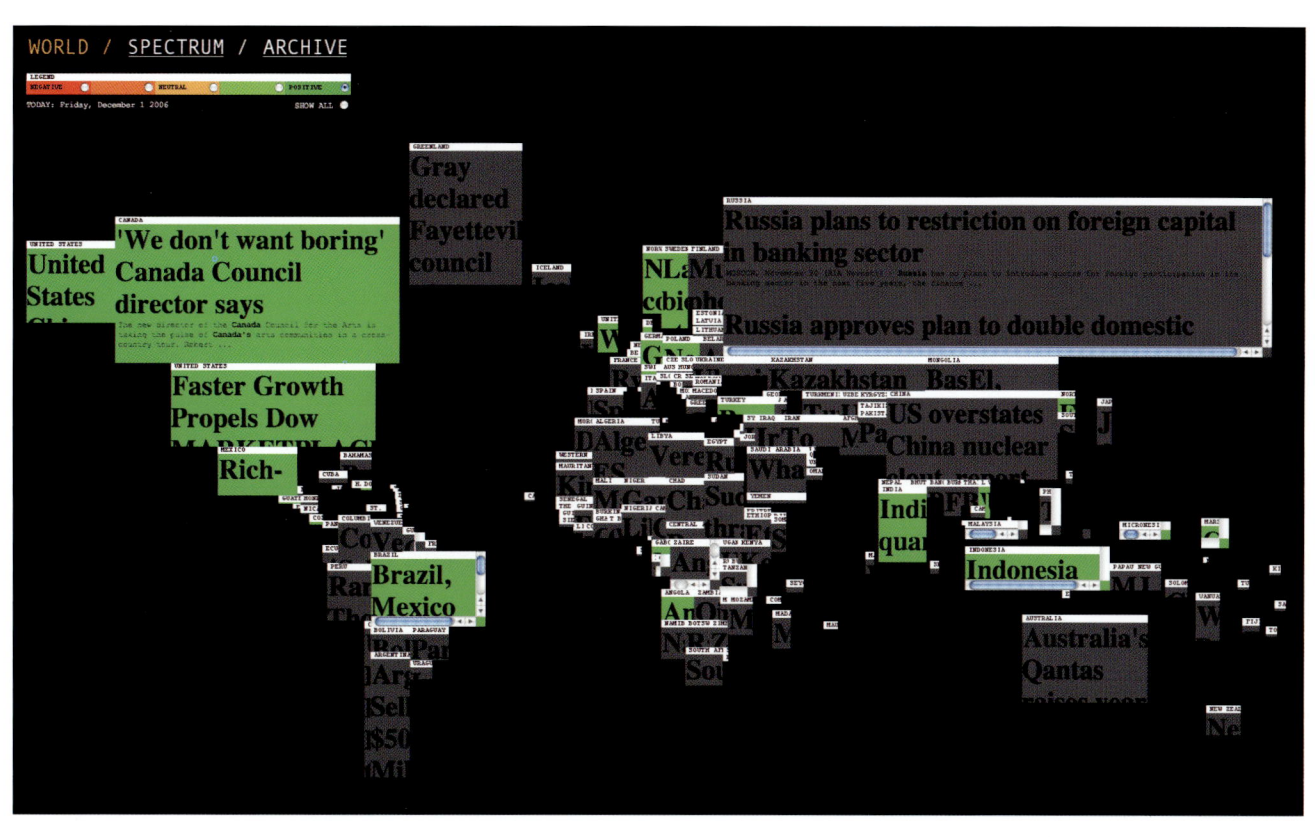

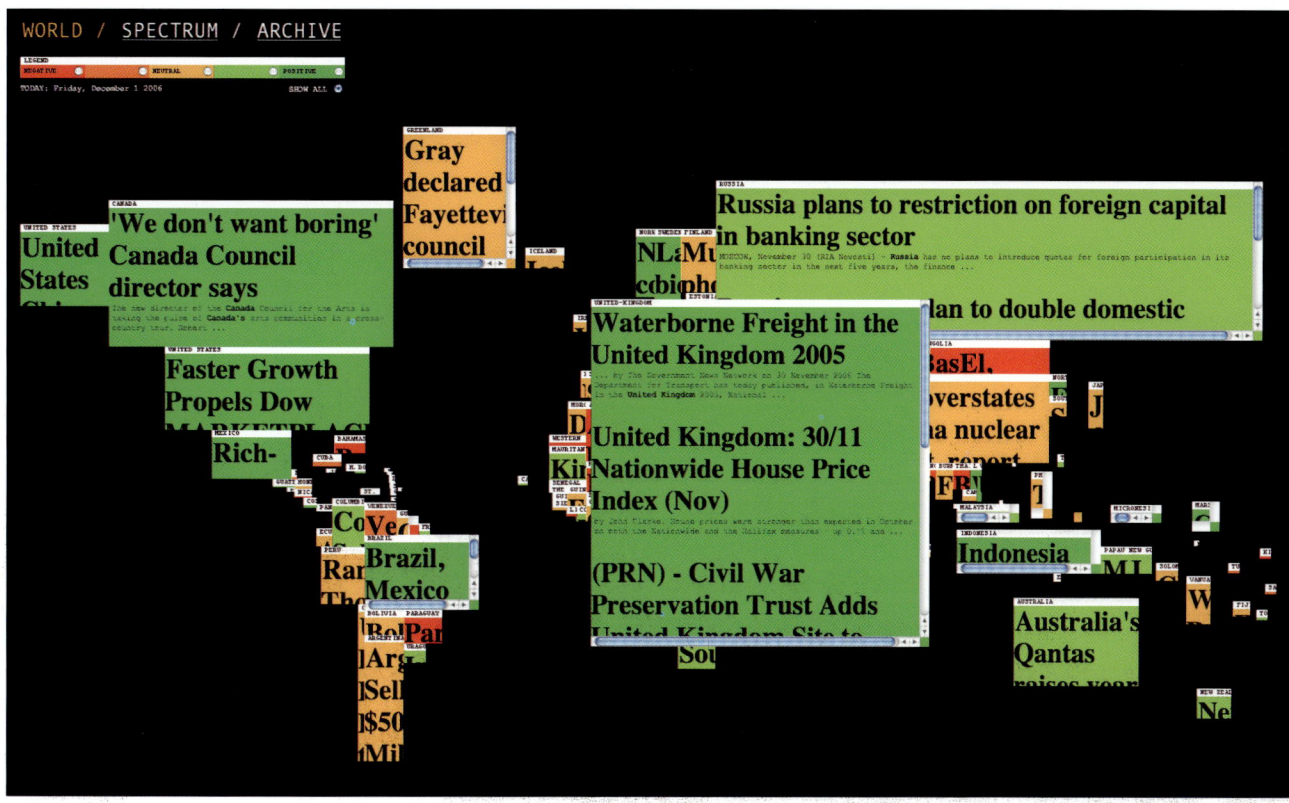

Pace of Design ::
Lichtwitz – Büro für visuelle Kommunikation :: www.lichtwitz.com ::

The purpose of this exhibition was to understand the pace of creation, and the development and production of a design project. With this in mind, the curator observed the work methods of seven big design studios around the world: Munich, New Delhi, San Francisco, Cape Town, Hong Kong, Tokyo, and São Paulo. The outcome of such analysis ended up being converted by the Lichtwitz designers into infographics like this map.

LUN

Mercados / Markets
100% Mundial / worldwide

Encomendas / Commissions
100% EUA / USA

CAM

100% Mundial / worldwide

15% Museus EUA e Europa / Museums in USA and Europe
35% Europa / Europe
50% Projectos auto-propostos / Self Commissioned projects

GRC

30%
70%
100%

MA

A diferença mais extraordinária verificou-se entre os Campanas a discutir o caos e Ichiro Iwasaki. Ouçam ou leiam as entrevistas
The most amazing difference was to be found between the Campanas discussing chaos and Ichiro Iwasaki. Listen to or read the interviews!

O Brasil, tal como a Índia e a China, é um dos mercados emergentes mais fortes, e de crescimento rápido – em São Paulo sente-se uma energia vital, com potencial para a violência, mas também muita positividade e criatividade.
Brazil, like India and China, is one of the strongest emerging markets, with rapid growth – being in São Paulo you can feel a vital energy, with the potential of violence, but so much positiveness and creativity as well.

MAPEAR › SETE › ESTÚDIOS › DE › DESIGN
MAPPING › SEVEN › DESIGN › STUDIOS

Além de São Francisco e Palo Alto, a Lunar tem mais dois escritórios – Munique e Hong Kong – alcançando clientes diferentes. (só mostramos clientes dos escritórios dos Estados Unidos).

Lunar has two more offices, besides San Franciso and Palo Alto – Munich and Hong Kong – reaching different clients there (we are only showing clients of the USA offices).

A Índia parece tão pequena neste mapa, mas na realidade é enorme, com mais de 100 línguas diferentes, 22 das quais são línguas oficiais de comunidades. No entanto, o Hindi (41%) e o Inglês são as mais comuns."

India looks so small on this map, but actually is huge, with over a 100 different languages, 22 of which are official community languages. Still Hindi (41%) and English are the most common.

Não me tinha dado conta do quão especial e diferente é o mercado japonês! Faz todo o sentido que o Iwasaki Design Studio receba encomendas do Japão e trabalhe para o Japão.

I was not aware how special and different the Japanese Market is! Its makes total sense that Iwasaki Design Studio gets its commissions from Japan and works for Japan.

- Japão / Japan — 100%
- Mundial / worldwide — 100%
- Índia / India — 100%
- Índia / India — 100%
- Japão / Japan — 100%
- Ásia / Asia — 50%
- Europa / Europe — 40%
- EUA / USA — 10%
- Europa, América do Norte / Europe, North America
- África do Sul / South Africa
- Projectos auto-propostos / Self Commissioned projects

CKS **YOU** **LU** **IWA**

Stroom Goes Underground ::
LUST :: www.lust.nl ::

On Architecture Day in 2006, organized by Stroom, attention was paid to the most invisible and clandestine sites in the city of The Hague. The map was designed as a guide for excursions; the only locations on the map are those that can be seen underground. With the use of overlay, the designers were able to create various shades of black, giving the design a feeling of depth.

UTRECHTSEBAAN

R

P
Q
Station
CS

LEKSTRAAT

7

S BINCKHORSTLAAN

6

WETERINGKADE

NIEUWE HAVEN

Stad-
huis
4
5
SPUI
PLETTERIJKADE
RIJSWIJKSE-
PLEIN
RIJSWIJKSEWEG

ORANJELAAN

STATIONSWEG
Station
HS
STATIONS-
PLEIN

WAGENSTRAAT
A'DAMSE VEERKADE
STILLE VEERKADE
WALDORPSTRAAT
NEHERKADE

WAGENSTRAAT

PAVILJOENSGRACHT
ORANJESTRAAT
ORANJE-
PLEIN
LEEGHWATERPLEIN

BOEKHORSTSTRAAT

Percentage of Pages Distributed by Subject

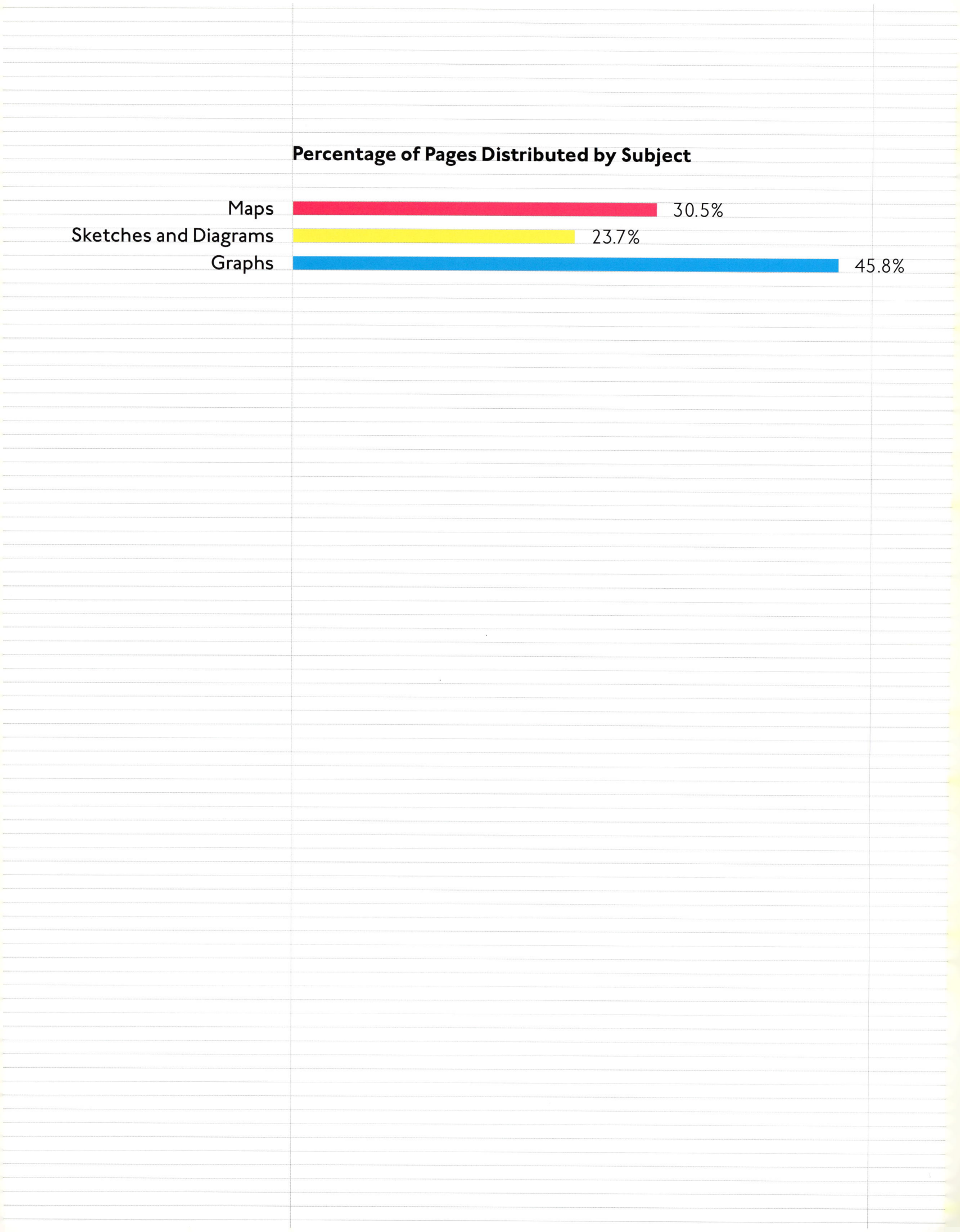

- Maps: 30.5%
- Sketches and Diagrams: 23.7%
- Graphs: 45.8%

sketch
n (from the German *schets*, and Italian *schizzo*) ❙ A rough drawing or outline representing the chief features of an object or scene.

diagram
n (from the Latin *diagramma*, and Greek: that which is marked out by lines) ❙ A drawing or plan that outlines and explains the parts, operation, etc., of something.

Visual explanations – Spinal Column ::
Cybu Richli :: www.c2f.to ::

This diagram forms part of a piece of research on infographics. The aim of the thesis is to explain scientific phenomena using easy-to-understand metaphors. To do this, real photographs of the processes or elements are used and reproduced with everyday objects and materials in new and diverse ways. In this particular case, the spinal column is represented by a means of gaskets.

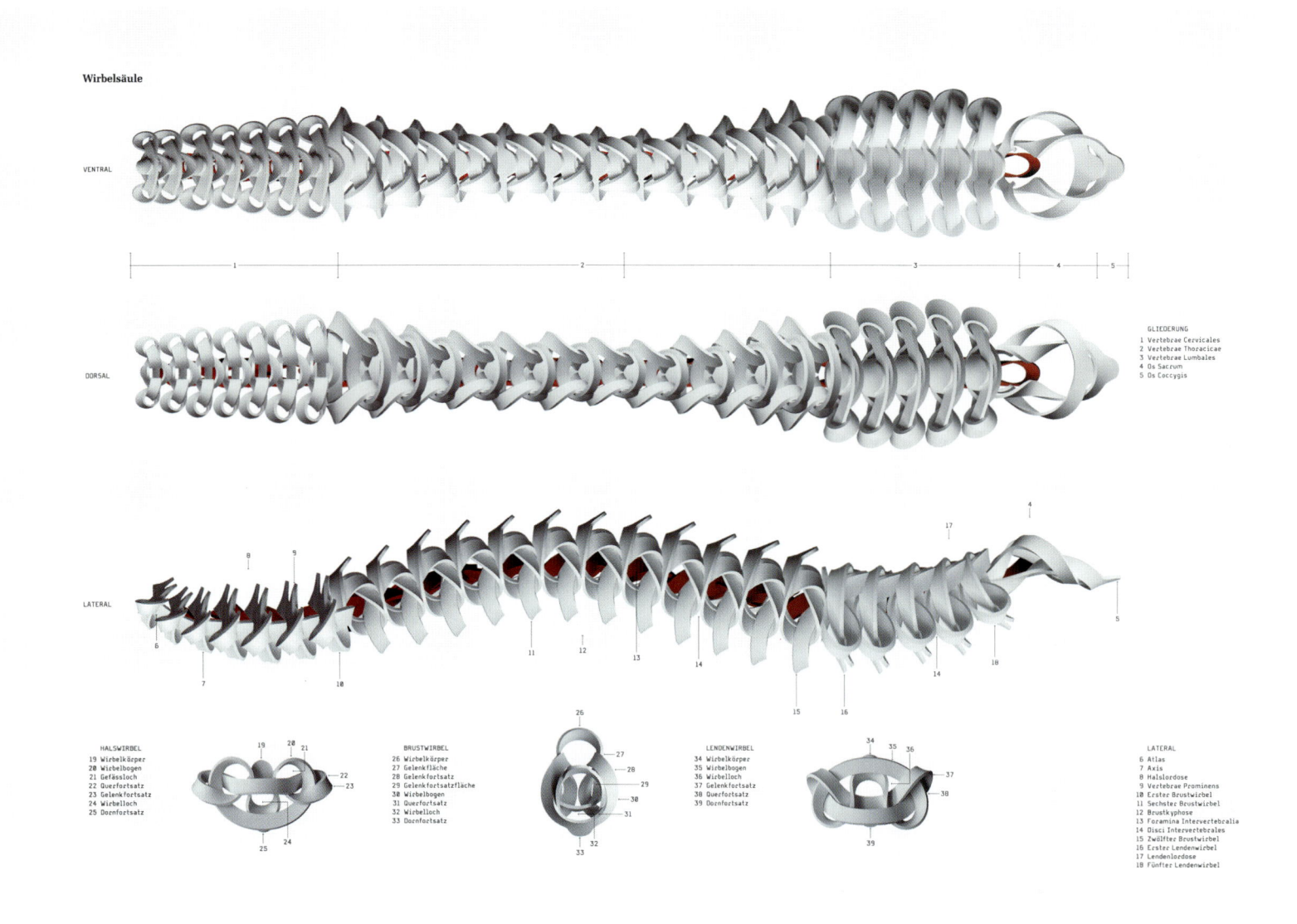

84 Sketches and Diagrams

Love Will Tear Us Apart ::
Martin Dominguez :: www.dominguezdesign.net ::

The song *Love Will Tear Us Apart* by Joy Division has an isolated sound. Martin Dominguez, a graphic designer from Philadelphia, PA, thought that mashing it up in a simple and mechanical fashion would capture its essence. This poster was designed in a similar manner. The grid is comprised of thirty columns—with each one representing one second of the song. Each instrument, in turn, is assigned a symbol to indicate exactly when it is heard in the song.

Joy Division. Love Will Tear Us Apart. 1979

00:00
Drums:
Vocals:
Guitars:
Keys:

00:30
Drums:
Vocals: Love, Love Will Tear Us Apart, Again.
Guitars:
Keys:

01:00
Drums:
Vocals: Love, Love Will
Guitars:
Keys:

01:30
Drums:
Vocals: Tear Us Apart, Again.
Guitars:
Keys:

02:00
Drums:
Vocals: Love, Love Will
Guitars:
Keys:

02:30
Drums:
Vocals: Tear Us Apart, Again. Love, Love Will Tear Us Apart, Again.
Guitars:
Keys:

03:00
Drums:
Vocals:
Guitars:
Keys:

Sketches and Diagrams 85

The City ::
Atelier Aquarium :: www.atelieraquarium.com ::

Every year the Graphisme dans la rue contest is held in the French city of Fontenay-sous-Bois, with designers from all over the world sending in their posters. Although it did not win a prize, Atelier Aquarium's poster depicts the disparity of wealth in Paris, indicating the distribution according to monthly income.

RÉPARTITION DES INDIVIDUS SELON LEURS REVENUS MENSUELS

© Simon Renaud, Jérémie Nuel/Atelier Aquarium

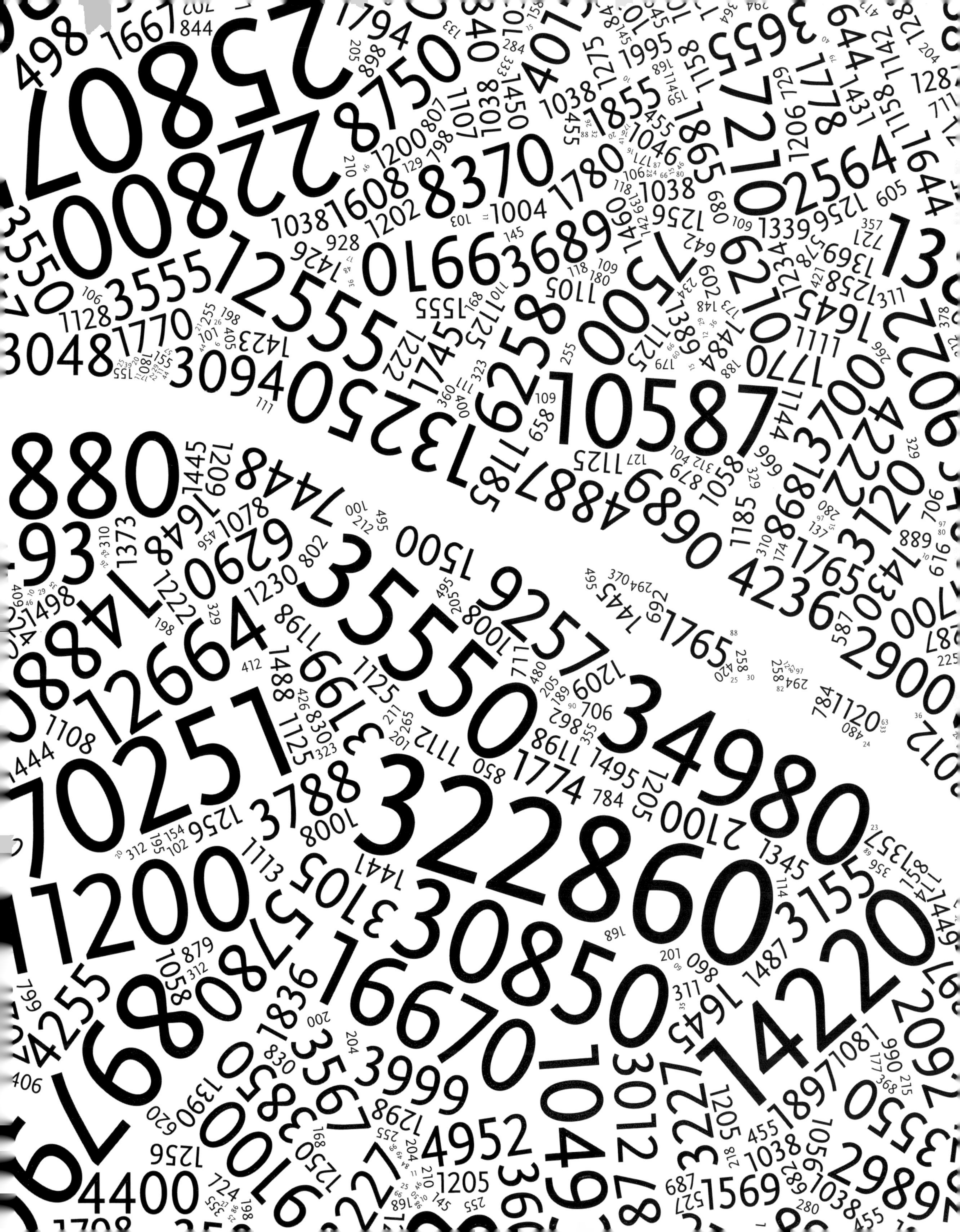

2003-2008 Kunsthaus Graz Annual Report ::
Lichtwitz – Büro für visuelle Kommunikation :: www.lichtwitz.com ::

This spectacular museum, devoted to temporary exhibitions of modern contemporary art, opened its doors in 2003, when Graz was the European capital of culture. This yearbook, which was compiled for its fifth anniversary, presents the activities performed in each of the seven spaces of the building organized in chronological order, and guided by a line of color that runs all the way through the book, much like a music score.

88 **Sketches and Diagrams**

Cayeli Process Diagram ::
Rose Zgodzinski :: www.chartsmapsdiagrams.com ::

This flowchart—compiled for a report for the mining company Inmet Mining—offers a detailed explanation of the work procedure for the Cayeli underground mine, located on the shores of the Black Sea, in northeastern Turkey. Copper and zinc are extracted from the mine.

This diagram illustrates the various phases—from the time the mineral is extracted from the tower until it is loaded and taken aboard ship in the port of Rize.

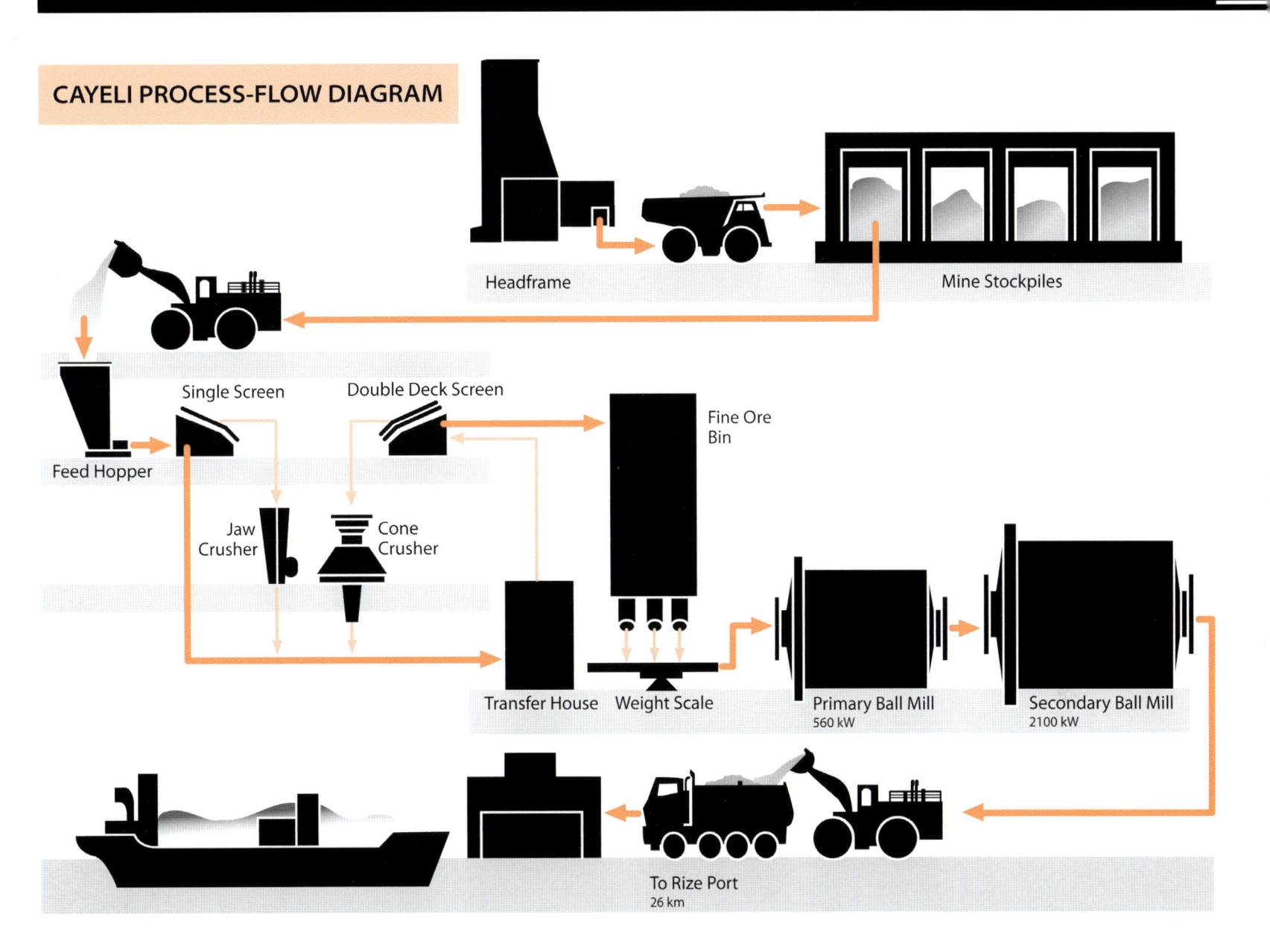

CAYELI PROCESS-FLOW DIAGRAM

Headframe

Mine Stockpiles

Feed Hopper

Single Screen

Double Deck Screen

Jaw Crusher

Cone Crusher

Fine Ore Bin

Transfer House

Weight Scale

Primary Ball Mill
560 kW

Secondary Ball Mill
2100 kW

To Rize Port
26 km

Sketches and Diagrams 89

Pace of Design ::
Lichtwitz – Büro für visuelle Kommunikation :: www.lichtwitz.com ::

The object of this exhibit was to analyze the connection between time, process, intensity, and creation when developing a project. After observing the day-to-day routine of seven big design studios, a huge spreadsheet was obtained, with interviews and photographs that formed the basis for developing a complex spatial and graphic structure. Each panel covers a topic, enabling comparisons to be made between the studios.

90 **Sketches and Diagrams**

Sketches and Diagrams 91

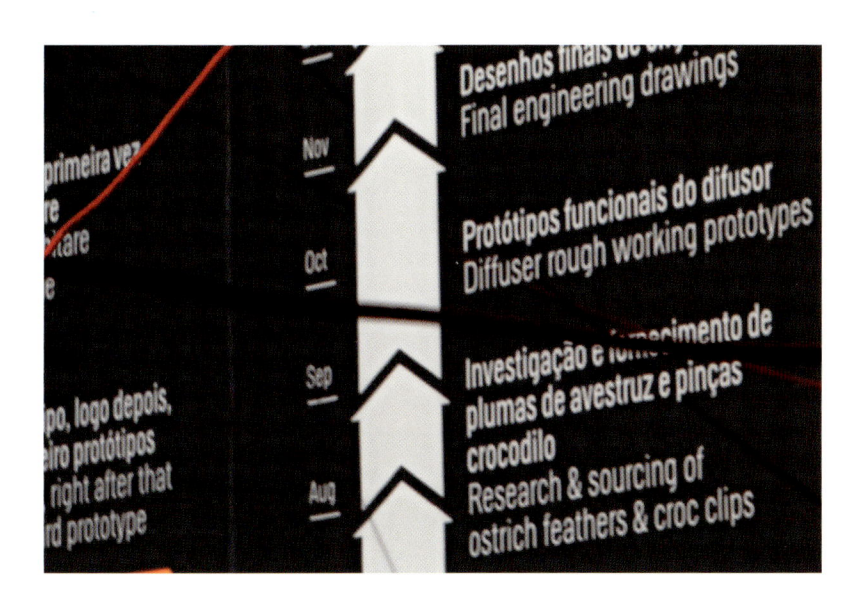

Organize Everything ::
Xavier Barrade :: www.xavierbarrade.com ::

This long-term, ambitious project attempts to organize everything—from the food that is bought on a monthly basis to the information that has already been put in order—into a hierarchical structure. The first step in this direction is looking at how organizers—those small books that include various blank flowcharts for the user to fill in—are distributed. The second step, which is much more universal in its approach, is the creation of a Web site where everyone can contribute.

Sketches and Diagrams 93

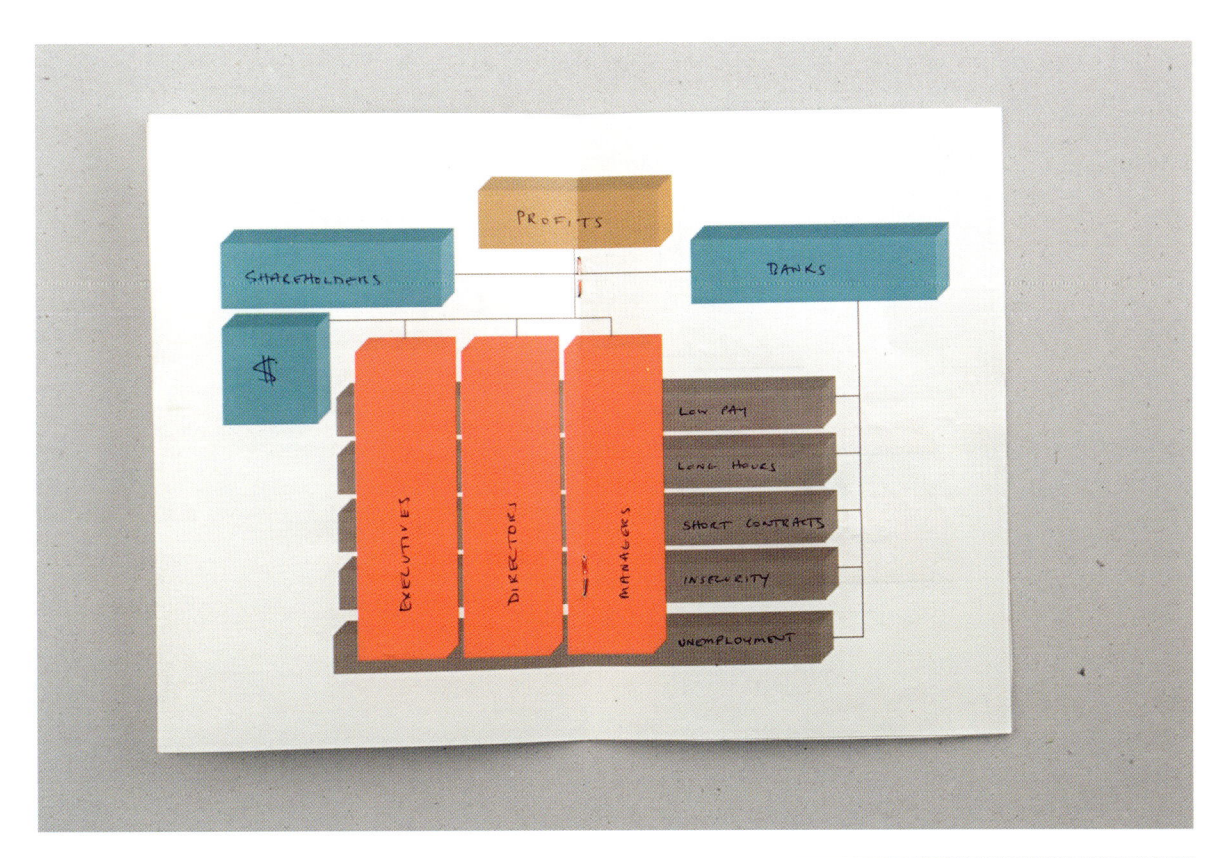

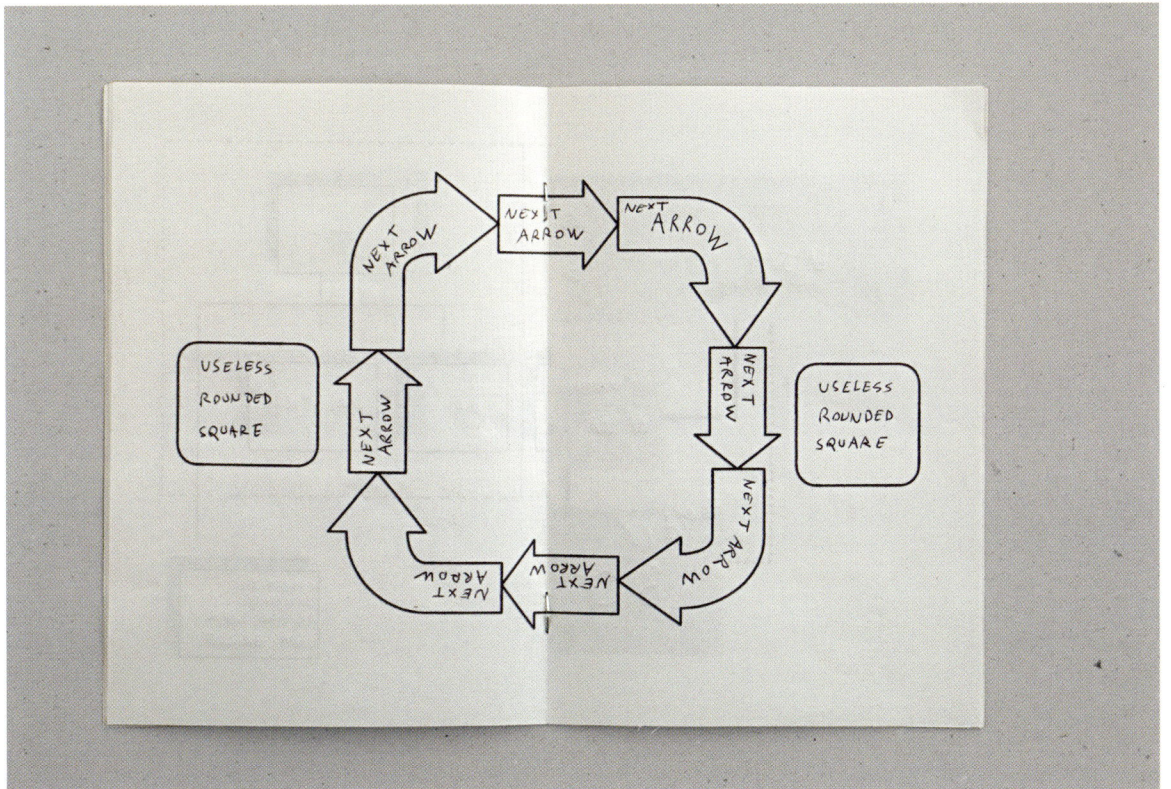

World of Violence ::
Lorenzo Geiger :: www.lorenzogeiger.ch ::

The red figures in the poster are based on an objective analysis of the number of violent cases present in a local newspaper in Berne, Switzerland, during a specific period of 2004. No moral statement is made; this poster is simply a graphic analysis of the facts. The color red is used to highlight violent acts covered by the media.

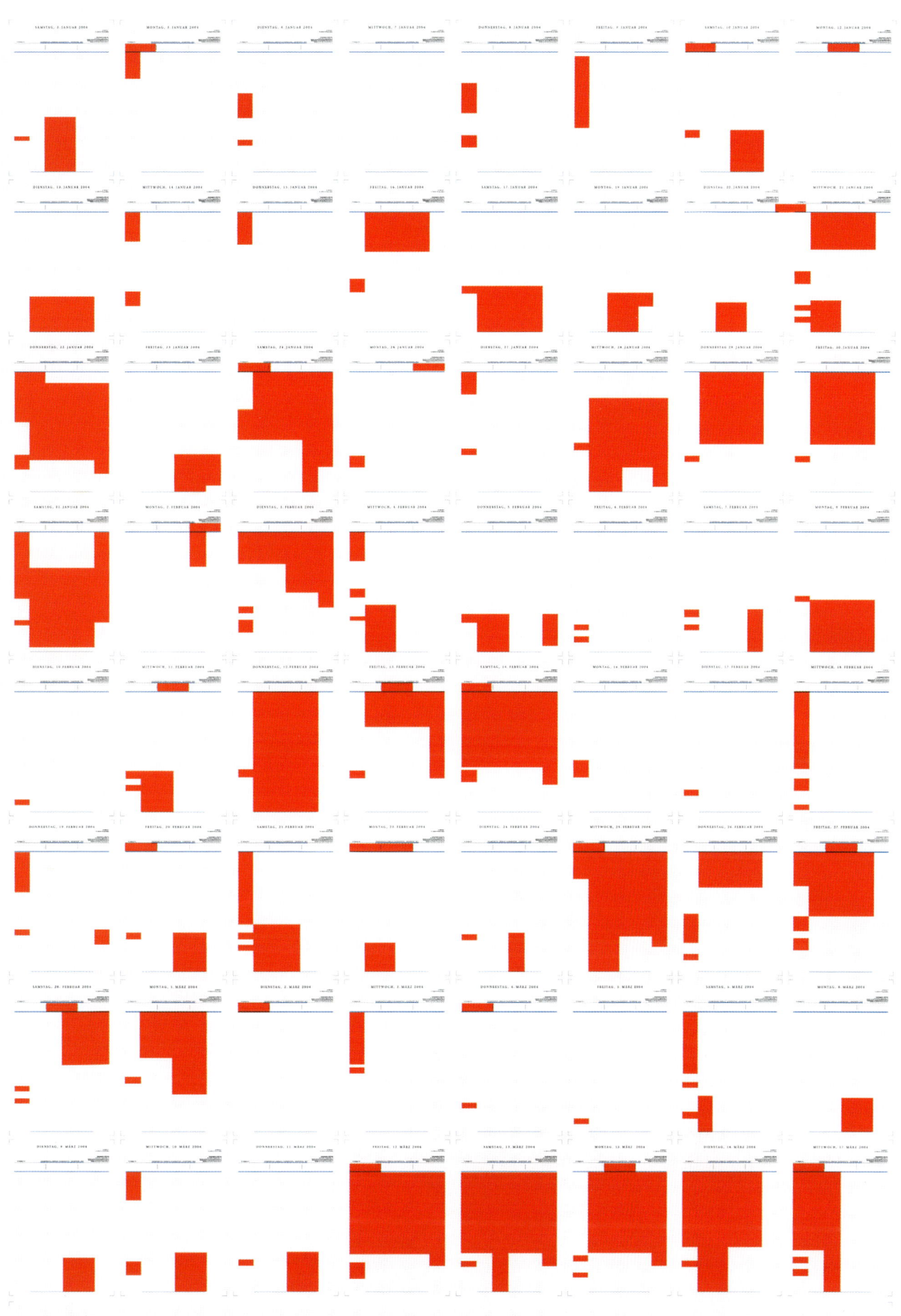

«The ‹Up & Down› of violence in our daily newspaper»

Focused ::
Cybu Richli, Fabienne Burri/C2F :: www.c2f.to ::

Research is like a machine. There are many parts to the machinery—sources, areas, topics, etc. Some of these parts fit together nicely, while others need to simply co-exist with one another. The design firm C2F utilized this analogy in their poster for the fourth Research Symposium on Design in Switzerland.

96 **Sketches and Diagrams**

Girl Talk Poster ::
Shane Long :: www.buddybogus.com ::

The songs of musician Girl Talk are *mashups*: songs created with parts of other songs. For his presentation at the 2009 Sasquatch! Festival, designer Shane Long made a Girl Talk poster designed using the same concept: He blended the faces and bodies of the musicians to create a new image. He also added a caption that invited viewers to guess who the different parts belonged to.

Sketches and Diagrams 97

Tomorrow#03 ::
Per Madsen/Scandinavian DesignLab :: www.scandinaviandesignlab.com ::

These pages form part of a biannual on trends written for Bestseller/Style Counsel. With respect to both format and content, it is a source of inspiration for music, fashion, retail, art, and sociology. The publication changes its appearance and the manner in which the information is presented, to adapt to the relevant trends being discussed.

Sketches and Diagrams 99

Lesley Moore Corporate Identity ::
Lesley Moore :: www.lesley-moore.nl ::

The good thing about small design studios is that they do not need to follow the same standards as large commercial companies. For instance, they can choose to have a corporate identity that is in a constant state of flux, as in the case of Lesley Moore. Visitors to her Web site can design a logo by choosing different graphic shapes; they can also choose the palette combination for the initials "L" and "M," which becomes the text for the company's sales sticker.

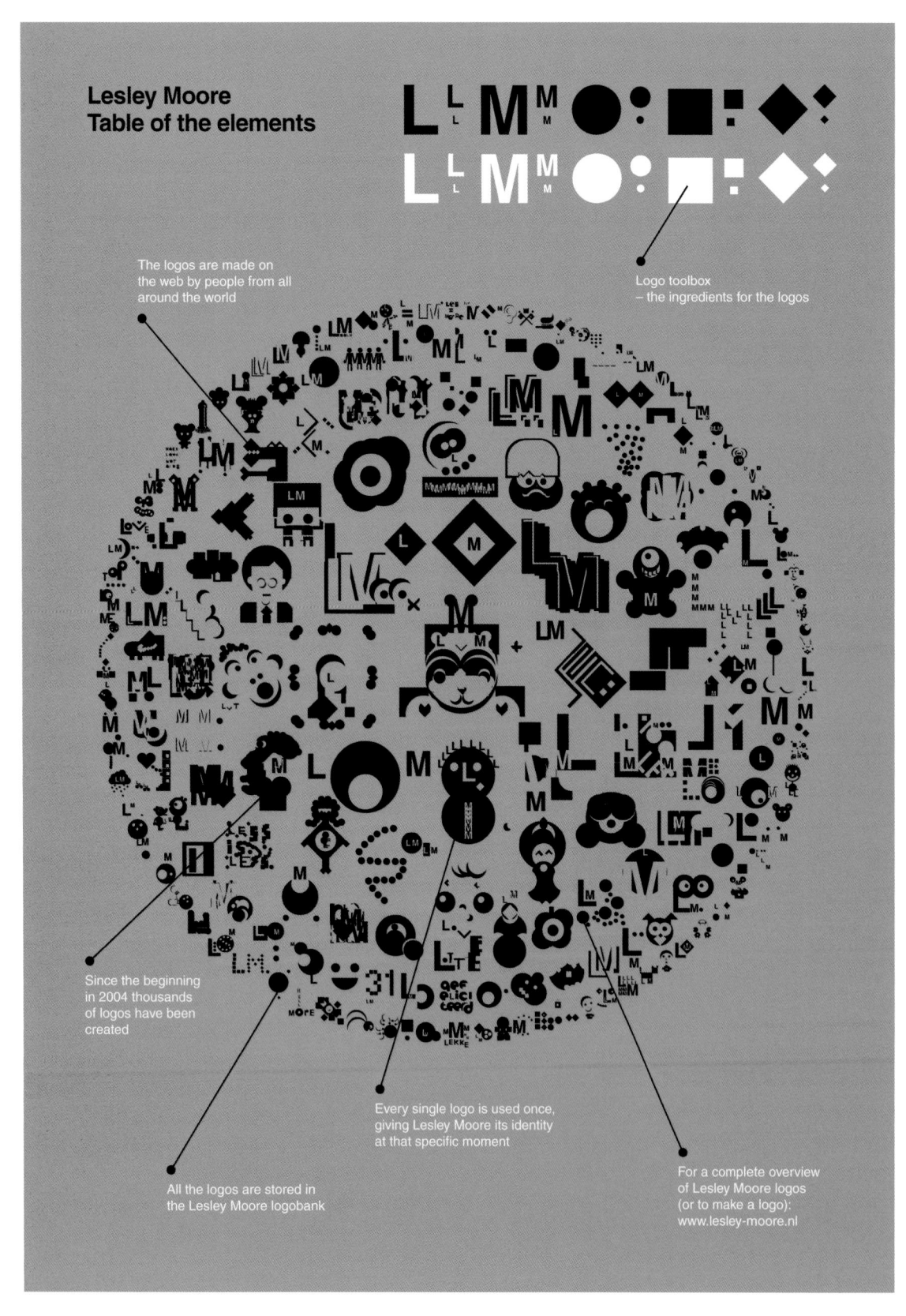

Lesley Moore
Table of the elements

The logos are made on the web by people from all around the world

Logo toolbox – the ingredients for the logos

Since the beginning in 2004 thousands of logos have been created

All the logos are stored in the Lesley Moore logobank

Every single logo is used once, giving Lesley Moore its identity at that specific moment

For a complete overview of Lesley Moore logos (or to make a logo): www.lesley-moore.nl

100 **Sketches and Diagrams**

Boobs ::
Jennifer Daniel :: httpcolonforwardslashforwardslashwwwdotjenniferdanieldotcom.com ::

While many people talk about women's breasts, it is a subject not easily broached everywhere and always, both in personal conversation and in the media. Designer Jennifer Daniel asked the following question: How can we show breasts without really showing them? The answer? By using literal illustrations of the many nicknames subscribed to them, which later became this diagram for the magazine *Latina*.

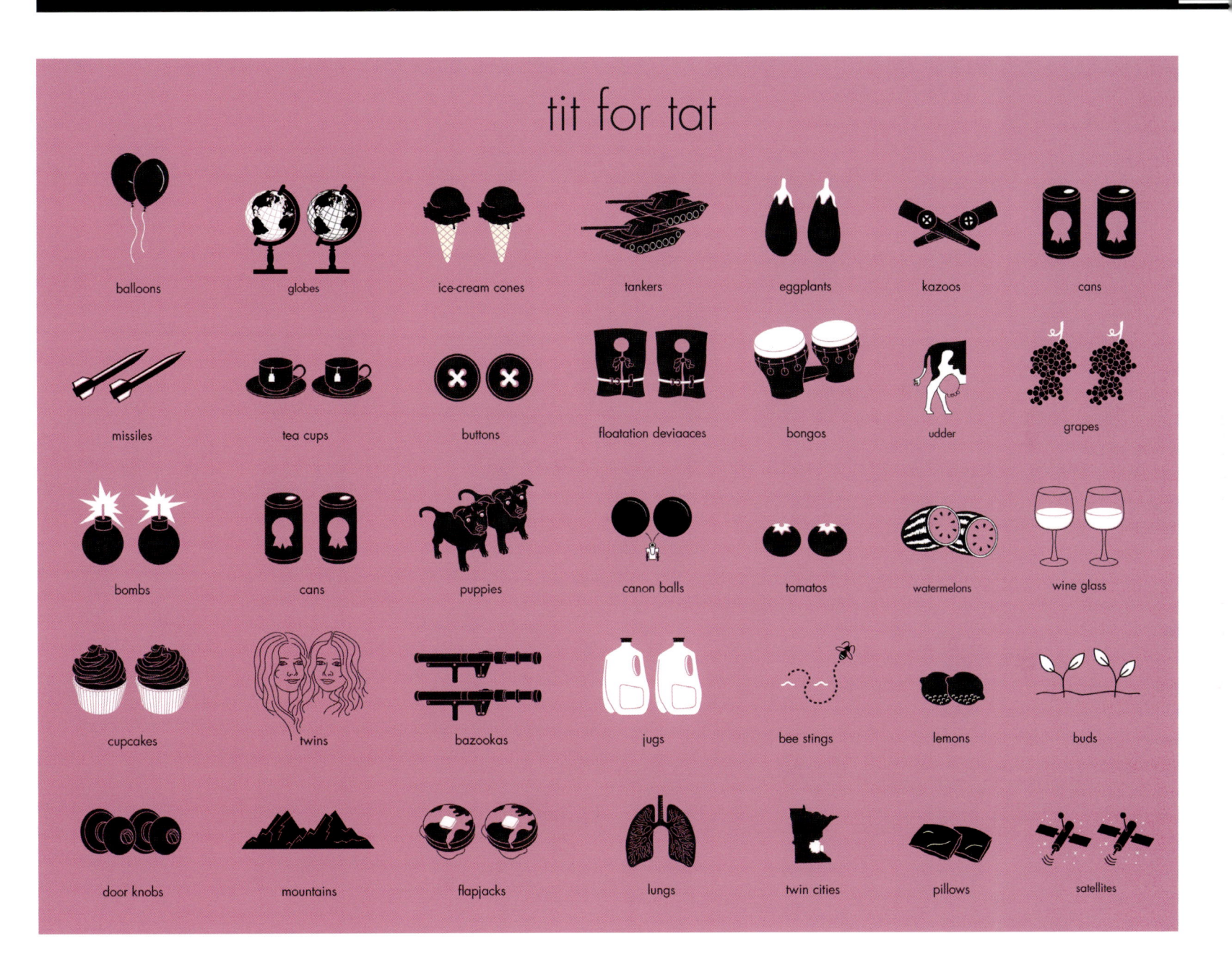

tit for tat

balloons	globes	ice-cream cones	tankers	eggplants	kazoos	cans
missiles	tea cups	buttons	floatation deviaaces	bongos	udder	grapes
bombs	cans	puppies	canon balls	tomatos	watermelons	wine glass
cupcakes	twins	bazookas	jugs	bee stings	lemons	buds
door knobs	mountains	flapjacks	lungs	twin cities	pillows	satellites

Sketches and Diagrams 101

Subjective Atlas of Serbia ::
Annelys de Vet :: www.subjectiveatlasofserbia.info ::

Dutch designer Annelys de Vet asked thirty young Serbian artists and designers about their country. She then illustrated their stories; in this case, through the creative use of a diagram, to communicate the artists' views of the nation. This diagram uses an analogy with the waltz to show how to behave in Serbia.

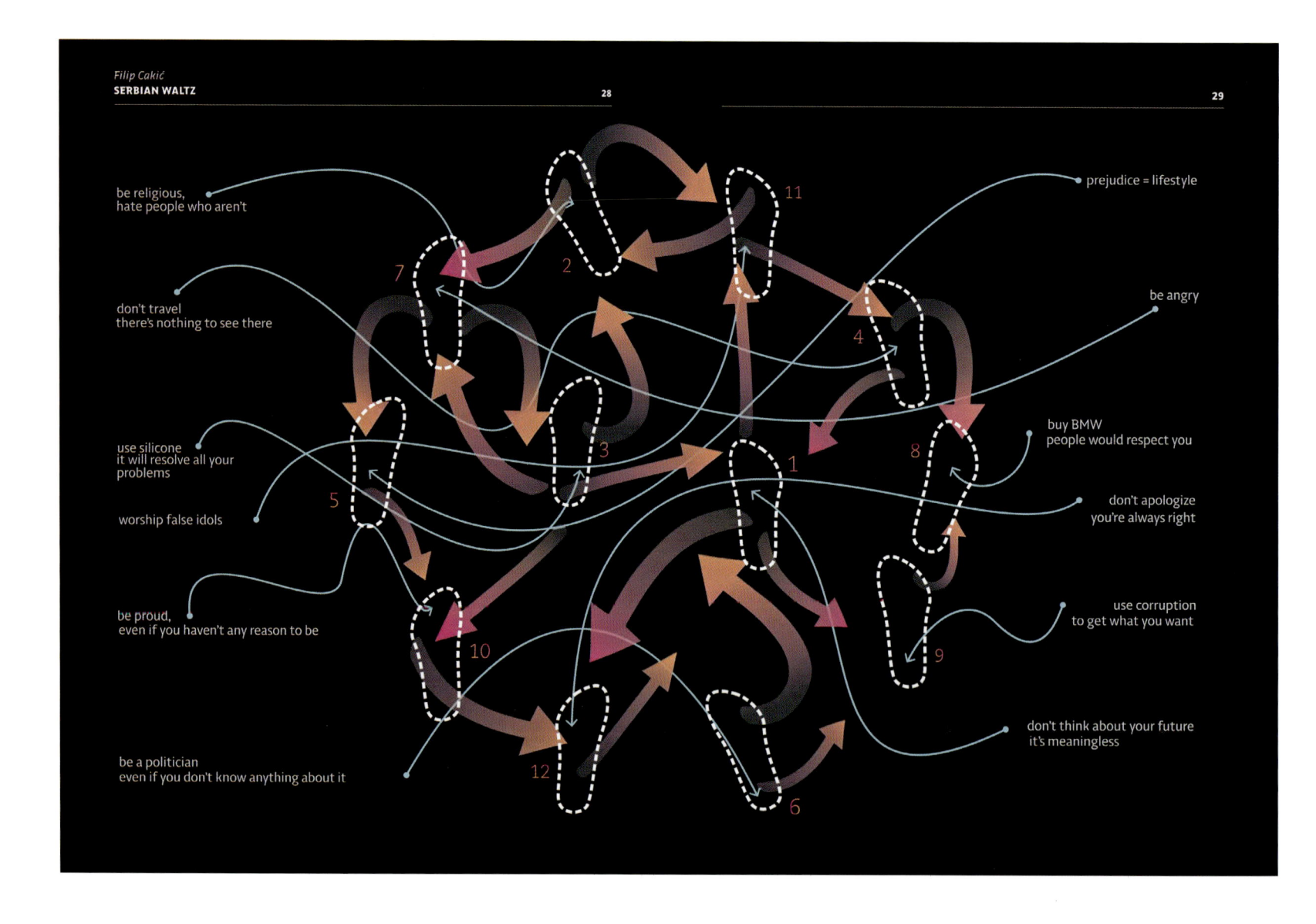

Filip Cakić
SERBIAN WALTZ

- be religious, hate people who aren't
- don't travel there's nothing to see there
- use silicone it will resolve all your problems
- worship false idols
- be proud, even if you haven't any reason to be
- be a politician even if you don't know anything about it
- prejudice = lifestyle
- be angry
- buy BMW people would respect you
- don't apologize you're always right
- use corruption to get what you want
- don't think about your future it's meaningless

Sketches and Diagrams

Interaction Design ::
Cybu Richli, Fabienne Burri/C2F :: www.c2f.to ::

Interaction design defines the behavior of the products and systems a user comes into contact with, such as software programs, cell phones, and MP3 players. It is an area of design that is growing quickly. Experts and enthusiasts on the subject are showing more interest in it as a discipline. This diagram is organized by subtopic and graphically illustrates the field's many sources.

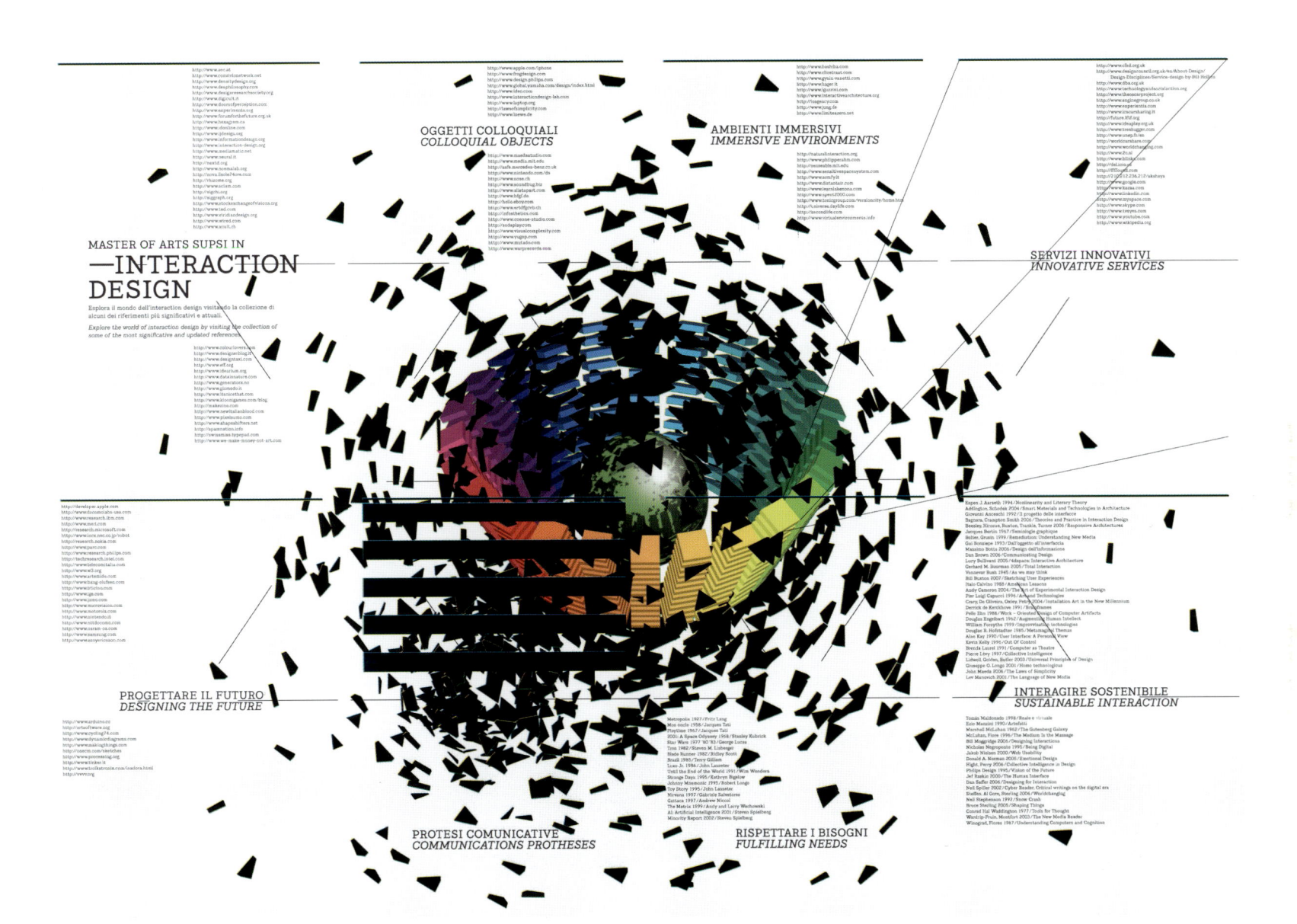

Sketches and Diagrams

Design Charts ::
Toxic Design :: toxicdesign.com ::

Every week this ranking system indicates the result of the Internet traffic generated on Web sites that deal with Web design associated with Design Charts. Each Toxic Design computer has a script installed, which monitors the clicks made by the users and stores them in the Toxic Design server. This information is then processed using algorithms on a weekly basis to obtain the list of the forty most visited Web sites.

Design Charts

Chart Control:
- THIS WEEK'S CHART »
- LAST WEEK'S CHART
- CHART ARCHIVE

Chart Menu:
- THE CHART SYSTEM
- THE NETWORK LIST

Chart News:

Every week DesignCharts scans the traffic generated from our Network of Websites that award website design. Using this data we publish a Top40 Chart every Monday at 6am GMT.

With our weekly charts designlovers and creatives alike have a new de facto standard for gaging which websites are truly a cut above the rest.

Enjoy!

Chart Adspace:

Your Rich List Position
Discover how rich you are! »

Advertise Here

Copyright 2006-2009
All Content Reserved.
DesignCharts is a Toxic Product
Advertising by Vantageous
Rockstar Hosting by MediaTemple
(mt)

Top 40 Websites For Week Ending Sunday July 19th 2009

#	Site	Status
1	TRIPLESKY	** NEW ENTRY ** / PEAK POSITION: 1
2	DIGITAL GURUS	LAST WEEK: 8 / PEAK POSITION: 2
3	POLDO UK	LAST WEEK: 1 / PEAK POSITION: 1
4	ETERNAL MOONWALK	** NEW ENTRY ** / PEAK POSITION: 4
5	PIXELINGLIFE	LAST WEEK: 3 / PEAK POSITION: 3
6	BABELO	** NEW ENTRY ** / PEAK POSITION: 6
7	HIISHII DESIGN	** NEW ENTRY ** / PEAK POSITION: 7
8	SPRINTER NEUHEITEN 20	<<< RE-ENTRY >>> / PEAK POSITION: 8
9	RUY ADORNO	LAST WEEK: 11 / PEAK POSITION: 9
10	SOCIETY6	** NEW ENTRY ** / PEAK POSITION: 10
11	TOYOTA SCREENSAVER	** NEW ENTRY ** / PEAK POSITION: 11
12	COCA COLA LIGHT	LAST WEEK: 27 / PEAK POSITION: 4
13	LE MEURICE	<<< RE-ENTRY >>> / PEAK POSITION: 13
14	TIN HUYNH'S PORTFOLIO	LAST WEEK: 7 / PEAK POSITION: 7
15	FORMTROOPERS	LAST WEEK: 12 / PEAK POSITION: 8
16	GUERRA CREATIVA	LAST WEEK: 15 / PEAK POSITION: 15
17	PHOTOGRAPHER FREDR	LAST WEEK: 21 / PEAK POSITION: 2
18	BYHOOK	LAST WEEK: 34 / PEAK POSITION: 3
19	LOADED	LAST WEEK: 2 / PEAK POSITION: 2
20	PRO PLAN	LAST WEEK: 4 / PEAK POSITION: 4
21	GREAT WORKS	** NEW ENTRY ** / PEAK POSITION: 21
22	CORNETTO	** NEW ENTRY **

104 Sketches and Diagrams

Lockstoffe Book ::
LIGALUX :: www.ligalux.de ::

LIGALUX decided to compile a book about the world of visual codes. In particular, the team wanted to know what attracts people and why only some things are retained in our memory. The book's title might be translated as "attractant," a term that is rather ad hoc since it combines properties inherent in bait, which are used to try to understand human feeling in an experimental and playful fashion.

Sketches and Diagrams 105

Artist Groups: Young Estonian Art ::
Margus Tamm :: www.tammtamm.net ::

The Estonian magazine *KUNST.EE* is about visual arts in that country. Margus Tamm, who has been in contact with the Estonian art scene for years, was asked to compile a visual index of contents for a special edition about the connections between artists and critics. He chose this circular diagram evocative of a core, in which it is easy to connect people.

weareallconnected ::
Artroom srl :: www.sergiocalatroni.com ::

"Once upon a time we all used to be connected, and we will be again." Each circle represents a community from which spheres are detached with the names of some of its members. These circles grow, move, and change color, just as happens in real life as the people forming part of a community opt for different activities. The design has been executed in 3-D to provoke the feeling of chaos.

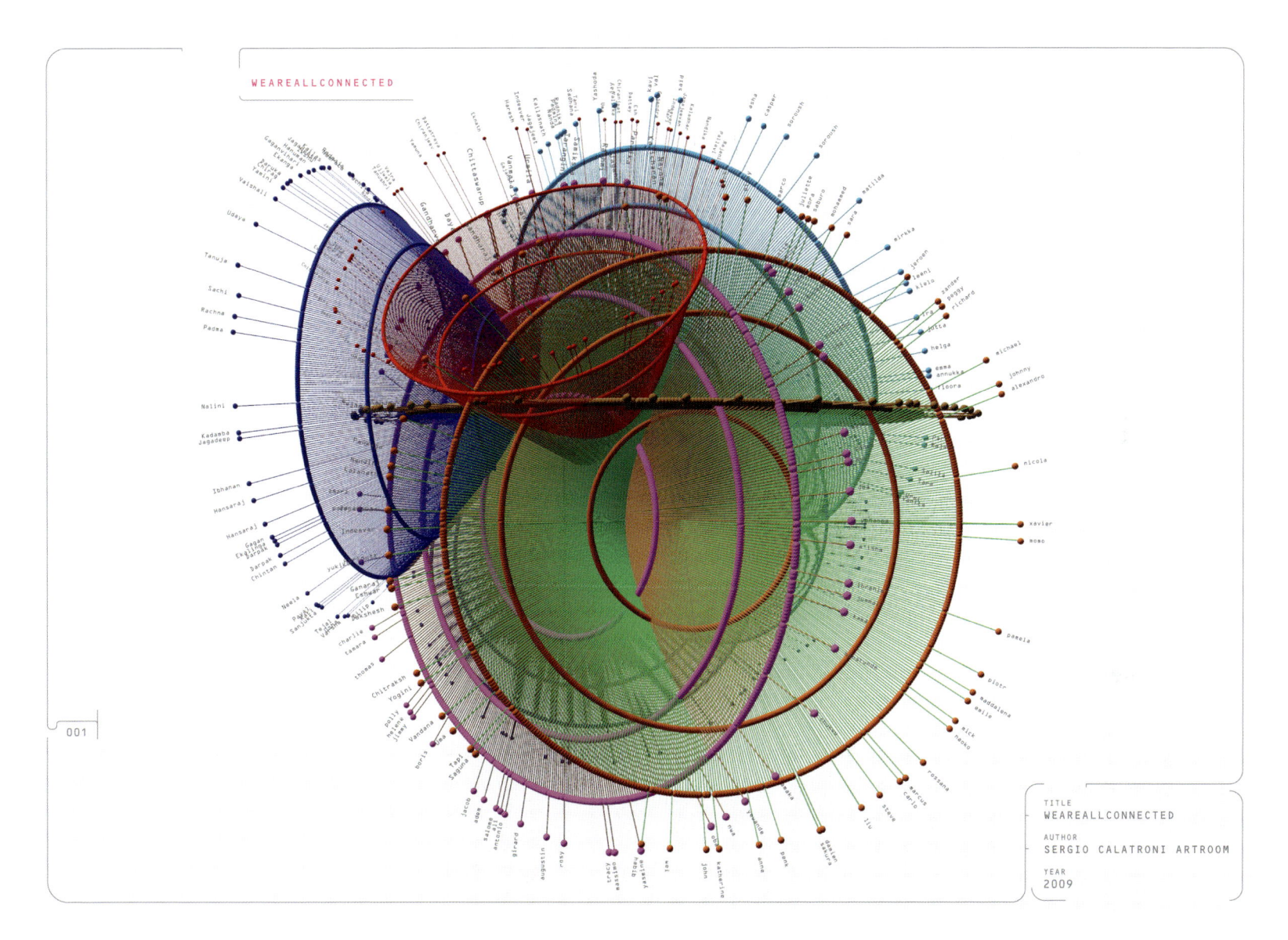

TITLE: WEAREALLCONNECTED
AUTHOR: SERGIO CALATRONI ARTROOM
YEAR: 2009

Art direction: Miyuki Yajima. Design: Hisayukia Amae, Yosuke Nakagawa. Rendering: Yosuke Nakagawa

Timeless ::
Andrej Filetin/Fiktiv :: www.fiktiv.hr ::

The leading quality paper dealer in Croatia, IGEPA Plana, commissioned these pages for their 2006 calendar to twelve design studios, one of which was Fiktiv. Their month—May—was based on a visualization of the results obtained from introducing the term *timeless* in the Google Sets application. This work won them the Young Gun Prize awarded by the Art Directors Club in New York.

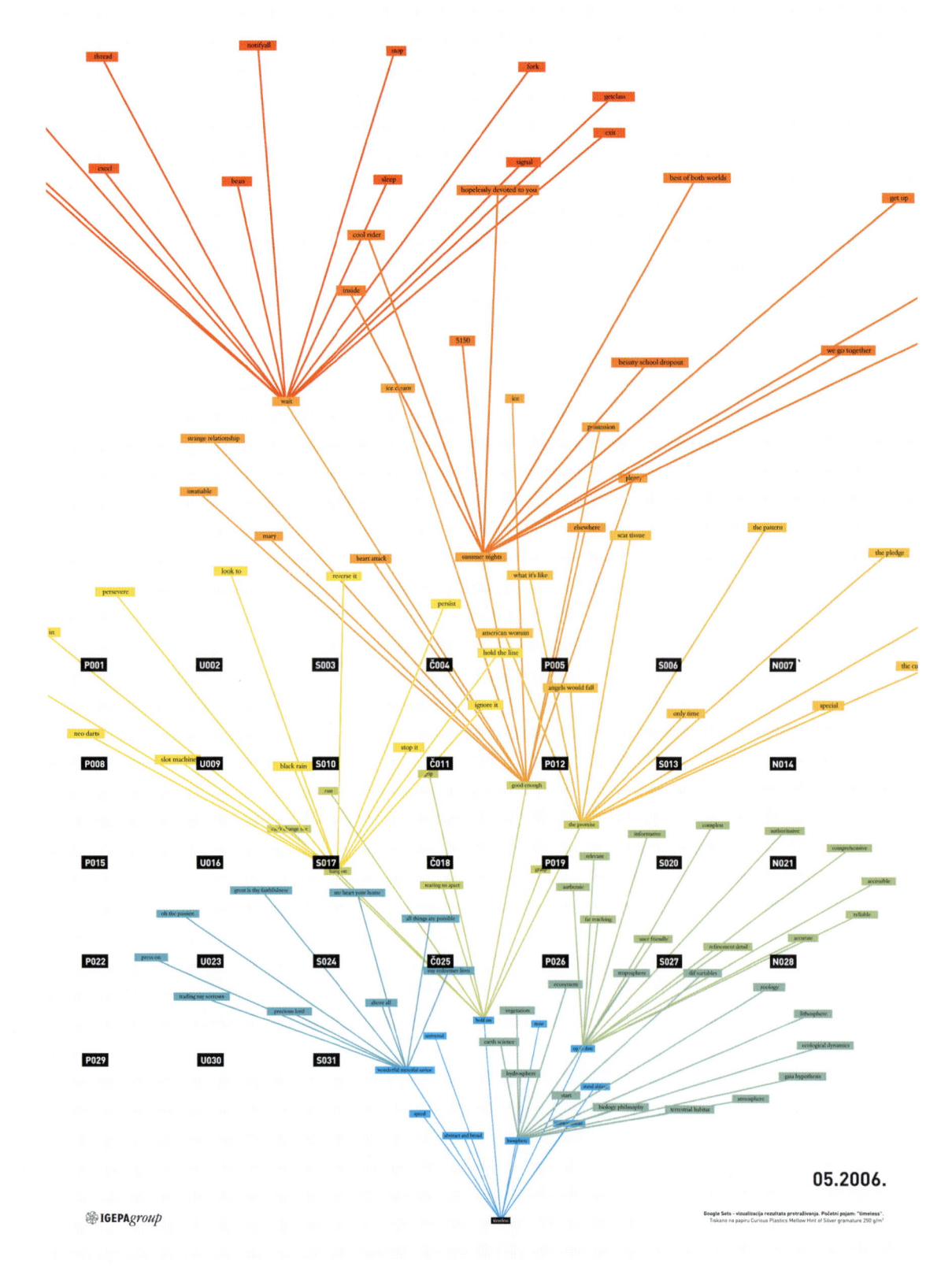

05.2006.

108 Sketches and Diagrams

elsewhere

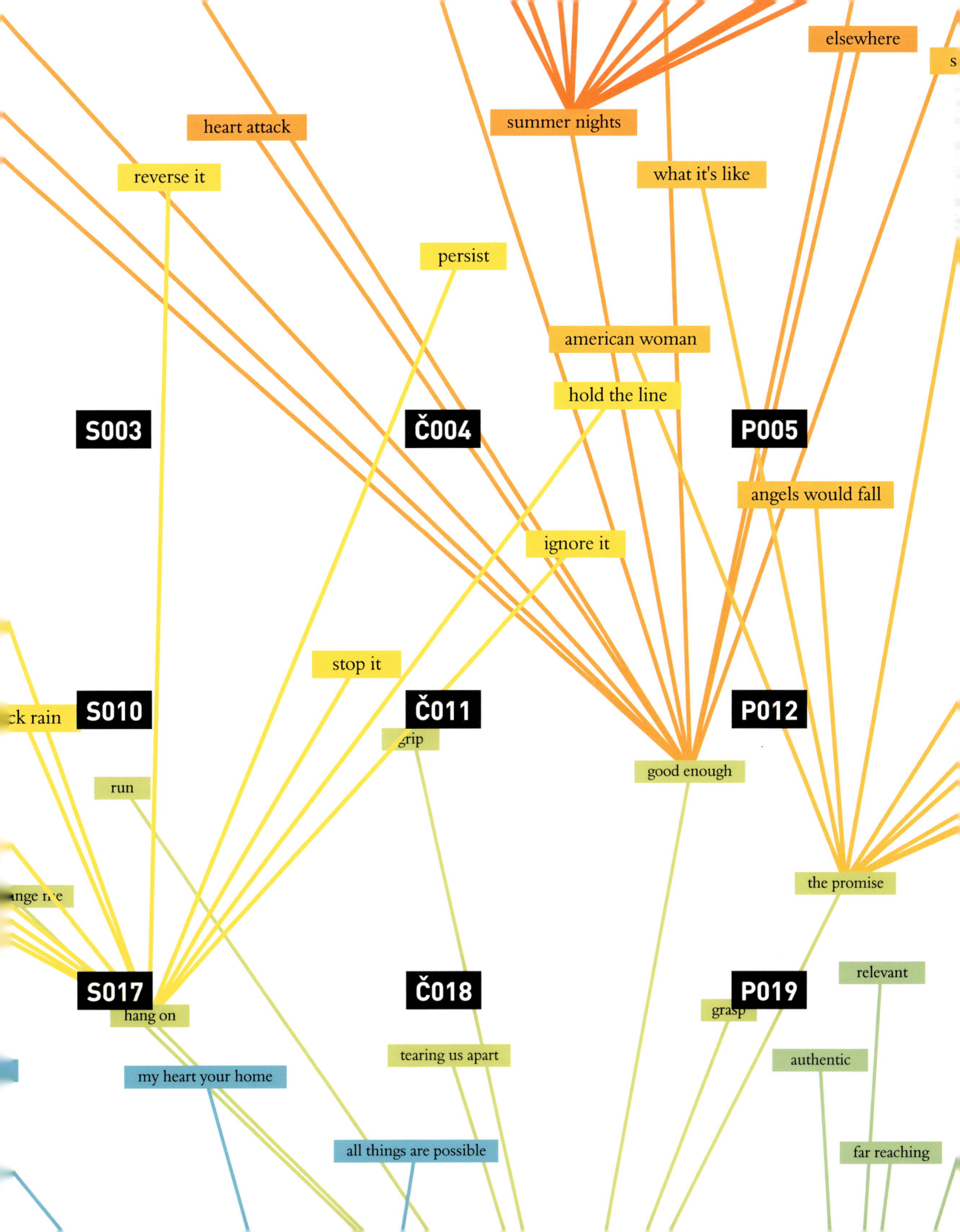

heart attack

summer nights

reverse it

what it's like

persist

american woman

hold the line

S003 **Č004** **P005**

angels would fall

ignore it

stop it

ck rain **S010** **Č011** **P012**

grip

run

good enough

the promise

relevant

S017 **Č018** **P019**

hang on

grasp

tearing us apart

authentic

my heart your home

all things are possible

far reaching

Flocking Diplomats 04 ::
Catalogtree :: www.catalogtree.net ::

This diagram draws attention to the offenses committed by New York diplomats in 1999. Working with the photographer Mikhail Iliatov, the designers depicted the top one hundred addresses involved in violating the transit laws in sizes comparable to the number of offenses. It can be seen, for instance, that the address 307 E 44 ST is the most affected, with a total of 2,014 violations.

© Mikhail Iliatov

110 **Sketches and Diagrams**

Il Mondo del Libro ::
Leftloft :: www.leftloft.com ::

Alterstudio Partners organized a travelling show-cum-workshop (promoted by ABCittà and the Fondazione Mondadori) for the purpose of raising children's awareness on the importance of reading books and informing them about their production process and uses. Leftloft was commissioned to develop the graphic material for the exhibit, such as this poster.

Une chronologie détaillée des événements dans la série télévisée Day Break ::
Julien Antonescu :: julien.antonescu.free.fr ::

Chronology is a subject that fascinates designer Julien Antonescu. His book, *Une chronologie détaillée des événements dans la série télévisée Day Break*, is folded like an accordion to facilitate the union between one day and the next, and represents the television series *Day Break*, using a sketch to show all the actions that could have happened on different days and at different times, but in the program occur on the same day.

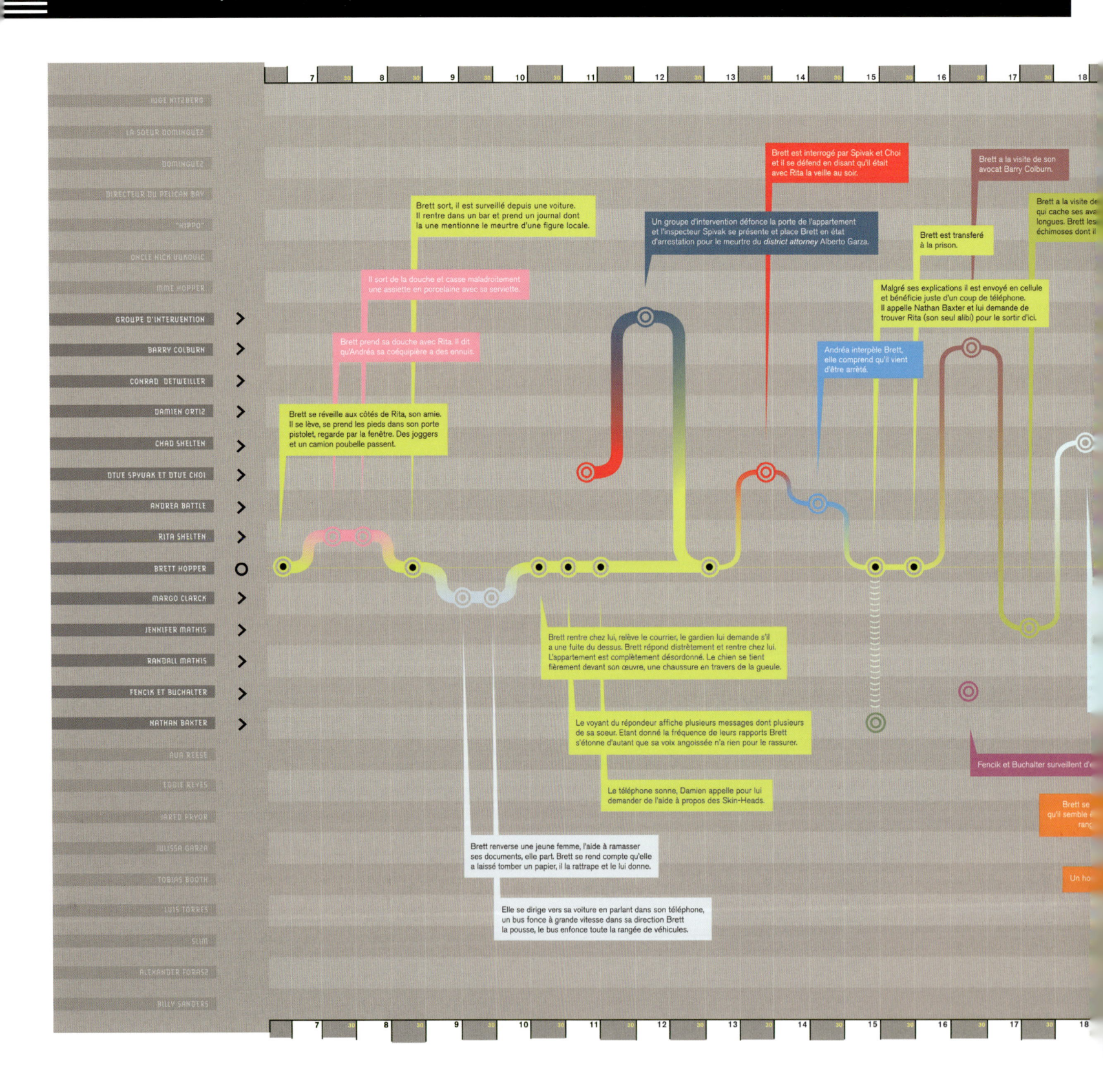

Sketches and Diagrams

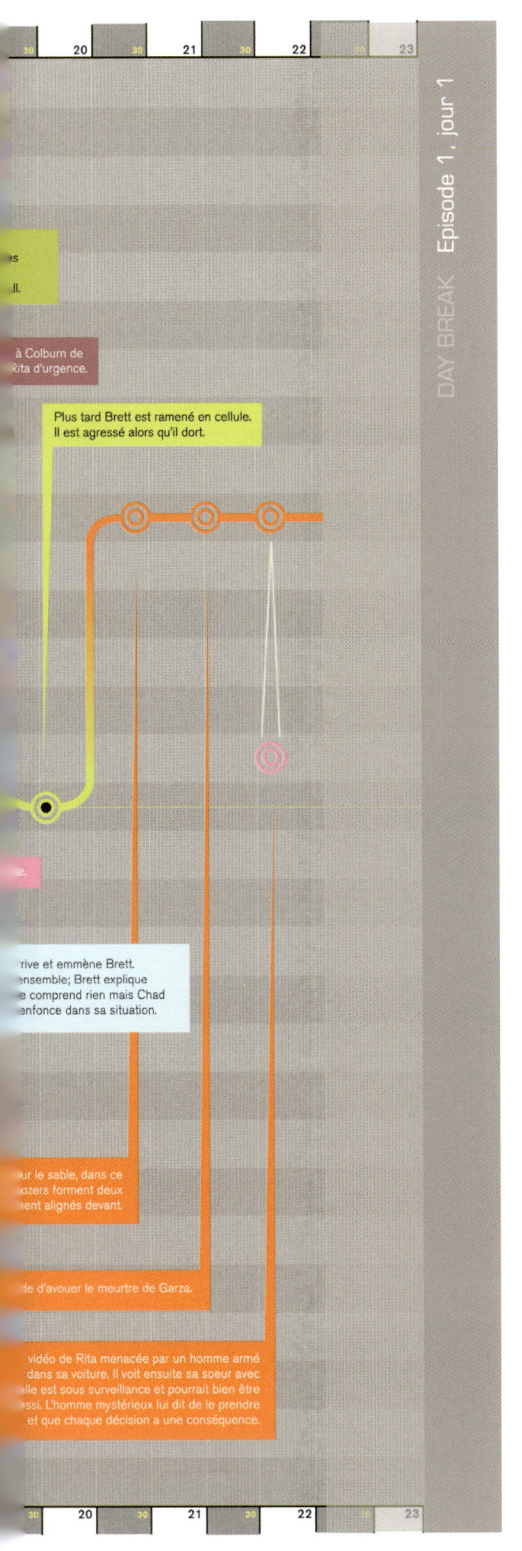

DAY BREAK Episode 1 . jour 1

Plus tard Brett est ramené en cellule.
Il est agressé alors qu'il dort.

...rive et emmène Brett.
...ensemble; Brett explique
...e comprend rien mais Chad
...enfonce dans sa situation.

...ur le sable, dans ce
...ozers forment deux
...ent alignés devant

...de d'avouer le meurtre de Garza.

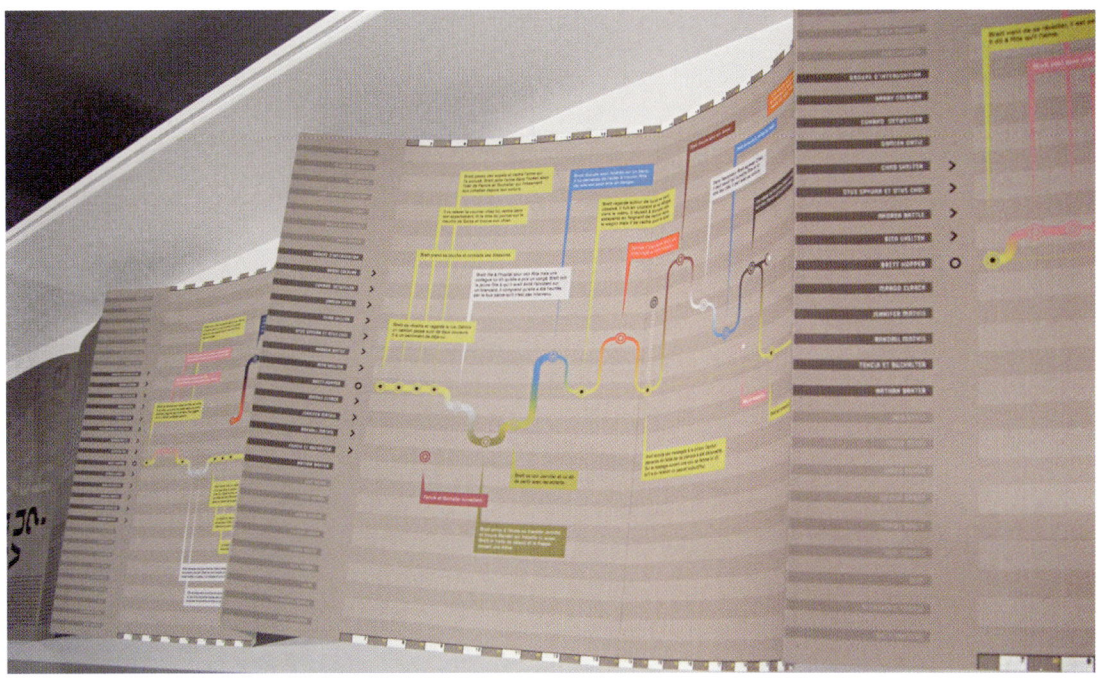

...vidéo de Rita menacée par un homme armé
...dans sa voiture. Il voit ensuite sa soeur avec
...lle est sous surveillance et pourrait bien être
...ssi. L'homme mystérieux lui dit de le prendre
...et que chaque décision a une conséquence.

Sketches and Diagrams | 113

fischerAppelt, profiling ::
LIGALUX :: www.ligalux.de, www.fischerappelt-profiling.de ::

While compiling a technical brochure for a firm, it is a good idea to find a way of making the information presented as clear and self-explanatory as possible. In this instance, the brief was to produce some prints to explain the key competences of a consultancy firm. The areas of work and the individual steps that need to be taken are described through graphs based on elements that are in the public domain.

Programmatik:
Die öffentliche Seite der
Unternehmensstrategie

Medien und
breite Öffentlichkeit

NGOs und Verbände

Kunden

Investoren

Mitarbeiter und
potentielle Mitarbeiter

Öffentliche Seite
Programmatik

Nichtöffentliche Seite
Interne Strategie

CORPORATE STRATEGY

Sketches and Diagrams

Sustainable Corporate Strategy: Drei Ebenen prägen ein nachhaltiges Profil

01
Nachhaltige Unternehmenspositionierung

– Strategische Gesamtausrichtung
– CR* Strategy
– Nachhaltigkeitsprofil

02
CSR-Portfoliomanagement

– CSR**-Aktivitäten
– CC***-Projekte
– CSR-Management-Systeme

03
Strategische CR-Kommunikation

– Kommunikationsplanung
– Stakeholderanforderungen
– CSR-Reporting

* Corporate Responsibility.
** Corporate Social Responsibility.
*** Corporate Citizenship.

SUSTAINABILITY

Management von Kommunikation: Prozesse effektiv steuern

01
Strategische Unternehmensziele

02
Vision & Werte

03
Kommunikationsziele & Dialoggruppen

04
Erfolgsfaktoren & Botschaften

05
Zieloperationalisierungen / KPIs

06
Kreativkonzept & Maßnahmen

07
Wirkungskontrolle

STRATEGIC PLANNING

Sketches and Diagrams

Chocolate Background Stories (Chocolate Wrapper Prototypes) ::
Arlene Birt :: www.backgroundstories.com ::

Consumers appreciate additional information when they are about to make a purchase, especially if what they are buying is food. If this information is even more extensive, that is to say, if it explains the whole product development process, they will be in a better position to understand the global impact of its hidden meaning on society and on the environment.

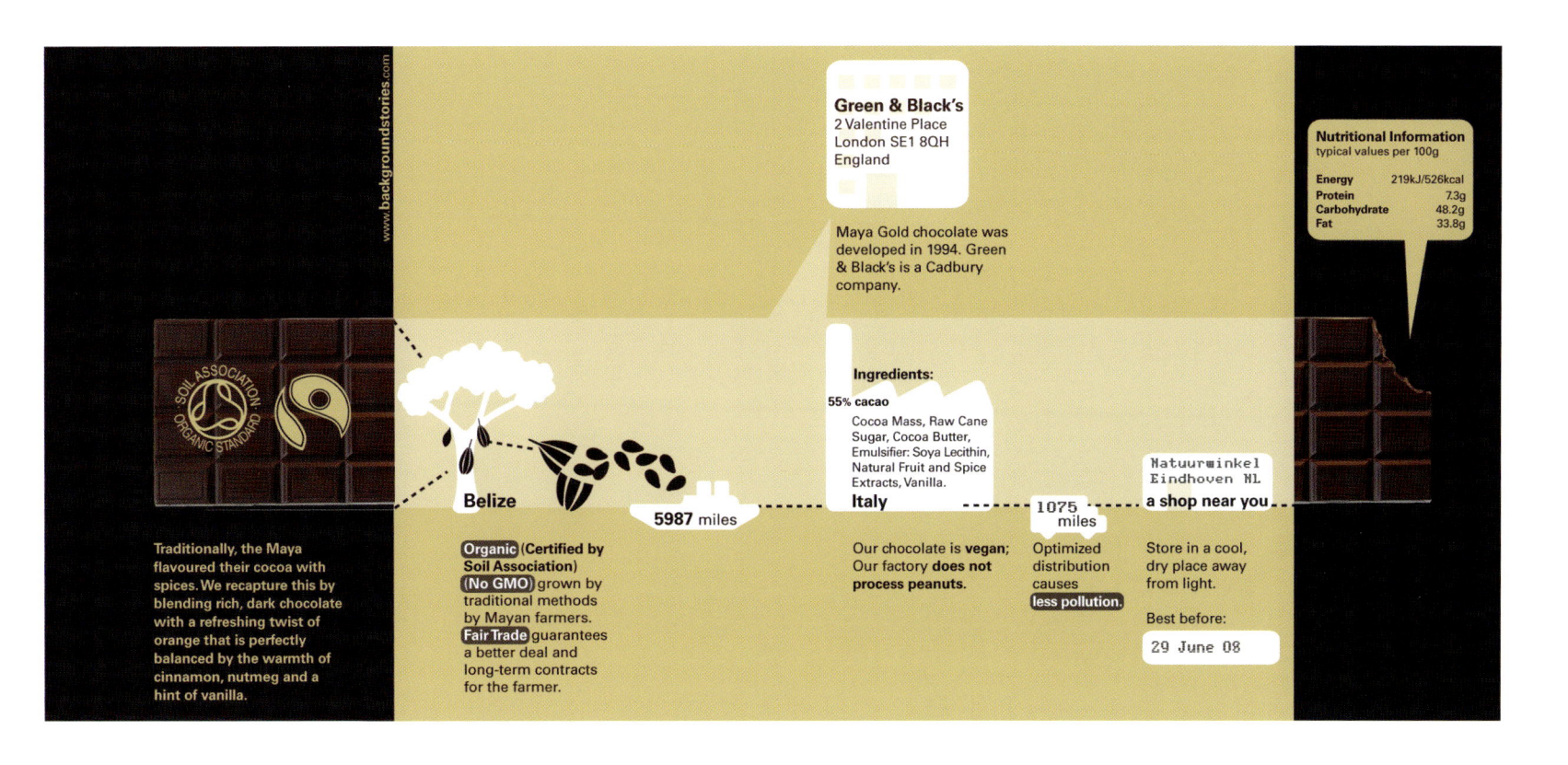

Green & Black's
2 Valentine Place
London SE1 8QH
England

Maya Gold chocolate was developed in 1994. Green & Black's is a Cadbury company.

Nutritional Information
typical values per 100g

Energy	219kJ/526kcal
Protein	7.3g
Carbohydrate	48.2g
Fat	33.8g

www.backgroundstories.com

Traditionally, the Maya flavoured their cocoa with spices. We recapture this by blending rich, dark chocolate with a refreshing twist of orange that is perfectly balanced by the warmth of cinnamon, nutmeg and a hint of vanilla.

Belize

Organic (Certified by Soil Association) **No GMO** grown by traditional methods by Mayan farmers. **Fair Trade** guarantees a better deal and long-term contracts for the farmer.

5987 miles

Ingredients:
55% cacao

Cocoa Mass, Raw Cane Sugar, Cocoa Butter, Emulsifier: Soya Lecithin, Natural Fruit and Spice Extracts, Vanilla.

Italy

Our chocolate is **vegan**; Our factory **does not process peanuts**.

1075 miles

Optimized distribution causes **less pollution**.

Natuurwinkel
Eindhoven NL
a shop near you

Store in a cool, dry place away from light.

Best before:
29 June 08

Sketches and Diagrams 117

Timemit ::
Studio Laucke Siebein :: www.studio-laucke.com ::

Timemit is a computer program, created by the German team Studio Laucke, that registers and administrates working hours. The German duo developed all the promotional materials, like the logo, Web site, packaging, and publicity campaign for the product. This flier-cum-instruction manual refers to the Web site, where visitors are invited to create their own time machine by putting absurd objects together.

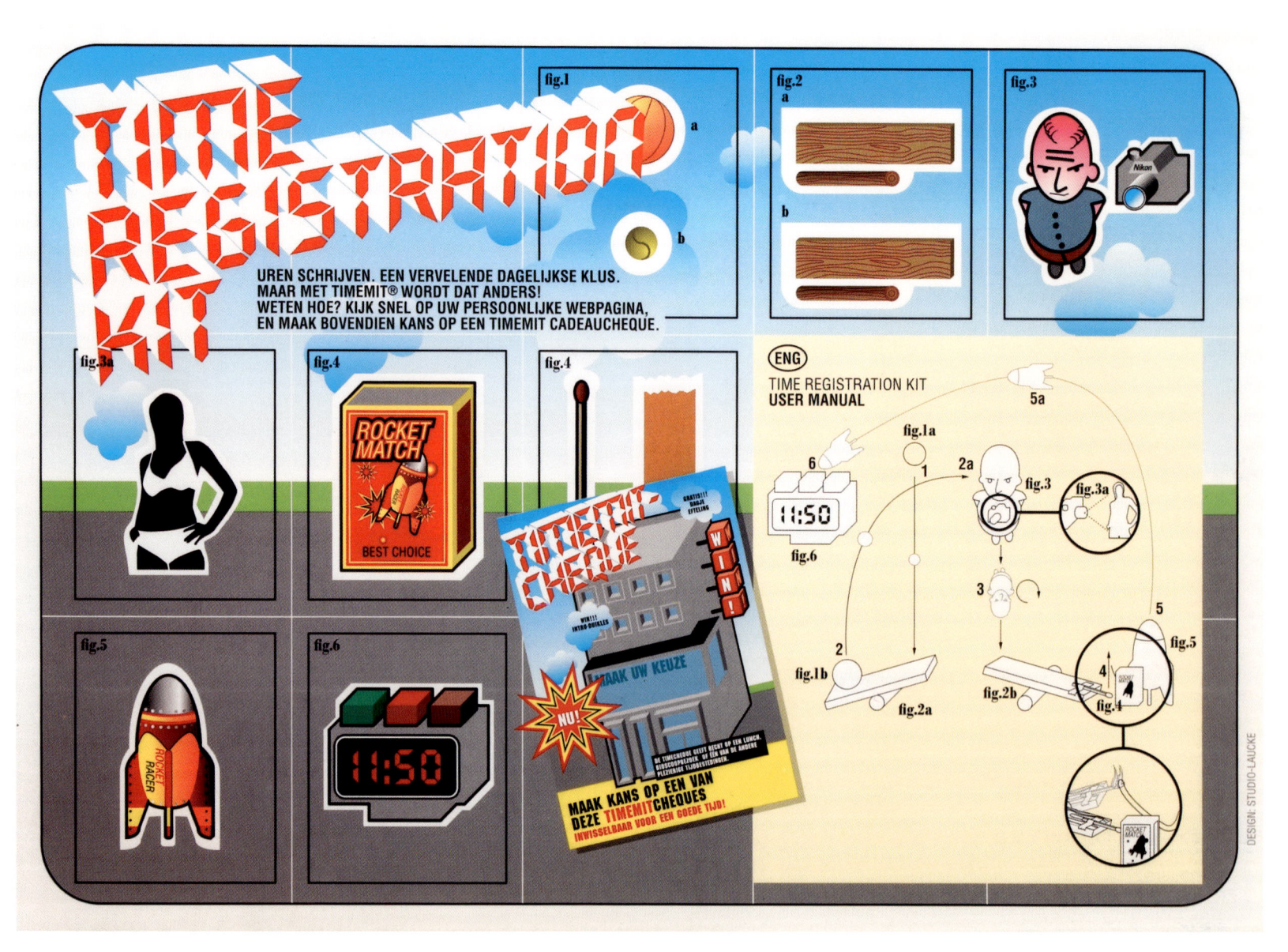

Creative direction and design: Dirk Laucke/Studio Laucke Siebein

118 Sketches and Diagrams

Illinois: Visualizing Music/Vocal Album Grid ::
Jax de León :: www.jaxdeleon.com ::

Based on Sufjan Stevens's album *Illinois*, this interesting project extracts visual interpretations of the music. In this particular diagram, seventy-four minutes and thirteen seconds of the album are represented with squares (each one is a second and each row, a minute); the colored ones indicate the piece that is being sung each second while the gray ones indicate the instrumental parts of the album.

Sketches and Diagrams

Science Infographics for *Seed* Magazine ::
Cybu Richli/C2F :: www.c2f.to ::

"Seeing is believing" is one of the phrases that best represents men of science, for whom faith is not sufficient since they need to check the facts. For this reason, the magazine *Seed*, which is about science, and the points at which this intersects with society and the people that make it possible, accompanies its articles with illustrations and explanatory diagrams so that, in some way, *quod erat demonstrandum*.

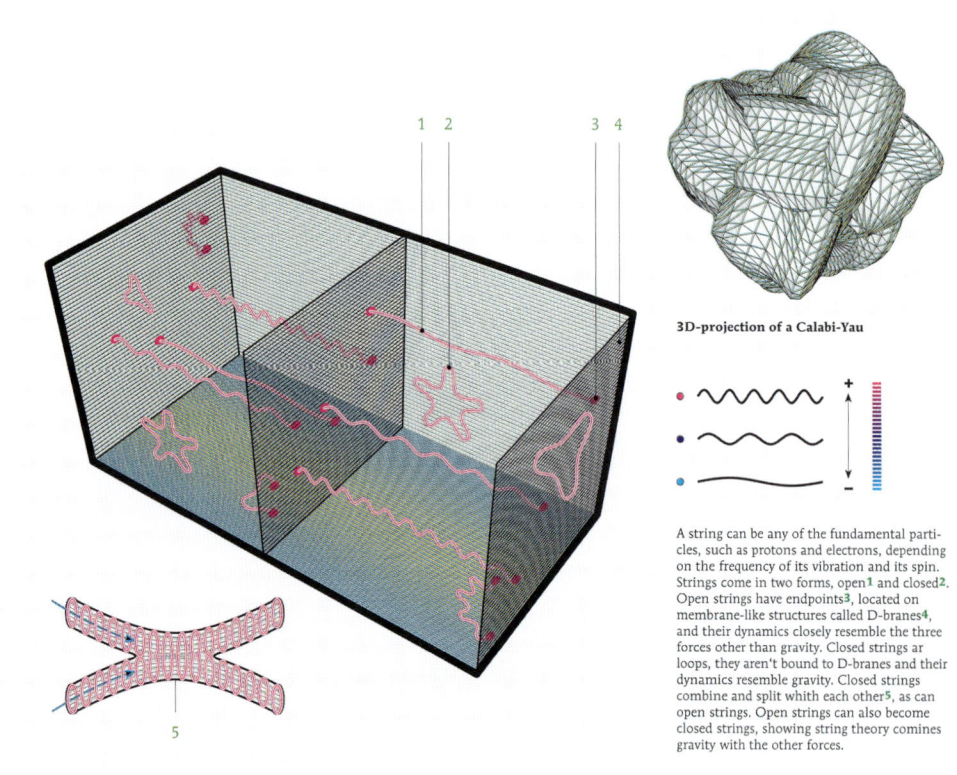

3D-projection of a Calabi-Yau

A string can be any of the fundamental particles, such as protons and electrons, depending on the frequency of its vibration and its spin. Strings come in two forms, open[1] and closed[2]. Open strings have endpoints[3], located on membrane-like structures called D-branes[4], and their dynamics closely resemble the three forces other than gravity. Closed strings ar loops, they aren't bound to D-branes and their dynamics resemble gravity. Closed strings combine and split whith each other[5], as can open strings. Open strings can also become closed strings, showing string theory comines gravity with the other forces.

120 **Sketches and Diagrams**

Legend
Batteries 1
Electric motor 2
Generator 3
Gasoline engine 4

Ring gear A
Planet carrier B
Sun gear C
Planets D

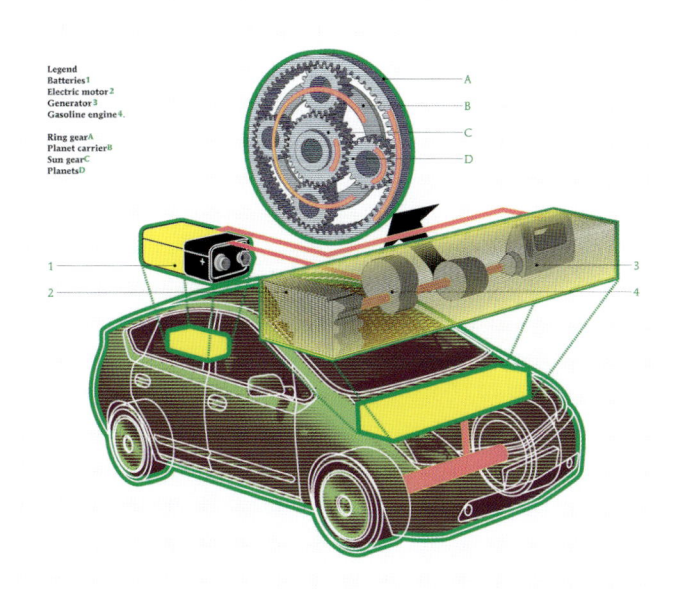

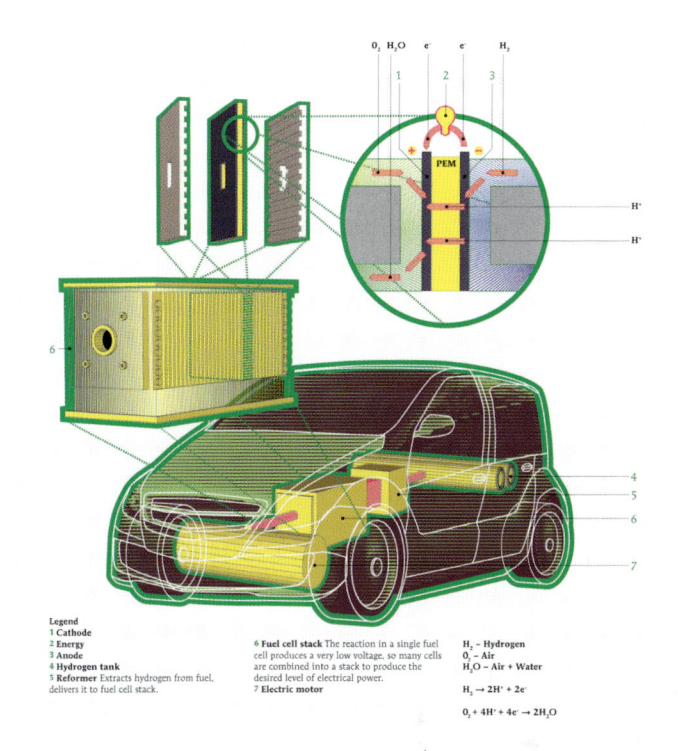

Legend
1 Cathode
2 Energy
3 Anode
4 Hydrogen tank
5 **Reformer** Extracts hydrogen from fuel, delivers it to fuel cell stack.
6 **Fuel cell stack** The reaction in a single fuel cell produces a very low voltage, so many cells are combined into a stack to produce the desired level of electrical power.
7 **Electric motor**

H_2 – Hydrogen
O_2 – Air
H_2O – Air + Water

$H_2 \rightarrow 2H^+ + 2e^-$

$O_2 + 4H^+ + 4e^- \rightarrow 2H_2O$

Sketches and Diagrams | 121

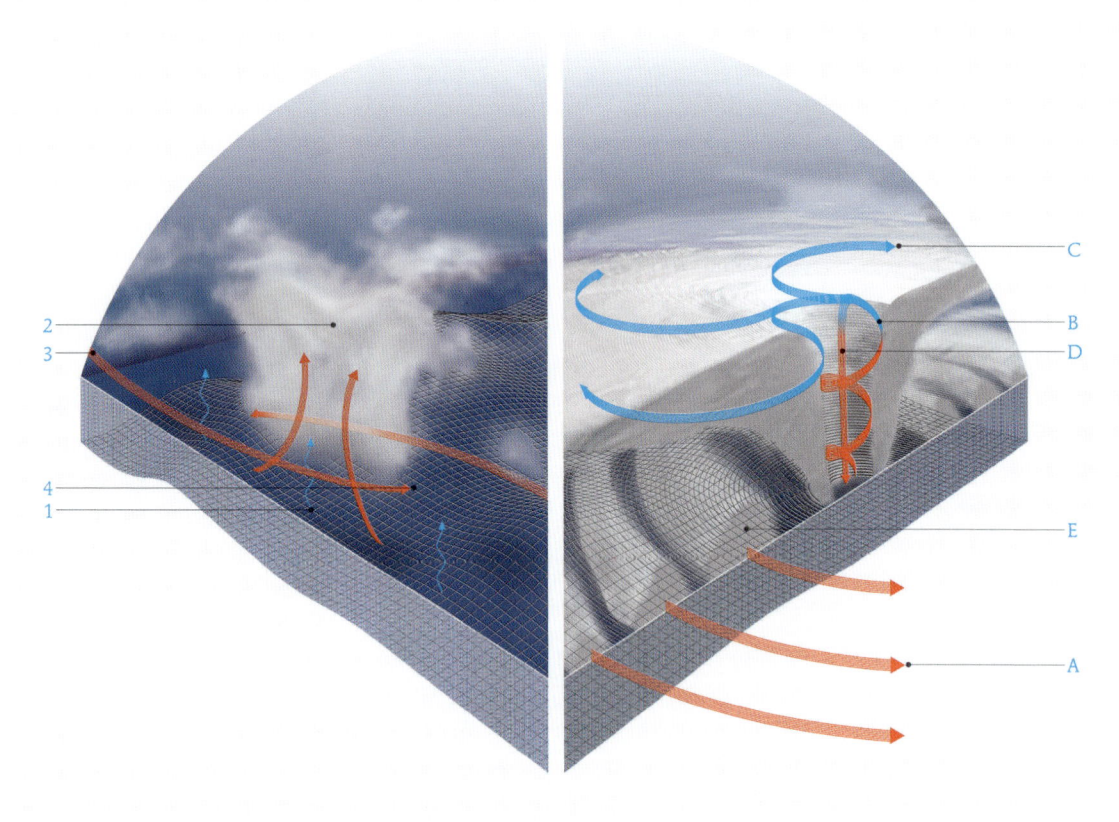

Process of Formation

1. Warm seawater evaporates. Moist, warm air rises and the water if carries condenses into droplets above to form rain clouds.
2. Condensing water gives off heat. As clouds form, the surrounding atmosphere warms and expands upward, pushing heavier air out of the way and leaving a lighter region of the atmosphere in its place. At low altitude, that means less total weight pushing down, creating a **low pressure zone**.
3. Sourrounding air rushes in to fill this low pressure zone, creating wind over the water. The wind increases the rate fo evaporation, creating more rainclouds. This **positive feedback loop** causes the storm›s intensity to increase. When winds reach 34 m/s (75 mph) the storm is called a hurricane.
4. If the Earth were stationary, wind would flow directly from the high pressure to the low pressure zone. but the Earth is spinning, so the inrushing wind misses its target (it appears to veer right). This is the **Coriolis effect**. Since the wind initially misses to the right of the low pressure zone, it ends up orbiting the zone counterclockwise. This is why hurricanes spin.

Storm structure

Usually, as a hurricane forms, distributed thunderstorm activity coalesces into a single large, spinning storm system.

A Spiraling winds: Water evaporates fastest end createst the most heat at the center of the storm. Winds gradually spiral inward toward the center, accelerating as they go. This is conservation of angular momentum, the same principle that causes an ice skater to spin faster as he pulls his arms in.

B Spreading winds: When they reach the eyewall, the heated winds begin to rise, spiraling upward. In the hot upper reaches of the hurricane, the pressure is actually higher than in the sourrounding atmosphere. Here the winds are pushed outward, slowing as they go, like an ice skater extending his arms.

C Anticyclonic rotation: Since the pressure is lower in every direction, the spreading winds have no particular target. They veer continually right due to the Coriolis effect, spinning in the opposite direction of the storm. This is anticyclonic rotation.

D Eye Formation: Some of the spreading winds are pushed back down into the center of the hurricane. As they descend, the pressure of the atmosphere above piles up, warming and drying them out. This creates a clear region called the eye.

E Rain bands: Throughout the hurricane, there are local areas of drying, descending air (which is referred to as subsidence) and local regions of evaporation and rain. The regions of heaviest rain and evaporation from rain bands.

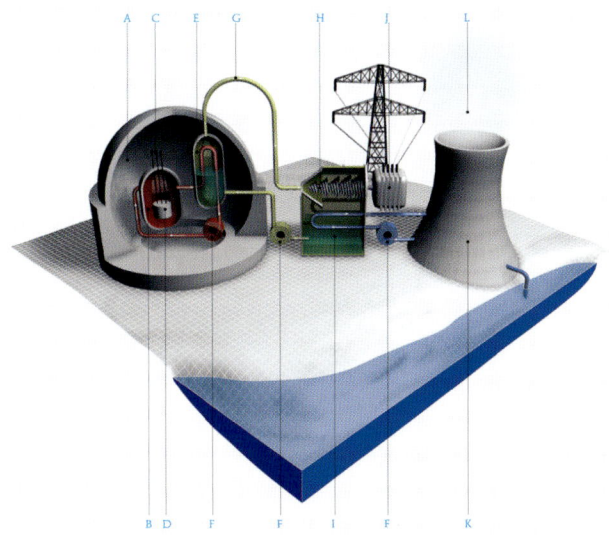

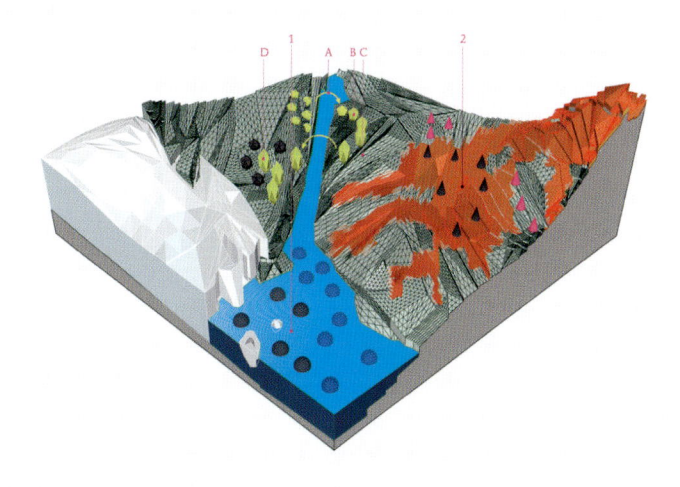

Parts
Containment structure A, reactor steel pressure vessel B, control rods C, reactor D, steam generator E, pumps F, streamline G, turbine H, cooling water condenser I, generator J, cooling tower K, steam/air L.

1 Glaciation slowly drains, cools, and deoxygenates an aquatic environment, threatening a species's survival.
2 A volcanic eruption rapidly wipes out a localized species.

A A newly formed river isolates some members of a species.
B Environmental pressures select for new traits.
C Over time a new species evolves.
D If beneficial adaptations have occurred, intermingling could eliminate the original species.

Sketches and Diagrams | 123

Ekens ::
Lotie :: www.lotie.com ::

Ekens is a Swedish brand devoted solely to bedroom furniture. Lotie made this illustration for the company to use on their Web site and catalog. All the key elements of the brand are represented and arranged in order in the illustration: the logo is in the center, then come the three main characteristics, with each of these being further divided into three more qualities.

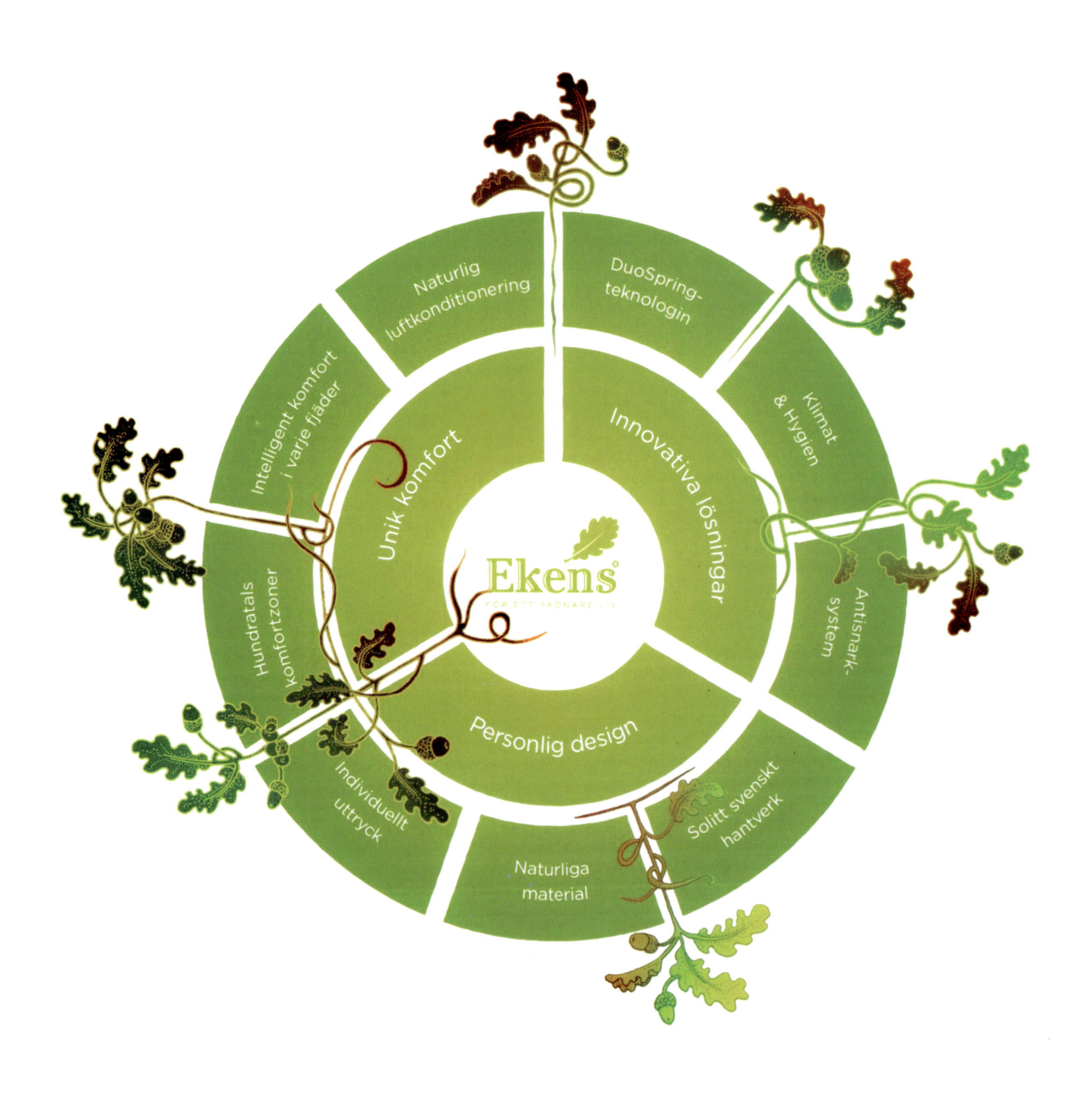

Visual Explanations — Growth of an Avocado ::
Cybu Richli :: www.c2f.to ::

There are many way to explain something, although the easiest way to understand a process is to visualize it. In this diagram, a balloon is used to represent the growth rate of an avocado as the days go by.

As the balloon inflates, it acquires the definitive shape and size of a seventy-day-old ripe avocado.

Wachstum einer Avocado

70 TAGE
63 TAGE
56 TAGE
49 TAGE
42 TAGE
35 TAGE
28 TAGE
21 TAGE
14 TAGE
7 TAGE
0 TAGE

Shale Gas ::
Apfel Zet :: www.apfelzet.de ::

The extraction of shale gas is a fairly new practice (it has been going on in the United States since the nineties and in Europe it is even more recent) since penetrating shale rock is very expensive. This flier was developed for one of the world's shale-extracting companies. The diagram illustrates the shale-extracting process. The flier was developed by Apfel Zet, a trio of designers.

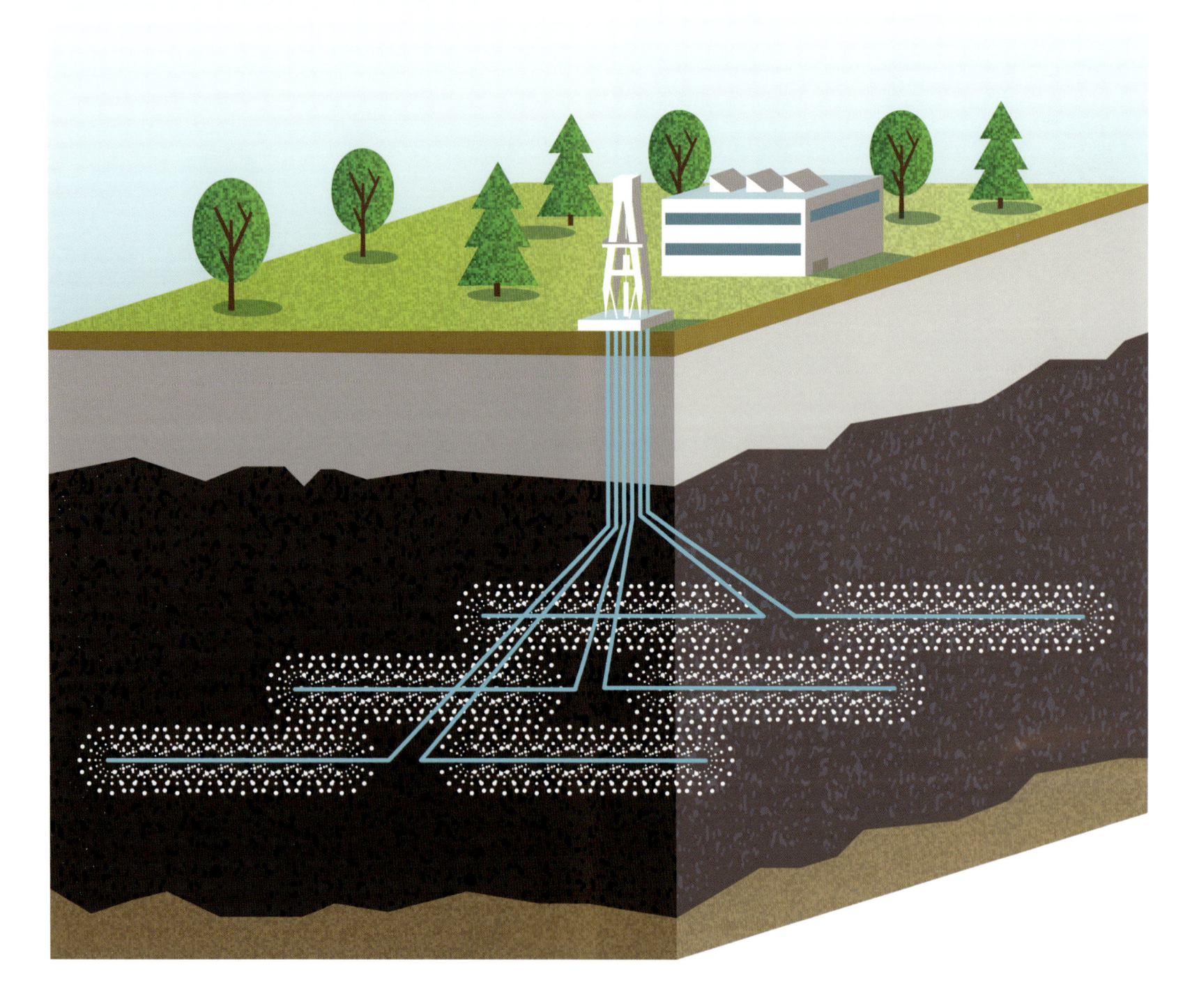

Das Baumhaus ::
Daniel Kaufmann :: www.danielkaufmann.ch ::

This poster is an instruction manual for building a treehouse. It gives instructions on how to build the construction (identifying each part with a letter), the amount of material used, and the weight the structure can withstand compared to other factors. Growth over the years is indicated by annual rings, just like those seen on trees.

Research in the Visualization of Financial Data ::
Cybu Richli/C2F :: www.c2f.to ::

In the financial world, there are many specific terms and processes in the sector that require a certain amount of knowledge to be able to understand what is being discussed. Morningstar, a company devoted to researching investments, is well aware of this fact. For this reason, they commissioned these diagrams to help readers visualize certain financial data, like the distribution of assets (left) or a complete portfolio (right).

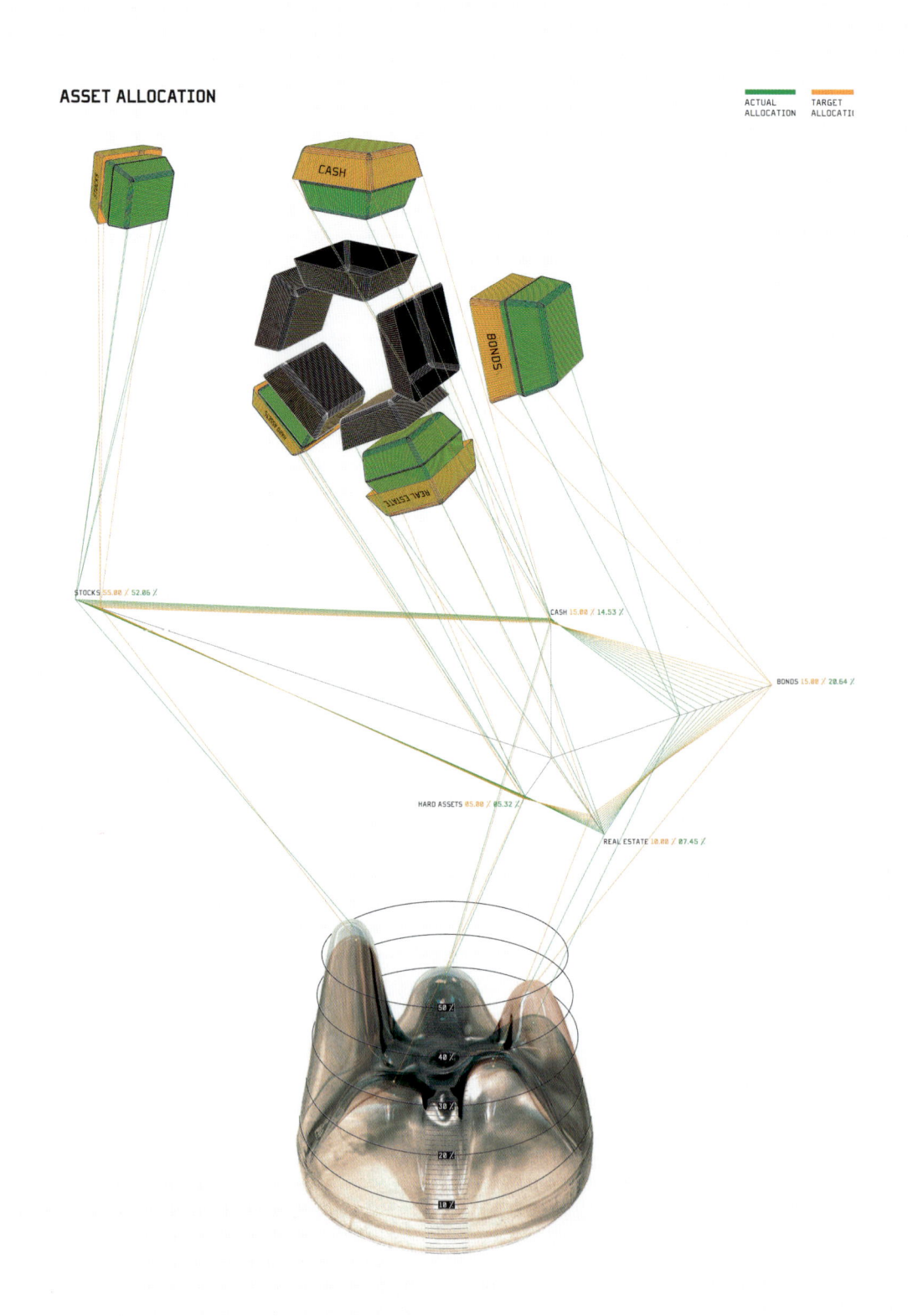

ASSET ALLOCATION

ACTUAL ALLOCATION / TARGET ALLOCATION

128 **Sketches and Diagrams**

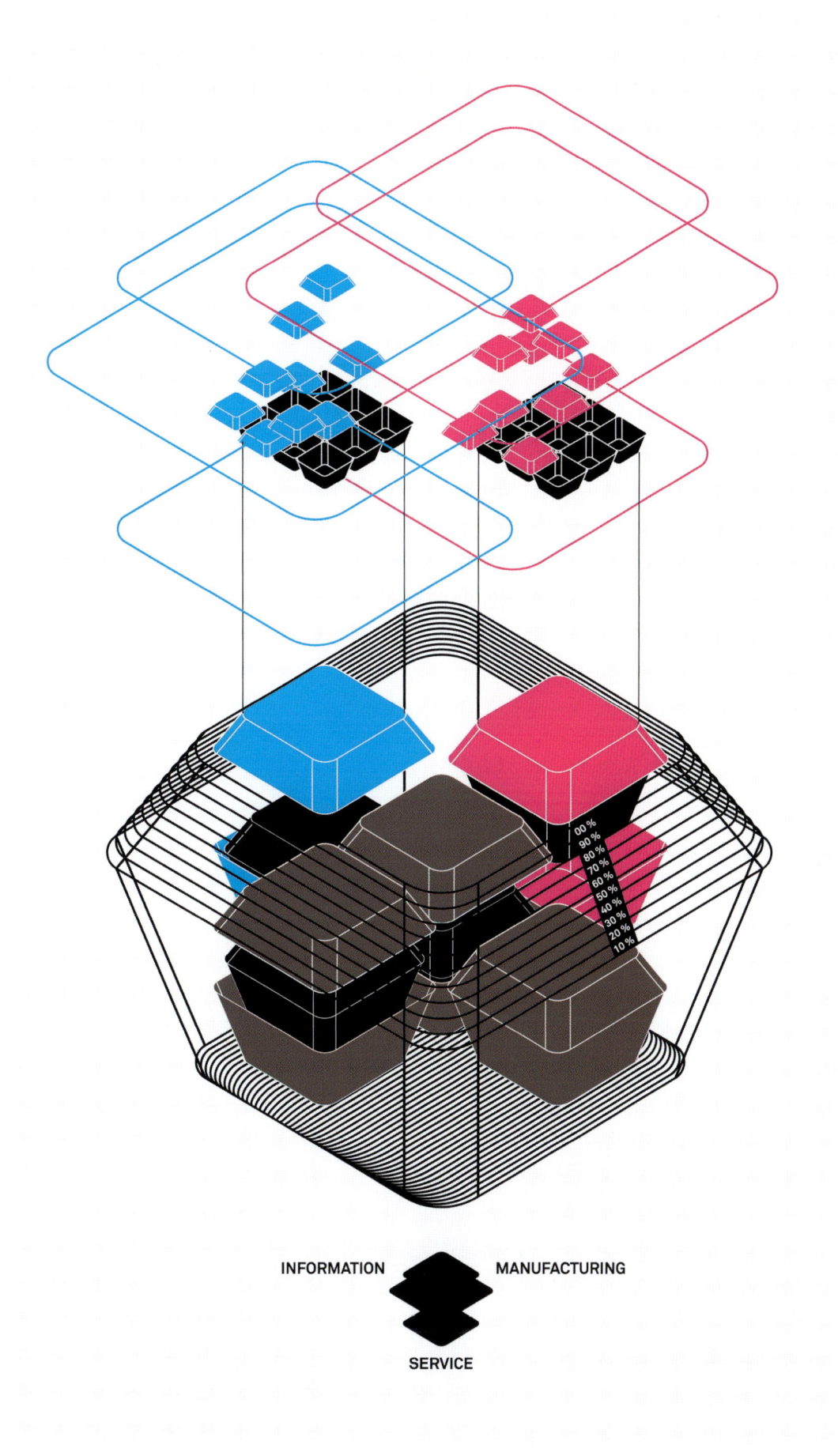

INFORMATION   MANUFACTURING

SERVICE

Sketches and Diagrams | 129

Impossibles possibles ::
Enric Jardí :: www.enricjardi.com ::

What do we get when a designer works hand in hand with a printing office? A book like this one, in which excellence is appreciated in both the way the information is presented graphically, along with the design of each page and the printing quality. To achieve this high level of quality, the latest printing and handling techniques were used, some of which had never before been done in Spain.

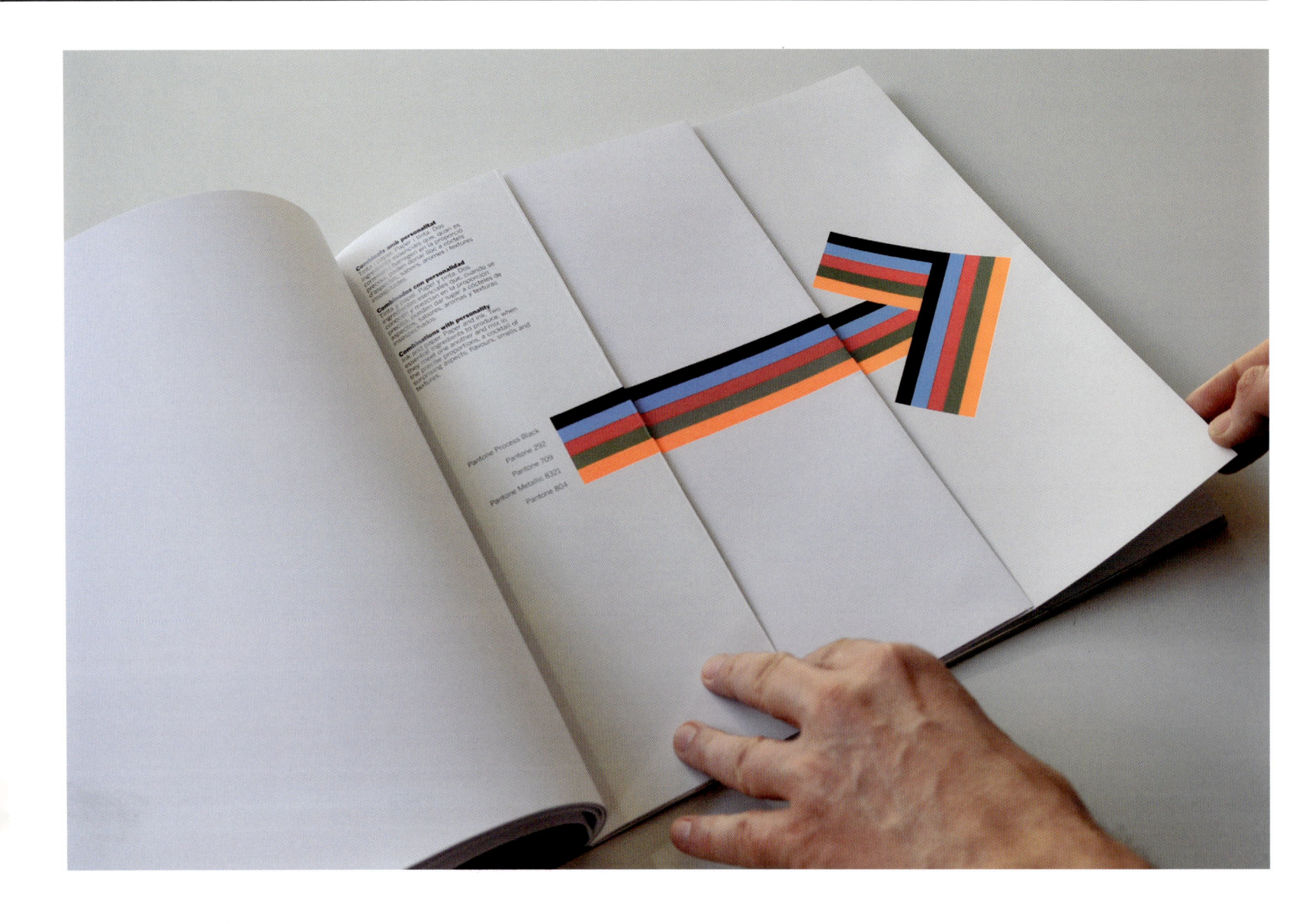

Sketches and Diagrams | 131

Virgin in Numbers ::
Andrio Abero :: www.andrioabero.com ::

The magazine *Roger* commissioned a diagram from Andrio Abero visualizing certain information, along with statistical data, on Virgin Airlines. The magazine wanted the information to be presented in a somewhat unconventional manner so it would be visually attractive to its readers. The result differs from conventional charts since the images take center stage, backed up by figures and hard data.

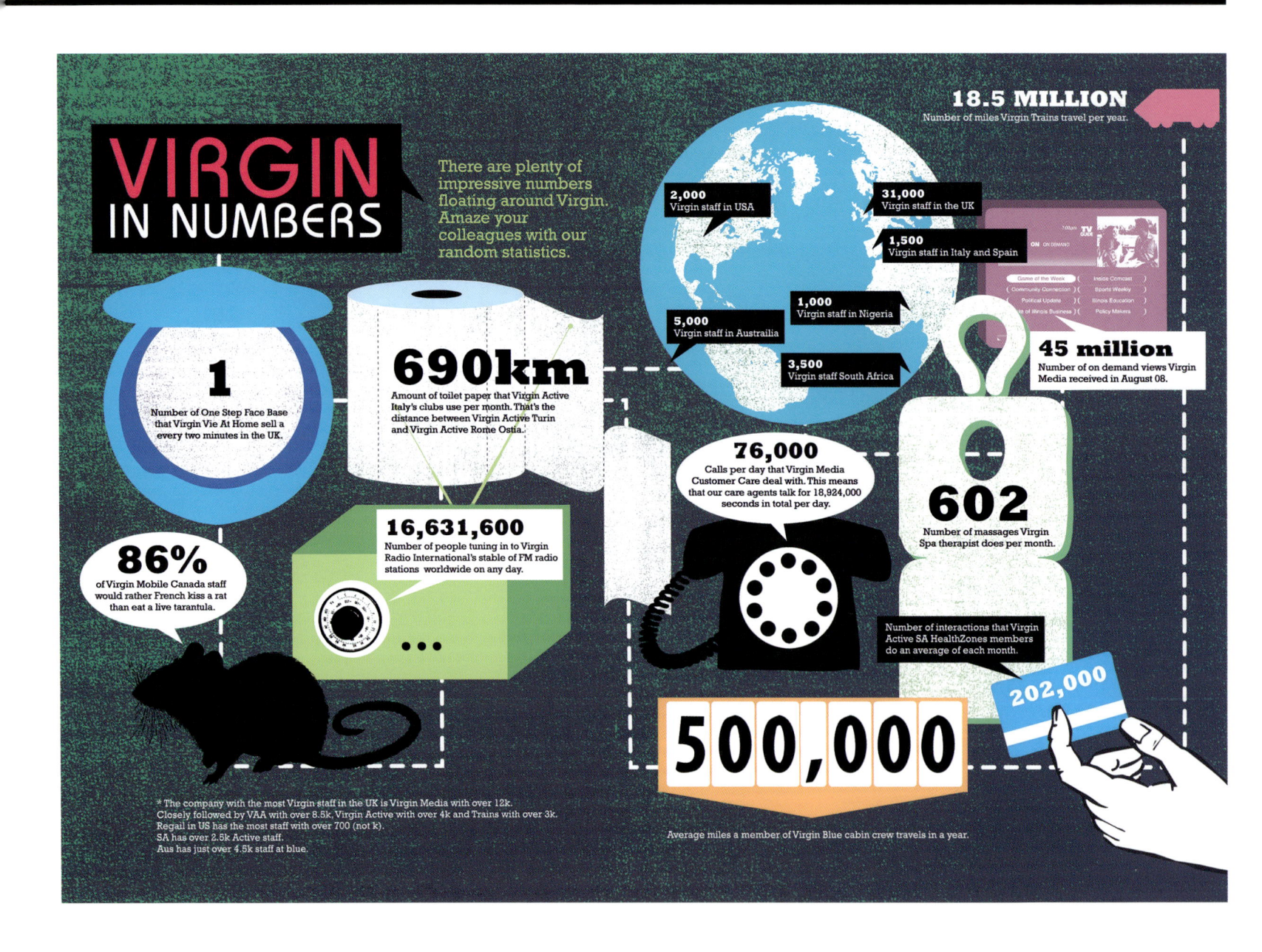

VIRGIN IN NUMBERS

There are plenty of impressive numbers floating around Virgin. Amaze your colleagues with our random statistics.

1 — Number of One Step Face Base that Virgin Vie At Home sell a every two minutes in the UK.

86% of Virgin Mobile Canada staff would rather French kiss a rat than eat a live tarantula.

690km — Amount of toilet paper that Virgin Active Italy's clubs use per month. That's the distance between Virgin Active Turin and Virgin Active Rome Ostia.

16,631,600 — Number of people tuning in to Virgin Radio International's stable of FM radio stations worldwide on any day.

2,000 Virgin staff in USA
31,000 Virgin staff in the UK
1,500 Virgin staff in Italy and Spain
5,000 Virgin staff in Austrailia
1,000 Virgin staff in Nigeria
3,500 Virgin staff South Africa

18.5 MILLION Number of miles Virgin Trains travel per year.

45 million Number of on demand views Virgin Media received in August 08.

76,000 Calls per day that Virgin Media Customer Care deal with. This means that our care agents talk for 18,924,000 seconds in total per day.

602 Number of massages Virgin Spa therapist does per month.

202,000 Number of interactions that Virgin Active SA HealthZones members do an average of each month.

500,000 Average miles a member of Virgin Blue cabin crew travels in a year.

* The company with the most Virgin staff in the UK is Virgin Media with over 12k. Closely followed by VAA with over 8.5k, Virgin Active with over 4k and Trains with over 3k. Regail in US has the most staff with over 700 (not k).
SA has over 2.5k Active staff.
Aus has just over 4.5k staff at blue.

100 Year Forecast ::
Jennifer Daniel :: httpcolonforwardslashforwardslashwwwdotjenniferdanieldotcom.com ::

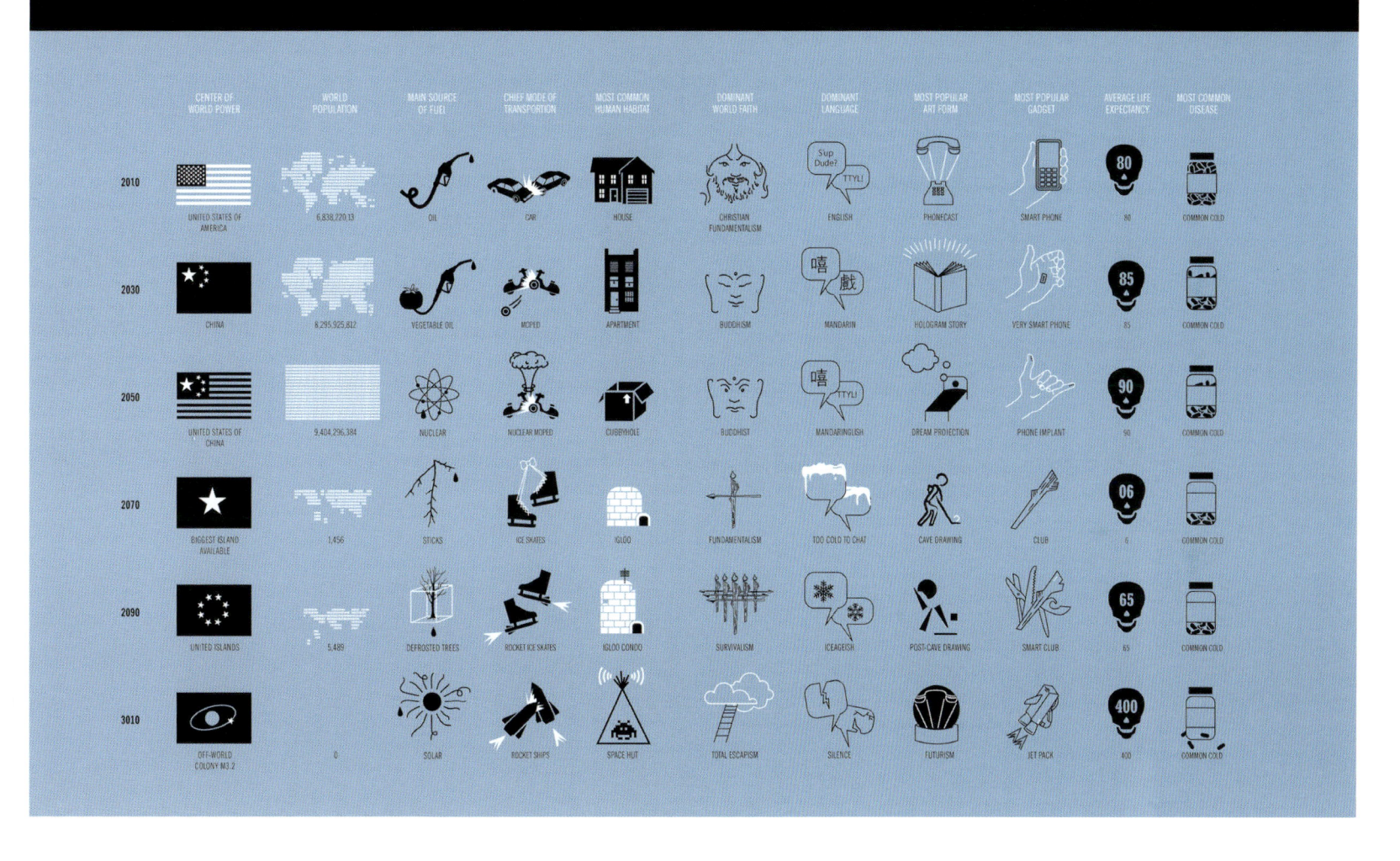

When watching the news about the economy, ecology, politics, or religion, the predictions regarding the earth and humanity are not exactly encouraging. In spite of the surrounding negativity, it is important to not lose one's sense of humor. This poster was created for the book *Forecast* from Princeton Architectural Press, and forecasts the world's future with a heavy dose of comedy.

Kulturband ::
Sweden Graphics :: www.nillesvensson.com ::

This diagram demonstrates how all the people in Sweden that belong to the intellectual and cultural elite (writers, journalists, artists, etc.) are connected in one way or another, whether by blood, love, business, or friendship, forming one big social circle.

The different colors used for each one indicate their professional field and the symbol they use to join their hands indicates their relationship with each other.

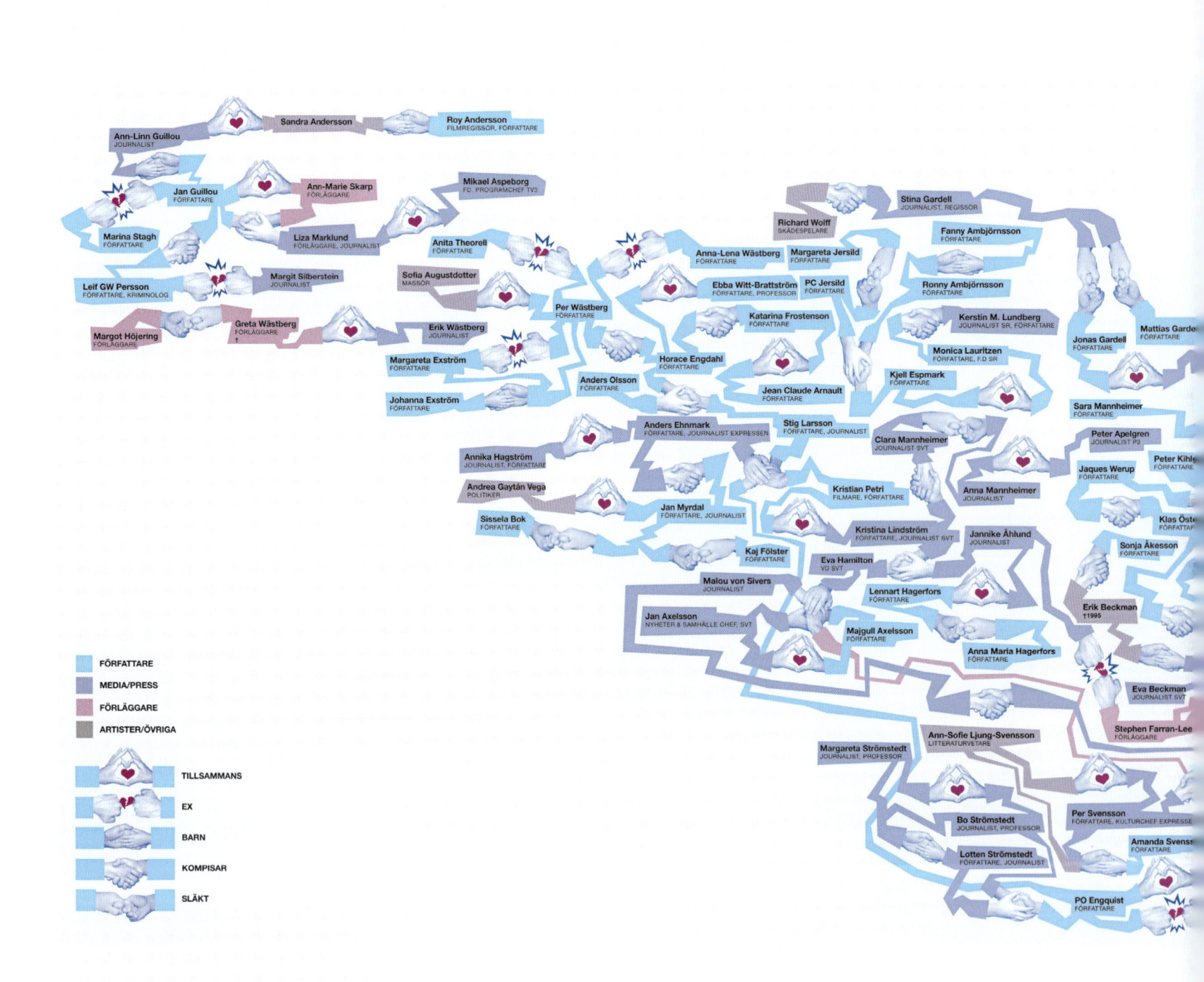

Sketches and Diagrams | 135

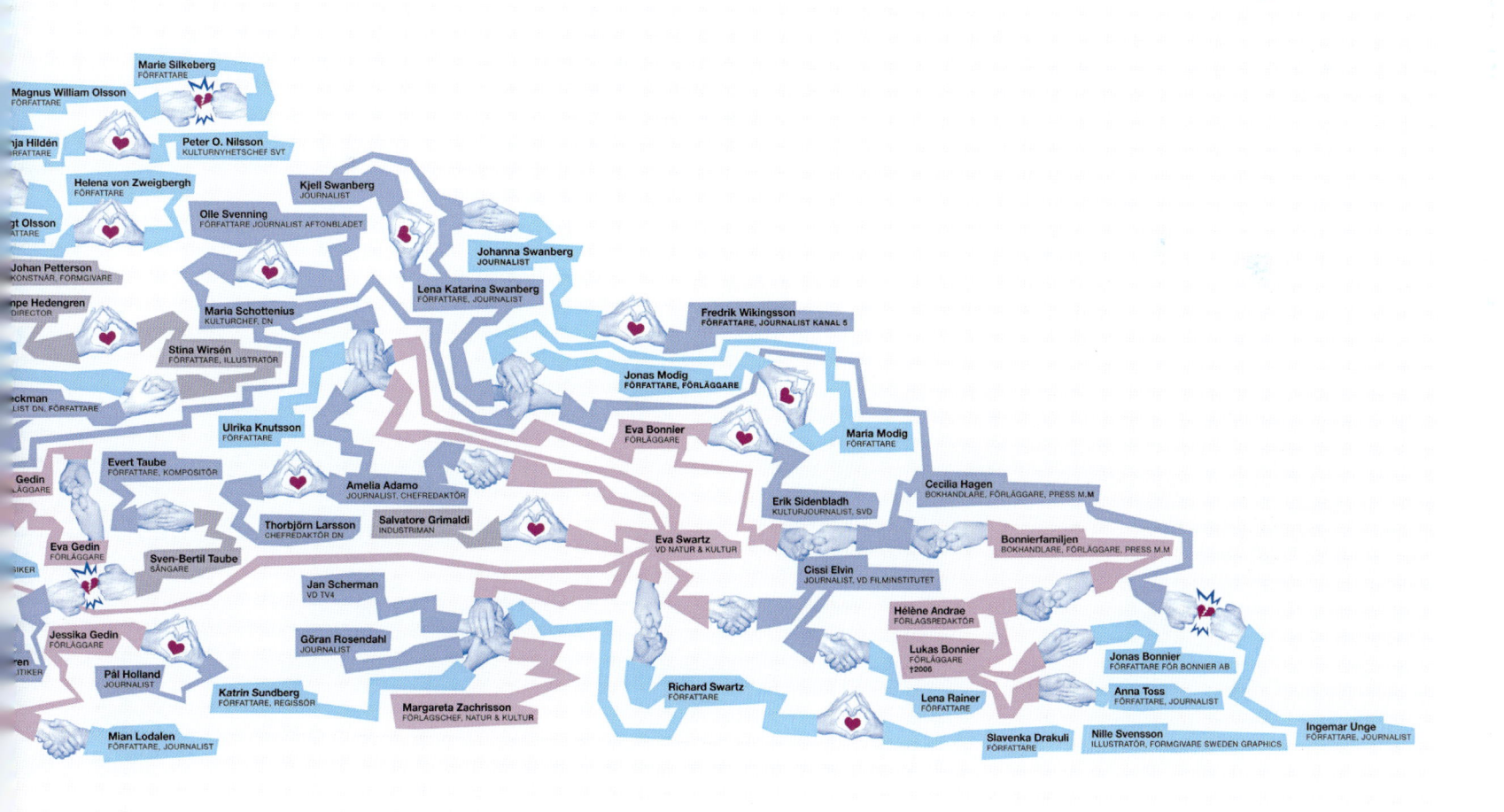

PlasticsGuide ::
Anna Filipova :: www.anfilip.com ::

The classifications in this diagram have been made based on the properties of the different plastics, gathering together those with a similar quality based on the specifications for their group. Those that are at the top are the ones that are more environmentally friendly and easy to recycle, whereas those that are at the bottom of the diagram are more contaminating and hazardous to the health.

PLASTICS GUIDE   PRICE | DISPOSAL | HEALTH RISK | RESISTANCE

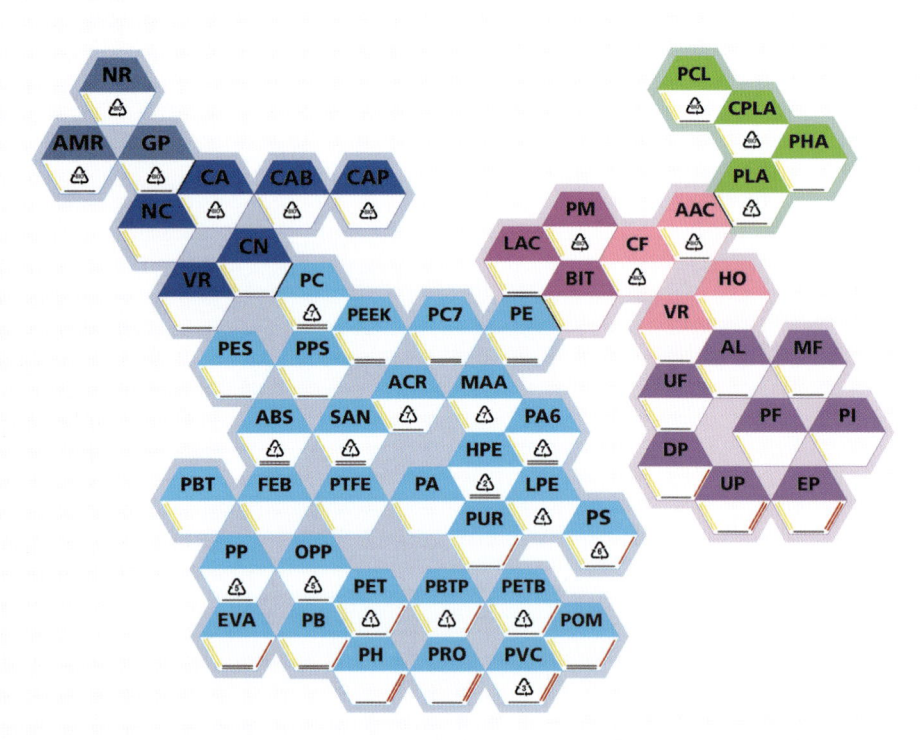

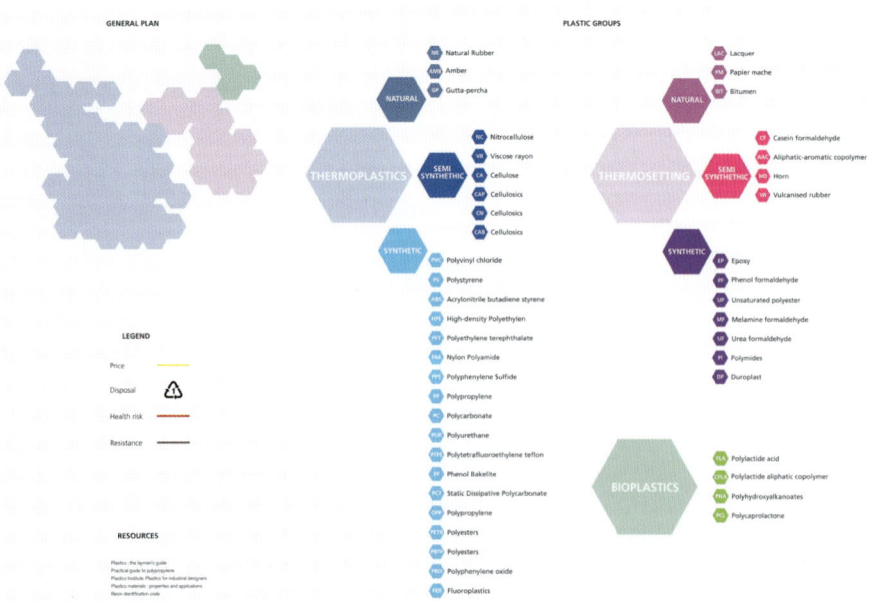

The classifications on the graph are made based on the plastic's properties. Plastics sitting next to each other has similar quality (based on specifications in their groups).
The plastics which are situated at the upper part are most environmental friendly, easy to recycle and disposable and viceversa, the plastics at the bottom part are dangerous for health and harm the environment.

136 Sketches and Diagrams

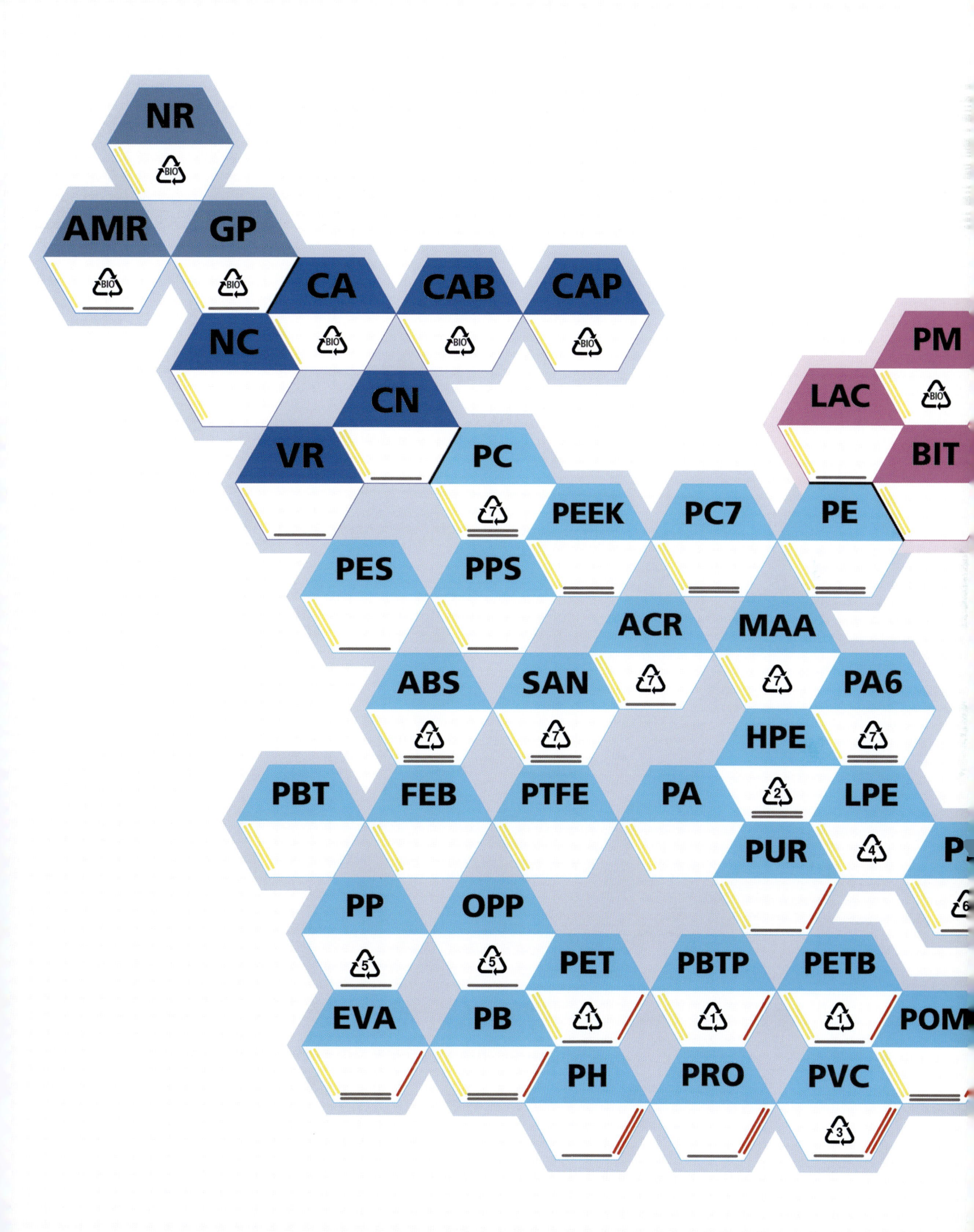

NR								
AMR	GP	CA	CAB	CAP				
	NC						PM	
		CN				LAC		
	VR	PC				BIT		
		PEEK	PC7	PE				
PES	PPS							
		ACR	MAA					
ABS	SAN		PA6					
		HPE						
PBT	FEB	PTFE	PA	LPE				
			PUR	P.				
PP	OPP							
		PET	PBTP	PETB				
EVA	PB			POM				
	PH	PRO	PVC					

Life-Cycle T-Shirt ::
Arlene Birt for Droog :: www.backgroundstories.com ::

The work of artist Arlene Birt for Droog focuses on communicating what lies behind everyday products, and offers an explanation of their origins using educational diagrams. Unlike the majority of charts, which focus on data, here history is given pride of place and then the data is included in context. In this example, the artist has illustrated the production process behind making a T-shirt. She has ingeniously printed the illustration on the garment itself.

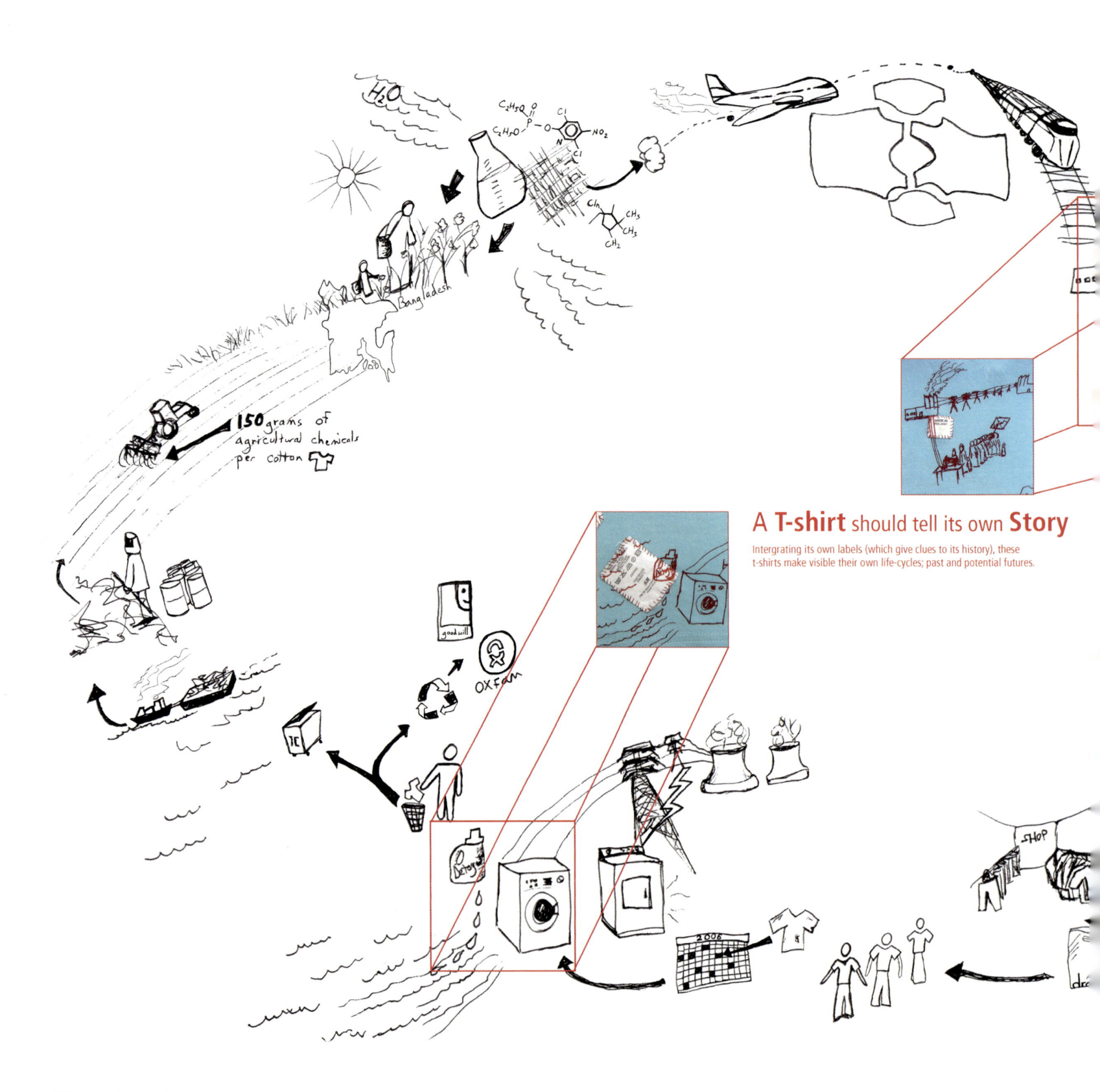

A **T-shirt** should tell its own **Story**

Intergrating its own labels (which give clues to its history), these t-shirts make visible their own life-cycles; past and potential futures.

138 Sketches and Diagrams

Sketches and Diagrams | 139

Eau Propre = Bonne Santé ::
Nathanaël Hamon, Jaana Davidjants/SLANG :: www.slanginternational.org ::

This informative poster was designed to show the people from a village in Africa's Togo how to use water properly. Eight points are covered—from how to wash your hands before cooking to how to boil water to why it is important not to drink from the rivers. Since the poster was distributed in several places (schools, hospitals, and to folk healers), icons were included so that the non-French speaking population could also understand.

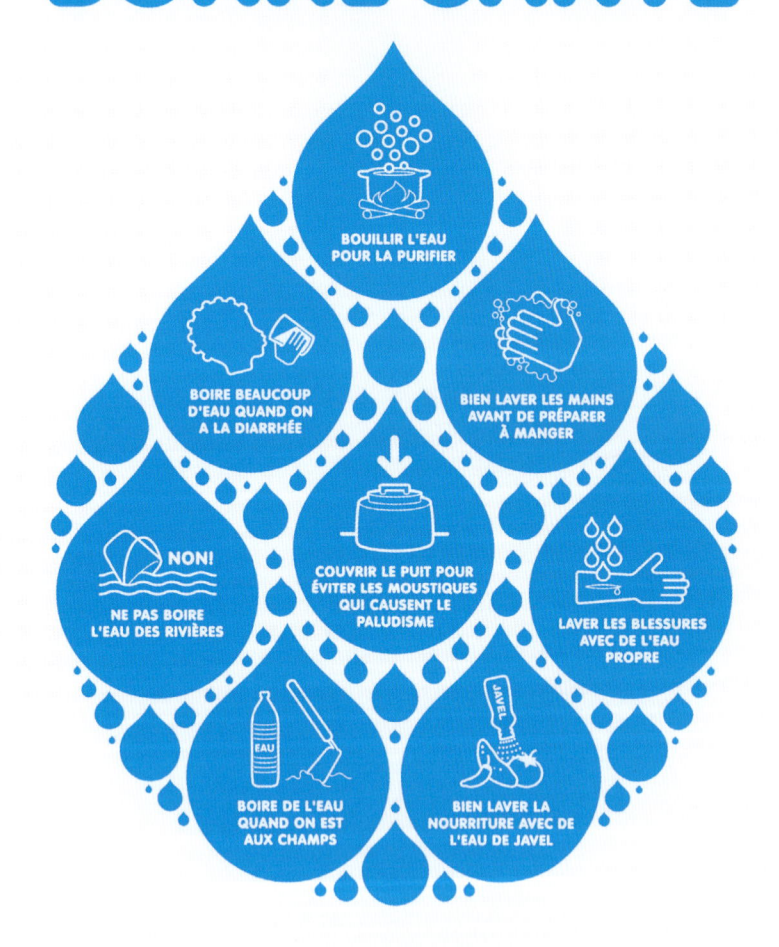

Models ::
Xavier Barrade :: www.xavierbarrade.com ::

A concept map is a diagram that is used to help people learn about a subject. It entails organizing the information in a hierarchical structure, putting the main concept right at the top, and connecting it to other concepts, which can then be subdivided until all the relevant information has been included.

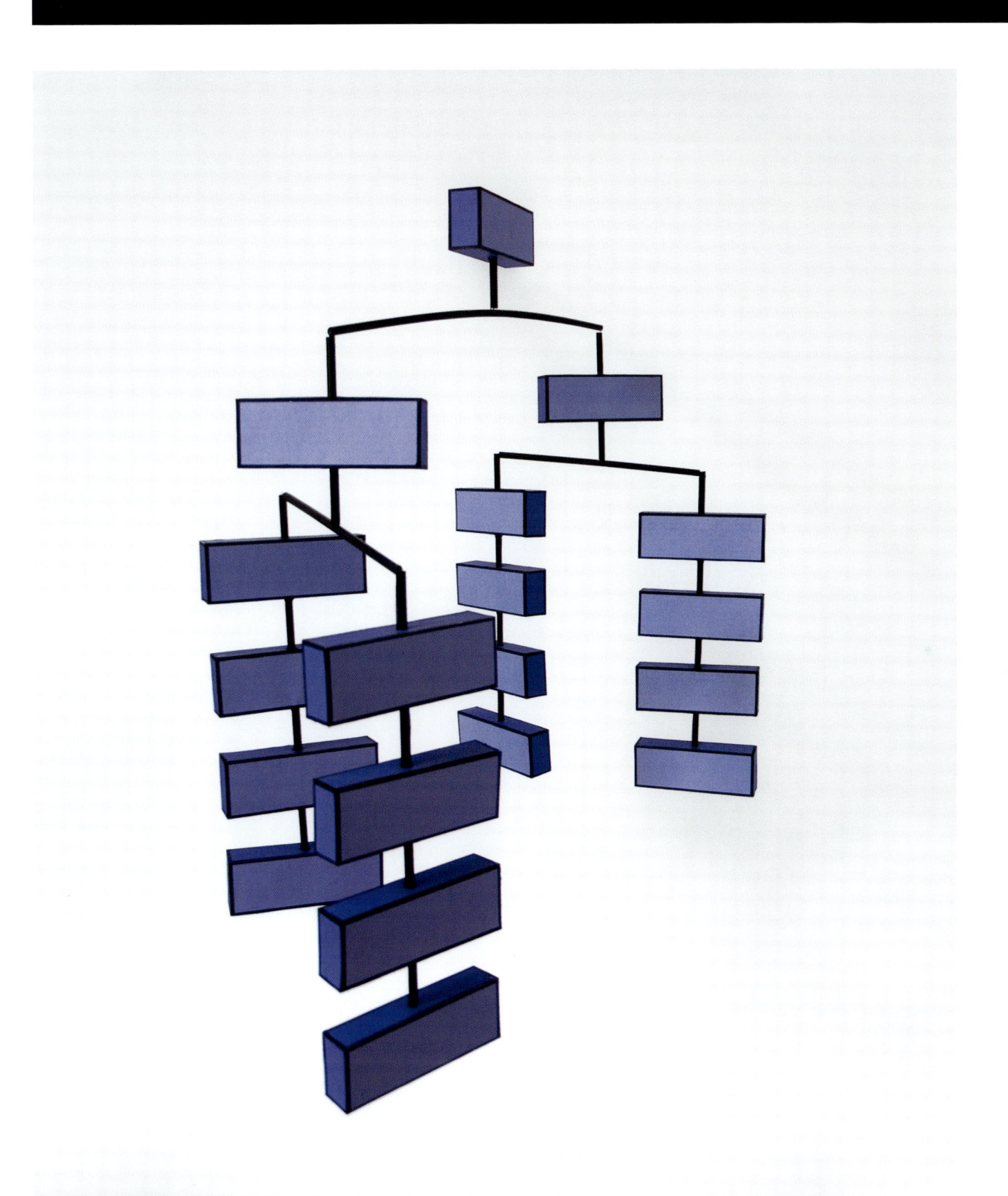

Sketches and Diagrams | 41

Wind Turbine ::
LIGALUX :: www.ligalux.de ::

When this new wind turbine came into operation, the Ligalux studio was asked to do an illustration showing how the machine worked, providing a detailed explanation of each of its parts, as well as telling the story of its development and the potential benefit the new technology had to offer for the future. A sample of the material was put on display at the visitors' center for the site.

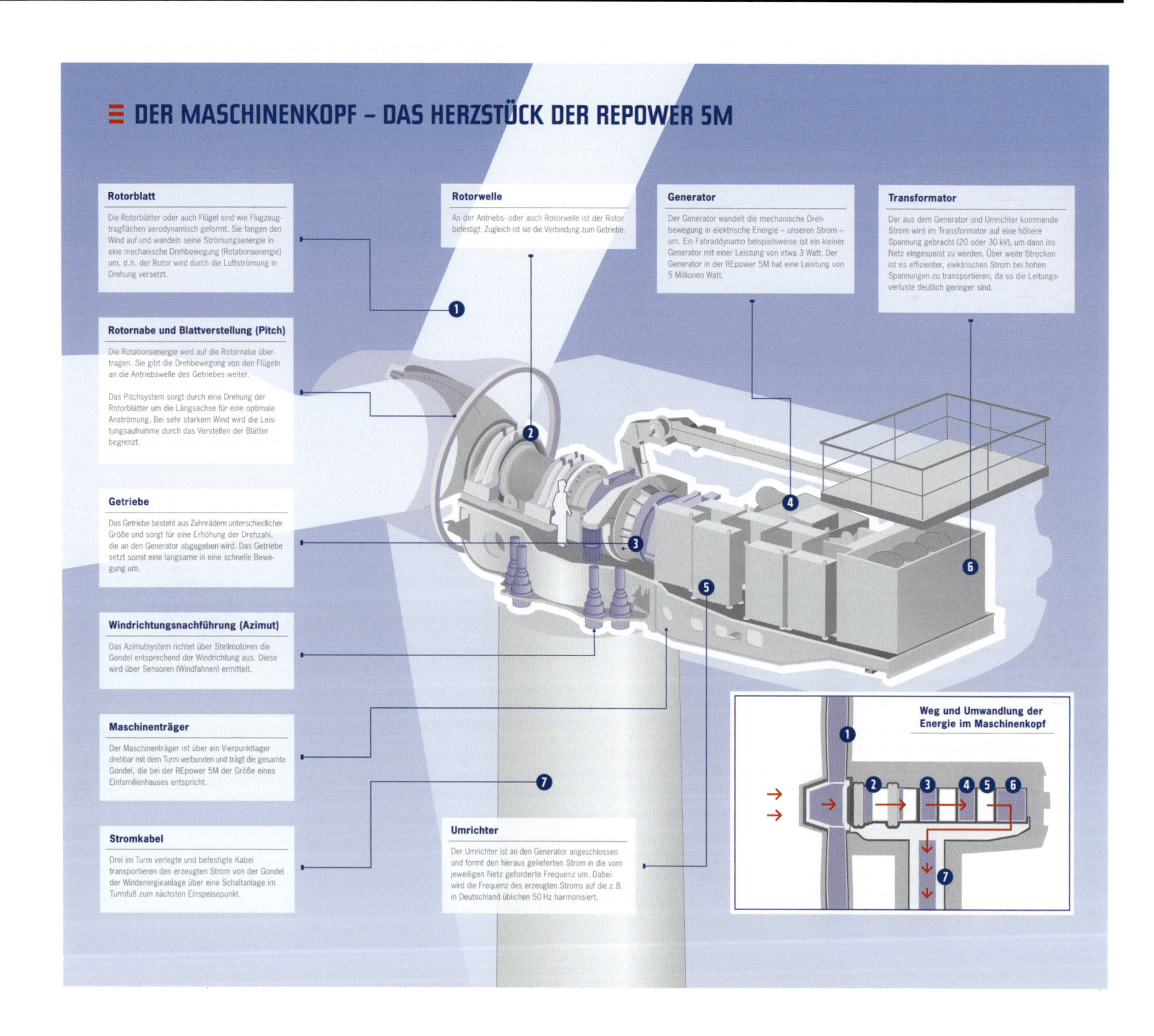

DER MASCHINENKOPF – DAS HERZSTÜCK DER REPOWER 5M

Rotorblatt

Die Rotorblätter oder auch Flügel sind wie Flugzeugtragflächen aerodynamisch geformt. Sie fangen den Wind auf und wandeln seine Strömungsenergie in eine mechanische Drehbewegung (Rotationsenergie) um, d.h. der Rotor wird durch die Luftströmung in Drehung versetzt.

Rotornabe und Blattverstellung (Pitch)

Die Rotationsenergie wird auf die Rotornabe übertragen. Sie gibt die Drehbewegung von den Flügeln an die Antriebswelle des Getriebes weiter.

Das Pitchsystem sorgt durch eine Drehung der Rotorblätter um die Längsachse für eine optimale Anströmung. Bei sehr starkem Wind wird die Leistungsaufnahme durch das Verstellen der Blätter begrenzt.

Getriebe

Das Getriebe besteht aus Zahnrädern unterschiedlicher Größe und sorgt für eine Erhöhung der Drehzahl, die an den Generator abgegeben wird. Das Getriebe setzt somit eine langsame in eine schnelle Bewegung um.

Windrichtungsnachführung (Azimut)

Das Azimutsystem richtet über Stellmotoren die Gondel entsprechend der Windrichtung aus. Diese wird über Sensoren (Windfahnen) ermittelt.

Maschinenträger

Der Maschinenträger ist über ein Vierpunktlager drehbar mit dem Turm verbunden und trägt die gesamte Gondel, die bei der REpower 5M der Größe eines Einfamilienhauses entspricht.

Stromkabel

Drei im Turm verlegte und befestigte Kabel transportieren den erzeugten Strom von der Gondel der Windenergieanlage über eine Schaltanlage im Turmfuß zum nächsten Einspeisepunkt.

Rotorwelle

An der Antriebs- oder auch Rotorwelle ist der Rotor befestigt. Zugleich ist sie die Verbindung zum Getriebe.

Generator

Der Generator wandelt die mechanische Drehbewegung in elektrische Energie – unseren Strom – um. Ein Fahrraddynamo beispielsweise ist ein kleiner Generator mit einer Leistung von etwa 3 Watt. Der Generator in der REpower 5M hat eine Leistung von 5 Millionen Watt.

Umrichter

Der Umrichter ist an den Generator angeschlossen und formt den hieraus gelieferten Strom in die vom jeweiligen Netz geforderte Frequenz um. Dabei wird die Frequenz des erzeugten Stroms auf die z.B. in Deutschland üblichen 50 Hz harmonisiert.

Transformator

Der aus dem Generator und Umrichter kommende Strom wird im Transformator auf eine höhere Spannung gebracht (20 oder 30 kV), um dann ins Netz eingespeist zu werden. Über weite Strecken ist es effizienter, elektrischen Strom bei hohen Spannungen zu transportieren, da so die Leitungsverluste deutlich geringer sind.

Weg und Umwandlung der Energie im Maschinenkopf

Sketches and Diagrams

Table of Elements Poster ::
Blok Design :: www.blokdesign.com ::

This project stands out for its simplicity, audacity, and clarity and for the right mix of concept and surprise, present in the fact that the whole organization is depicted as if it were the periodic table. The information is structured on various levels in such a way that the directors become elements that, when matched correctly against the needs of the clients, can trigger creativity.

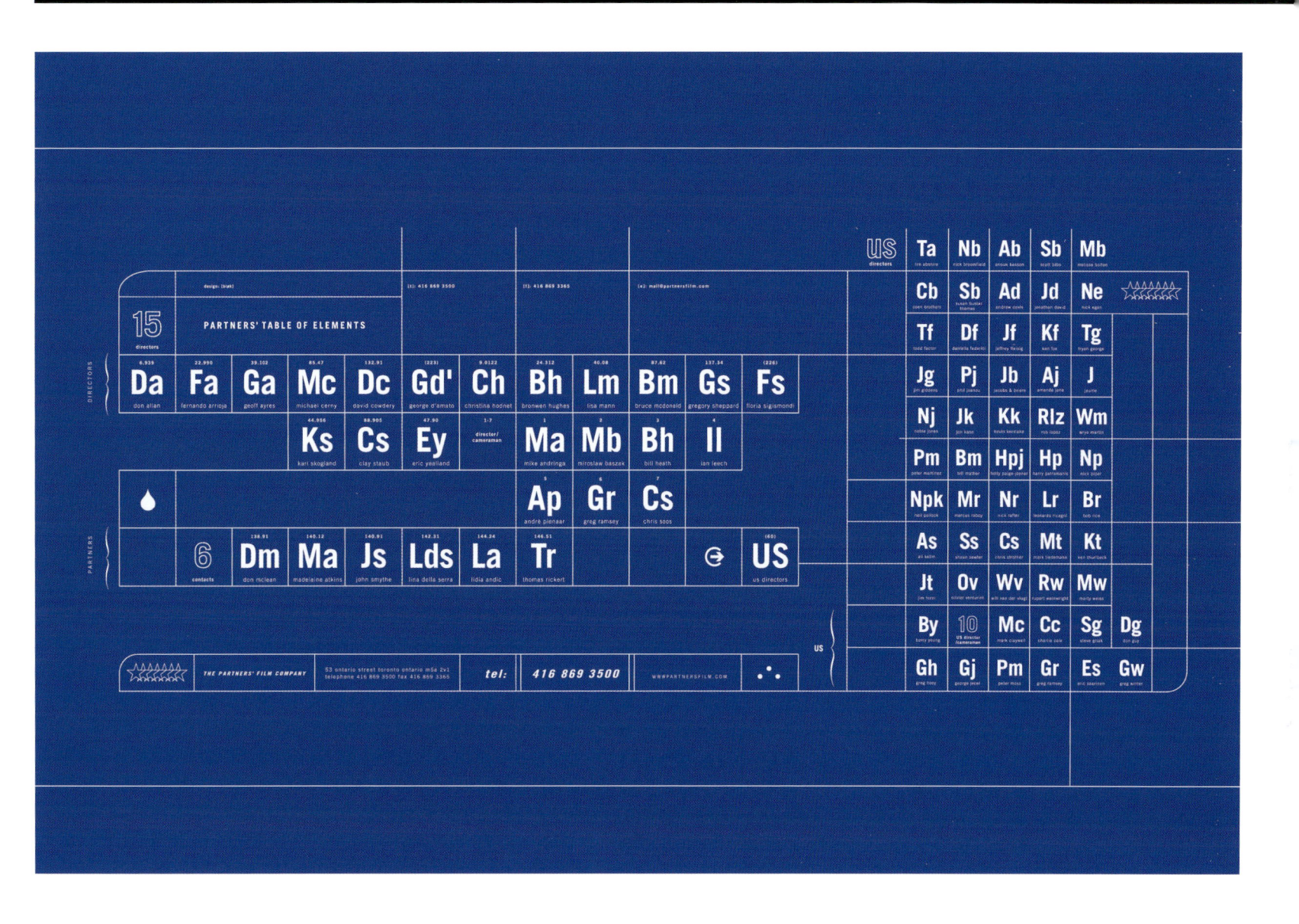

Sketches and Diagrams | 43

Percentage of Pages Distributed by Subject

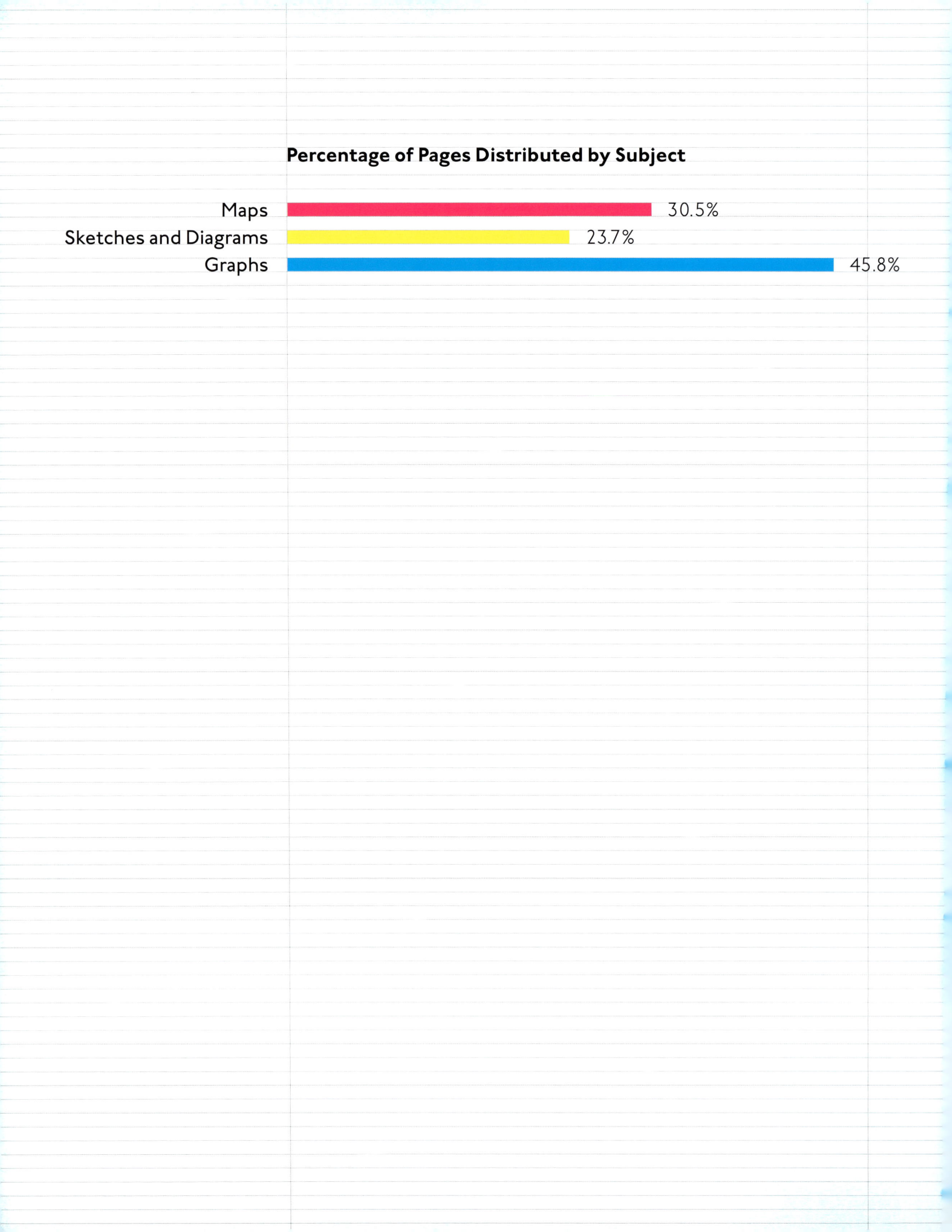

- Maps — 30.5%
- Sketches and Diagrams — 23.7%
- Graphs — 45.8%

graph
n (short for graphic formula) **1** A series of points each of which represents a value of a given function. **2** A network of lines connecting points.

Les cauchemars de l'enfant ::
Jessica Scheurer :: www.kaysl.ch ::

Children's nightmares form the subject of the content and illustrations of this publication. It is based on the numerous statistics that appear in the book *Les cauchemars de l'enfant* by Michel Zlotowicz, which are transformed into highly visual and interactive graphs. Each graph depicts one of the actions recurring in children's dreams and shows which characters are involved and with what frequency.

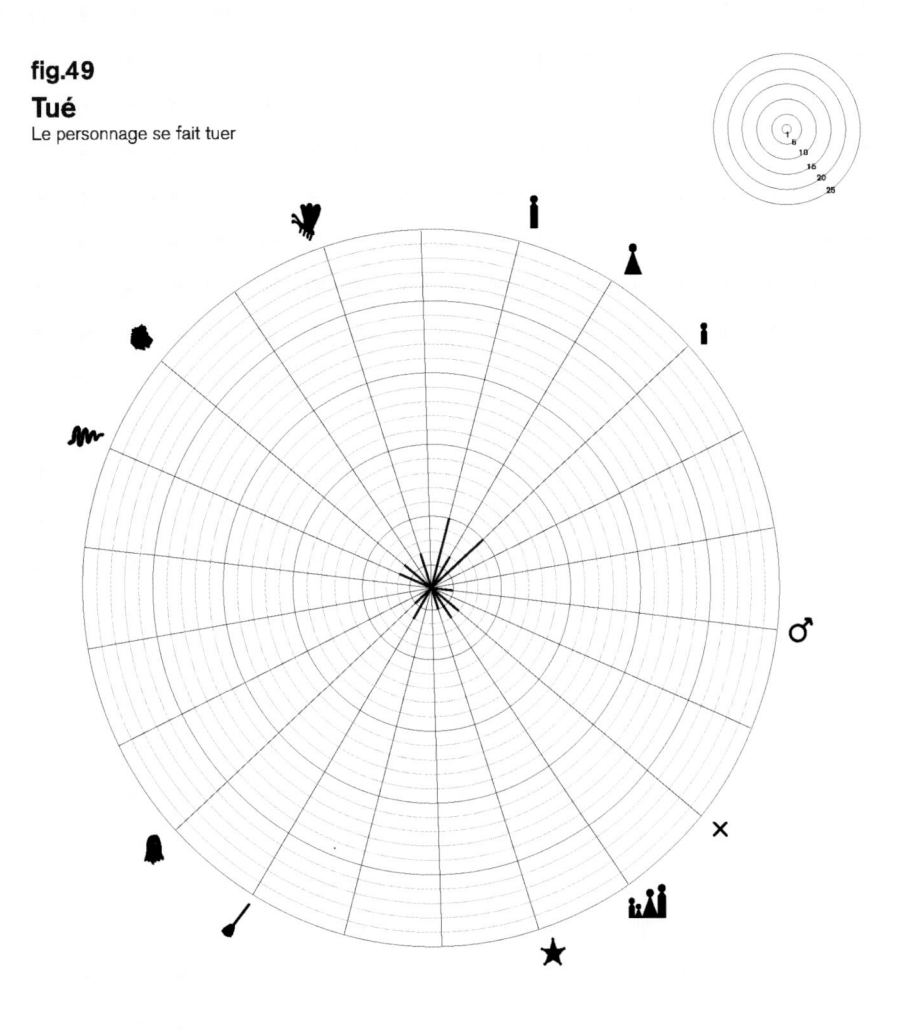

fig.49
Tué
Le personnage se fait tuer

76

Sujet [—]	Hommes [01]	Voleurs [—]	Serpents [02]
Père [05]	Femmes [—]	Sorcières [02]	Lions [02]
Mère [02]	Inconnus [02]	Fantômes [01]	Crocodiles [—]
Frère [05]	Famille [02]	Araignée géante [—]	Autres Animaux [02]
Soeur [—]	Policiers [01]	Autres créatures [—]	
Enfants [—]	Autres humains [—]	Loups [—]	

146 **Graphs**

🐾	autres animaux	?	indeterminés
	autres créatures fantastiques	▲	indiens
	autres humains		lions
	amis		loups
	araignée géante		maîtresse
	chasseurs		mère
	cowbows		objets
	crocodiles		père
	enfants	★	policiers
	grand-mère		pompiers
	famille		prussien
	fantômes		serpents
♀	femmes		sorcières
	france		soeur
	frère	○	sujet
♂	hommes		tante
×	inconnus	∞	voleurs

16   les personnages du cauchemar enfantin

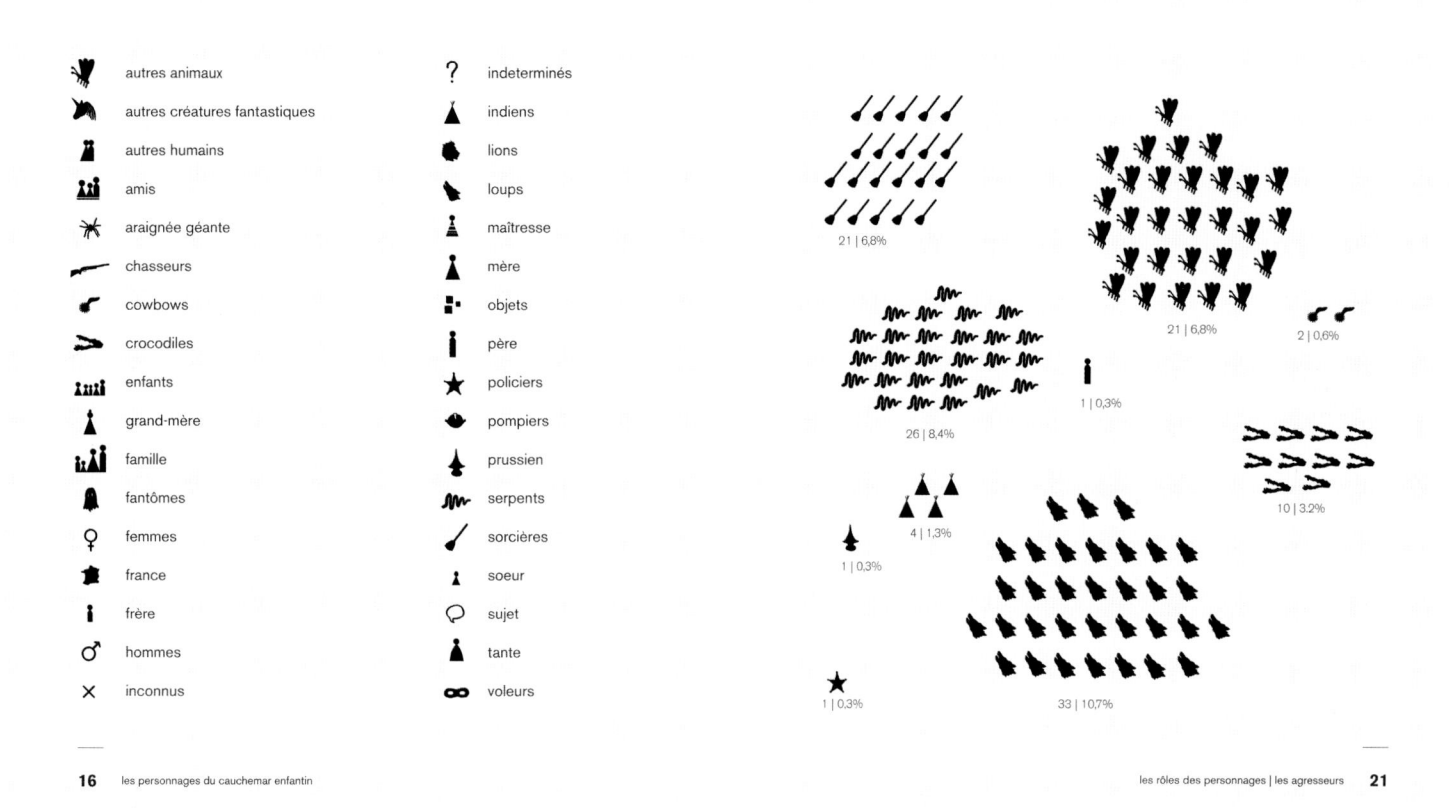

les rôles des personnages | les agresseurs   21

21 | 6,8%

21 | 6,8%

2 | 0,6%

26 | 8,4%

1 | 0,3%

4 | 1,3%

10 | 3,2%

1 | 0,3%

1 | 0,3%

33 | 10,7%

Graphs | 47

Weißensee brochure ::
Ariane Spanier :: www.arianespanier.com ::

This is a prospectus for the Kunsthochschule Berlin-Weißensee, a school of art and design, which has been designed in two languages: English and German. To avoid any confusion with respect to information or language, Ariane Spanier has opted to change the format of the text for each of them. These sample pages show graphs with data for the students and teachers at the school in 2008.

ZAHLEN

Allen Studenten der Kunsthochschule Berlin-Weißensee wird ein eigener Arbeitsplatz zur Verfügng gestellt.

GAST-STUDENTEN AUS DEM AUSLAND
40
630
107 (17%) AUSLÄNDISCHE STUDIERENDE

STUDENTEN UND STUDENTINNEN
STAND SOMMERSEMESTER 2008

34 **8** **60**

PROFESSOREN, GASTPROFESSOREN UND -DOZENTEN

KÜNSTLERISCHE MITARBEITER/INNEN UND KÜNSTLERISCHE LEHRKRÄFTE

LEHRBEAUFTRAGTE PRO STUDIENJAHR

FIGURES

All students at the Berlin Weissensee School of Art are provided with their own workspace.

60 ASSOCIATE LECTURERS PER ACADEMIC YEAR

34 **8** ARTWORK TEACHERS

PROFESSORS IN PERMANENT EMPLOYMENT, VISITING PROFESSORS AND TEACHERS

EXCHANGE OR VISITING STUDENTS
40
630
107 (17%) STUDENTS FROM ABROAD

STUDENTS
AS OF SUMMER SEMESTER 2008

The Top Concerns of Journalists by Percentage ::
Topos Graphics :: www.toposgraphics.com ::

Louise Ma and Richard Watts commissioned Topos Graphics to design this graph showing how journalists' interests have evolved in recent years. The image was then printed on a T-shirt designed to display the statistics showing that newspapers are nearing the end of their life, hence the brilliant heading *Death of News*.

The Top Concerns of Journalists by Percentage

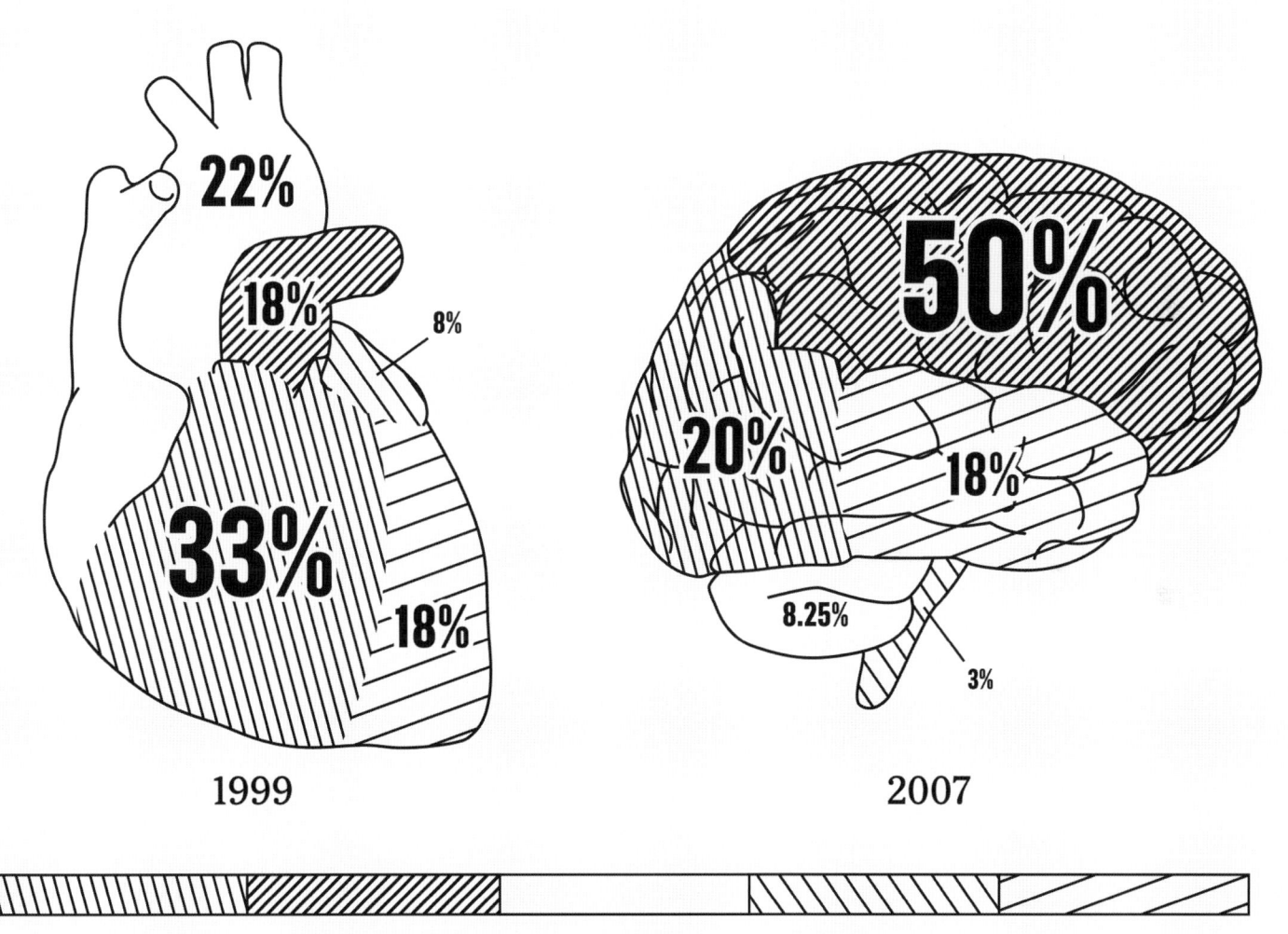

1999
- 22%
- 18%
- 8%
- 33%
- 18%

2007
- 50%
- 20%
- 18%
- 8.25%
- 3%

QUALITY OF COVERAGE | BUSINESS & FINANCE | LOSS OF CREDIBILITY | ETHICS & STANDARDS | MEDIA ENVIRONMENT

A_B_ Peace & Terror etc. The Computational Aesthetics of Love & Hate ::
The Luxury of Protest :: www.theluxuryofprotest.com ::

A geopolitical survey conducted among the 192 members of the United Nations on their level of contribution both to world peace and terror led to this two-sided poster. Side A measures the levels of peace and side B the levels of terror. Each chart has been divided into three rings corresponding to quantitative outcomes obtained from the research: the thicker the line, the greater its value.

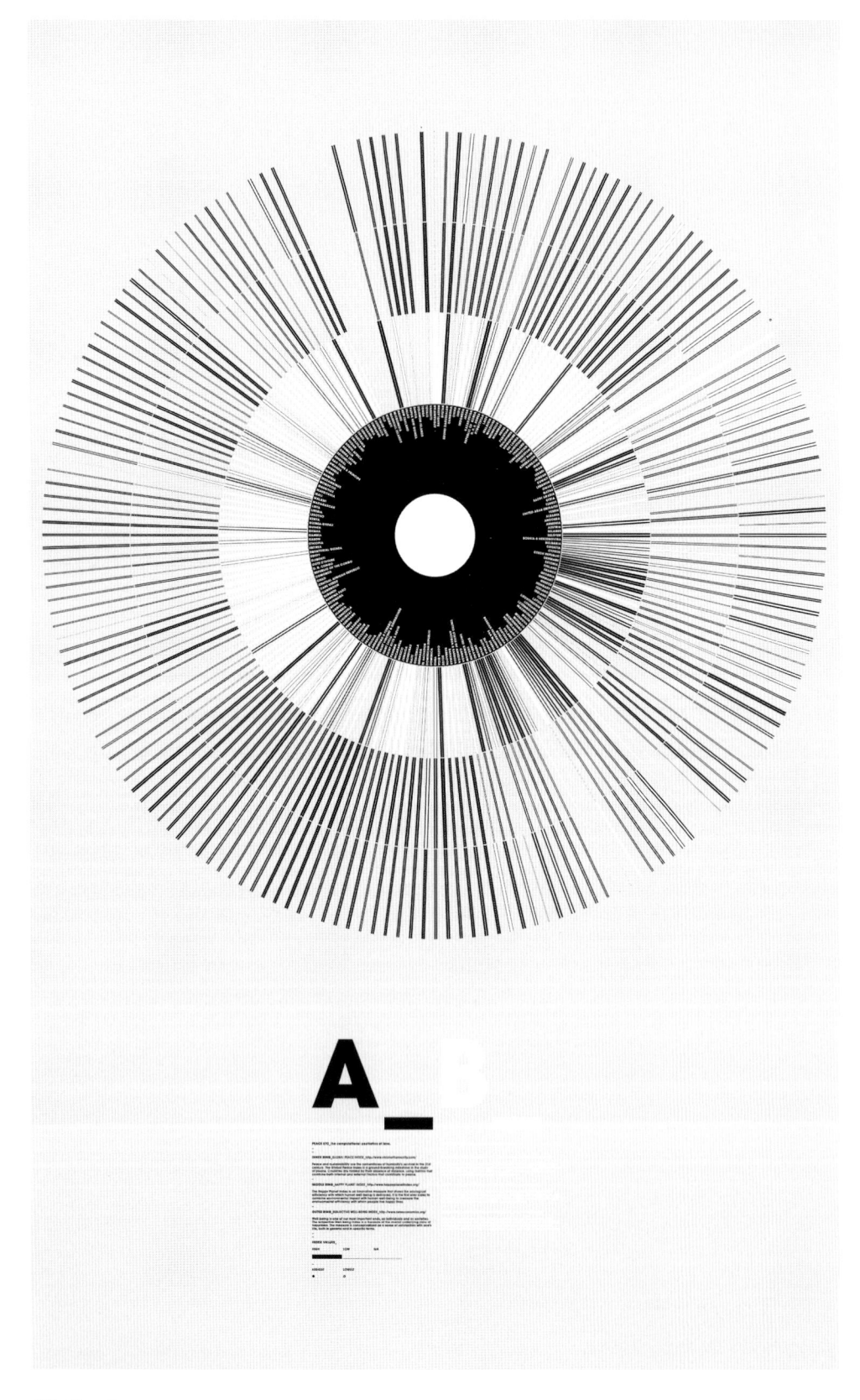

Graphs 151

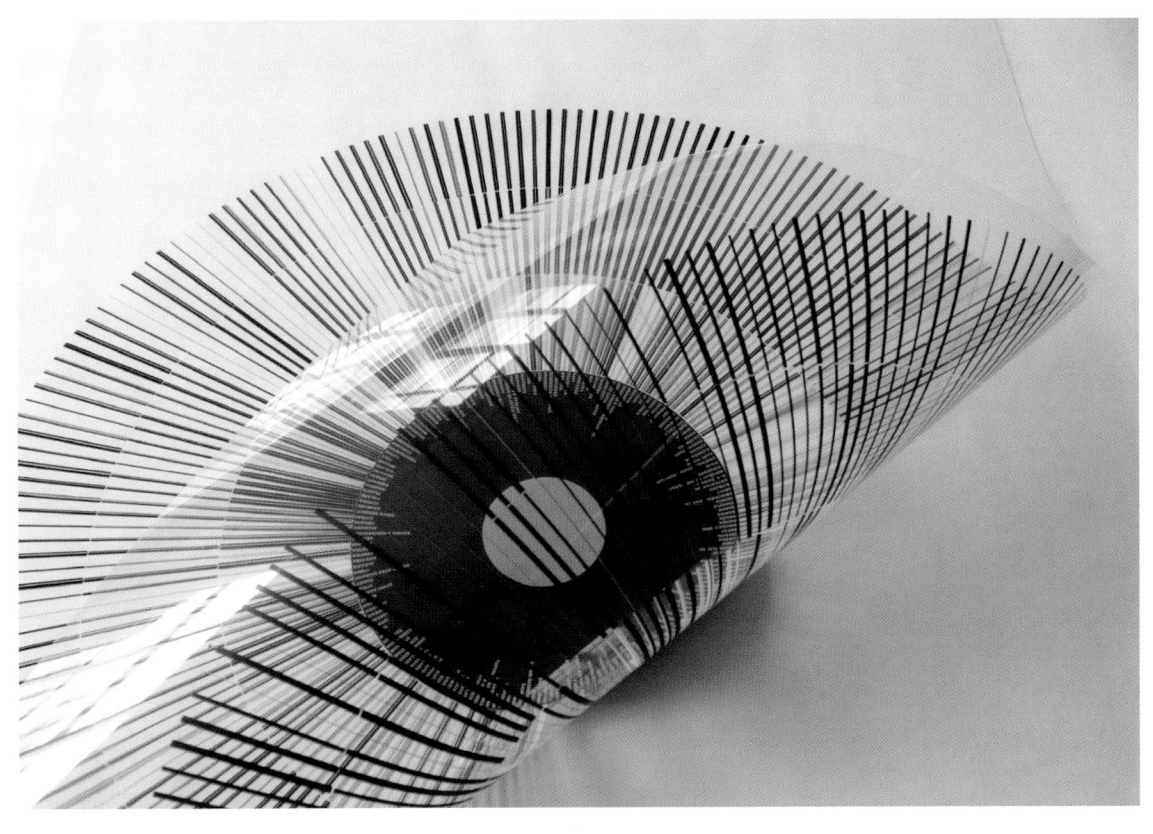

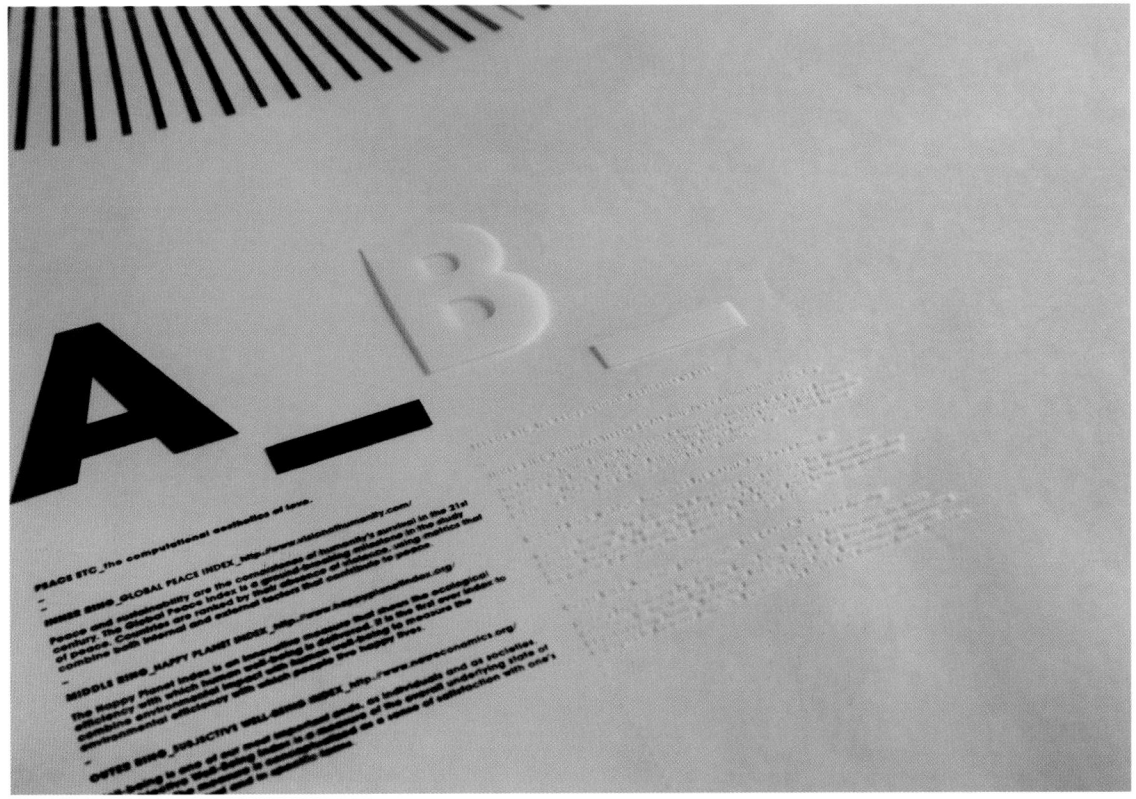

A Typographic Interpretation, Obama's Speech ::
me studio :: www.mestudio.info ::

The purpose of this assignment for the Dutch design magazine *Creatie* was to do something with President Obama's inaugural speech, just using fonts without any images. The approach chosen was to analyze the video of the speech so as to be able to depict the emphasis in his words graphically: the strongest and most passionate were written in larger, bold type whereas those that were almost whispered were drawn very small.

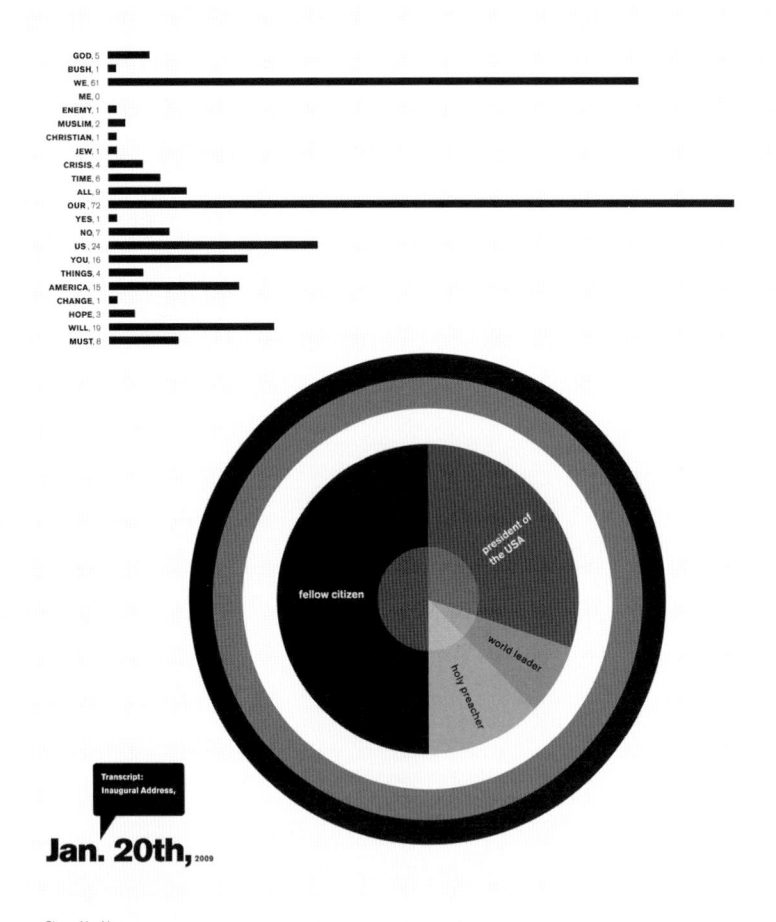

Word frequency counts:
- GOD, 5
- BUSH, 1
- WE, 61
- ME, 0
- ENEMY, 1
- MUSLIM, 2
- CHRISTIAN, 1
- JEW, 1
- CRISIS, 4
- TIME, 6
- ALL, 9
- OUR, 72
- YES, 1
- NO, 7
- US, 24
- YOU, 16
- THINGS, 4
- AMERICA, 15
- CHANGE, 1
- HOPE, 3
- WILL, 19
- MUST, 8

Transcript: Inaugural Address, Jan. 20th, 2009

Font weights shown:
- Obama Humble
- Obama Regular
- Obama Medium
- **Obama Bold**
- **Obama Black**

CROWD: Obama! Obama! Obama! **Obama! Obama! Obama!** Obama! Oba...

Thank you. **Thank you.** CROWD: Obama! Oba...

My fellow citizens: I stand here today humbled by the task before us, **grateful** for the trust you have bestowed, **mindful** of the **sacrifices** borne by our ancestors.
I thank President **Bush** for his service to our nation...
(APPLAUSE)

... as well as the generosity and cooperation he has shown throughout this transition. **Forty-four** Americans have now *taken* the presidential oath.

The words have been *spoken* during rising tides of **prosperity** and the still waters of **peace.** Yet, every **so often** the oath is taken amidst gathering clouds and raging storms. **At these** moments, America has carried on not simply because of the **skill** or vision of those in high office, but because

We the People have
remained faithful to the ideals of our forbearers, and *true* to our founding documents.

So it has **been.** So it must **be** with this generation of Americans.

That we are in the **midst of crisis** is now well understood. Our nation is at war against a far-reaching network of **violence** and **hatred.** Our economy is badly weakened, a consequence of **greed and irresponsibility** on the part of some but also our collective failure to make hard **choices** and prepare the nation for a new age.

Homes have been lost, jobs
shed, businesses shuttered. Our health care is too costly, our schools fail **too many**, and each day brings further evidence that the **ways** we use energy strengthen our adversaries and threaten our planet.

These are the indicators of crisis, subject to data and statistics. Less **measurable**, but no less profound, is a sapping of confidence across our land; a nagging **fear** that America's decline is inevitable, that the next generation must lower its sights. **Today I say to you** that the **challenges we face are real,** they are serious and they are many. They will not be met easily or in a short span of time. But know this America:

They will be met. (APPLAUSE)

On this day, we gather because we have chosen **hope** over fear, unity of purpose over conflict and discord.

On this day,
we come to proclaim an end to the petty grievances and false promises, the recriminations and worn-out dogmas that for far too long have strangled our politics.

We remain a young nation, but in the words of Scripture, **the time has come** to set aside childish things. **The time has come** to reaffirm our enduring spirit; to choose our better history; to carry forward that precious gift, that noble idea, passed on from generation to generation: the **God-given** promise that **all** are

equal, **all are free, and all** deserve a chance to pursue their full measure of **happiness.**

(APPLAUSE)

In **reaffirming** the greatness of our nation, we understand that greatness is never a given. It must be earned. Our journey has never been one of **shortcuts** or settling for less.

It has not been the path for the faint-hearted, for those who prefer **leisure over work,** or seek only the pleasures of **riches and fame.**

Rather, it has been the **risk-takers, the doers,**
the makers of things
- some celebrated, but more often men and women obscure in their labor - who have **carried us** up the long, rugged path towards prosperity and freedom.

For us,
they packed up their few worldly possessions and traveled across oceans in search of a new life.

For us,
they toiled in sweatshops and settled the West, endured the lash of the whip and plowed the hard earth.

For us,
they fought and died in places like Concord and Gettysburg; Normandy and **Khe Sahn.**

Time and again these men and women struggled and sacrificed and worked **till their hands were raw** so that we might live a better life. They saw America as **bigger** than the sum of our individual ambitions; **greater** than all the differences of **birth or wealth or faction.**

This
is the journey we continue today. We remain the most prosperous, powerful nation on Earth. Our workers are no less productive than when this crisis began. Our minds are no less inventive, our goods and services no less needed than they were **last week** or **last month** or **last year.** Our capacity remains undiminished. But our time of standing pat, of protecting narrow interests and putting off unpleasant decisions - **that time has surely passed.**

Starting **today,** we must pick ourselves **up,** dust ourselves **off,** and begin again the work of remaking America.

(APPLAUSE)

For everywhere we look, there is work to be done.

The state of our economy calls for action: **bold** and **swift.** And we **will act** not only to create new jobs but to lay a new foundation for growth.

We will build the roads and bridges, the electric grids and **digital lines** that feed our commerce and bind us together.

We will restore science to its rightful place and wield technology's **wonders** to raise health care's quality... (APPLAUSE) ... and lower its costs.

We will harness the sun and the winds and the soil to fuel our cars and run our factories. And we will transform our schools and colleges and universities to meet the **demands** of a new age.

All this we can do.
All this we will do.

Now, there are some who question the scale of our ambitions, who suggest that our system cannot tolerate too many big plans. Their memories are short, for they have forgotten what this country has already done, what free men and women can achieve **when imagination** is joined to common purpose and necessity to courage.

152 **Graphs**

What the cynics **fail** to understand is that the ground has shifted beneath them, that the stale political arguments that have consumed us for so long, no longer apply.

The question we ask **today is not whether our government is too big or too small, but whether it works,** whether it helps families find jobs at a decent wage, care they can afford, a **retirement** that is dignified.

Where the answer is **yes,** we intend to move forward. Where the answer is **no,** programs will end.

And those of us who manage the public's knowledge will be held to account, **to spend wisely,** reform bad habits, and **do our business in the light of day,** because only then can we restore the vital trust between a people and their government.

Nor is the question before us whether the market is a force for good or ill. Its power to generate wealth and expand freedom is unmatched.

But this crisis has reminded us that **without a watchful eye,** the market can spin out of control. **The nation cannot prosper long when it favors only the prosperous.**

The success of our economy has **always** depended not just on the size of our gross domestic product, but on the **reach** of our prosperity; on the ability to extend opportunity to every willing heart - not out of charity, but because it is the surest route to our common good.

(APPLAUSE)

As for our common defense, we reject as false the choice between our safety and our ideals.

(APPLAUSE)

Our founding fathers...

(APPLAUSE)

Our founding fathers faced with **perils** that we can scarcely imagine, drafted a charter to assure the rule of law and the rights of man, a charter expanded by the blood of generations.

Those ideals still light the world, and we will not give them up for expedience's sake.

And so, **to all the other** peoples and **governments who are watching today,** from the grandest capitals to the small village where my father was born:

know that America is a friend of each nation and every man, woman and child who seeks a future of peace and dignity, and we are ready to lead once more!

(APPLAUSE)

Recall that earlier generations faced down **fascism and communism** not just with missiles and tanks, but with the sturdy alliances and enduring convictions.

They understood that our power alone cannot protect us, nor does it entitle us to do as we **please.** Instead, they knew that our power grows through its **prudent use.** Our security emanates from the justness of our cause; **the force of our example; the tempering qualities of humility and restraint.**

We are the keepers of this legacy, guided by these principles once more, **we can meet those new threats that demand even greater effort,** even greater cooperation and understanding between nations. We'll begin to responsibly leave Iraq to its people and forge a hard-earned **peace** in Afghanistan.

(APPLAUSE)

With **old friends** and former foes, we'll work tirelessly to lessen the nuclear threat and **roll back** the specter of a warming planet.

We will not apologize for our way of life nor will we waver in its defense.

And for **those** who seek to advance their aims by inducing terror and slaughtering innocents, we say to you now that,

"Our spirit is stronger and cannot be broken. You cannot outlast us, and we will defeat you."

(APPLAUSE)

For we know that our patchwork heritage is a strength, not a weakness.

We are a nation of **Christians and Muslims, Jews and Hindus,** and nonbelievers. **We are shaped by every language and culture, drawn from every end of this Earth.**

And because we have tasted **the bitter swill of civil war** and segregation and emerged from that dark chapter **stronger** and **more united, we cannot help** but believe that the old hatreds shall someday pass; **that the lines of tribe shall soon dissolve; that as the world grows smaller, our common humanity shall reveal itself;** and that America must play its role in ushering in a new era of peace.

To the Muslim world, we seek a new way forward, based on mutual interest and mutual respect.

To those leaders around the globe who seek to sow conflict or blame their society's ills on the West, know that your people will judge you on what you can build, not what you destroy. To those...

(APPLAUSE)

To those who cling to power through corruption and deceit and the silencing of dissent, know that you are on the wrong side of history, **but that we will extend a hand if you are willing to unclench** your fist.

(APPLAUSE)

To the **people** of poor nations, we pledge to work alongside you to make your farms flourish and let clean waters flow; to **nourish** starved bodies and **feed** hungry minds.

Field Guide: How to Be a Graphic Designer ::
José Manuel Hortelano :: www.zapbookseries.es ::

For this practical guide on how to be a graphic designer, these illustrations were produced plotting the replies on the work routine of 2,096 designers and students and the opinions and secrets of thirty-one successful studios and designers. The book is written in an unassuming manner to encourage those visiting the world of design for the first time. The visualization of the data was executed in the same vein.

Do you stick to your deadlines?

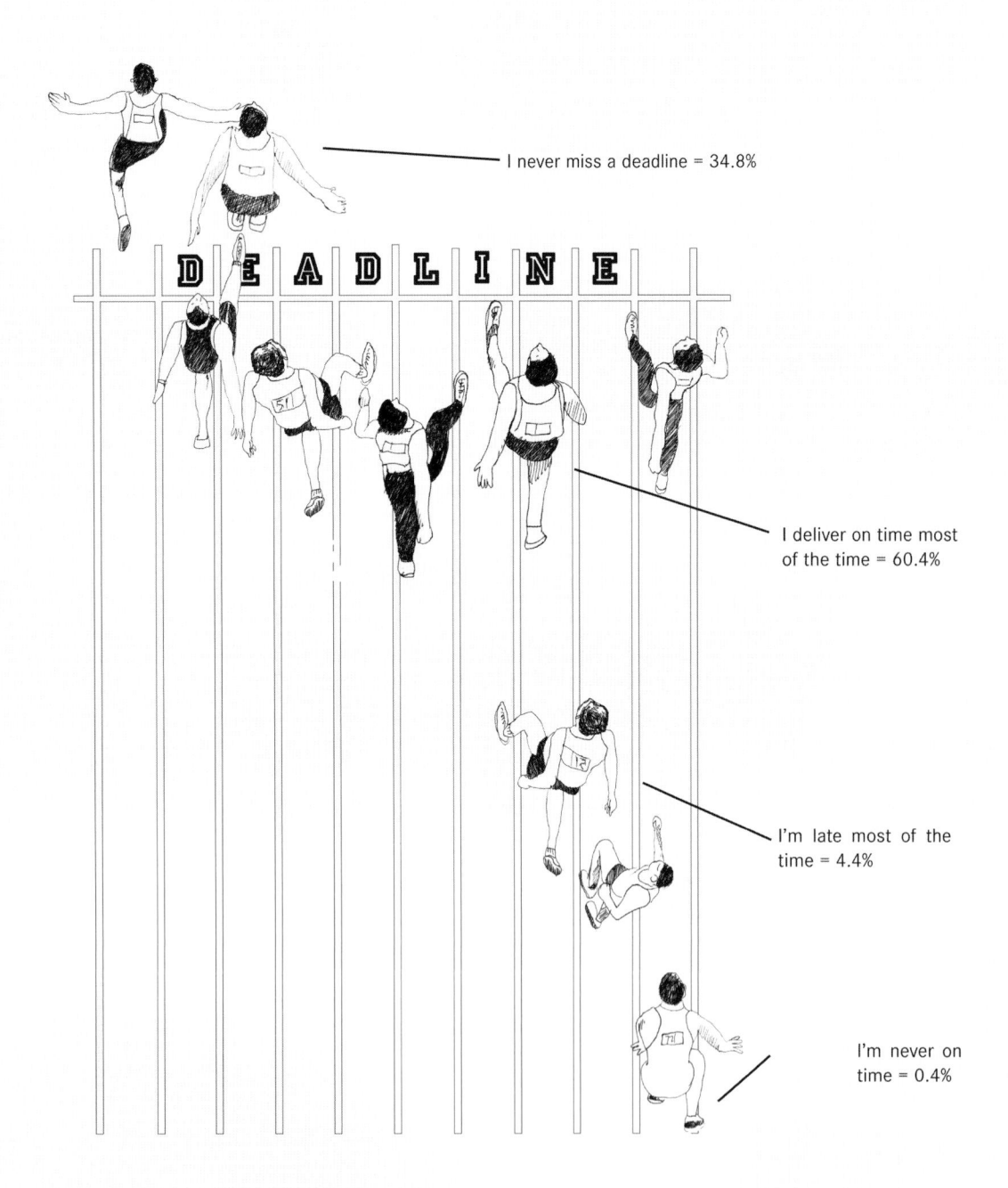

I never miss a deadline = 34.8%

I deliver on time most of the time = 60.4%

I'm late most of the time = 4.4%

I'm never on time = 0.4%

Which way do you prefer working?

Alone = 27.3%

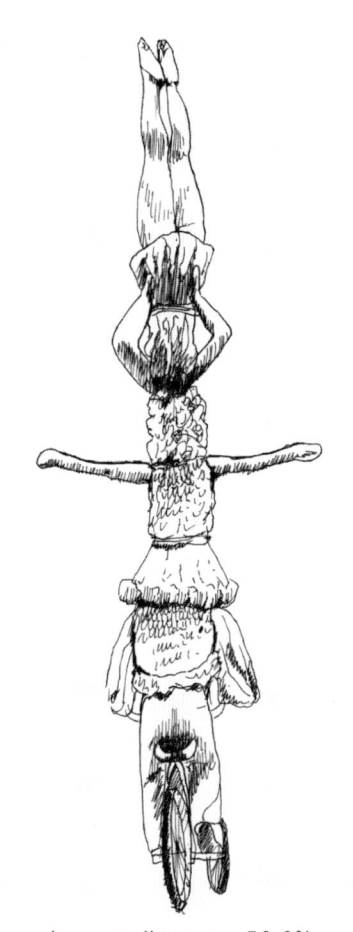

In a small team = 58.0%

In a big team = 1.1%

Paired up = 13.5%

DG STATS ::
+ WONKSITE STUDIO + :: www.wonksite.com ::

The originality of this piece of furniture, designed by mySHELF, lies in the chart, which is not only used to present the data, but also to decorate the back of one of its modules. To develop this idea, the team at + WONKSITE STUDIO + took some questionnaires issued to various graphic designers from Colombia about their likes and dislikes regarding design as their starting point. The results were used to create this interesting compostion, which was then screenprinted on this background.

156 **Graphs**

FAVORITE BRANDS

- Sony
- Custo Barcelona
- Diesel
- Abercrombie & Fitch
- National Geographic Channel
- Coca-Cola
- MTV
- adidas
- Harley-Davidson Motor Cycles
- Dreamworks Pictures
- D&G Dolce & Gabbana
- Rolling Stones
- FOX
- Apple
- Converse
- Playboy

&MAGA

IDENTITY | 10% FILM | 6% ARTS | 5% BRANDING | 1% WHATEVER

Für uns alle. Der IdeenPark :: häfelinger + wagner design :: www.hwdesign.de ::

With the aim of advancing Germany's potential as a land of innovation, ThyssenKrupp launched the Discovering Future Technology initiative. The idea was to promote the appeal and social acceptance of science and technology, along with the importance of teaching these subjects. This book aims to illustrate such a philosophy, by presenting the information through the use of graphs that are both dynamic and original.

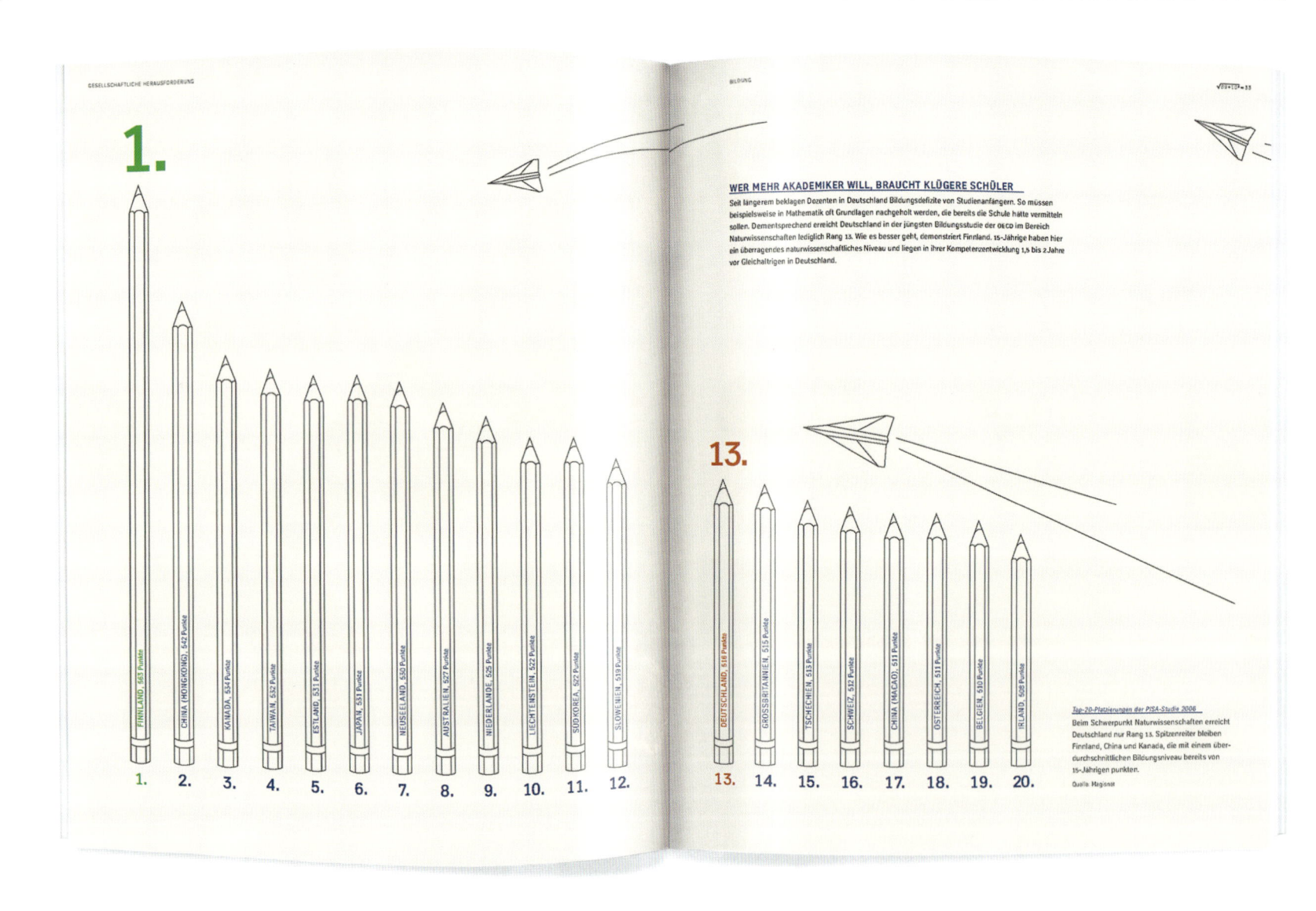

Graphs | 159

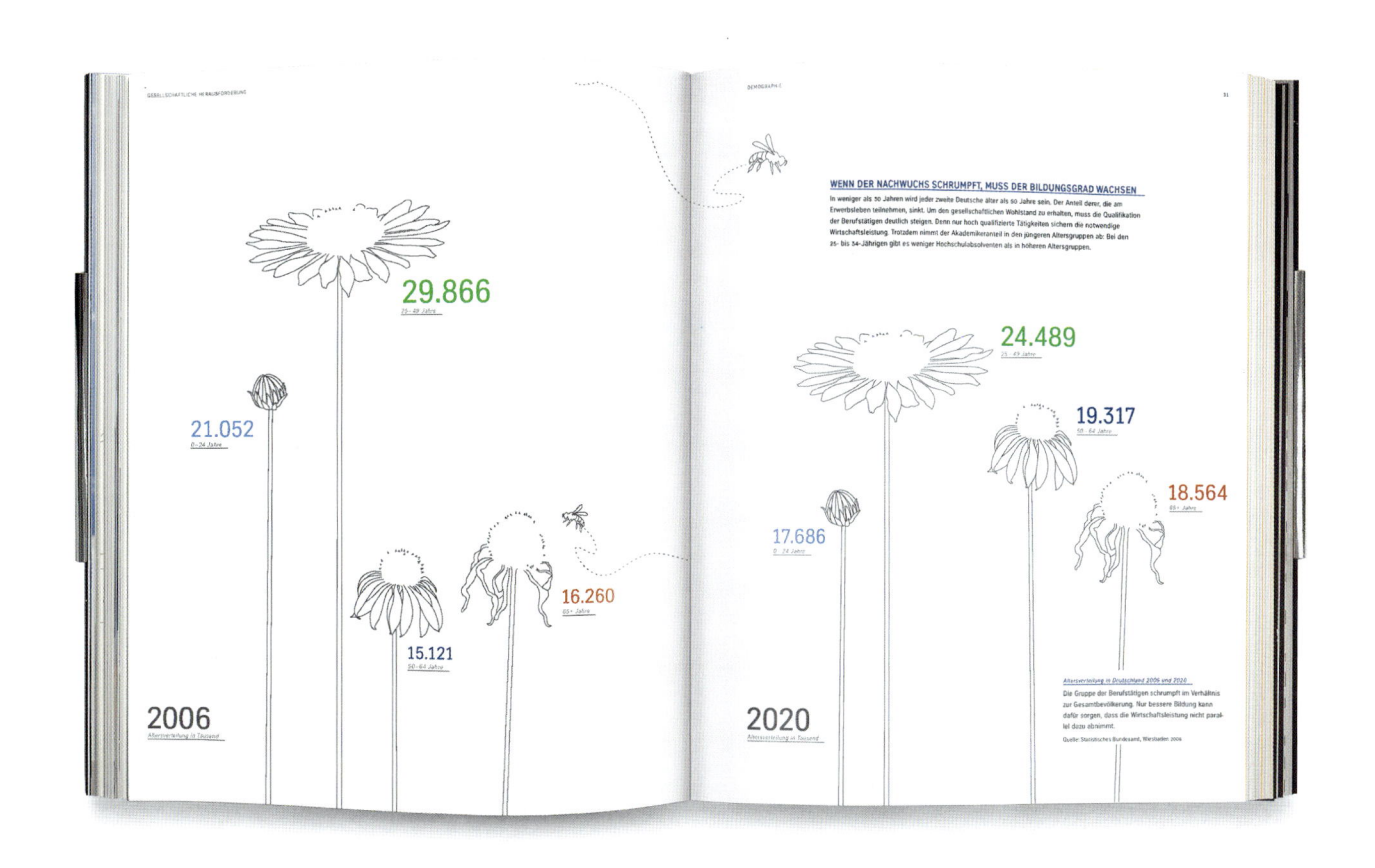

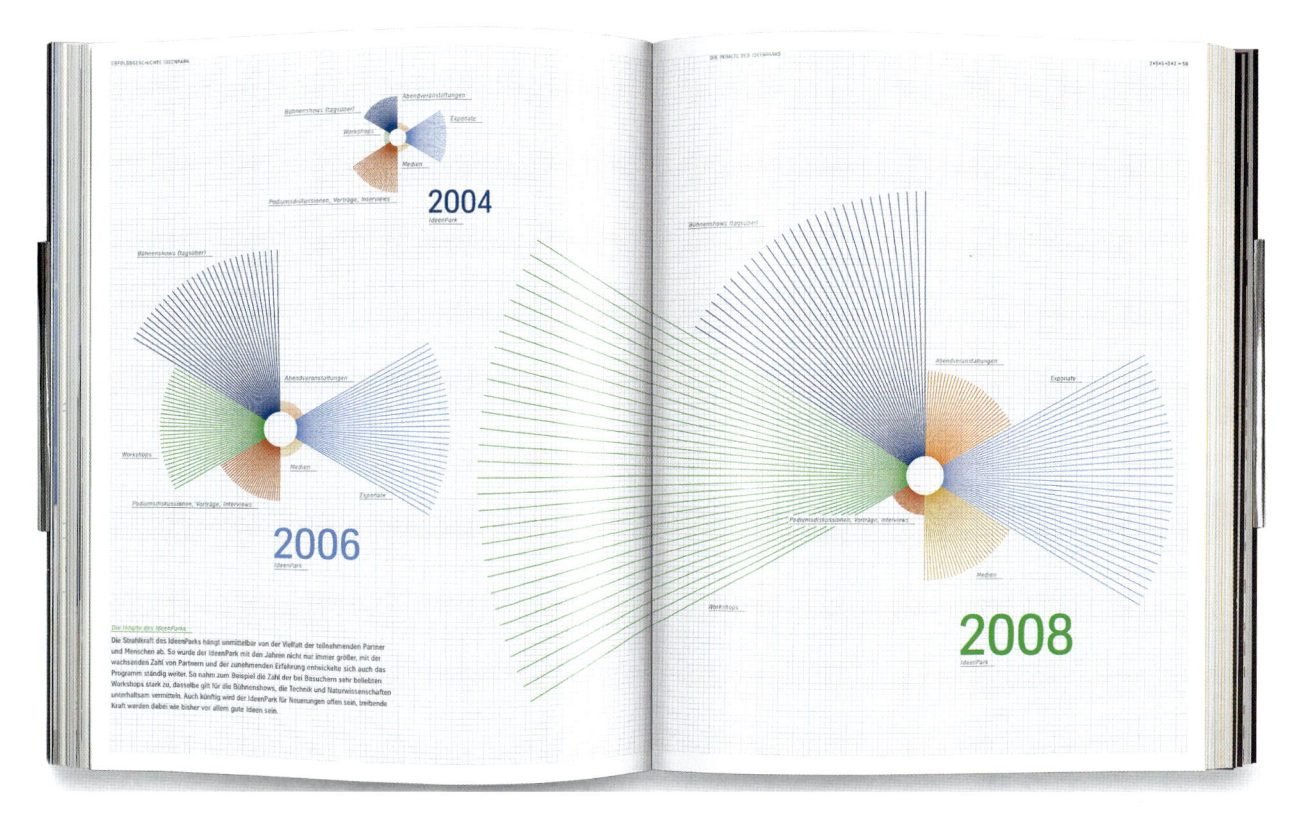

Simple Twist of Fate ::
Studio8 Design :: www.studio8design.co.uk ::

The brief for this poster called for the visual representation of a song. To comply, Studio8 Design decided to use an audiogram indicating the threshold of a person's hearing capacity at various strengths and frequencies, which enabled them to plot each letter (vowels and consonants) pronounced in the song *Simple Twist of Fate* by Bob Dylan, focusing, on the one hand, on listening level (in decibels) and frequency on the other (in hertz).

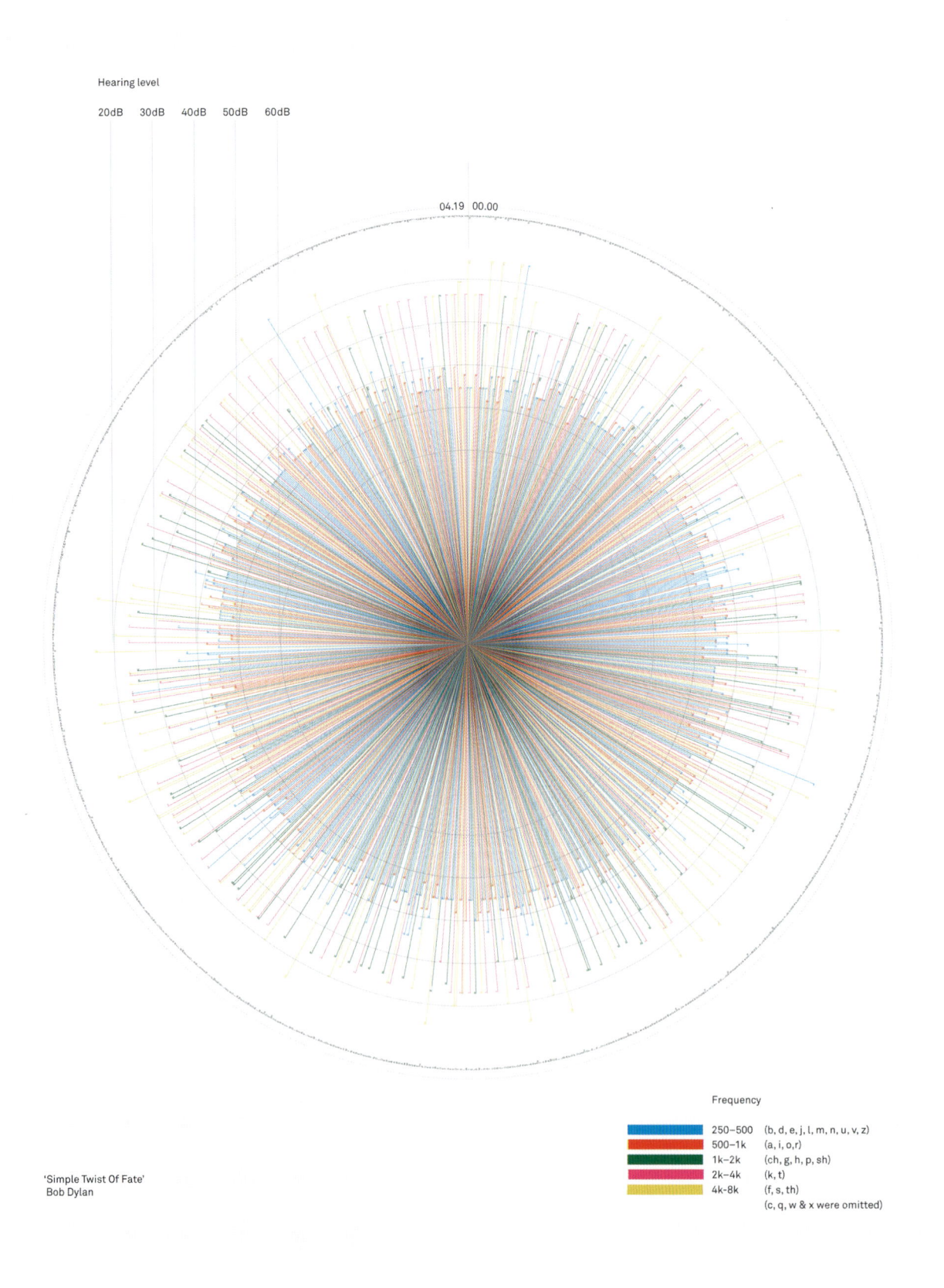

Hearing level

20dB   30dB   40dB   50dB   60dB

04.19   00.00

'Simple Twist Of Fate'
Bob Dylan

Frequency

	250–500	(b, d, e, j, l, m, n, u, v, z)
	500–1k	(a, i, o, r)
	1k–2k	(ch, g, h, p, sh)
	2k–4k	(k, t)
	4k–8k	(f, s, th)
		(c, q, w & x were omitted)

Design and Sustainability ::
LUST :: www.lust.nl ::

This complex and somewhat chaotic web of information shows the relationship that exists between design and sustainability in the Netherlands. Organizations—ranging from NGOs to stores promoting fair trade—are on the left axis and designers and design studios on the right; products or projects are at the bottom, while at the top there are tags from del.icio.us, with the lines indicating the links between them.

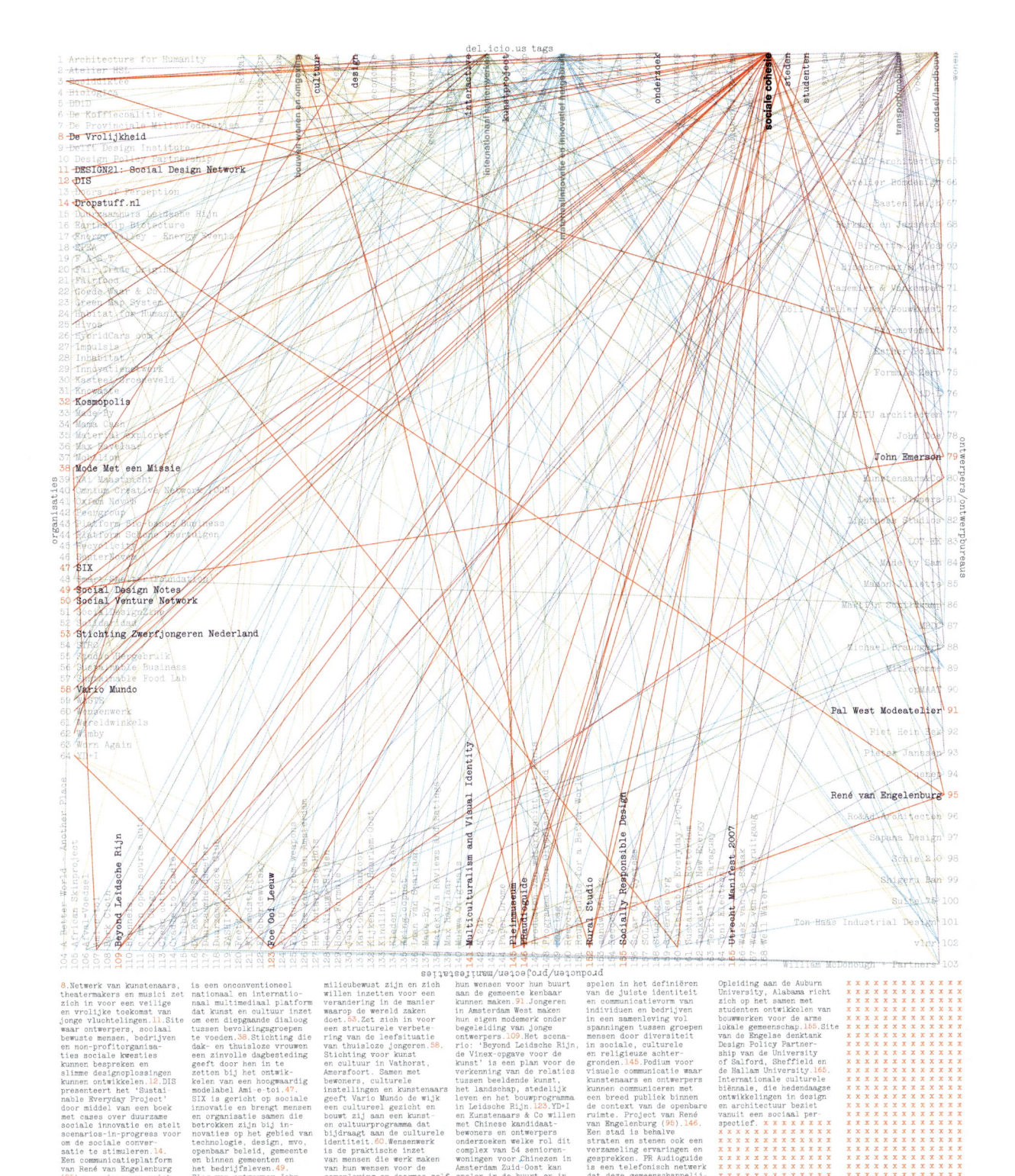

2008 VSB Foundation Annual Report ::
Stout/Kramer :: www.stoutkramer.nl ::

The annual report for 2008 for the VSB Foundation focuses on the financial crisis as its main theme—since it was in this year that it surfaced on a worldwide scale. The report explains the projects that were undertaken that year by this Dutch foundation to ride the storm and manage to stay afloat. Thus the design adhered to the concept of maximizing resources and opting for a reliable, minimalist graph.

OPBRENGSTEN VOOR DE SAMENLEVING

TOTAAL DONATIEVOLUME VERDEELD OVER DE AANDACHTSGEBIEDEN
(bedragen in 1000 euro)

2008
10.103 | 8.223 | 5.397 | 34.040 | 1.935 | 6.390

2007
10.062 | 7.853 | 4.883 | 31.612 | 1.645 | 3.972

2006
8.729 | 4.710 | 3.871 | 24.131 | 1.600 | 0

- Mens & maatschappij
- Natuur & milieu
- Sport
- Kunst & cultuur
- Beurzen
- Wetenschappelijk onderzoek

OPBRENGSTEN VOOR DE SAMENLEVING

TOTAAL DONATIEVOLUME PER REGIO
(bedragen in 1000 euro)

Regiokantoor	2008	2007	2006
Noord	3.506	3.371	2.421
ZuidOost	1.491	1.724	1.552
ZuidWest	3.112	2.049	1.584
NoordWest	537	627	693
Overige regio's	5.255	4.101	4.307

ORGANISATIE

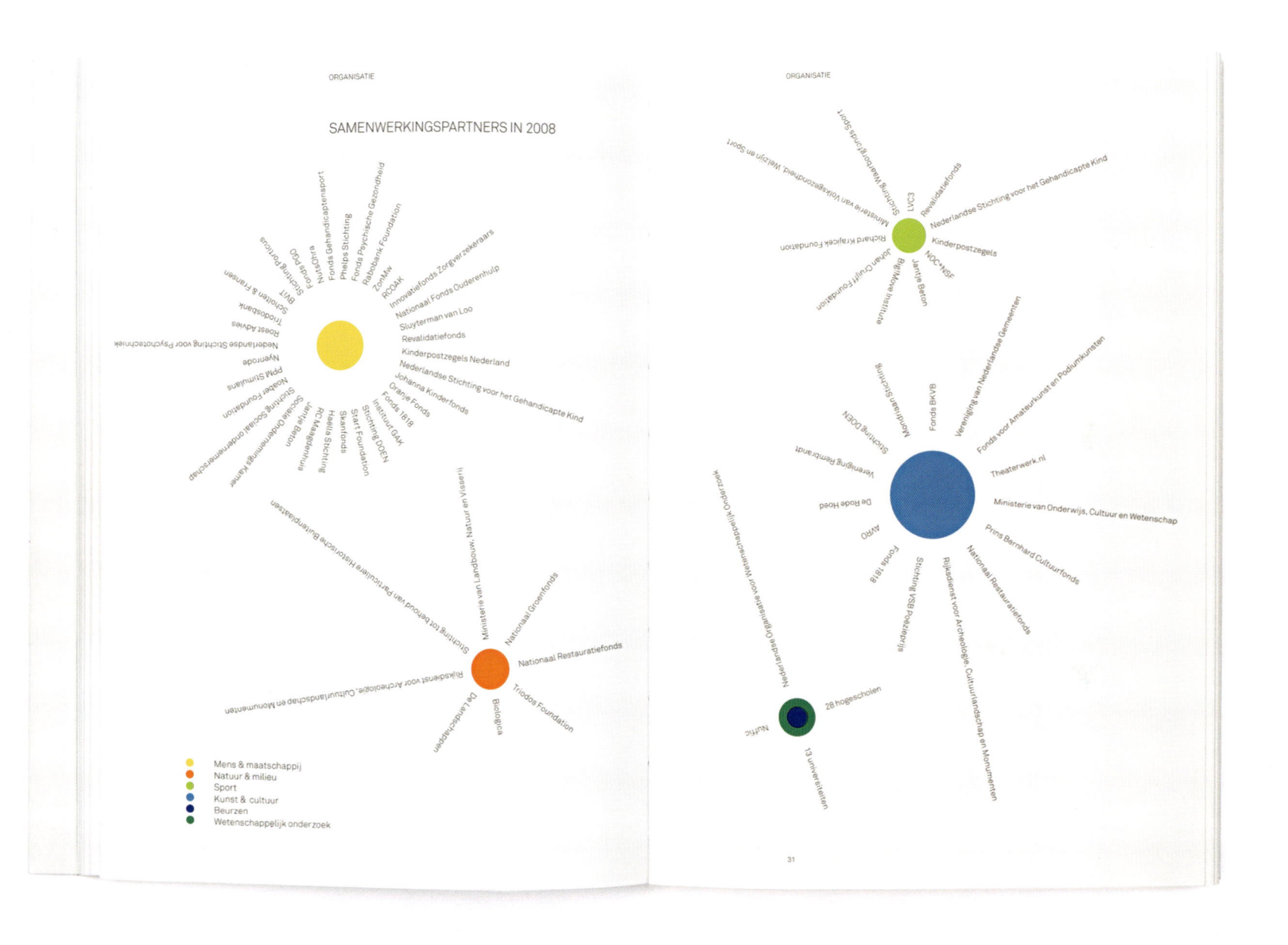

SAMENWERKINGSPARTNERS IN 2008

- Mens & maatschappij
- Natuur & milieu
- Sport
- Kunst & cultuur
- Beurzen
- Wetenschappelijk onderzoek

Mark – Another Architecture ::
Lesley Moore :: www.lesley-moore.nl ::

Vertical bar charts display data in columns, grouped according to category, and are used to compare elements with reference to a specific variable. Lesley Moore's team decided to alter the appearance of the columns in the design of these graphics for *Mark*, the innovative magazine on architecture, using symbols related to the items shown in the charts, with the data being classified according to continent.

WHERE STUDENTS DREAM

EDUCATION PROVIDES A GOLDEN KEY TO THE FUTURE. BUT EXACTLY HOW MANY SCHOOLS OF ARCHITECTURE ARE THERE?

GRAPHIC LESLEY MOORE

A thorough preparation for your career in the globalizing profession of architecture cannot begin soon enough. It starts with the educational institution you select. Any prospective student with a bit of sense bypasses the cosily familiar college town a couple of hours' drive from home and steps into the big, wide world. It's a question of shopping around before making a definitive choice. Orientation visits to schools in England or the United States seem like the obvious way to go, but while you're at it, why not browse around in Japan (no other country can top 195 architecture schools) or Germany (with 82 schools, your best bet in Europe)?

Got your degree way back when? No problem. Every self-respecting university offers summer courses, postgraduate and post-doctoral programmes and, for the stayers, of course, opportunities for those wanting PhDs. Even if you have no plans to further your education, an occasional visit to an architecture school can do no harm. As Cincinnati Art Museum director Aaron Betsky wrote in an Archiprix catalogue: 'Students know best. If you want to know what is going on in the world of architecture, find your way to the nearest design school and wander around the tables and the model shops, the canteen, and the lecture halls. There you will find the latest experiments. Students can still dream, and they don't yet know what is impossible.'

Source: Archiprix International, www.archiprix.org

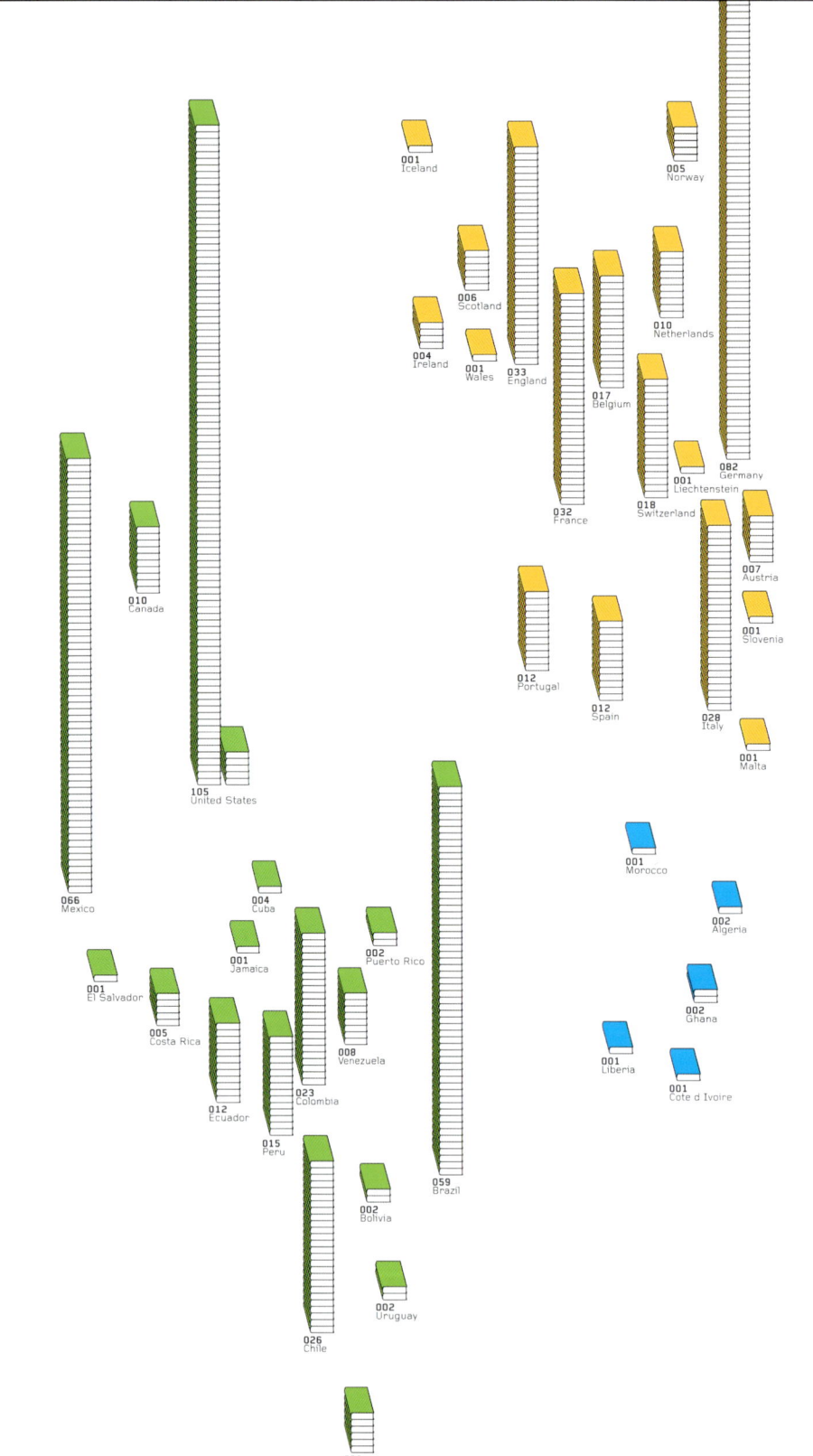

Country	Schools
Iceland	001
Norway	005
Scotland	006
Ireland	004
Wales	001
England	033
Netherlands	010
Belgium	017
France	032
Germany	082
Liechtenstein	001
Switzerland	018
Austria	007
Slovenia	001
Portugal	012
Spain	012
Italy	028
Malta	001
Canada	010
United States	105
Mexico	066
El Salvador	001
Cuba	004
Jamaica	001
Puerto Rico	002
Costa Rica	005
Venezuela	008
Ecuador	012
Colombia	023
Peru	015
Brazil	059
Bolivia	002
Uruguay	002
Chile	026
Argentina	006
Morocco	001
Algeria	002
Ghana	002
Liberia	001
Cote d Ivoire	001

CROSS SECTION

Schools of architecture
Source: Archiprix International

- 042 Africa
- 531 Asia
- 422 Europe
- 347 America
- 022 Oceania
- 1364 World

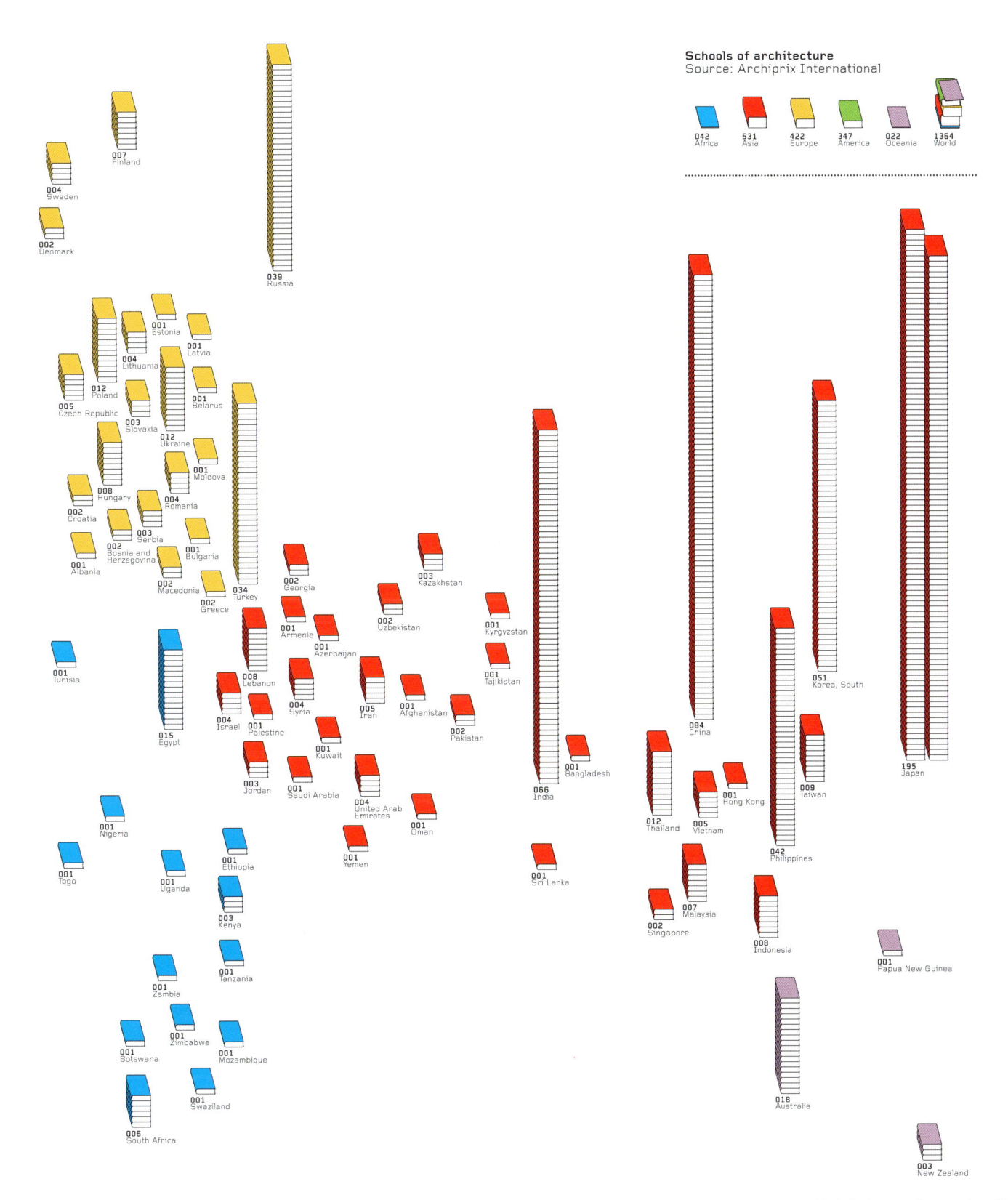

Mark 9, August–September 2007

36

DENCITIES

GRAPHIC LESLEY MOORE

Anyone under the impression that New York is one of the world's most densely developed cities is mistaken. Assuming that the density of development increases in line with the number of inhabitants per square metre, the Big Apple is ranked a paltry 44th. The majority of the most densely developed cities in the world are in Asia and Africa. The high ranking of some Asian cities is due to extensive residential areas with high-rise apartments (the most usual habitat of the middle classes, the antithesis of American suburbs), while for many African cities the high metropolitan density is, unfortunately, primarily thanks to their slums. The shanty town as a blueprint for the most efficient and ecologically sound form of community: there's something you never hear anyone talking about.

Source: Arjen van Susteren, Metropolitan World Atlas (Rotterdam: 010 Publishers, 2005)

(Note: The Metropolitan World Atlas makes a distinction between Residential and Metropolitan Density. The data mentioned here uses the Metropolitan Density, unless the data is unavailable.)

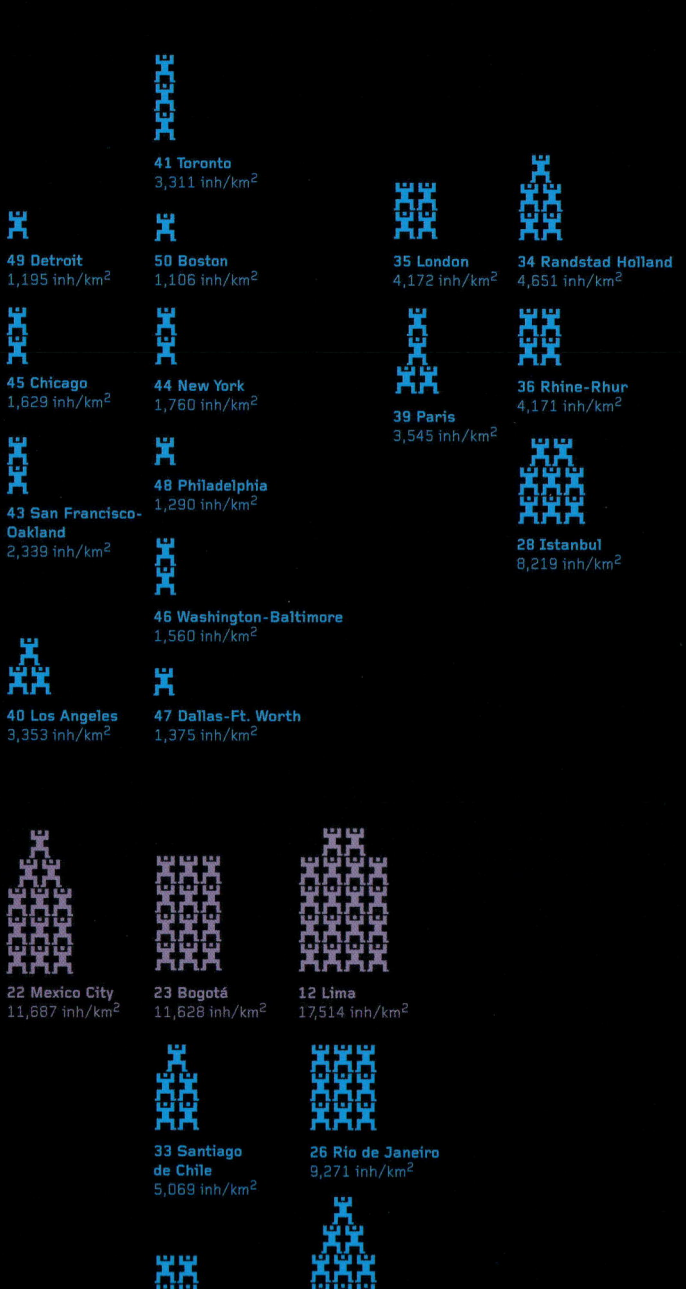

- 50,000 – 100,000 inhabitants/km²
- 40,000 – 30,000 inhabitants/km²
- 30,000 – 40,000 inhabitants/km²
- 20,000 – 30,000 inhabitants/km²
- 10,000 – 20,000 inhabitants/km²
- 1,000 – 20,000 inhabitants/km²

41 Toronto 3,311 inh/km²
49 Detroit 1,195 inh/km²
50 Boston 1,106 inh/km²
35 London 4,172 inh/km²
34 Randstad Holland 4,651 inh/km²
21 St Petersburg 12,692 inh/km²
25 Moscow 10,064 inh/km²
45 Chicago 1,629 inh/km²
44 New York 1,760 inh/km²
39 Paris 3,545 inh/km²
36 Rhine-Rhur 4,171 inh/km²
43 San Francisco-Oakland 2,339 inh/km²
48 Philadelphia 1,290 inh/km²
28 Istanbul 8,219 inh/km²
18 Baghdad 13,430 inh/km²
06 Tehran 25,359 inh/km²
46 Washington-Baltimore 1,560 inh/km²
40 Los Angeles 3,353 inh/km²
47 Dallas-Ft. Worth 1,375 inh/km²
22 Mexico City 11,687 inh/km²
23 Bogotá 11,628 inh/km²
12 Lima 17,514 inh/km²
07 Lahore 24,345 inh/km²
33 Santiago de Chile 5,069 inh/km²
26 Rio de Janeiro 9,271 inh/km²
02 Lagos 41,752 inh/km²
37 Buenos Aires 4,042 inh/km²
27 São Paulo 8,945 inh/km²
38 Johannesburg 3,923 inh/km²

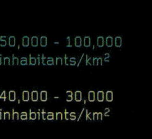

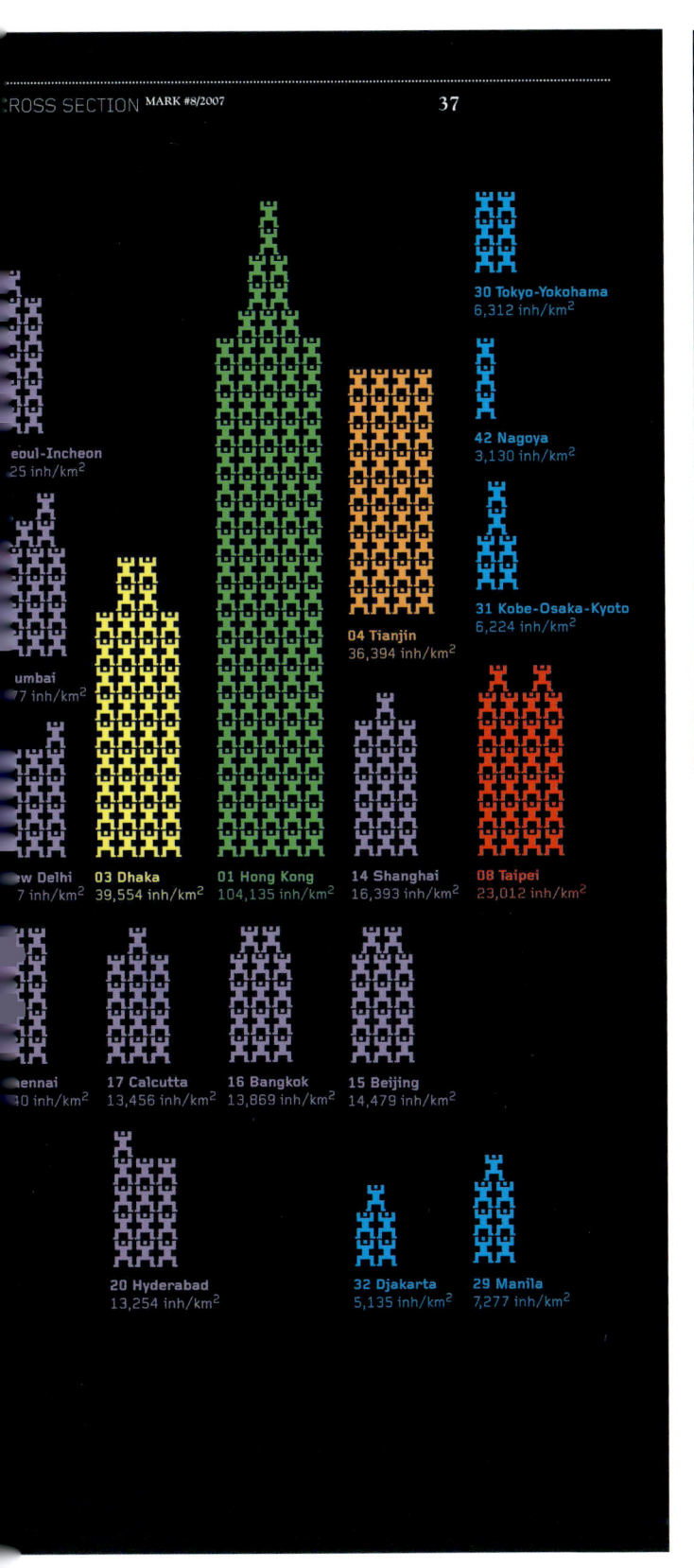

Mark 12, February–March 2008

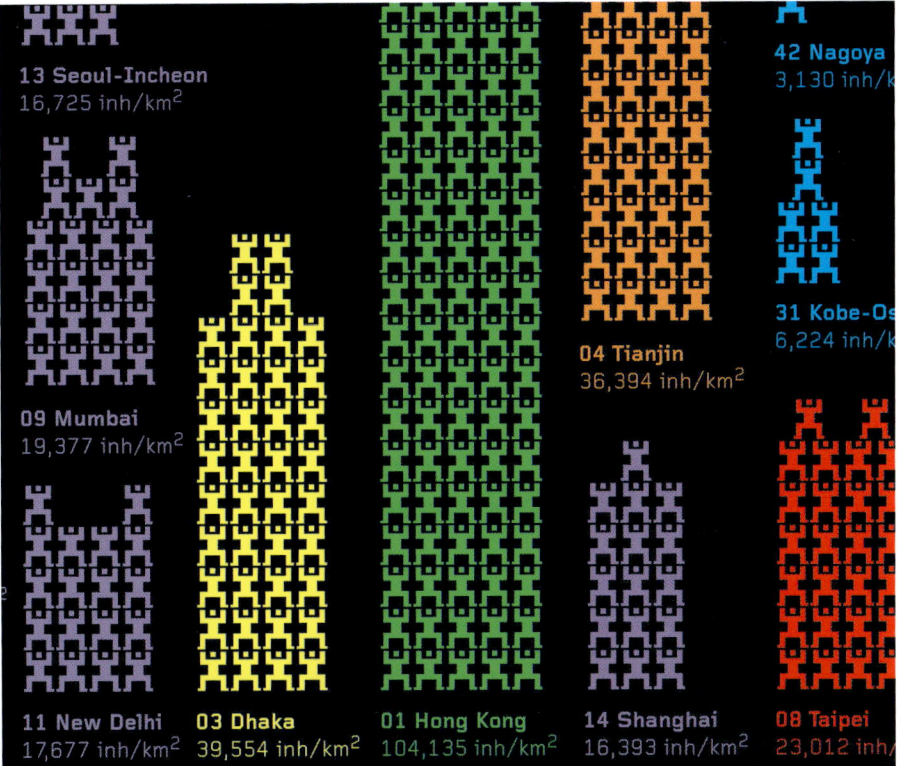

Research in the Visualization of Technology and Communication Data ::
Cybu Richli :: www.c2f.to ::

Swisscom, Switzerland's leading telecommunications company, is seeking for solutions that are more far-reaching than the obvious answers, and is therefore surveying and observing the behavior of various people with respect to how they use technology, accessories, social networks, and in the general day-to-day running of their affairs. These graphs collate the information obtained, using different colors to separate the themes to make them easier to read.

Time of SMS sessions in comparison to the Timecircle of all collected data

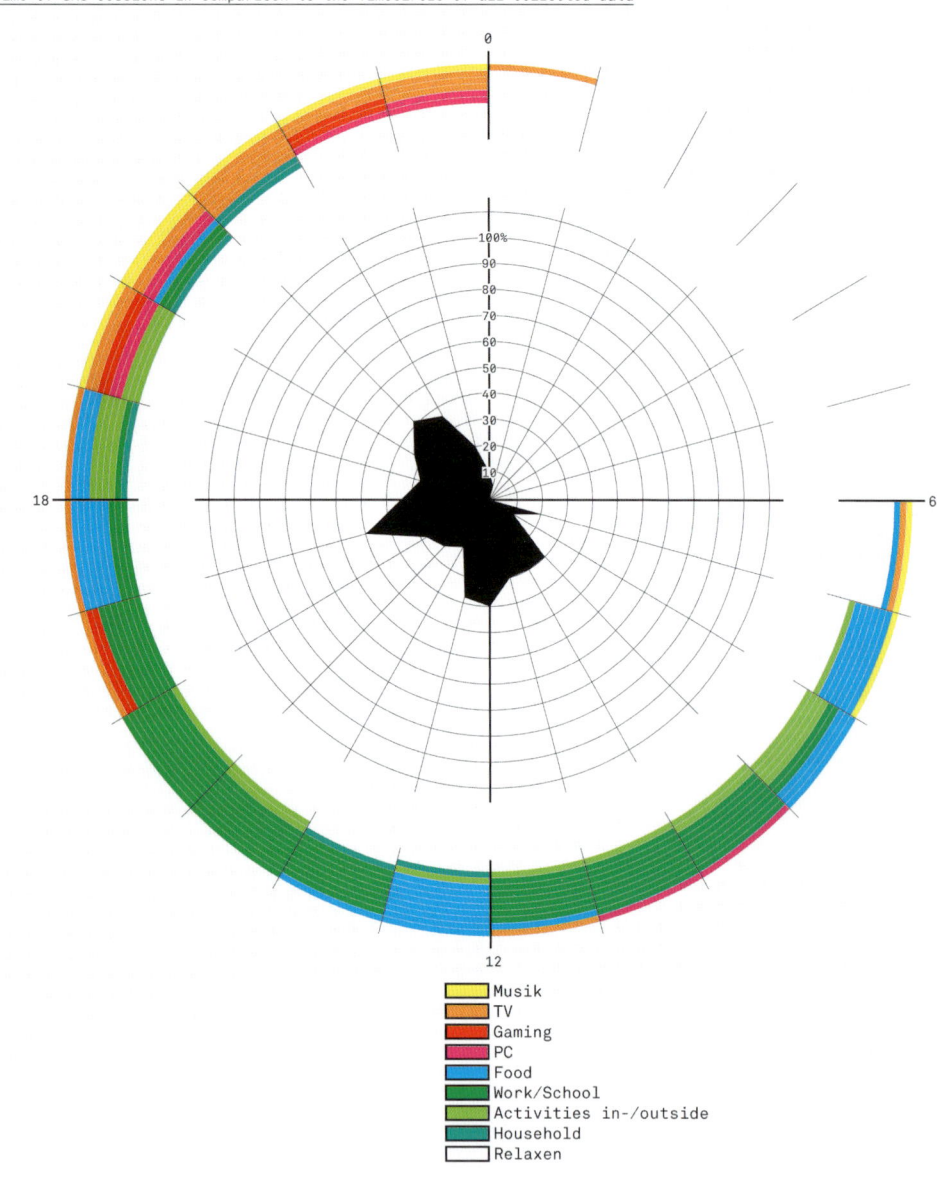

- Musik
- TV
- Gaming
- PC
- Food
- Work/School
- Activities in-/outside
- Household
- Relaxen

168 **Graphs**

Timecircle 24 hours week day in connection to the activity of technologies

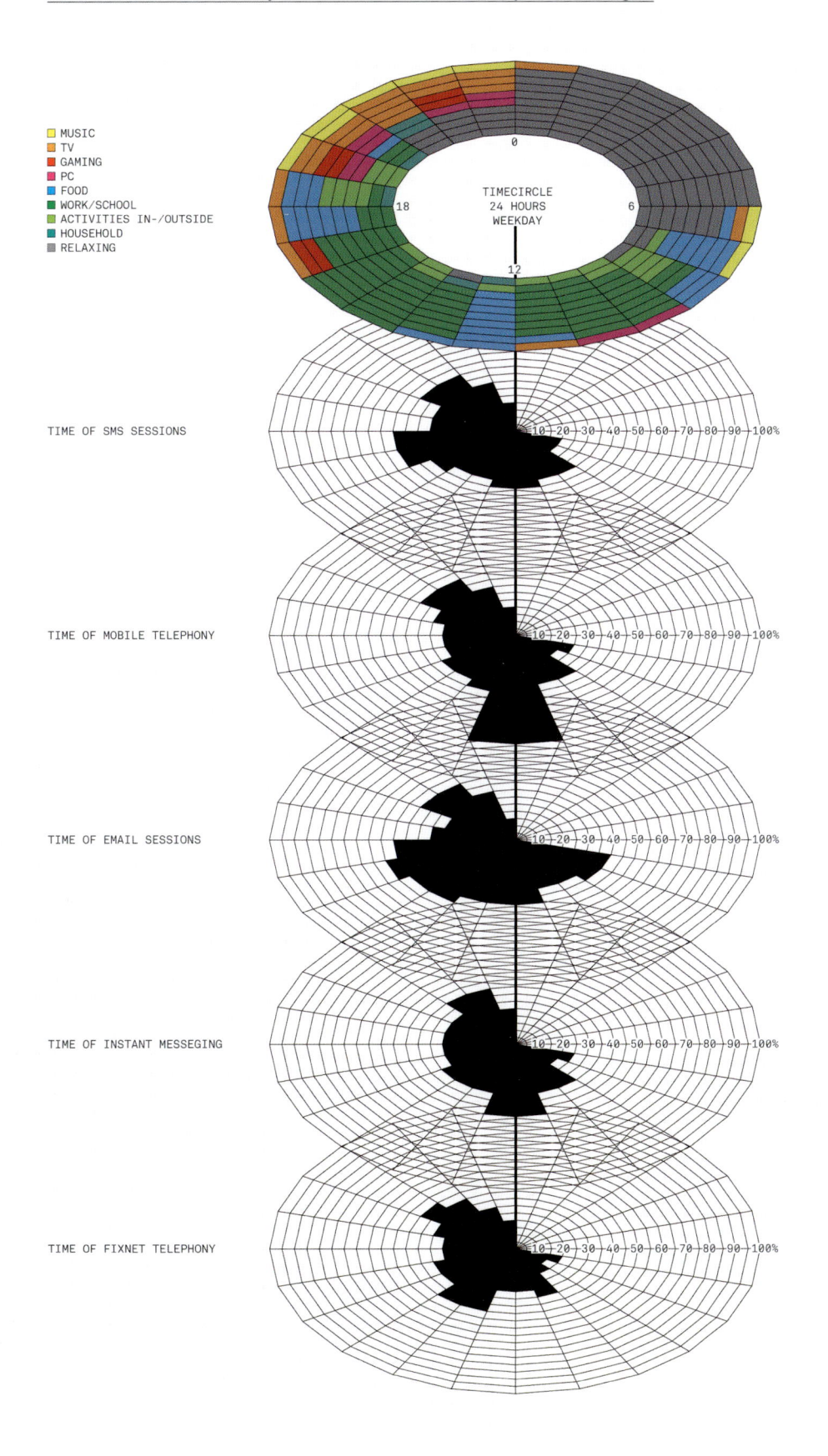

- ☐ MUSIC
- ☐ TV
- ☐ GAMING
- ☐ PC
- ☐ FOOD
- ☐ WORK/SCHOOL
- ☐ ACTIVITIES IN-/OUTSIDE
- ☐ HOUSEHOLD
- ☐ RELAXING

TIMECIRCLE 24 HOURS WEEKDAY

TIME OF SMS SESSIONS

TIME OF MOBILE TELEPHONY

TIME OF EMAIL SESSIONS

TIME OF INSTANT MESSEGING

TIME OF FIXNET TELEPHONY

Graphs | 69

2008 Getxo Kirolak (Deportes) Informe Anual ::
Supperstudio :: www.supperstudio.com ::

New year, new image. This was just what the people from Supperstudio thought when Getxo Town Council, in the Basque Country, asked them to draw up their annual report for 2008. To design it, they used elements belonging to the world of sports (the markings on pitches, courts, or swimming pools) as a graphic reference, along with the colors of the Olympic rings for each of the sections. The result: a real designer report.

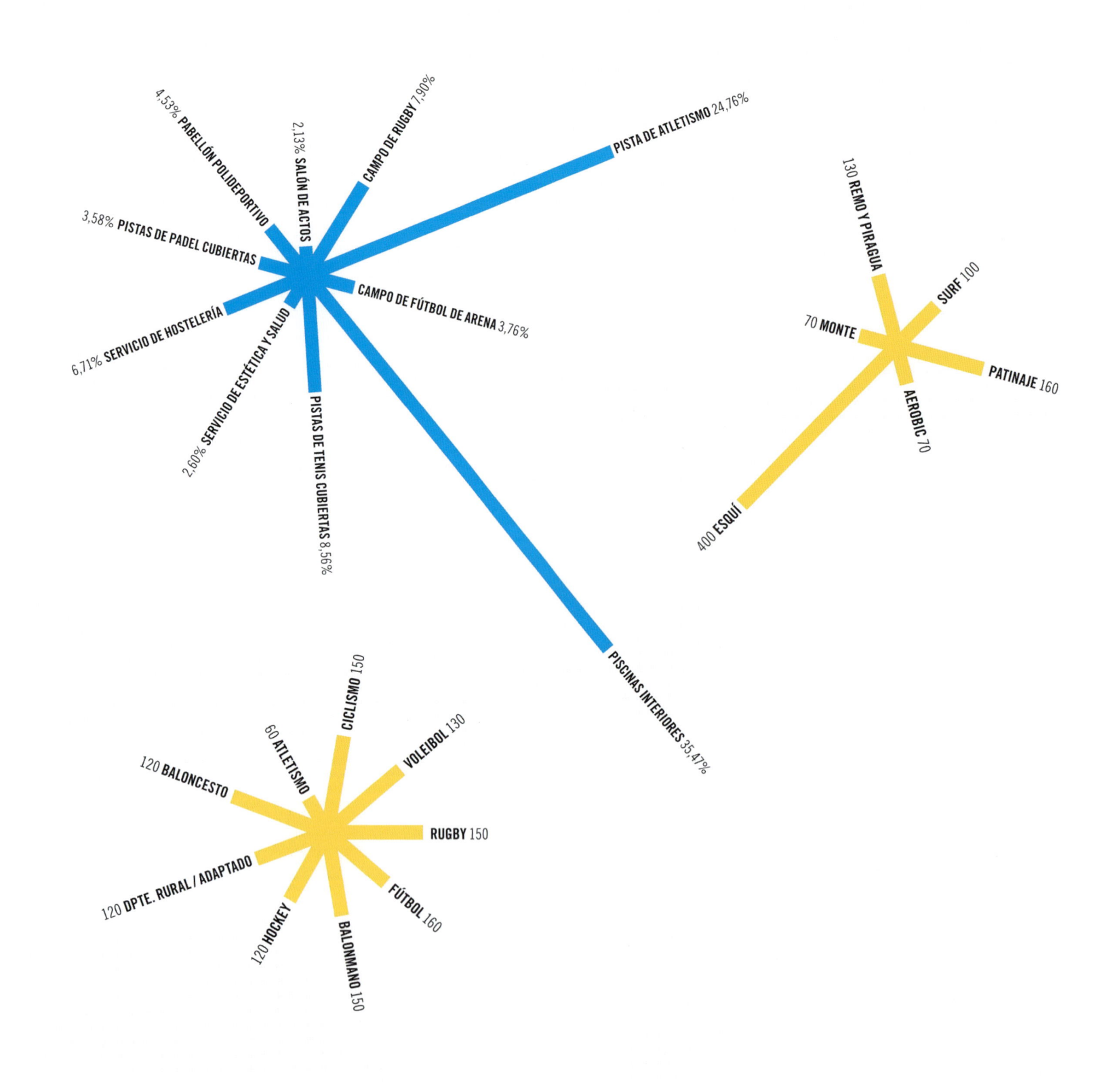

4,53% PABELLÓN POLIDEPORTIVO
2,13% SALÓN DE ACTOS
CAMPO DE RUGBY 7,90%
PISTA DE ATLETISMO 24,76%
3,58% PISTAS DE PADEL CUBIERTAS
6,71% SERVICIO DE HOSTELERÍA
CAMPO DE FÚTBOL DE ARENA 3,76%
2,60% SERVICIO DE ESTÉTICA Y SALUD
PISTAS DE TENIS CUBIERTAS 8,56%
PISCINAS INTERIORES 35,47%

130 REMO Y PIRAGUA
SURF 100
70 MONTE
PATINAJE 160
AEROBIC 70
400 ESQUÍ

150 CICLISMO
VOLEIBOL 130
60 ATLETISMO
120 BALONCESTO
RUGBY 150
120 DPTE. RURAL / ADAPTADO
FÚTBOL 160
120 HOCKEY
BALONMANO 150

2.4.1. NATACIÓN ESCOLAR

En esta apartado incluimos también el programa de Natación escolar, en el que participaron 1.030 niños y niñas de 14 centros escolares, a los que también agradecemos la confianza que depositan en Getxo Kirolak: C. AZKORRI, CEP ANDRA MARI, CEP JUAN BAUTISTA ZABALA, CEP ROMO, C. MADRE DEL DIVINO PASTOR, C. NUESTRA SEÑORA DE EUROPA, STMA. TRINIDAD, CEP LARRAÑAZUBI, CEP SAN IGNACIO, CEP ZUBILLETA, GE ROMO/IES JULIO CARO BAROJA, IKASTOLA GOBELA, IKASTOLA GEROA E IKASTOLA SAN NIKOLAS.

2.5. ASOCIACIONES DEPORTIVAS Y DEPORTE FEDERADO

El municipio de Getxo cuenta con 60 asociaciones deportivas registradas. Además, el deporte federado agrupa a 34 clubes que engloban 163 equipos.
Getxo Kirolak albergó un total de 1.881 competiciones.

	FADURA	GOBELA	ANDRA MARI	TOTAL
Fútbol sala	34	35	9	78
Baloncesto	60	44	-	104
Fútbol	580	254	-	834
Rugby	56	-	-	56
Tenis	330	-	-	330
Natación	1	-	-	1
Waterpolo	6	-	-	6
Balonmano	-	33	-	33
Pádel	148	-	-	148
Pelota	218	-	17	235
Ciclismo	2	-	-	2
Hockey	14	-	-	14
Voleibol	29	-	-	29
Atletismo	1	-	-	1
Herri Kirolak	1	-	5	6
Deporte adaptado	1	3	-	4
TOTAL	1.481	369	31	1.881

NÚMERO DE COMPETICIONES CELEBRADAS EN CADA POLIDEPORTIVO

1.481 FADURA   **369** GOBELA   **31** ANDRA MARI

COMPETICIONES CELEBRADAS EN EL POLIDEPORTIVO DE FADURA

218 PELOTA, 60 BALONCESTO, FÚTBOL SALA 34, 580 FÚTBOL, OTROS* 26, PÁDEL 148, VOLEIBOL 29, 56 RUGBY, 330 TENIS

*El apartado Otros incluye 26 competiciones: 14 de hockey, 1 natación, 6 de waterpolo, 2 de ciclismo, 1 de atletismo, 1 de deporte adaptado y 1 de herri kirolak.

COMPETICIONES REGISTRADA EN EL POLIDEPORTIVO DE GOBELA

33 BALONMANO, DEPORTE ADAPTADO 3, 35 FÚTBOL SALA, BALONCESTO 44, FÚTBOL 254

COMPETICIONES ORGANIZADAS EN EL POLIDEPORTIVO DE ANDRA MARI

17 PELOTA   **9** FÚTBOL SALA   **5** HERRI KIROLAK

Graphs | 71

34 kg de CO$_2$ ::
Pau de Riba, Guillem Cardona :: www.pauderiba.com ::

These graphs form part of a book published by the Generalitat de Catalunya on sustainable architecture. Working with experts forced the designers to immerse themselves in the subject to be able to prioritize the most relevant themes and thus set a schematic limit on complexity. That said, they had to discard fantastic charts, which on account of their density would have required instructions to be interpreted properly.

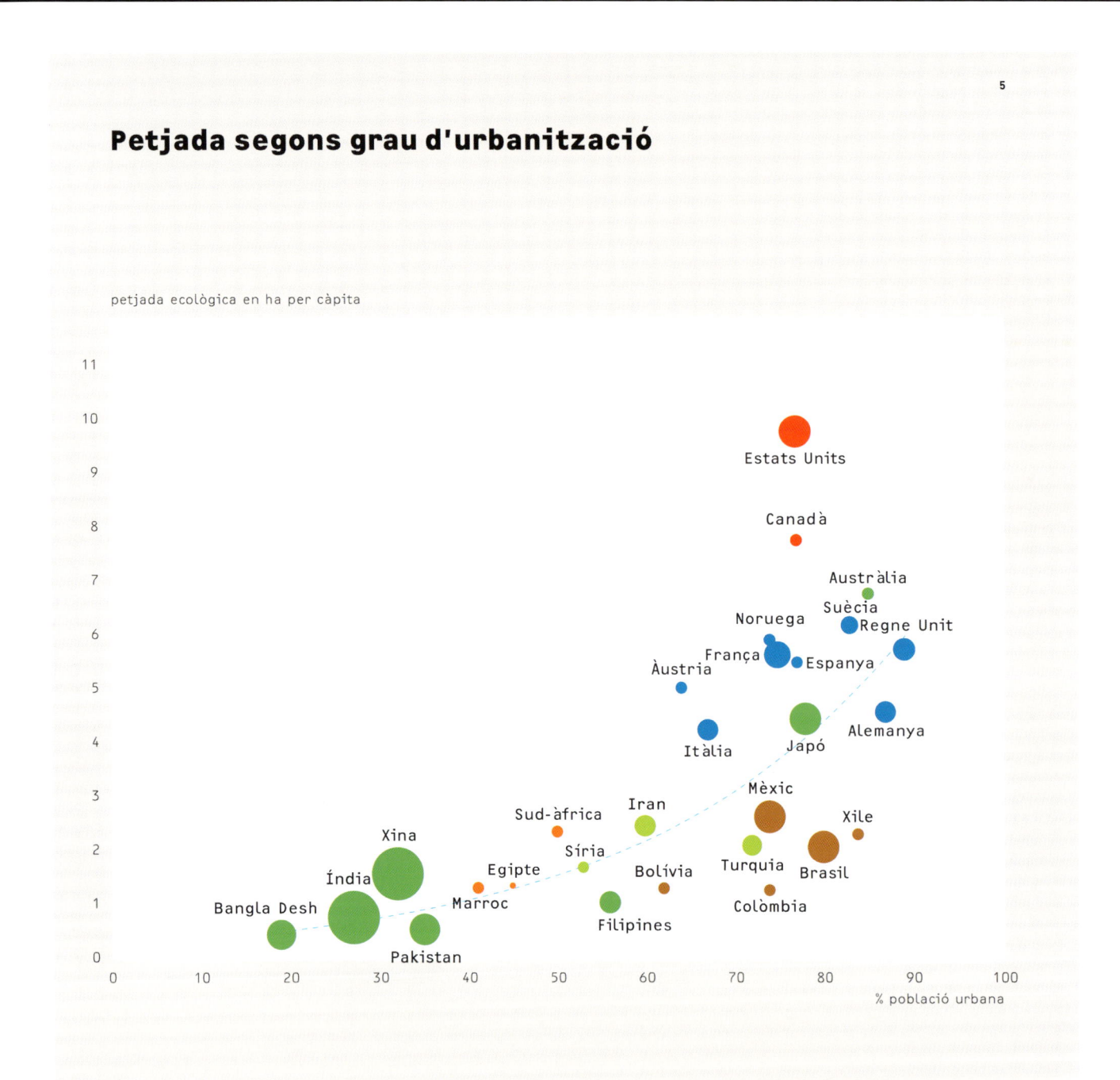

Petjada segons grau d'urbanització

petjada ecològica en ha per càpita

% població urbana

Petjada ecològica de Barcelona

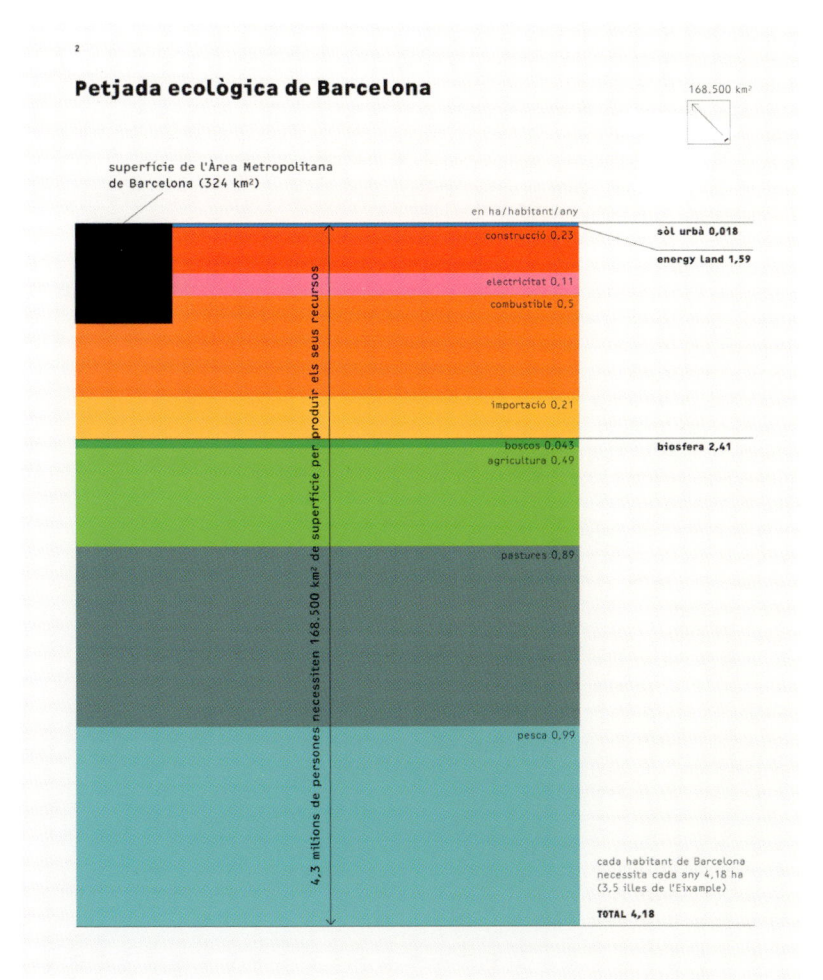

168.500 km²

superfície de l'Àrea Metropolitana de Barcelona (324 km²)

en ha/habitant/any

construcció 0,23	sòl urbà 0,018
electricitat 0,11	energy land 1,59
combustible 0,5	
importació 0,21	
boscos 0,043	biosfera 2,41
agricultura 0,49	
pastures 0,89	
pesca 0,99	

4,3 milions de persones necessiten 168.500 km² de superfície per produir els seus recursos

cada habitant de Barcelona necessita cada any 4,18 ha (3,5 illes de l'Eixample)

TOTAL 4,18

Emissions de CO_2 per ciutats

consum energètic vinculat al transport gigajoules per habitant

- Houston
- Phoenix
- Detroit
- Denver
- Los Angeles
- San Francisco
- Boston
- Washington
- Chicago
- Nova York
- Toronto — **Amèrica del Nord**
- Perth
- Brisbane
- Melbourne — **Austràlia**
- Sydney
- Hamburg, Estocolm
- Paris, Zürich
- Londres, Munich
- Berlin oest
- Viena — **Europa**
- Amsterdam
- Tokio
- Singapur — **Àsia**
- Moscou
- Hong Kong

densitat urbana habitants per hectàrea

Graphs | 173

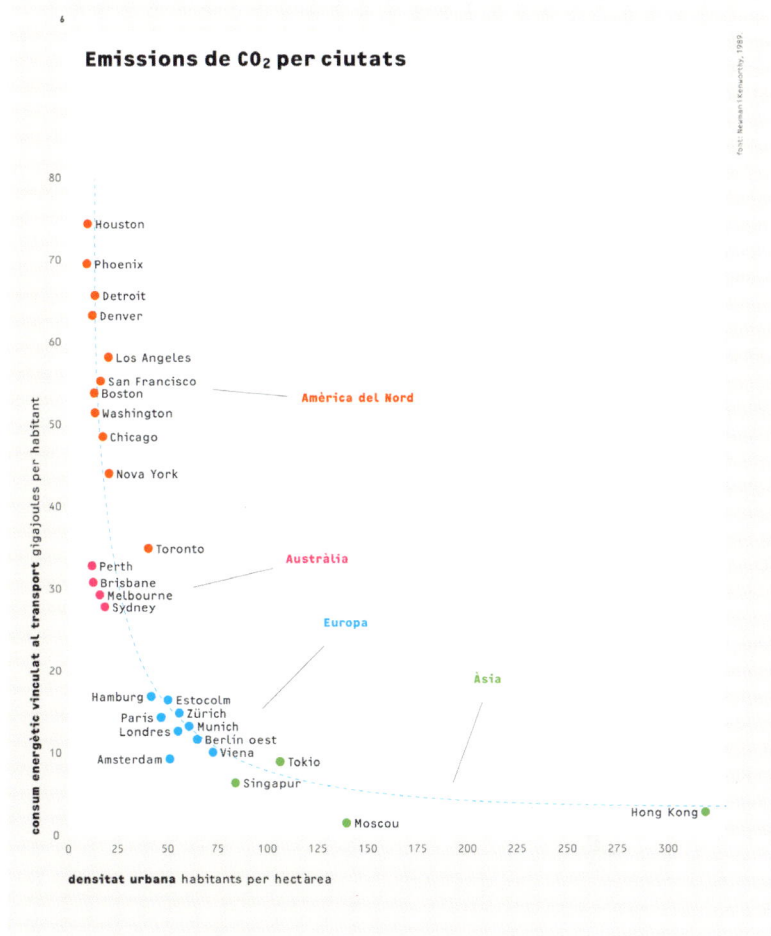

Atlas on Public Housing ::
Peter van den Hoogen, Erica Terpstra/Coup :: www.coup.nl ::

For an atlas on public housing, this pair of graphic designers created a series of infographics that stand out for their fresh approach. The data on the Dutch population is given according to age group, the sales figures for family housing in recent years or their prices, and is displayed in vivid colors and bold shapes that invite the reader to take a look and compare the information.

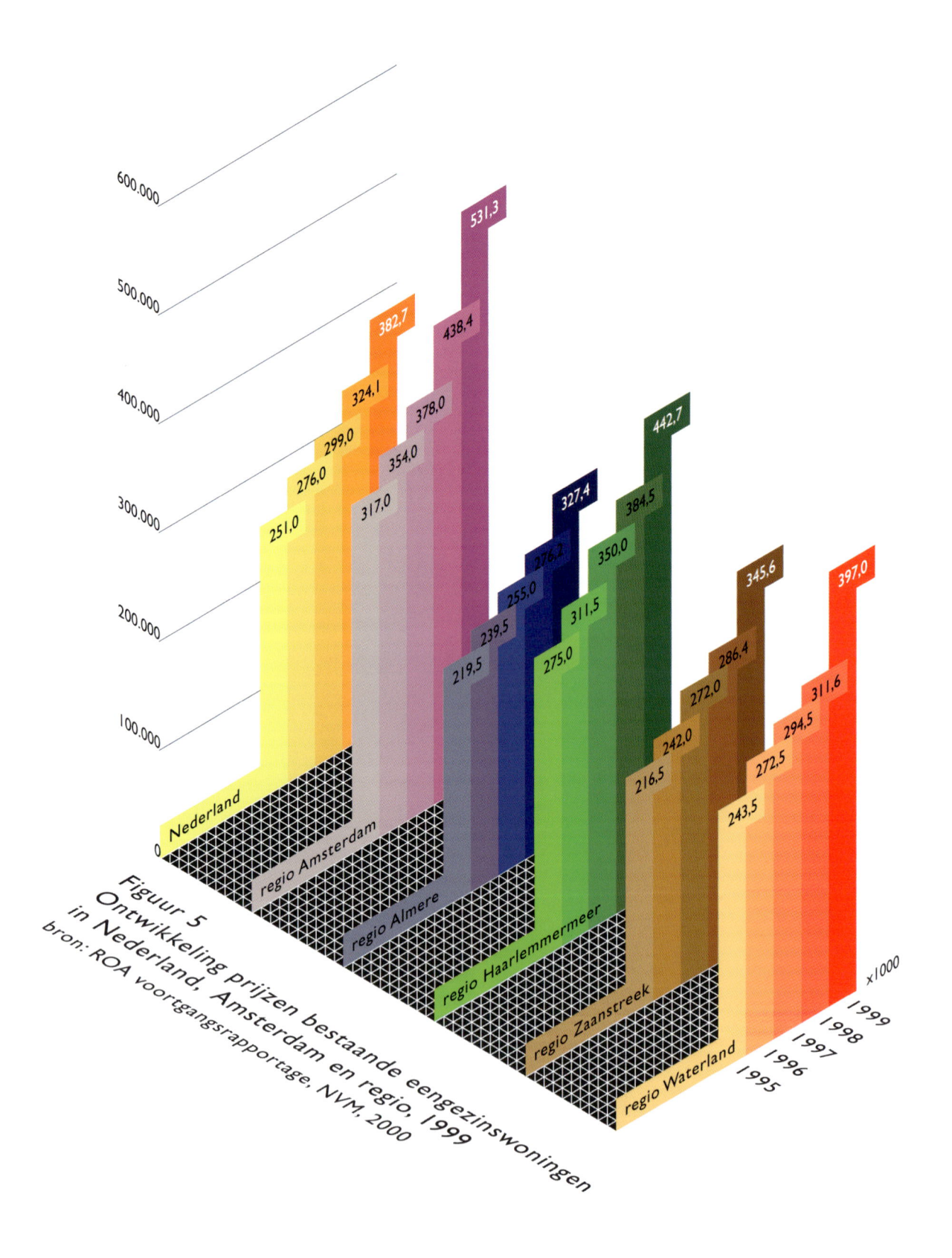

Figuur 5
Ontwikkeling prijzen bestaande eengezinswoningen in Nederland, Amsterdam en regio, 1999
bron: ROA voortgangsrapportage, NVM, 2000

Regio	1995	1996	1997	1998	1999
Nederland	251,0	276,0	299,0	324,1	382,7
regio Amsterdam	317,0	354,0	378,0	438,4	531,3
regio Almere	219,5	239,5	255,0	276,2	327,4
regio Haarlemmermeer	275,0	311,5	350,0	384,5	442,7
regio Zaanstreek	216,5	242,0	272,0	286,4	345,6
regio Waterland	243,5	272,5	294,5	311,6	397,0

×1000

Graphs 175

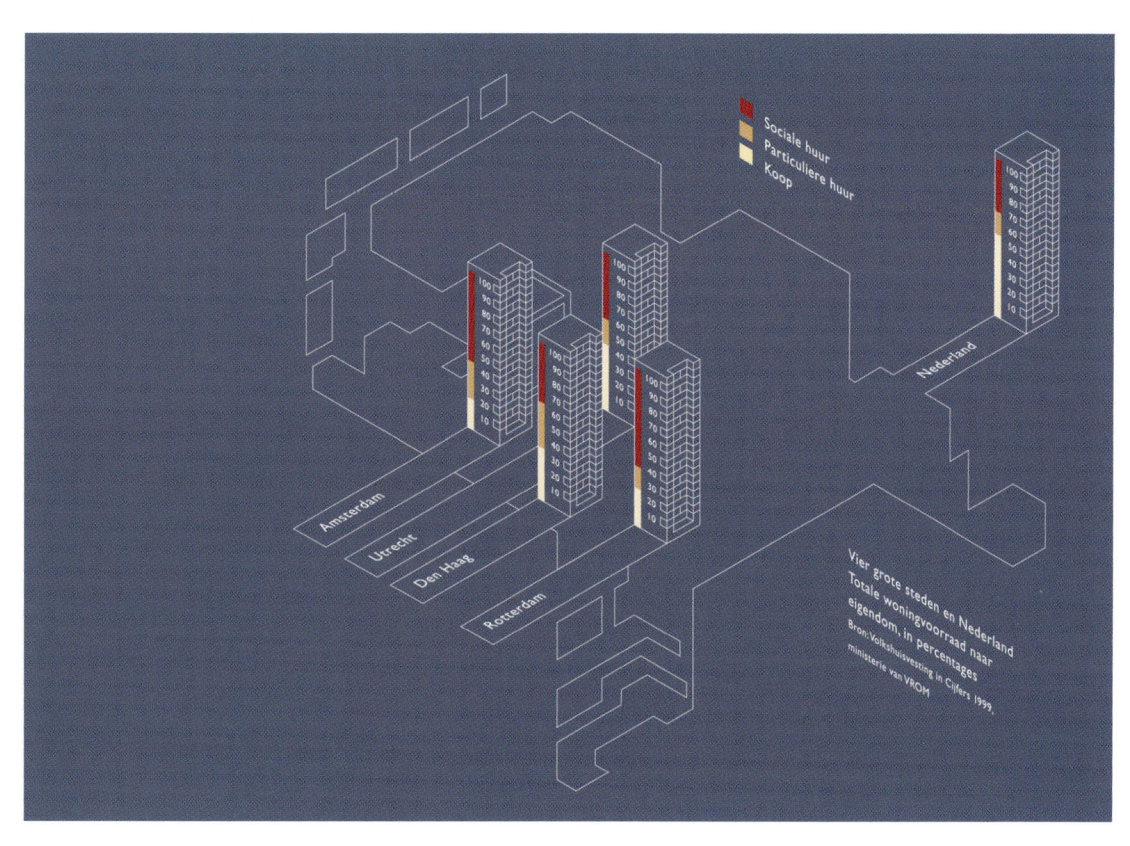

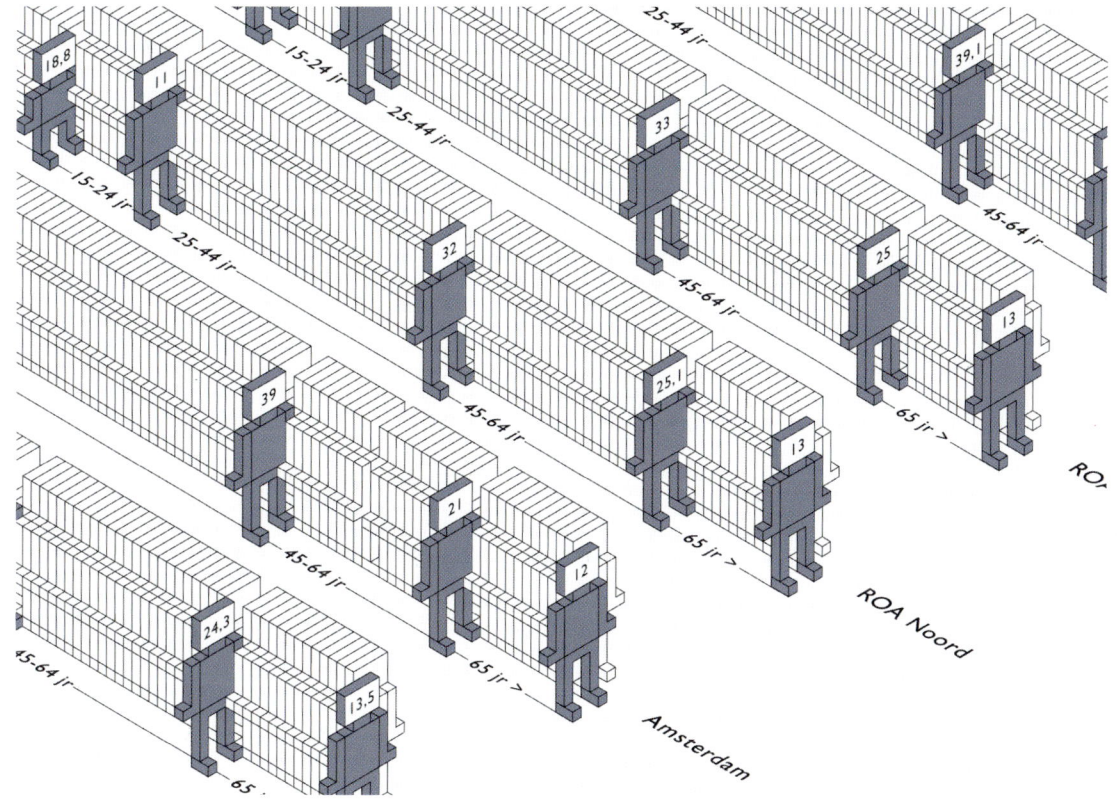

FUTU ::
Studio8 Design :: www.studio8design.co.uk ::

The purpose of these graphs is to show the intangible value enjoyed by some brands. The best way to do this is by means of a bar chart: each color represents an industrial sector (clothing, technology, fast food, beverages, and cars) and each bar, a brand from this sector. The originality of this design lies in the way the bars are displayed as having different layers of volume.

These are a series of graphs based on the intangible value of different brands. The graphs are not based on the parent companies overall worth. Brand value in US$

Apparel

Technology

Fast food

Soft drinks

Cars

Graphs | 177

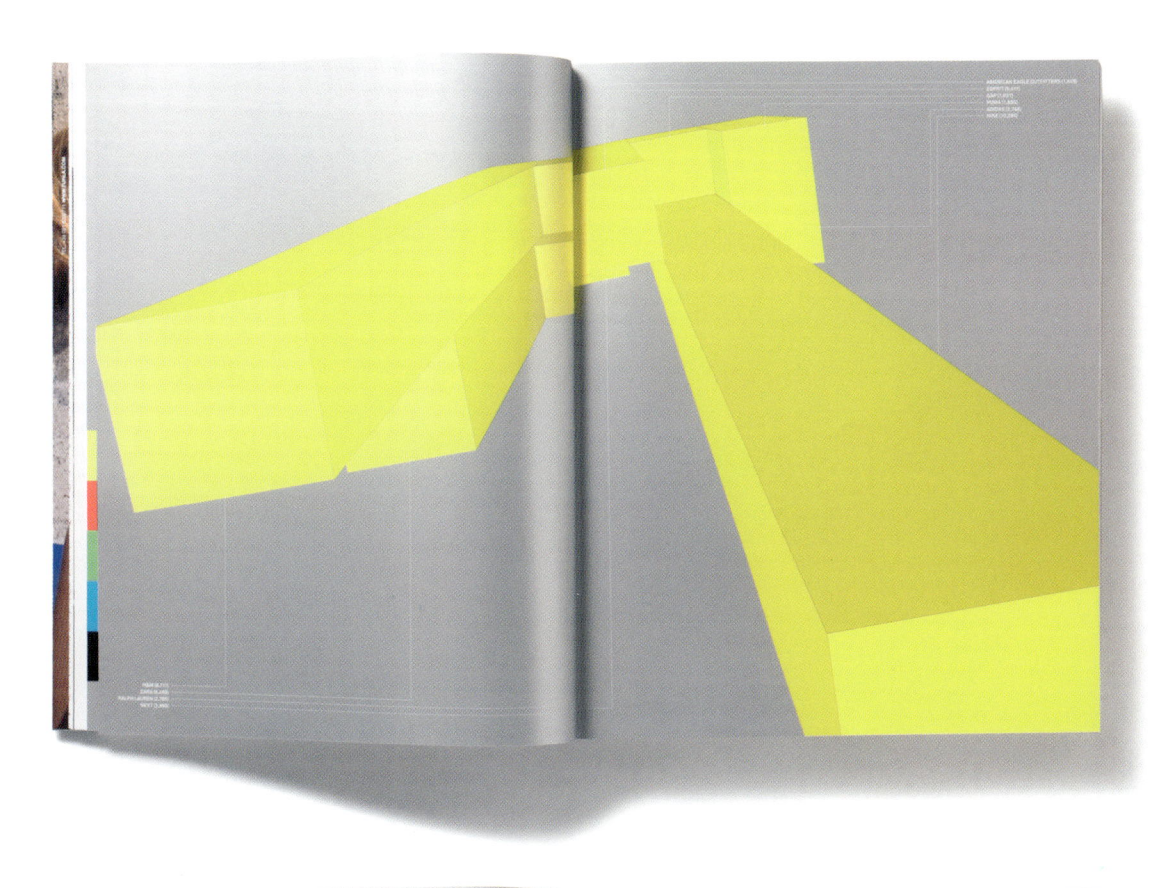

The Hague Catered Capital ::
LUST :: www.lust.nl ::

For the Foodprint program, which focuses on food and its impact in cities, LUST put together a series of graphs, using the city of The Hague as an example. They demonstrate food consumption in different ministries. A meal is used as a vehicle to compare the menus offered by the various catering services, the number of diners, and the dishes served.

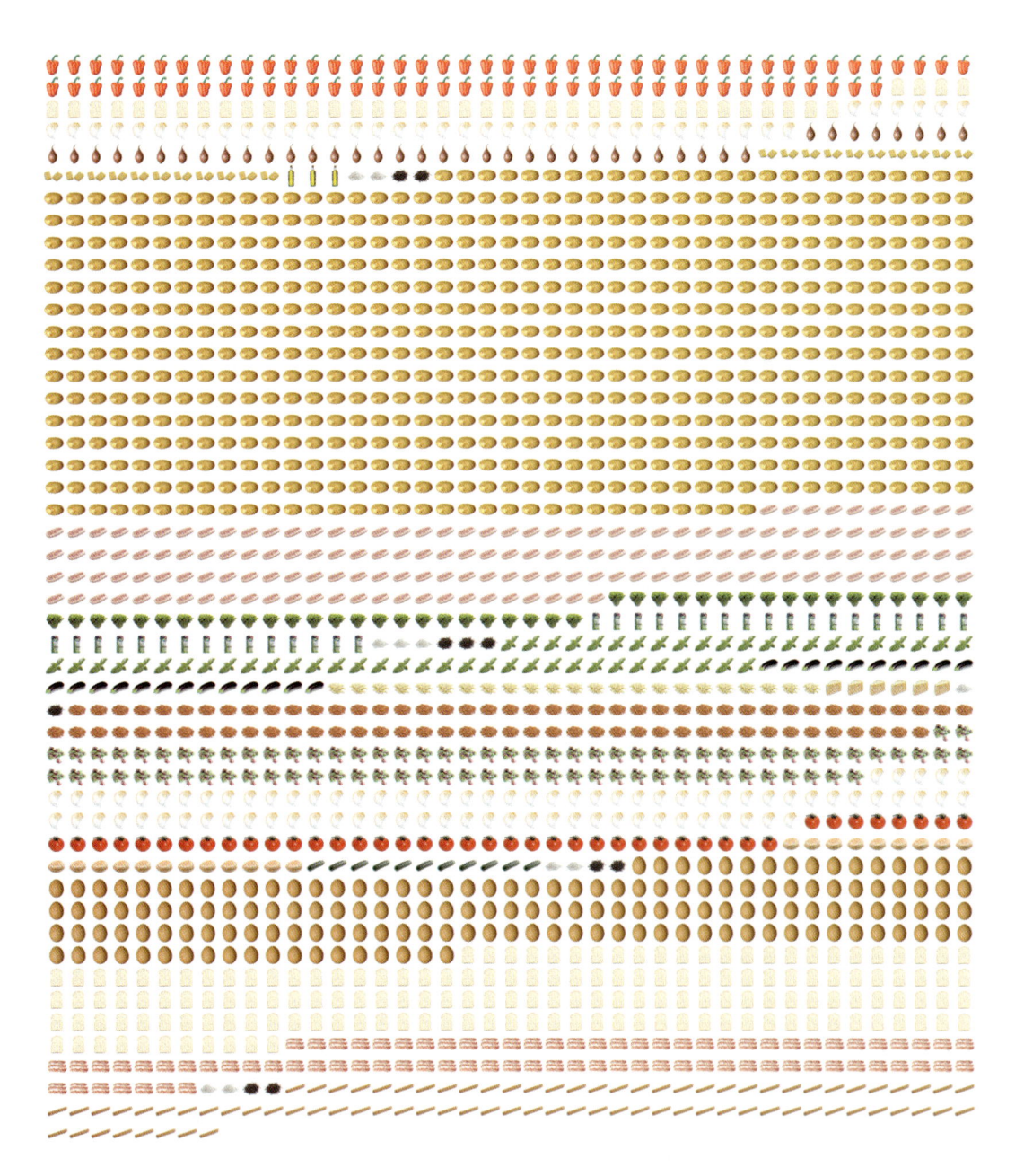

Ministerie van Financiën

Cateraar
ISS
Aantal ambtenaren
33851
Aantal lunch-deelnemers
+/- 550

Menu
Paprikasoep
Andijviestamppot met speklap
Pasta met aubergine en pesto
Broodje gyros met salade
Gebakken ei met spek
Frikandel

Feiten
Het Ministerie van Financiën is het enige ministerie waar ISS de catering verzorgd. Het Ministerie van Financiën is met de renovatie het eerste kantoorgebouw van de rijksoverheid dat in de vorm van publiek-private samenwerking (PPS) is aanbesteed. ISS is niet alleen verantwoordelijk voor het onderhoud en beheer van het Ministerie van Financiën, maar ook voor het ontwerp en de realisatie, voor een looptijd van 25 jaar.

Ministerie van Landbouw, Natuur en V

Cateraar
Albron
Aantal ambtenaren
7534
Aantal lunch-deelnemers
+/- 450

Menu
Goulash
Kip tando
Gebakke
pesto en
Salade m
Gebakke
Broodje f

178 Graphs

Woensdag 20 mei 2009

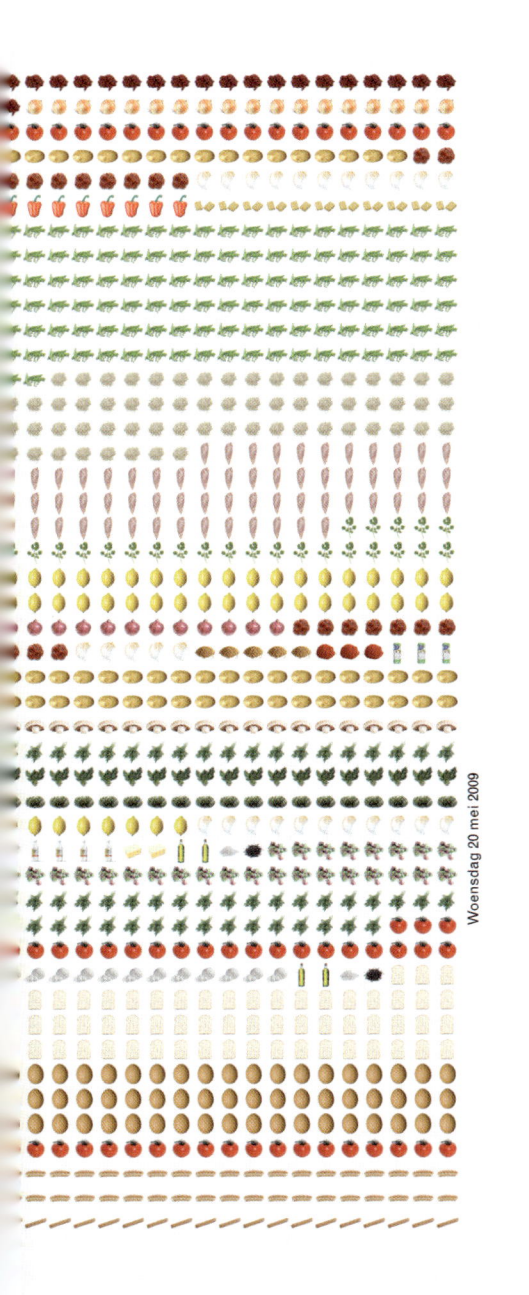

Feiten
Een Nederlander eet zo'n 18,4 kilogram kip per jaar, dat komt neer op ruim 300.000 ton kip landelijk per jaar. Een 'reguliere' kip heeft een leefruimte van nog geen 23 bij 23 centimeter, een biologische kip heeft twee keer zo veel ruimte. Op 20 mei werden er op het Ministerie van LNV zo'n 135 kipfilets gegeten, afkomstig van 68 kippen. Alleen in Nederland zijn er al 29,6 miljoen kippen, voor vlees en eieren.

Graphs | 179

State of Change Web ::
André Pahl :: www.primeclub.org ::

The idea for this Web site grew out of the intention to show the artists' individual careers online without losing sight of the group they belong to. The outcome is this book of diagrams in a state of constant growth, in this case bringing together nine artists from various places around the world, and illustrated as a graph on which the variables are the year and city where their work has been shown.

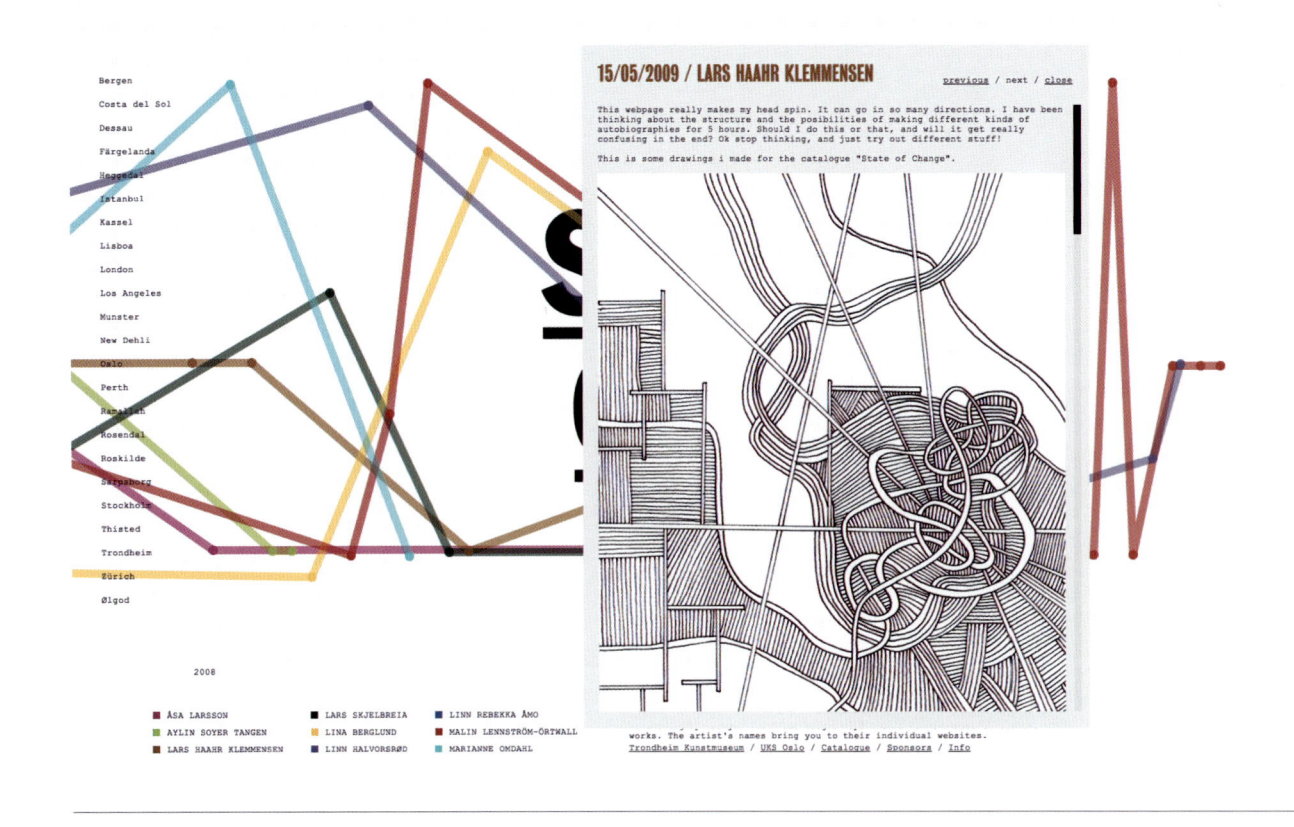

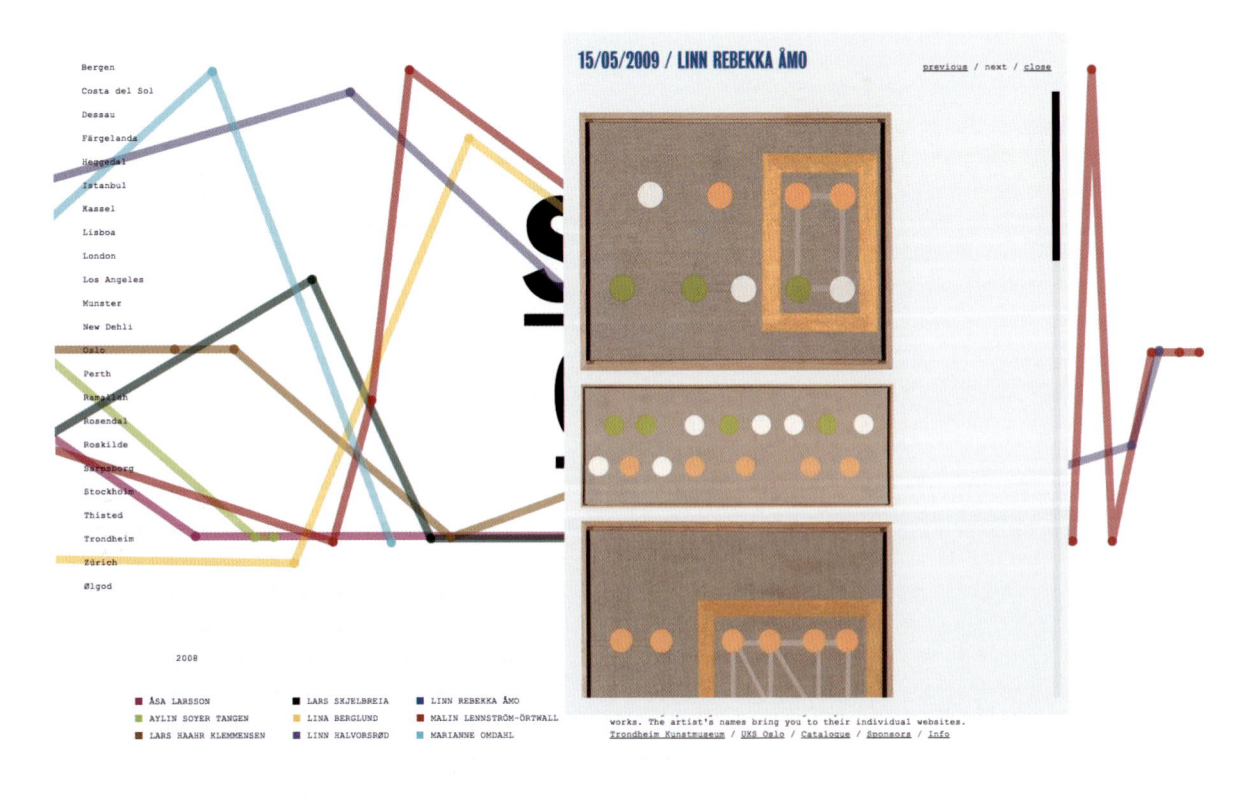

America 2030 ::
Cybu Richli/C2F :: www.c2f.to ::

This chart was commissioned by Pentagram, Abbott Miller's design studio in New York, and was included in the first issue of *Architect*, a new magazine on architecture. It compares the land developed in the USA before 2000 with the land expected to be used for building by 2030. What makes this chart different from the others in this book is the perspective used in drawing the bars.

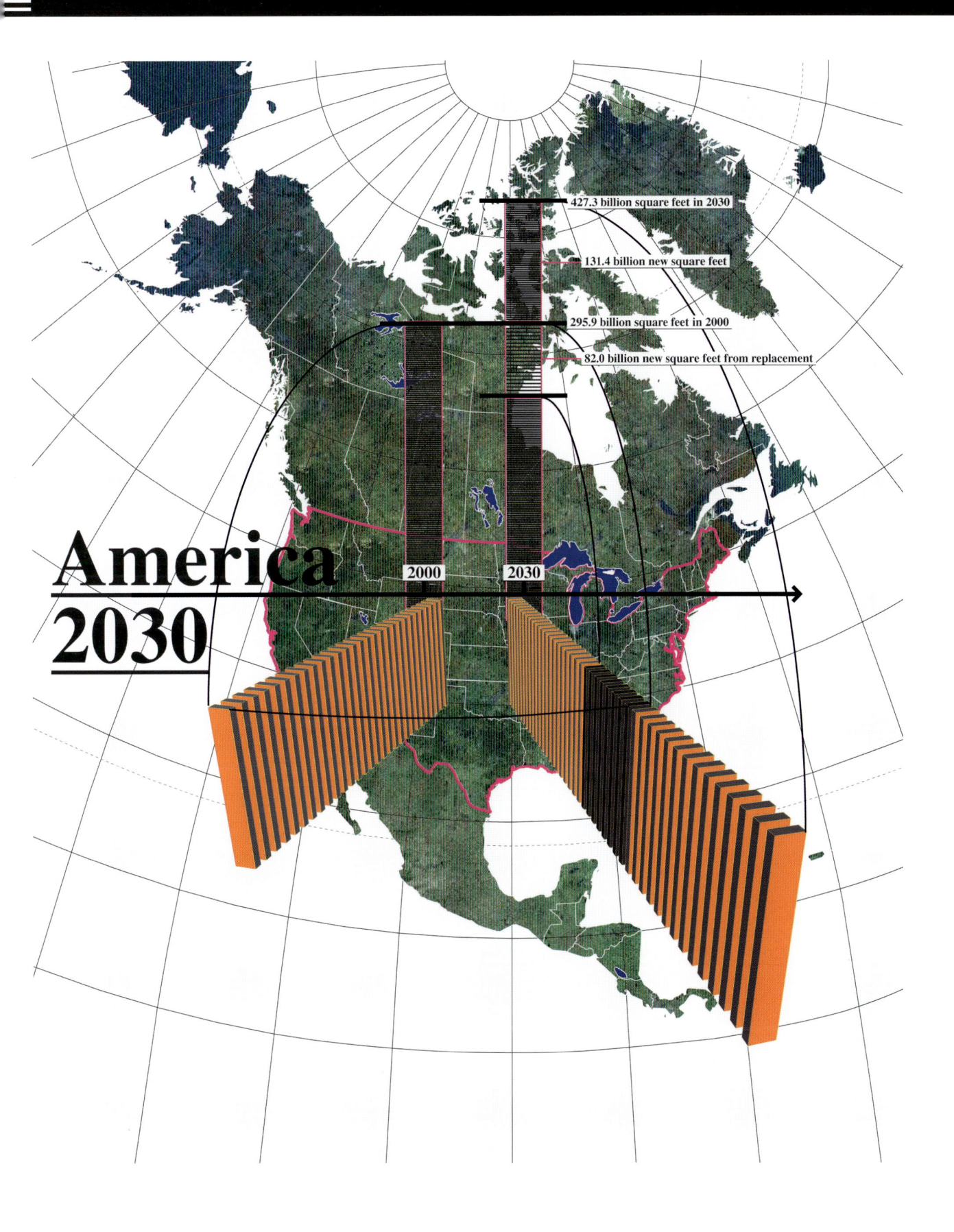

- 427.3 billion square feet in 2030
- 131.4 billion new square feet
- 295.9 billion square feet in 2000
- 82.0 billion new square feet from replacement

America 2030

2000   2030

Time Project ::
Anna Filipova :: www.anfilip.com ::

The brief for this project was to create a graphic representation of time which was unique. So the designer decided to do this by using the sins that appear in the Bible. In the graph, these are associated with longevity: this decreases from Adam to Moses, whereas the level of sin rises, and this was demonstrated by the designer through the use of quotations from the Bible. Each circle represents the age of the person and the color, the number of sins committed.

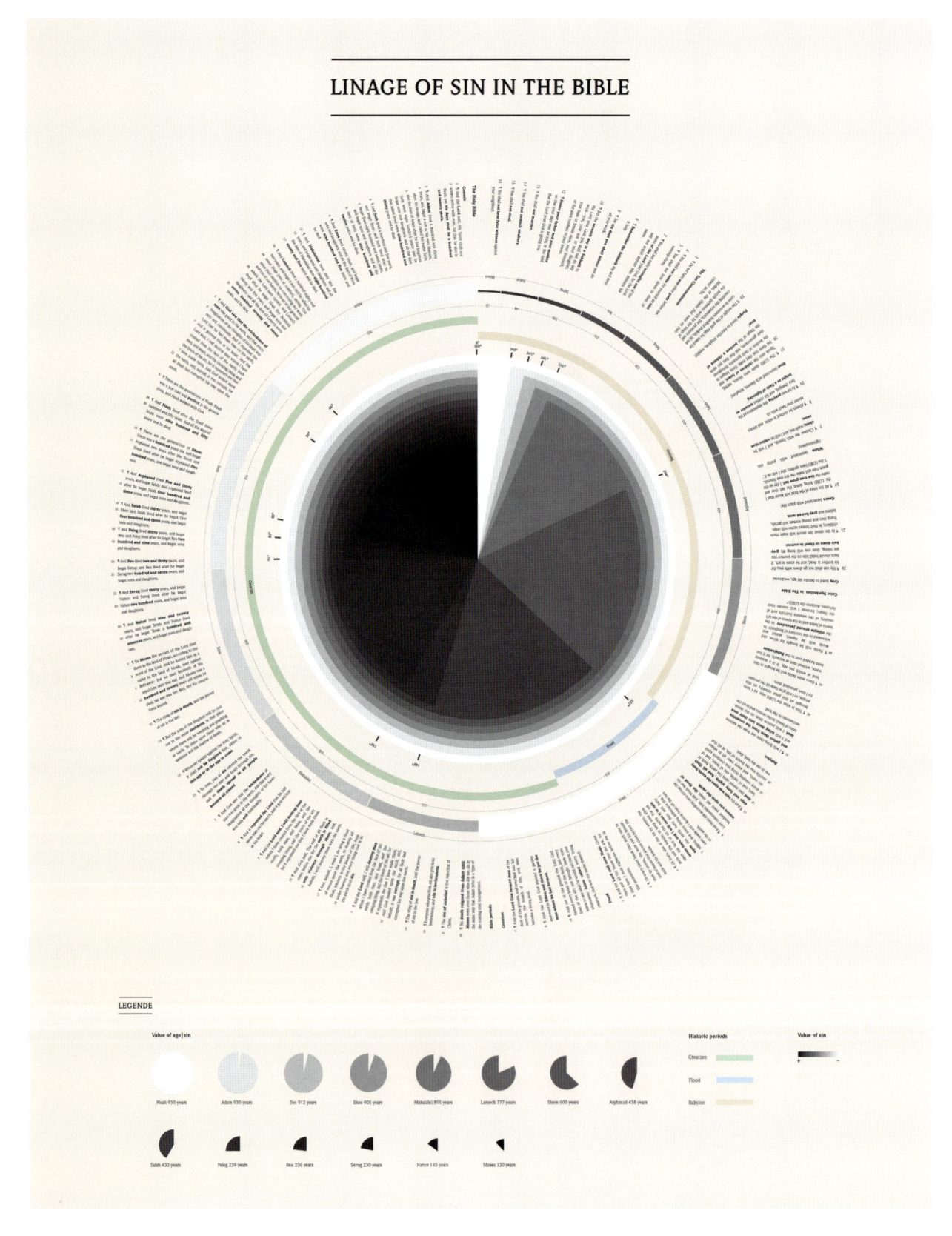

LINAGE OF SIN IN THE BIBLE

Zandstad ::
LUST :: www.lust.nl ::

Zandstad is a region located in Holland that is currently going through the process of reconverting and diversifying a predominantly agricultural area. The project works with the concepts concerning the human geography of the area, such as population, livestock, or land use, which have all been converted into graphs. The idea is to encourage designers and historians to work together to develop new projects in regions that are similar to this one.

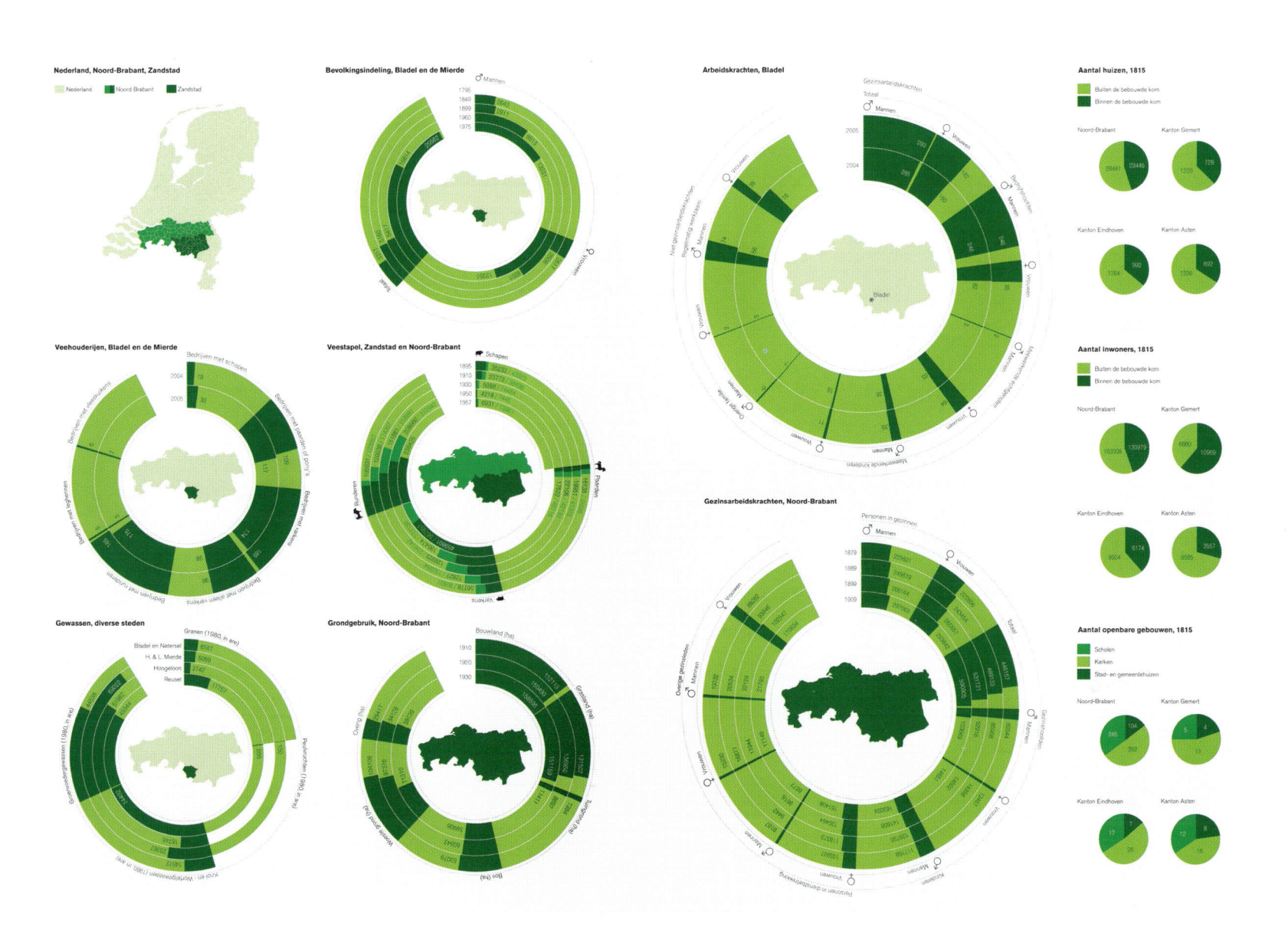

Association Nationale pour la Formation permanente du personnel Hospitalier (ANFH) ::
Atelier Chévara etc :: www.atelier-chevara.com ::

The brochures and posters devoted to health generally have a fairly clean, tidy appearance, with communication being given top priority. The people from Atelier Chévara etc respected these principles to develop the publications of this association, but removed the seriousness that should be implicit in this type of project, opting instead to have fun with 3-D charts, symbols, colors, and volumes.

2008 LA RÉFORME DE LA FORMATION PROFESSIONNELLE
RAPPORT D'ACTIVITÉ
ASSOCIATION NATIONALE POUR LA FORMATION PERMANENTE DU PERSONNEL HOSPITALIER

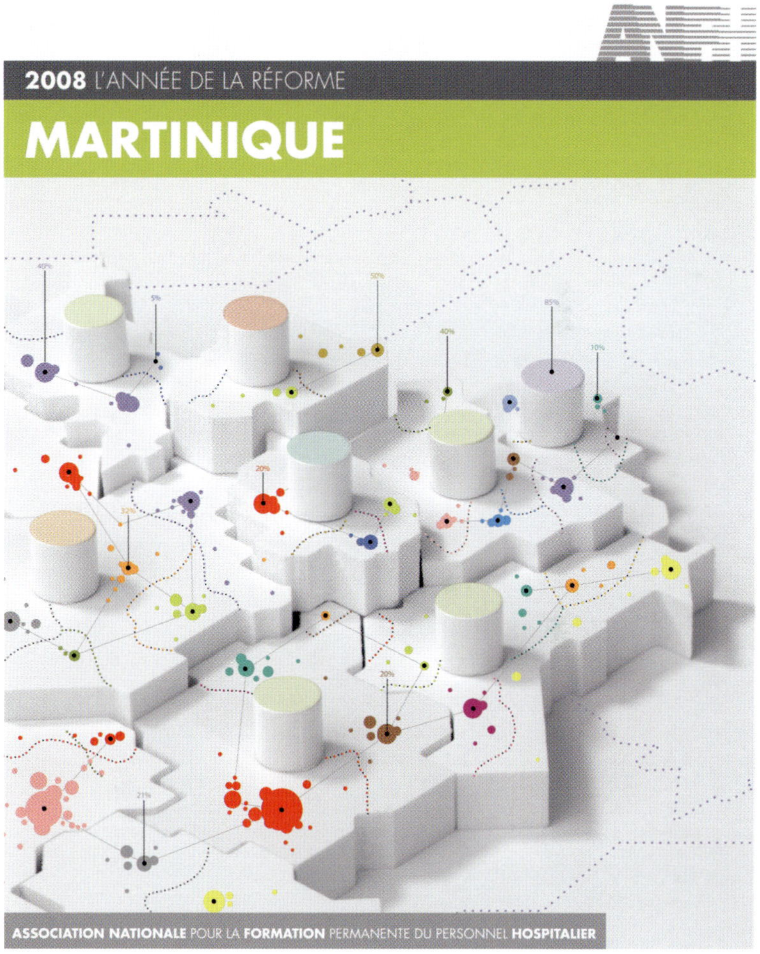
2008 L'ANNÉE DE LA RÉFORME
MARTINIQUE
ASSOCIATION NATIONALE POUR LA FORMATION PERMANENTE DU PERSONNEL HOSPITALIER

ESADE Presentation ::
TwoPoints.Net :: www.twopoints.net ::

The idea of this presentation was to use graphs to portray the creative environment of the Elisava school of design with its four specialties: technical architecture, automotive engineering, graphics design, and industrial design. They are alluded to in the form of related objects made of extruded polystyrene foam or plexiglass, which also give an idea of the atmosphere of design that permeates the school.

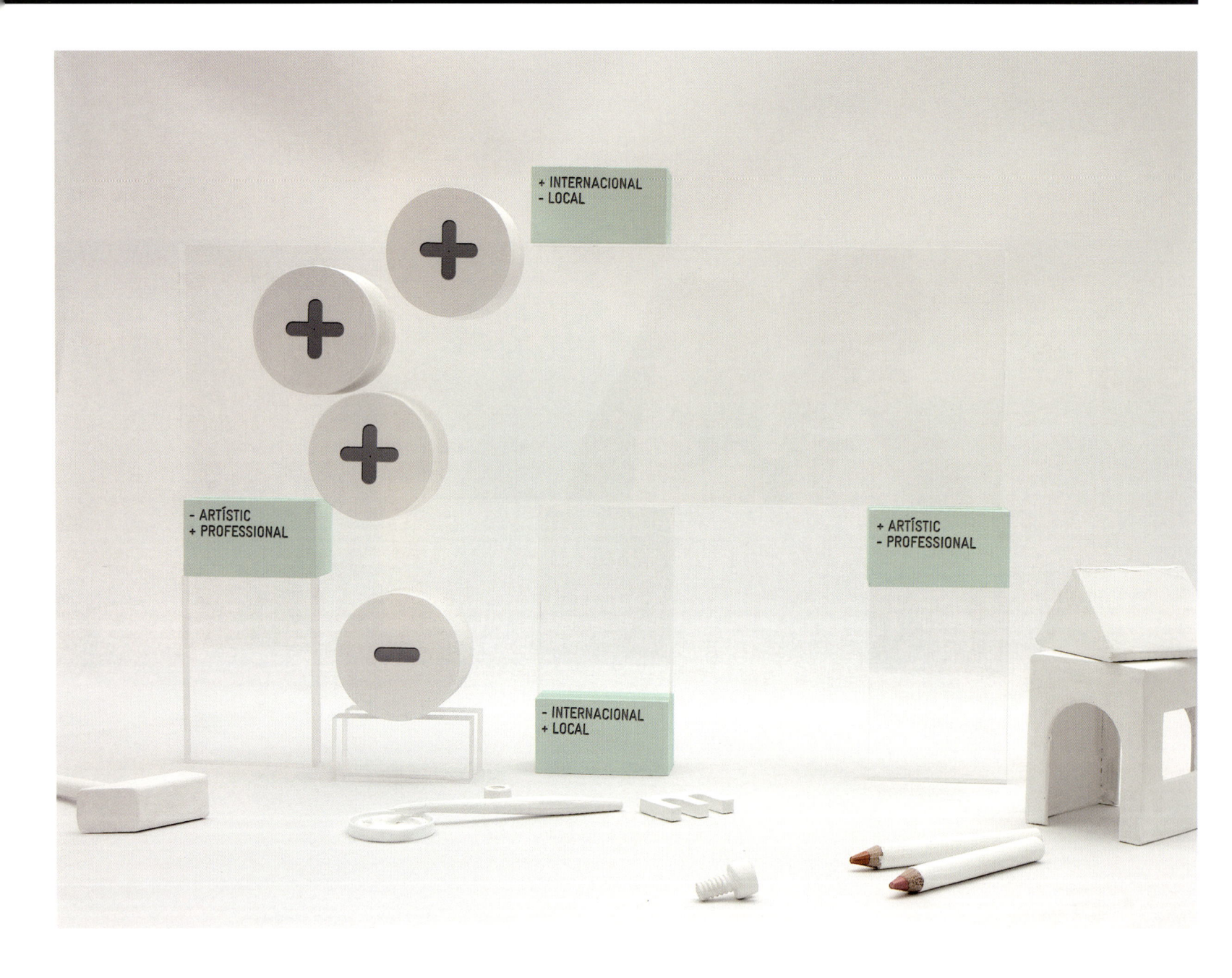

Objectius:

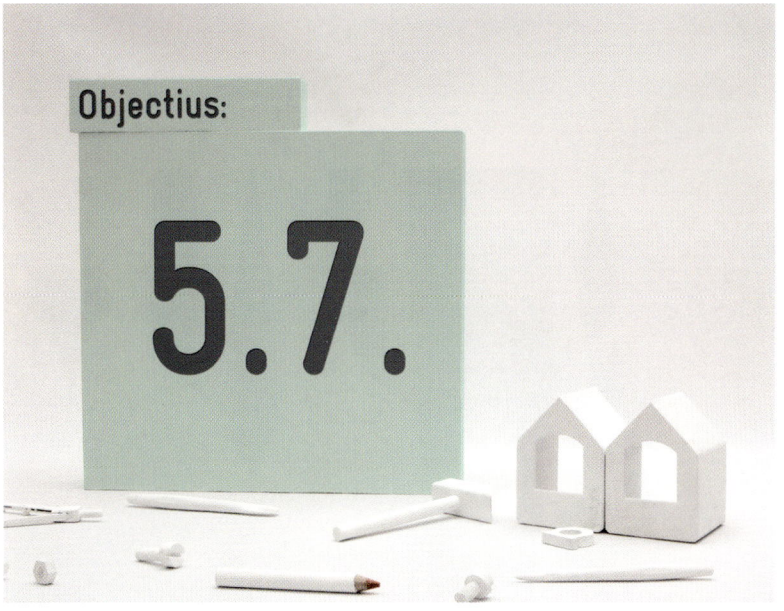

5.7.

Graphs | 87

Artist Groups: Possibility of Collaboration in Contemporary Art of Estonia ::
Margus Tamm :: www.tammtamm.net ::

These charts—used in posters and as the cover of a book—illustrate the contributions made by groups of artists on the Estonian scene in the 1990s. In its design, it was decided to depict a topic forming part of the sphere of art with shapes that are more closely associated with the scientific world, as if they were bodies in evolution. The size and volume of these shapes represent the group's activity and influence at each moment in time.

Table 1.
groupings in contemporary Estonian art*

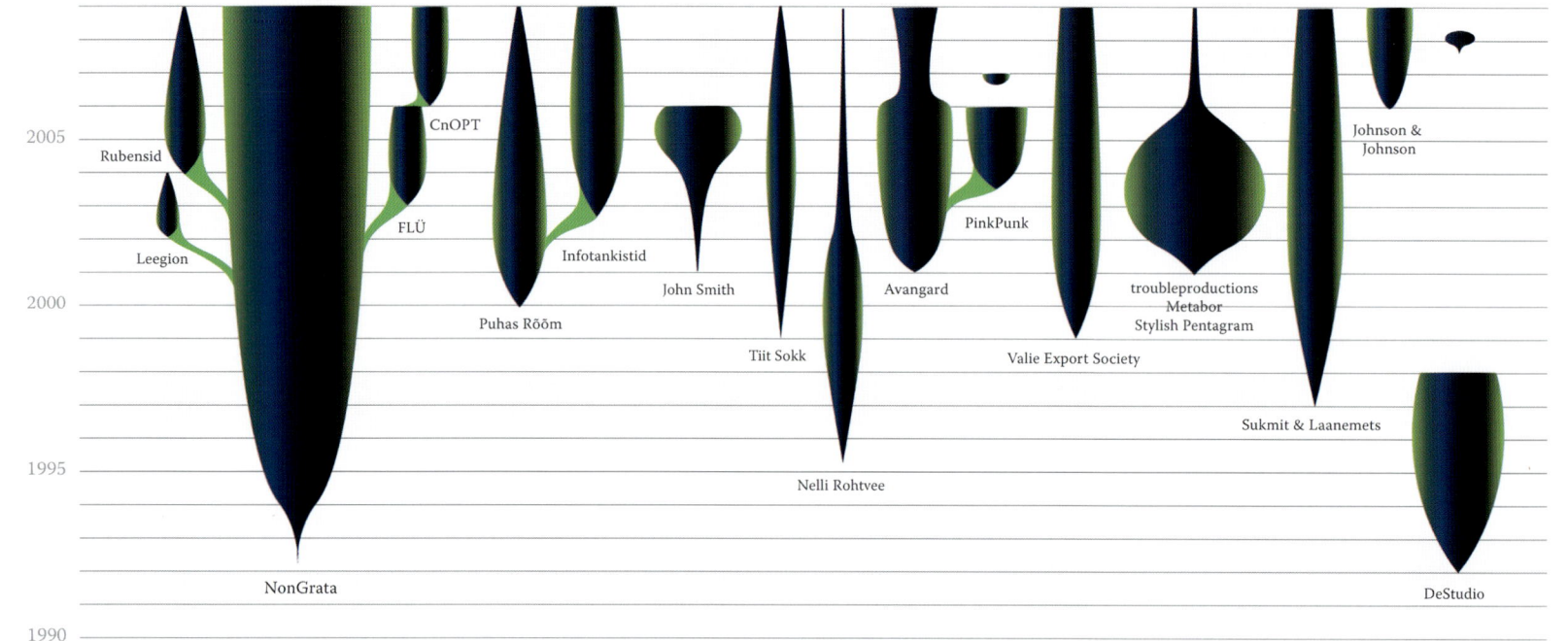

2005 — Rubensid, CnOPT, FLÜ, Infotankistid, PinkPunk, Johnson & Johnson
Leegion, Puhas Rõõm, John Smith, Avangard, troubleproductions, Metabor, Stylish Pentagram
2000 — Tiit Sokk, Valie Export Society
Sukmit & Laanemets
1995 — Nelli Rohtvee
NonGrata, DeStudio
1990

* this list remains open and will be continiouslycomplemented

Centre of Contemporary Art Estonia presents
"Appendages to history of Estonian art" 5th seminar:
"Groupings: exploring the possibilities for
collaborative practices in Estonian contemporary art"
7th Novembre 2008 TU Academic Library

KAASAEGSE KUNSTI EESTI KESKUS
CENTER FOR CONTEMPORARY ARTS, ESTONIA

11.00-11.15 Introduction
11.15-12.00 Anu Allas: Vanishing author and destroyed artefact.
12.00-12.45 Elnara Taidre: The role of fiction in collaborative practices

12.45-13.00 coffee break

13.00-13.45 Maarin Ektermann: Non Grata: Alternative practices as form of neo-tribalism
13.45-14.30 Airi Triisberg: Collective work, grass-roots democracy and visual forms of counterculture in contemporary Estonia

14.30- ... open discussion

Artist Groups:
Possibility of Collaboration in Contemporary Art of Estonia
Addenda to Estonian Art History

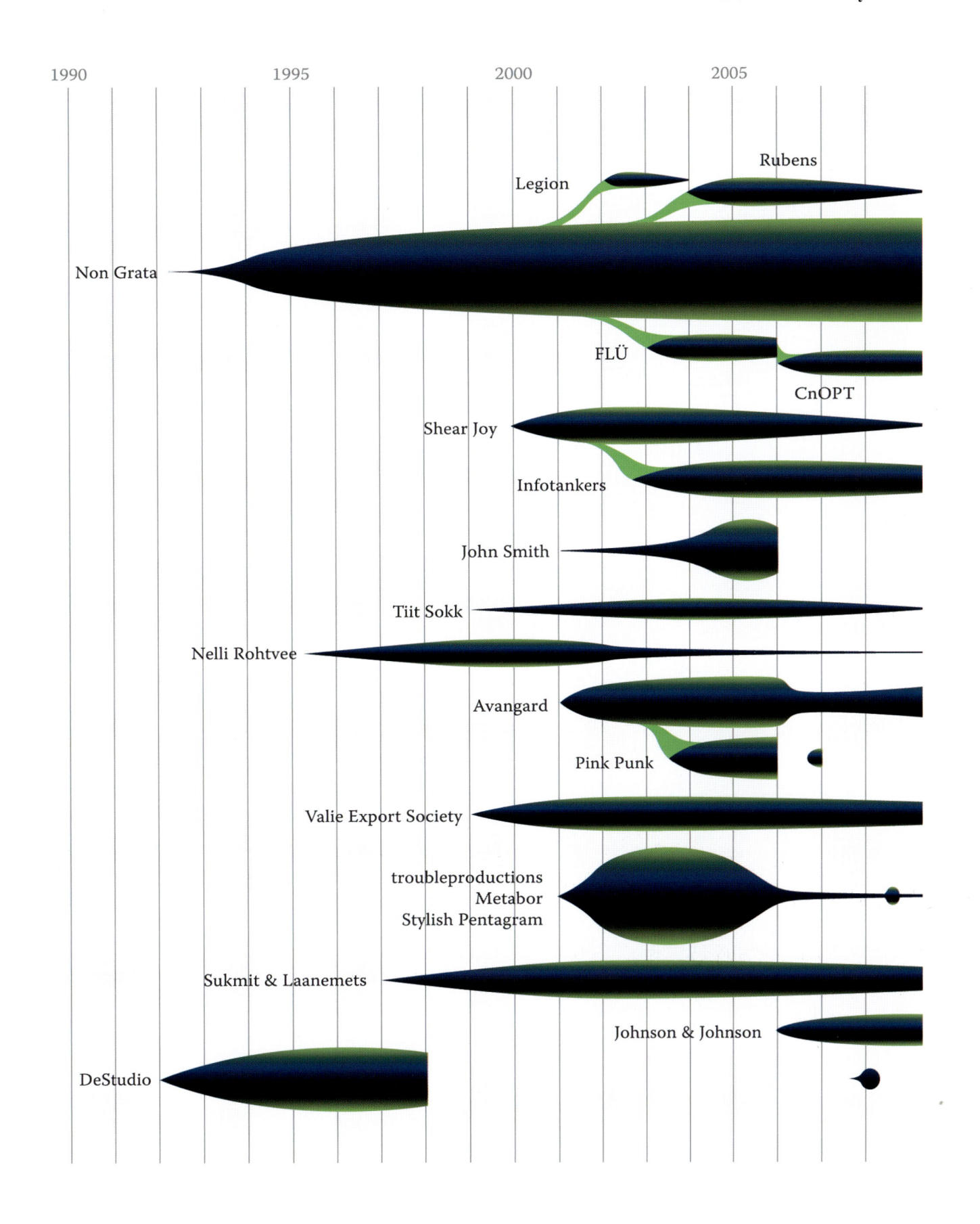

1990　　1995　　2000　　2005

Rubens
Legion
Non Grata
FLÜ
CnOPT
Shear Joy
Infotankers
John Smith
Tiit Sokk
Nelli Rohtvee
Avangard
Pink Punk
Valie Export Society
troubleproductions
Metabor
Stylish Pentagram
Sukmit & Laanemets
Johnson & Johnson
DeStudio

Graphs 189

2008 CeMM Annual Report ::
Lichtwitz – Büro für visuelle Kommunikation :: www.lichtwitz.com ::

The type of graphics applied in the charts and diagrams in the annual report of this biomedical research institute were developed in line with its corporate identity. The relevant items for the design were its logo, with the company's initials being arranged like a molecular formula, and the silhouettes of people drawn with texts that combine the nomenclature for proteins.

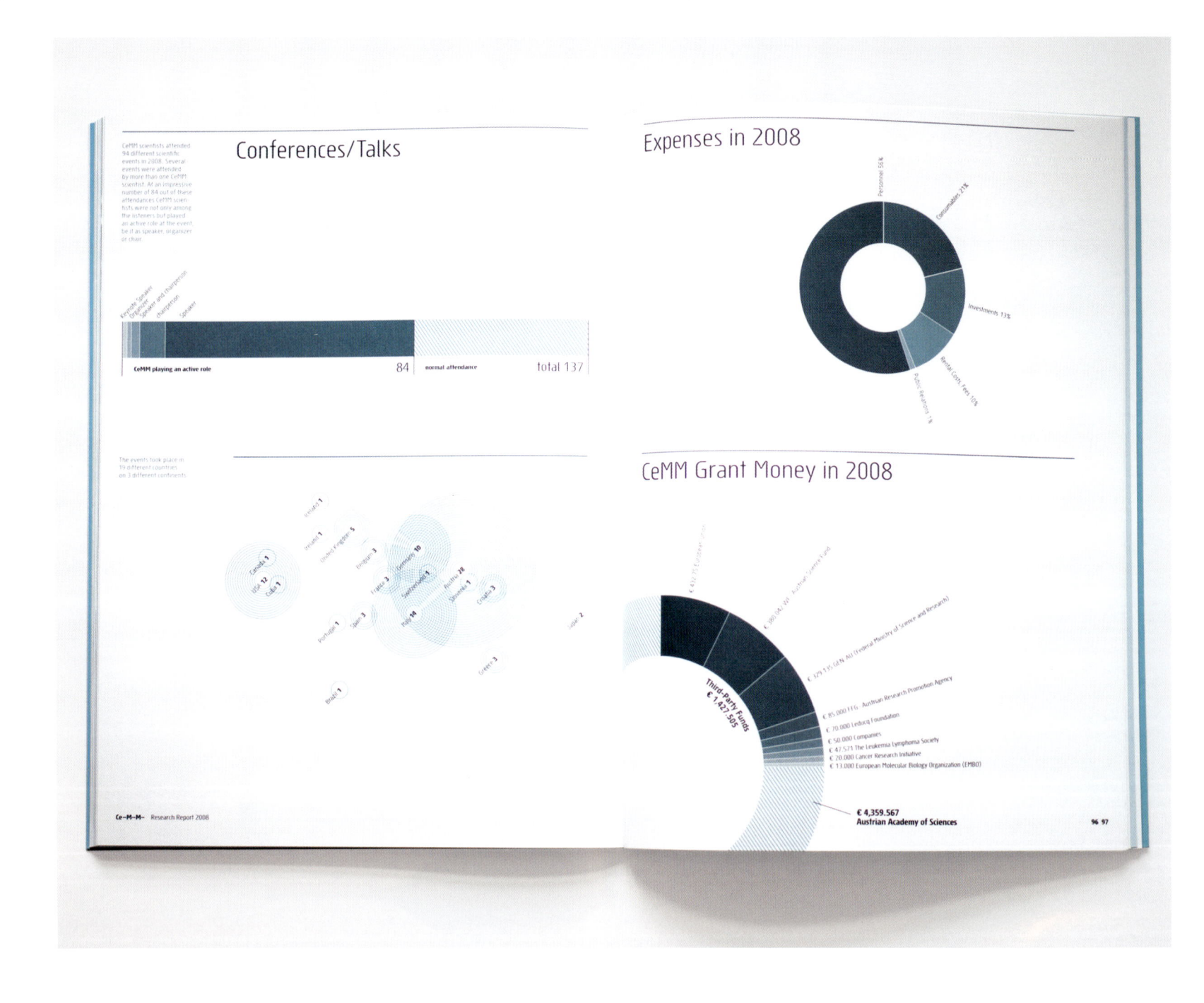

190 **Graphs**

Graphs | 91

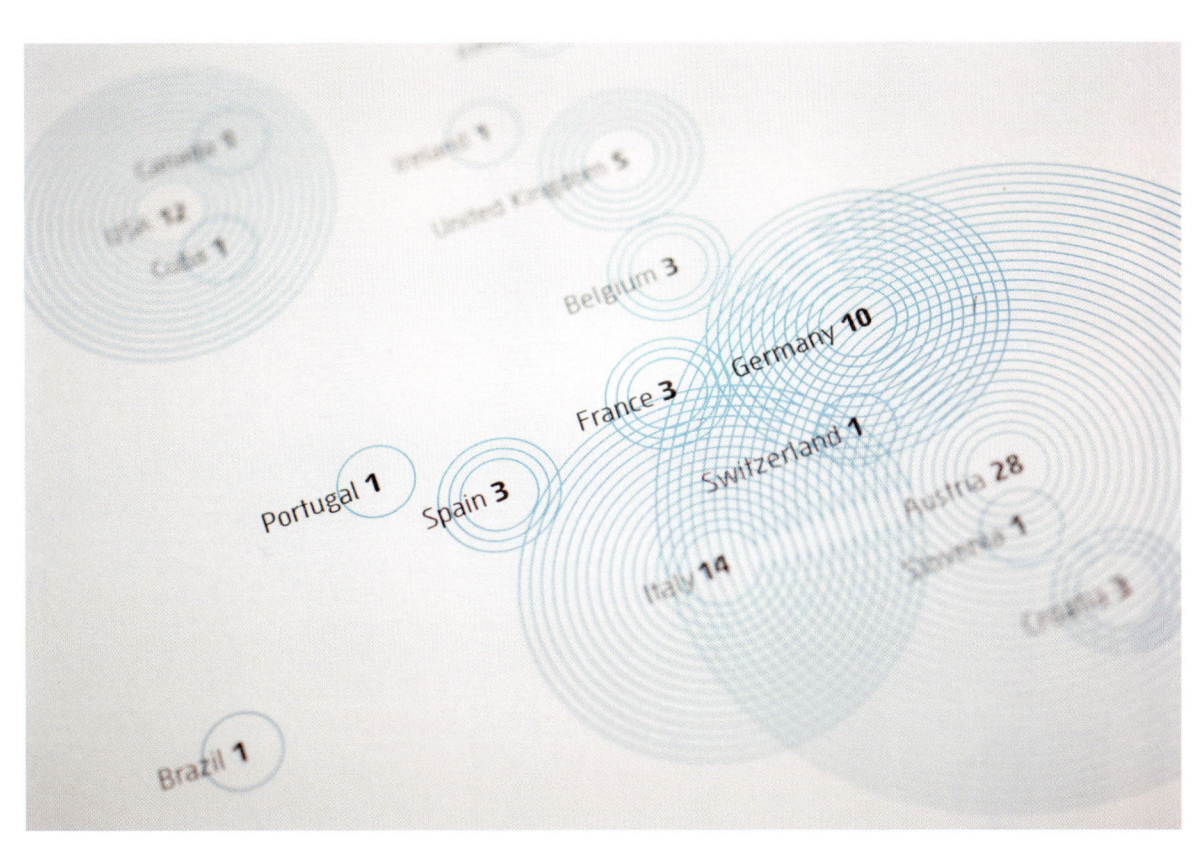

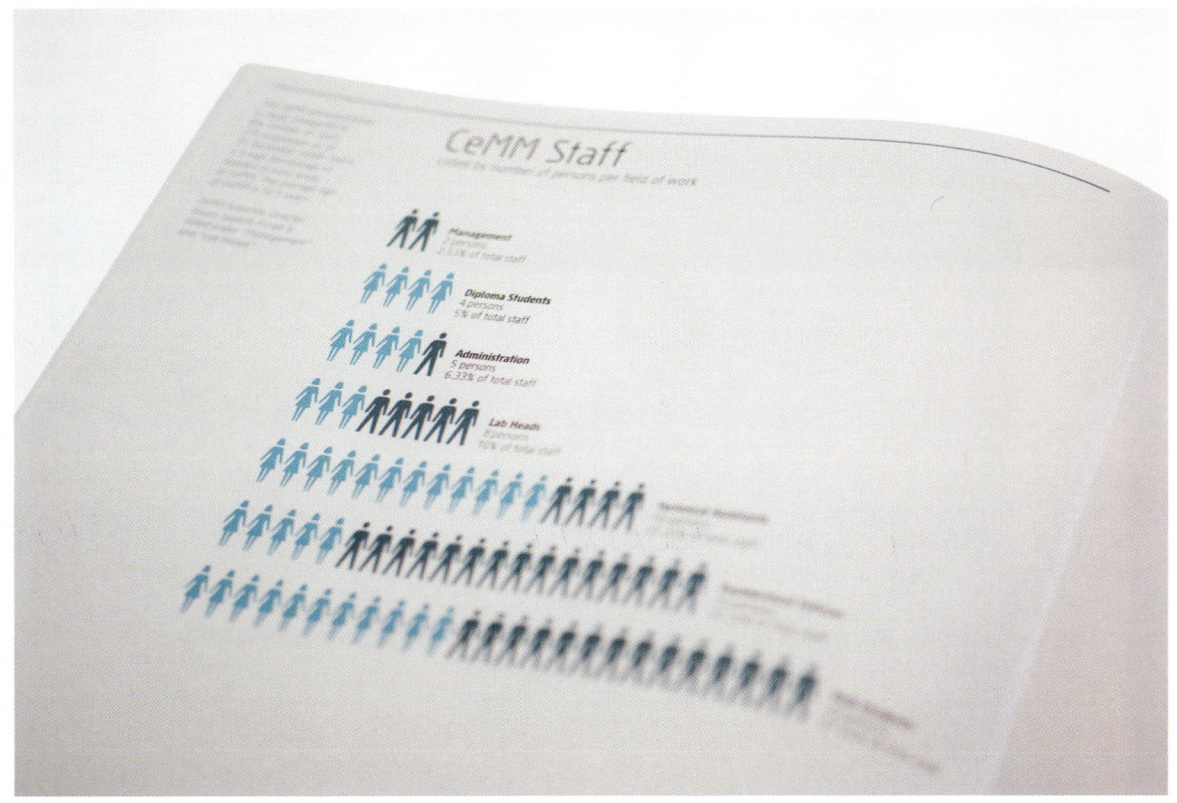

At Random? Networks and Cross-pollinations ::
LUST :: www.lust.nl ::

The Museum De Paviljoens staged an exhibition with eighty thousand folios forming a paper sculpture. These were created with a photocopier, with visitors being able to print their own copy of the exhibition catalog, using a program created specifically for this occasion, as well as posters, invitations, and texts taken from the exhibition. The piles of paper are a visual representation of the quantities of paper printed.

Graphs | 193

Teenage Pregnancy ::
Rose Zgodzinski :: www.chartsmapsdiagrams.com ::

This was a commission for *The Toronto Star*, a newspaper in Canada. Many readers of this type of paper just flick through the articles without reading them thoroughly. Designer Rose Zgodzinski was clever in the way she went about communicating the information, using the classic line graph (containing the information) as part of the illustration of a pregnant girl, which forms the main subject of the report.

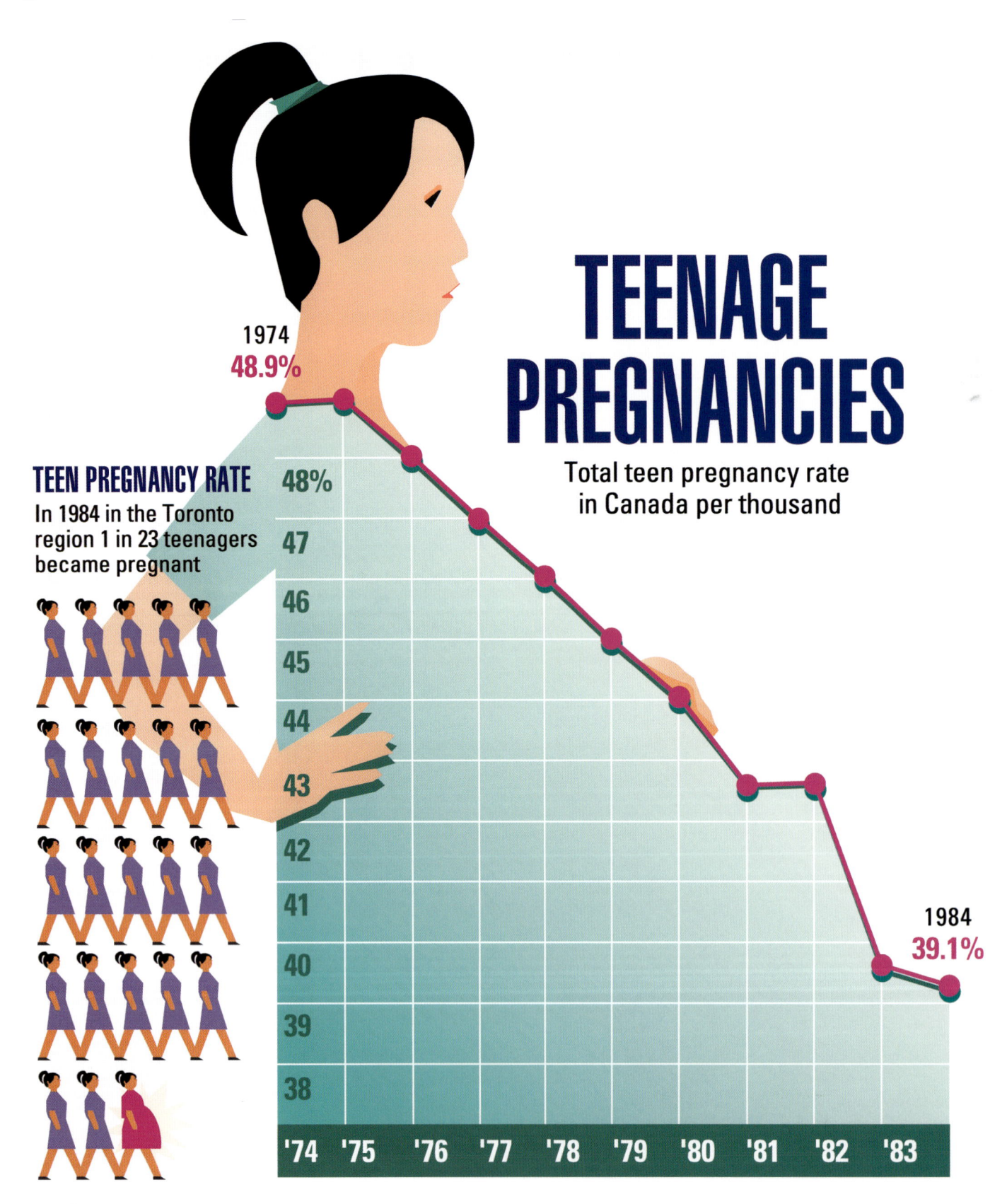

TEENAGE PREGNANCIES

Total teen pregnancy rate in Canada per thousand

1974
48.9%

1984
39.1%

TEEN PREGNANCY RATE
In 1984 in the Toronto region 1 in 23 teenagers became pregnant

'74 '75 '76 '77 '78 '79 '80 '81 '82 '83

194 Graphs

Access to Safe Drinking Water ::
Nathanaël Hamon/SLANG :: www.slanginternational.org ::

The infographics here show the percentage of the world's population that has access to drinking water. They have been divided into zones and each couple of glasses show the countries with the greatest and least amount of access. In this way, it is particularly easy to see the inequality that exists between the most developed and least developed countries, where the difference is so obvious that it is not a matter of seeing the glass half full or half empty.

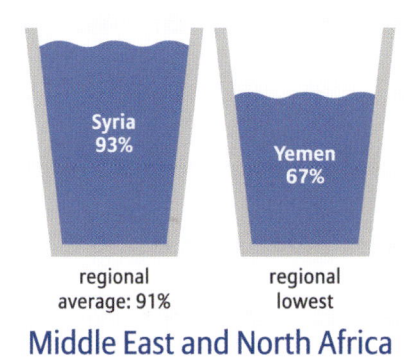

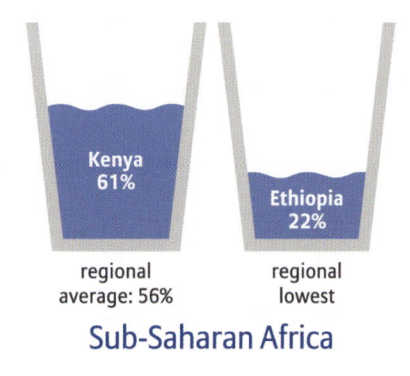

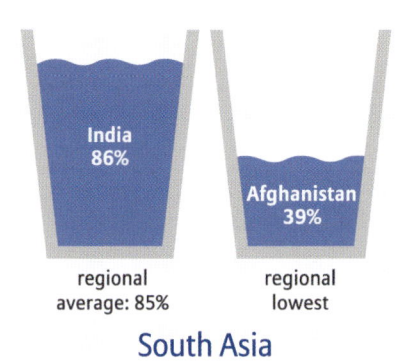

Access to Safe Drinking Water

Allianz

Percentage of population living within one kilometer from a source likely to provide 20 liters of safe drinking water per person per day

Middle East and North Africa
- Syria 93% — regional average: 91%
- Yemen 67% — regional lowest

Sub-Saharan Africa
- Kenya 61% — regional average: 56%
- Ethiopia 22% — regional lowest

East Asia
- China 77% — regional average: 78%
- Mongolia 62% — regional lowest

South Asia
- India 86% — regional average: 85%
- Afghanistan 39% — regional lowest

Latin America & Caribbean
- Brazil 90% — regional average: 91%
- Haiti 54% — regional lowest

Developed Countries
- USA 100% — group average: 99%
- Romania 57% — group lowest

Source: WHO / UNICEF Joint Monitoring Programme for Water Supply & Sanitation (statistics show situation in 2004)
The publication of this graphic is free of charge provided that users credit Allianz SE. Graphics are available in the media section of the Allianz Knowledge Partnersite: www.knowledge.allianz.com/en/media/graphics

CEOs Were Asked ::
Rose Zgodzinski :: www.chartsmapsdiagrams.com ::

This pie chart, which was commissioned by the *CEO Magazine*, has been converted into an illustration that draws its inspiration from the subject of the questionnaire: CEOs. Therefore, the pie chart doubles up as an office desk, the stage of the scene that is being depicted.

When it came to choosing colors, the designer decided just to use two in different proportions, so as not to add any more elements, but to keep the information nice and simple.

CEOs Were Asked

To whom does the most senior information technology official in your company report?"

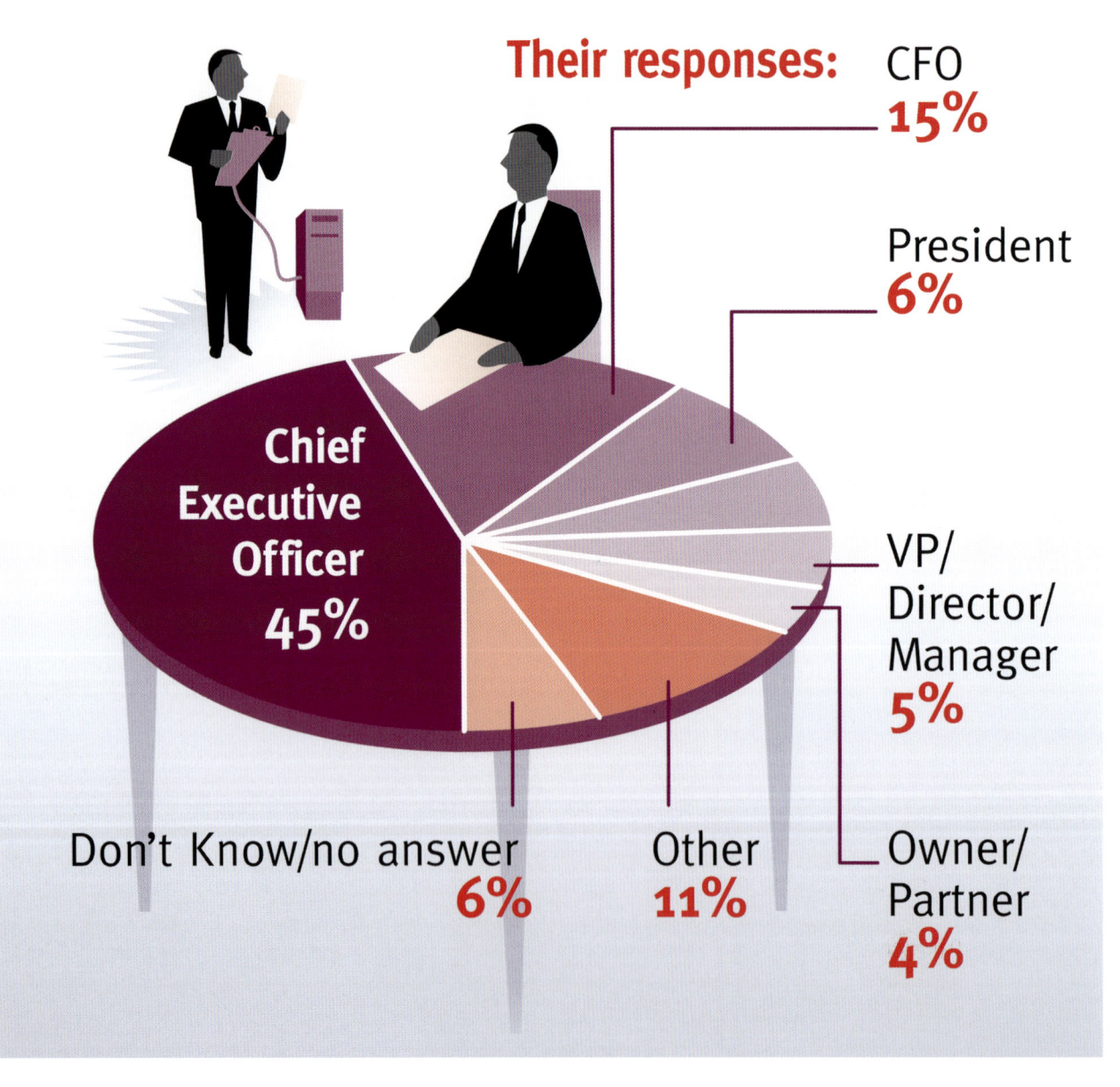

Their responses:

- CFO **15%**
- President **6%**
- VP/Director/Manager **5%**
- Owner/Partner **4%**
- Other **11%**
- Don't Know/no answer **6%**
- Chief Executive Officer **45%**

Grand ::
Letterbox :: www.letterbox.net.au ::

Grand is a publication that focuses on the relationships between typography and socio-economic conditions, based on a study recording all the fonts used within a heterogeneous kilometer in the city of Melbourne, Australia. The result, illustrated by this study specializing in typographic projects, draws attention to how trends evolve in Melbourne's visual environment.

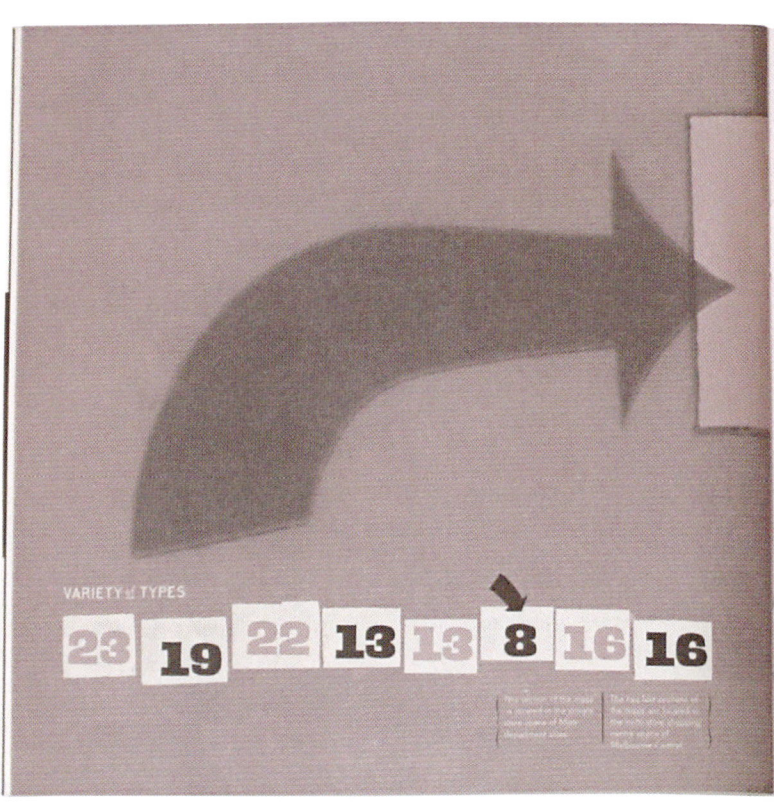

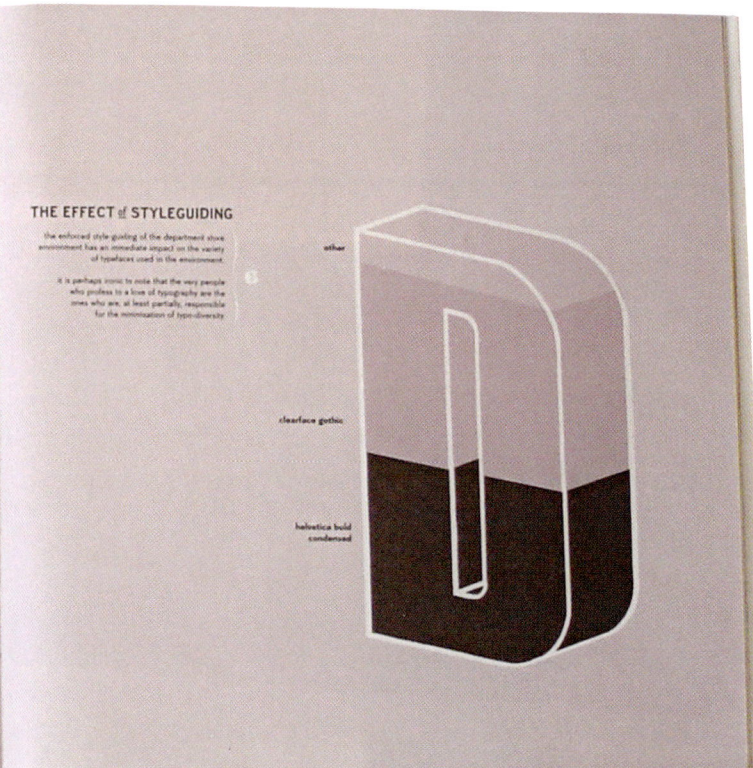

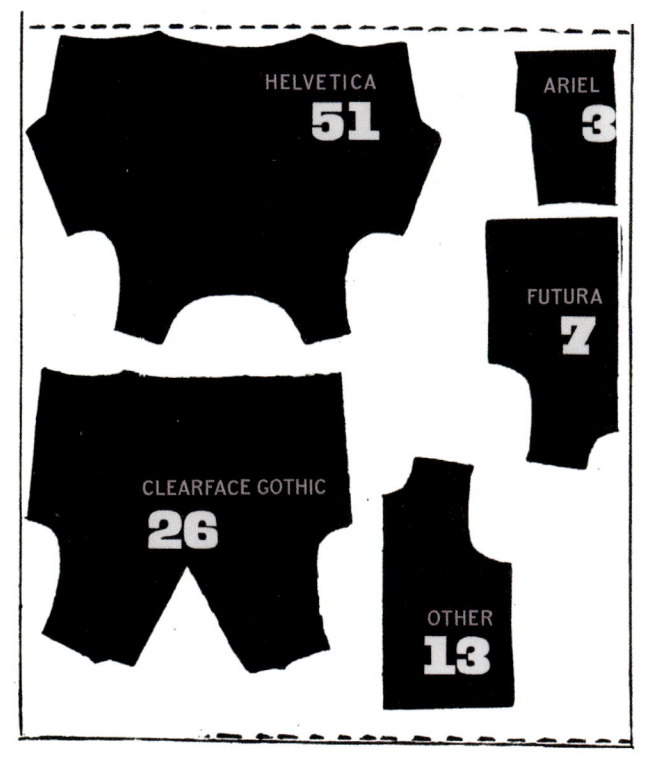

Pechos ::
Fábio Prata, Flávia Nalon/ps.2 arquitetura + design :: www.ps2.com.br ::

Breasts were the main subject of the first conference staged in Latin America on design and gender. As a subject for their poster, Fábio Prata, Flávia Nalon/ps.2 arquitetura + design developed this original poster where several graphs—whose colors and shape are reminiscent of a womans breasts—show the difference in the perception of various social, cultural, and behavioral aspects between the men and women of Brazil.

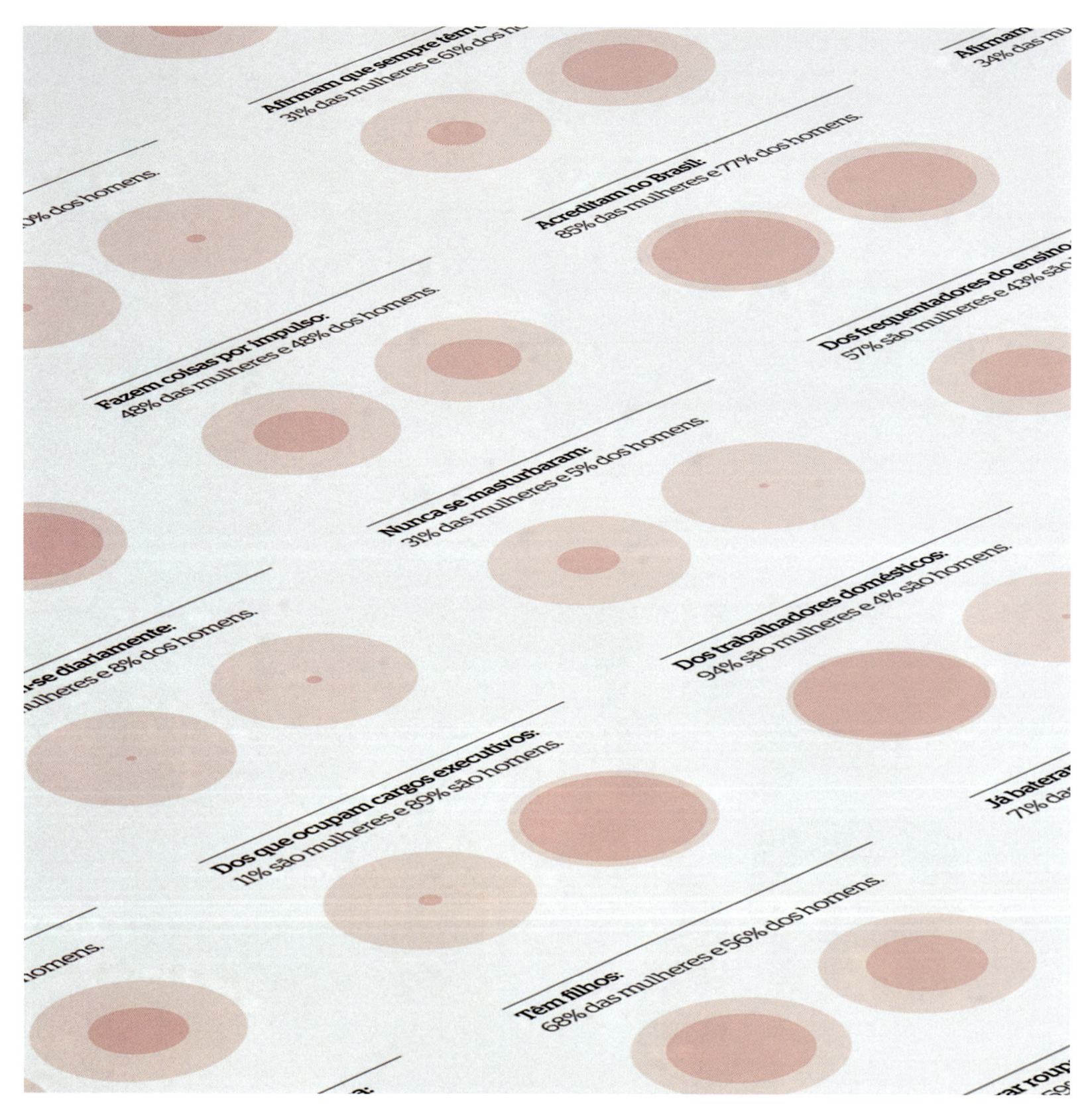

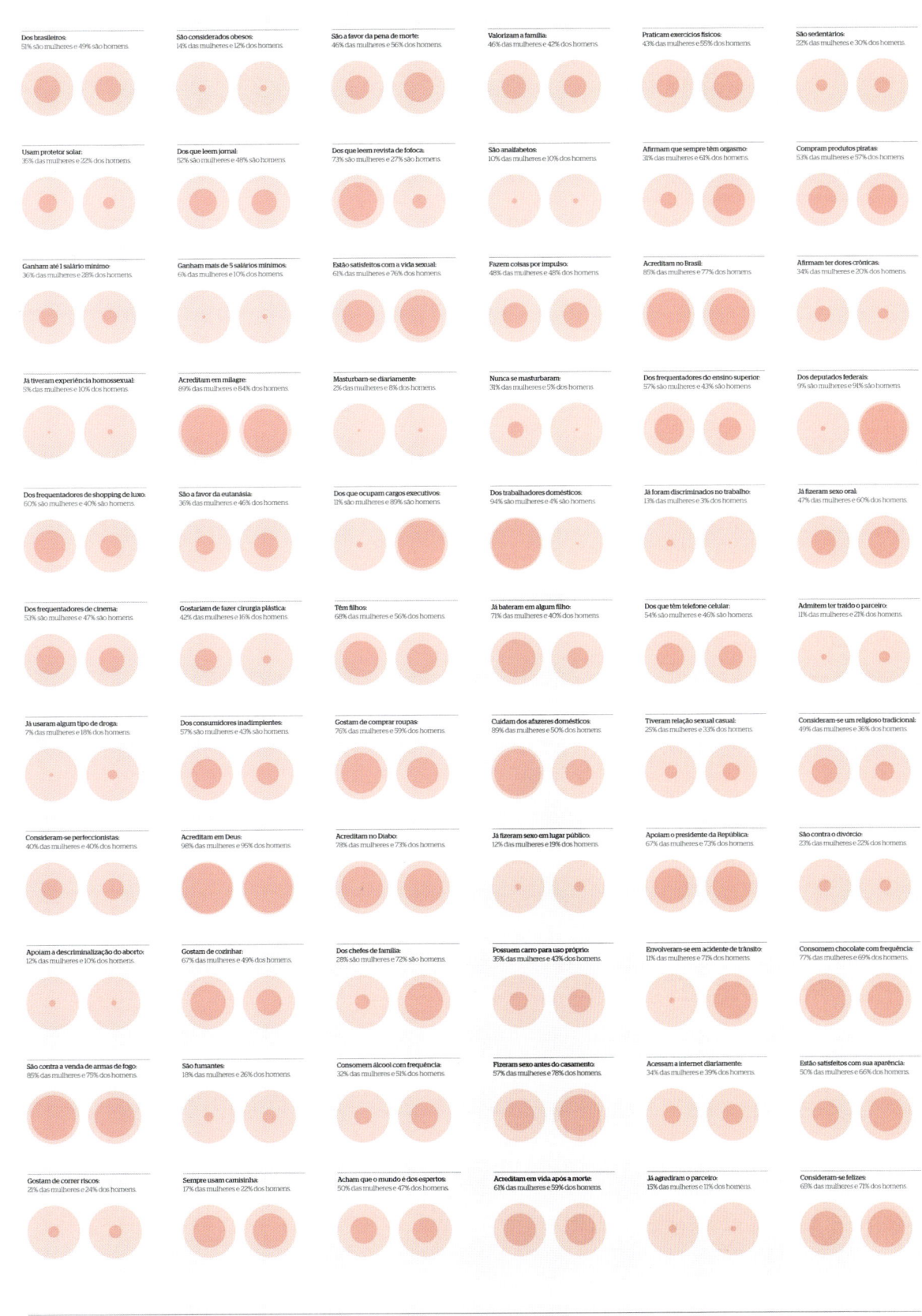

Dos brasileiros: 51% são mulheres e 49% são homens.	**São considerados obesos:** 14% das mulheres e 12% dos homens.	**São a favor da pena de morte:** 46% das mulheres e 56% dos homens.	**Valorizam a família:** 46% das mulheres e 42% dos homens.	**Praticam exercícios físicos:** 43% das mulheres e 55% dos homens.	**São sedentários:** 22% das mulheres e 30% dos homens.
Usam protetor solar: 35% das mulheres e 22% dos homens.	**Dos que leem jornal:** 52% são mulheres e 48% são homens.	**Dos que leem revista de fofoca:** 73% são mulheres e 27% são homens.	**São analfabetos:** 10% das mulheres e 10% dos homens.	**Afirmam que sempre têm orgasmo:** 31% das mulheres e 61% dos homens.	**Compram produtos piratas:** 53% das mulheres e 57% dos homens.
Ganham até 1 salário mínimo: 36% das mulheres e 28% dos homens.	**Ganham mais de 5 salários mínimos:** 6% das mulheres e 10% dos homens.	**Estão satisfeitos com a vida sexual:** 68% das mulheres e 76% dos homens.	**Fazem coisas por impulso:** 48% das mulheres e 48% dos homens.	**Acreditam no Brasil:** 85% das mulheres e 77% dos homens.	**Afirmam ter dores crônicas:** 34% das mulheres e 20% dos homens.
Já tiveram experiência homossexual: 5% das mulheres e 10% dos homens.	**Acreditam em milagre:** 89% das mulheres e 84% dos homens.	**Masturbam-se diariamente:** 2% das mulheres e 8% dos homens.	**Nunca se masturbaram:** 31% das mulheres e 5% dos homens.	**Dos frequentadores do ensino superior:** 57% são mulheres e 43% são homens.	**Dos deputados federais:** 9% são mulheres e 91% são homens.
Dos frequentadores de shopping de luxo: 60% são mulheres e 40% são homens.	**São a favor da eutanásia:** 36% das mulheres e 46% dos homens.	**Dos que ocupam cargos executivos:** 11% são mulheres e 89% são homens.	**Dos trabalhadores domésticos:** 94% das mulheres e 4% dos homens.	**Já foram discriminados no trabalho:** 17% das mulheres e 3% dos homens.	**Já fizeram sexo oral:** 47% das mulheres e 60% dos homens.
Dos frequentadores de cinema: 53% são mulheres e 47% são homens.	**Gostariam de fazer cirurgia plástica:** 42% das mulheres e 16% dos homens.	**Têm filhos:** 68% das mulheres e 56% dos homens.	**Já bateram em algum filho:** 71% das mulheres e 40% dos homens.	**Dos que têm telefone celular:** 54% das mulheres e 46% dos homens.	**Admitem ter traído o parceiro:** 11% das mulheres e 25% dos homens.
Já usaram algum tipo de droga: 7% das mulheres e 18% dos homens.	**Dos consumidores inadimplentes:** 57% são mulheres e 43% são homens.	**Gostam de comprar roupas:** 76% das mulheres e 59% dos homens.	**Cuidam dos afazeres domésticos:** 89% das mulheres e 50% dos homens.	**Tiveram relação sexual casual:** 25% das mulheres e 70% dos homens.	**Consideram-se um religioso tradicional:** 49% das mulheres e 36% dos homens.
Consideram-se perfeccionistas: 40% das mulheres e 40% dos homens.	**Acreditam em Deus:** 98% das mulheres e 95% dos homens.	**Acreditam no Diabo:** 78% das mulheres e 73% dos homens.	**Já fizeram sexo em lugar público:** 12% das mulheres e 59% dos homens.	**Apoiam o presidente da República:** 67% das mulheres e 73% dos homens.	**São contra o divórcio:** 23% das mulheres e 22% dos homens.
Apoiam a descriminalização do aborto: 12% das mulheres e 10% dos homens.	**Gostam de cozinhar:** 67% das mulheres e 49% dos homens.	**Dos chefes de família:** 28% são mulheres e 72% são homens.	**Possuem carro para uso próprio:** 35% das mulheres e 43% dos homens.	**Envolveram-se em acidente de trânsito:** 11% das mulheres e 71% dos homens.	**Consomem chocolate com frequência:** 77% das mulheres e 69% dos homens.
São contra a venda de armas de fogo: 85% das mulheres e 75% dos homens.	**São fumantes:** 18% das mulheres e 26% dos homens.	**Consomem álcool com frequência:** 32% das mulheres e 51% dos homens.	**Fizeram sexo antes do casamento:** 57% das mulheres e 78% dos homens.	**Acessam a internet diariamente:** 34% das mulheres e 39% dos homens.	**Estão satisfeitos com sua aparência:** 50% das mulheres e 66% dos homens.
Gostam de correr riscos: 21% das mulheres e 24% dos homens.	**Sempre usam camisinha:** 17% das mulheres e 22% dos homens.	**Acham que o mundo é dos espertos:** 50% das mulheres e 47% dos homens.	**Acreditam em vida após a morte:** 61% das mulheres e 59% dos homens.	**Já agrediram o parceiro:** 15% das mulheres e 11% dos homens.	**Consideram-se felizes:** 65% das mulheres e 71% dos homens.

Pechos

Percepção de diferentes aspectos sociais, econômicos, culturais e comportamentais, em comparação simples por gênero, entre mulheres e homens do Brasil.

Fontes: Os dados utilizados constam de levantamentos realizados entre 1999 e 2009, em diferentes amostragens de população e regiões brasileiras, pelo IBGE, Datafolha, Vigitel Brasil, Editora Abril, Sense, FSP-USP, Sistema PED, Marplan, Ibope, Uniad, Unesco, ONU, Qualibest, Fundação Carlos Chagas, FIBGE/PNAD's, Denatran, Fundação Getúlio Vargas, e entre funcionários e amigos da ps:2. Os dados foram adaptados e não têm qualquer precisão para fins oficiais.

Random Walk ::
Daniel A. Becker :: www.daniel-a-becker.de ::

There is something surprising in randomness as its existence is neither proven nor disproven, and yet it can be seen every day in science and also in daily life. This project simulates chance through the use of displays that are easy to understand; for example, true chaos and absolute order have been depicted harnessing an element of chance using purely numerical information and software simulations.

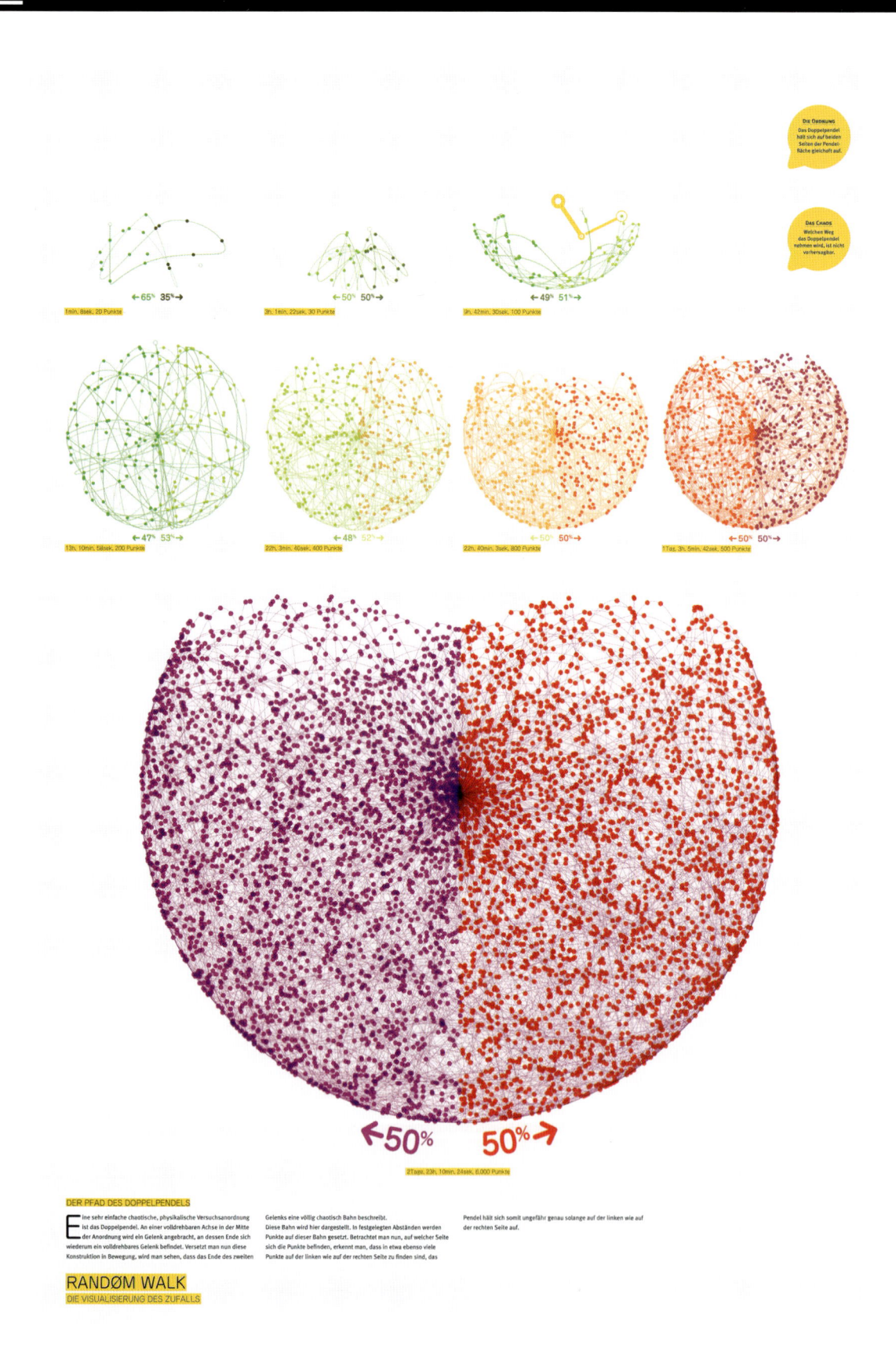

200 Graphs

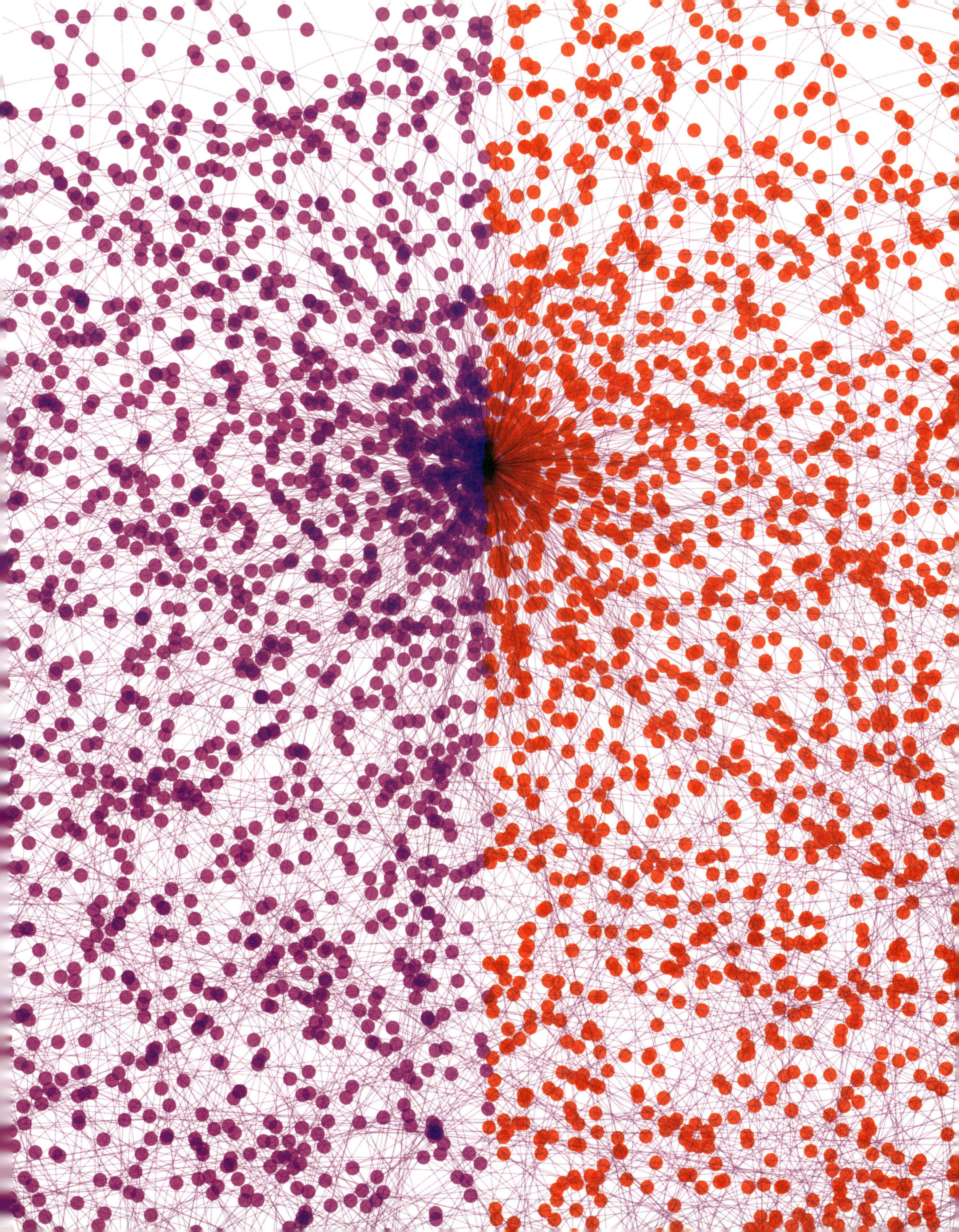

DIE ORDNUNG
Die Häufigkeit der Ziffern von 0-9 wird mit zunehmender Ziffernmenge immer ausgewogener.

DAS CHAOS
Verteilung, Häufigkeit und Abfolge der Ziffern in Pi unterliegen keiner Regelmäßigkeit.

1.000.000 STELLEN VON PI

Die Konstante Pi hat unendlich viele Nachkommastellen, wobei es keine bestimmte Reihenfolge in der Ziffernfolge gibt. Dennoch ist die Häufigkeit jeder Ziffer von 0 bis 9 – zumindest in diesem dargestellten Bereich bis 1.000.000 Stellen von Pi – recht ausgewogen. Für die Ziffern von 0 bis 9 werden Richtungen von 0° bis 360° festgelegt. Erscheint die 0, wird beispielsweise ein Strich mit der Gradzahl 0° gezeichnet. Am Ende des Striches beginnt wiederum der nächste Strich. Die Länge des Striches ist dabei bei jeder Ziffer gleich. Auf diese Weise entsteht ein Pfad, der sogenannte „Random Walk".

Die farbigen Flächen beziehen sich auf Abschnitte der Zahl Pi, die pro Schritt von 0 beginnend um jeweils 10.000 zunehmen. Diese Flächen legen sich um die äußeren Punkte des Random Walk. Man kann erkennen, dass mit zunehmender Größe immer rundere Formen entstehen. Die Häufigkeit der Ziffern von 0 bis 9 wird immer ausgewogener, je größer der betrachtete Zahlenbereich wird.

RANDØM WALK
DIE VISUALISIERUNG DES ZUFALLS

60 Felder, 100 Punkte

15 Felder, 100 Punkte

110 Felder, 200 Punkte

Die Ordnung
Die Anzahl von Trefferhäufigkeiten folgt der Poisson-Verteilung.

Das Chaos
Es gibt keine bewusste Steuerung der Verteilung der Zufallspunkte.

15 Felder, 50 Punkte

110 Felder, 1.000 Punkte

60 Felder, 200 Punkte

60 Felder, 500 Punkte

DIE POISSON-VERTEILUNG

Lässt man auf eine hingelegte Dartscheibe mit gleichgroßen Feldern Reiskörner rieseln und zählt anschließend, wie viele Körner jeweils auf den einzelnen Feldern liegen, stellt man nach einigen Wiederholungen eine gewisse Regelmäßigkeit in der Größe der Reiskornhaufen auf den Feldern fest. Diese Regelmäßigkeiten werden durch die sogenannte „Poisson-Verteilung" beschrieben. Mit ihrer Hilfe kann man die Wahrscheinlichkeit berechnen, auf wie vielen Feldern eine bestimmte Anzahl von Körnern liegen wird. Welches konkrete Feld eine bestimmte Menge an Körnern aufweisen wird, ist selbstverständlich nicht vorhersagbar.

Die Felder der Dartscheibe in der Mitte der Visualisierungen haben alle dieselbe Flächengröße. Darauf fallen zufällig Punkte, und es wird gezählt, wie viele Treffer auf jedes einzelne Feld gefallen sind. Diese Treffermengen werden durch die farbigen Blätter angezeigt. Je größer das Blatt, desto mehr Felder gab es beispielsweise, die die Treffermenge Eins aufweisen. Die Anzahl der Blätter zeigt die Anzahl der Treffermengen. Die graue Linie zeigt die errechnete Annahme nach der Poisson-Formel. Natürlich kommen Blätter und Linie nie ganz zur Deckung, da die Menge an Zufallspunkten sehr klein ist, aber man kann erkennen, dass die Simulation der Poisson'schen Annahme folgt.

RANDØM WALK
DIE VISUALISIERUNG DES ZUFALLS

Graphs 203

Impossibles possibles ::
Enric Jardí :: www.enricjardi.com ::

This is a joint project conducted by the Catalan designer Enric Jardí, winner of the National Culture Award, and the printing house Arts Gràfiques Orient. The project presents interesting charts regarding all kinds of details relating to paper, like the price of the sheet being printed, how much its consumption has increased per person over the past few years, or the drying time for the various types of paper.

Graphs 205

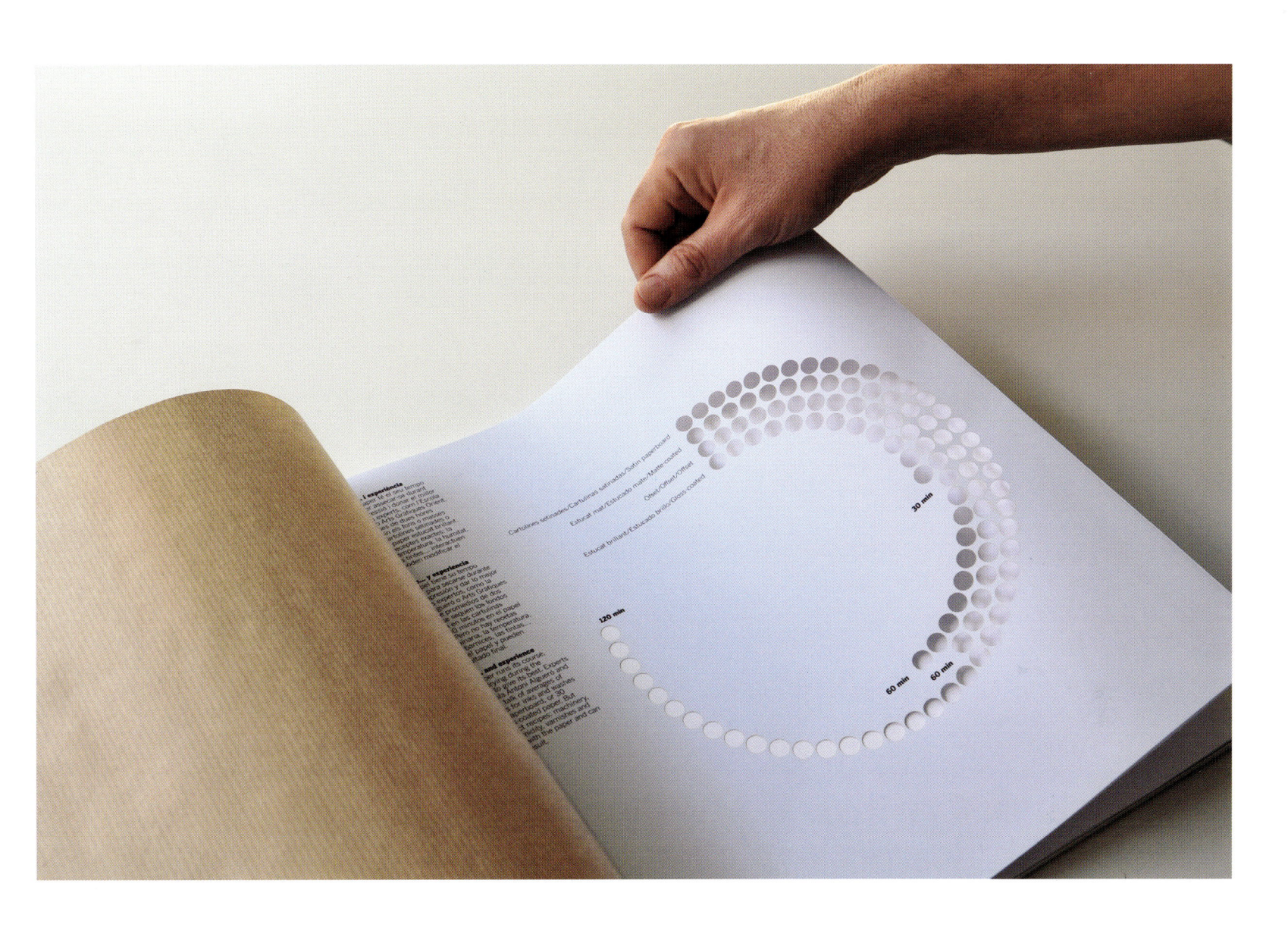

Nine Planets Wanted! ::
Zago :: zagollc.com ::

This is the booklet for an installation organized by the United Nations Program for Development on climate change and CO_2 emissions, in which the visitors could physically experience the quantitative information relating to this issue. The format of a newspaper was chosen to reflect the constantly evolving situation of the earth and to endow the message with a sense of urgency.

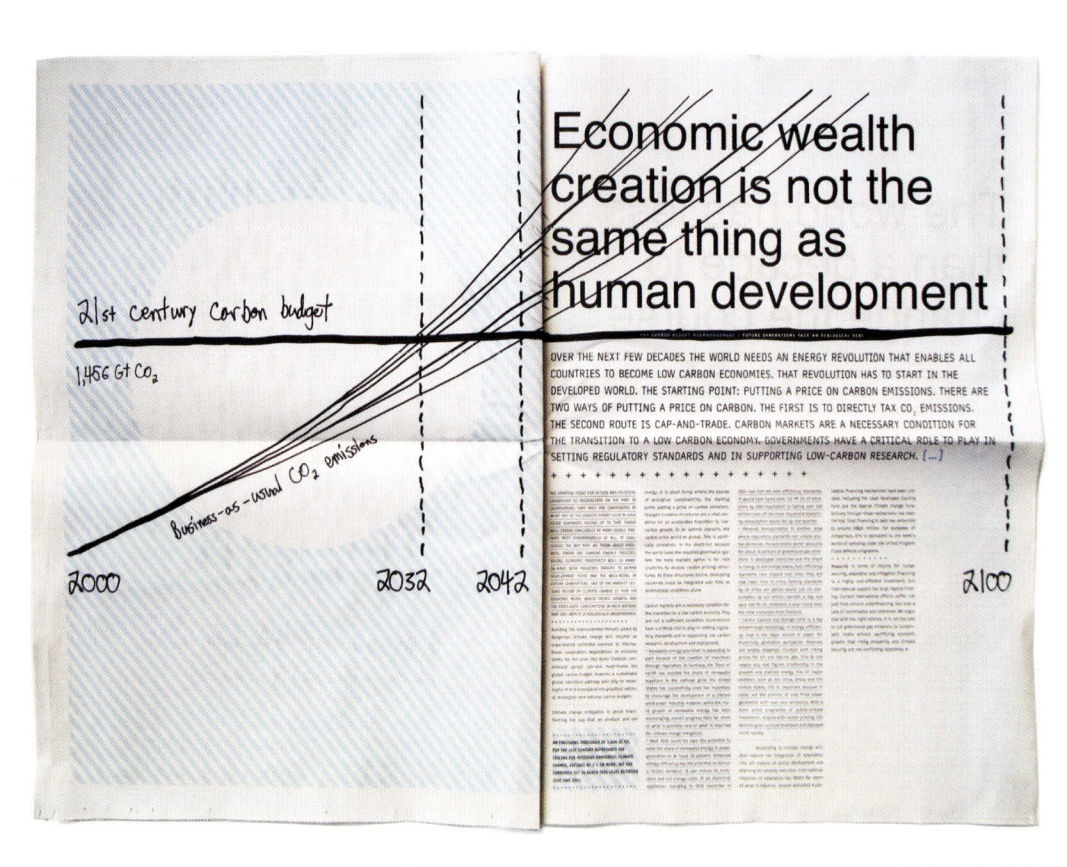

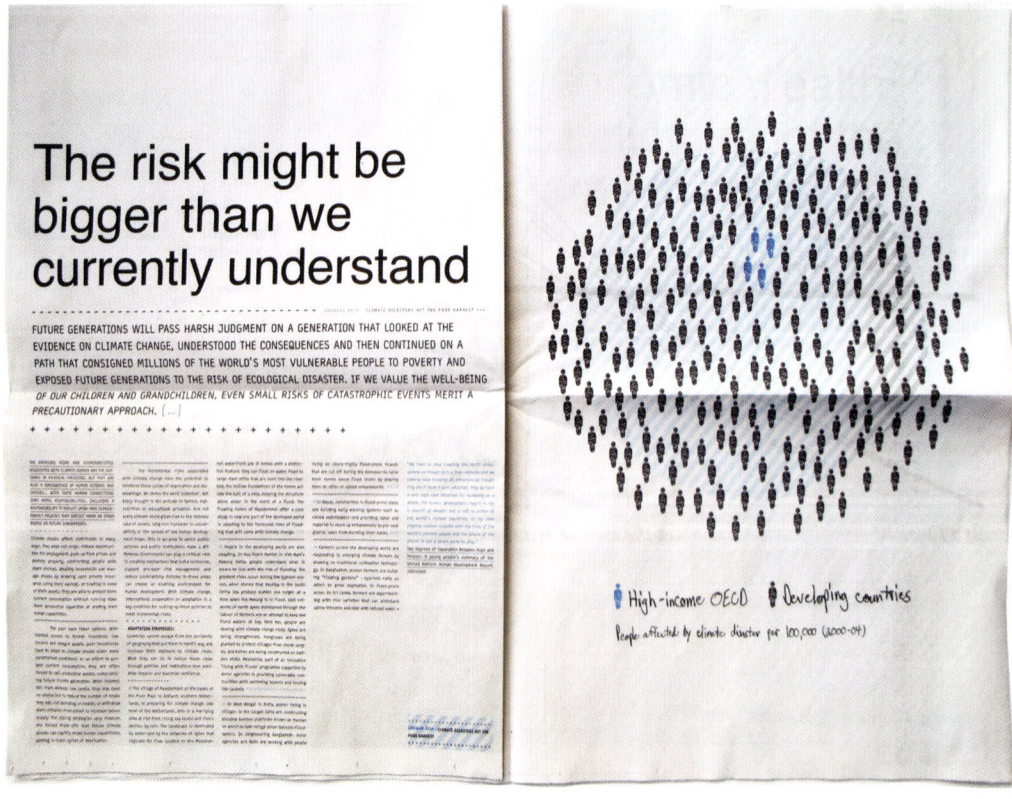

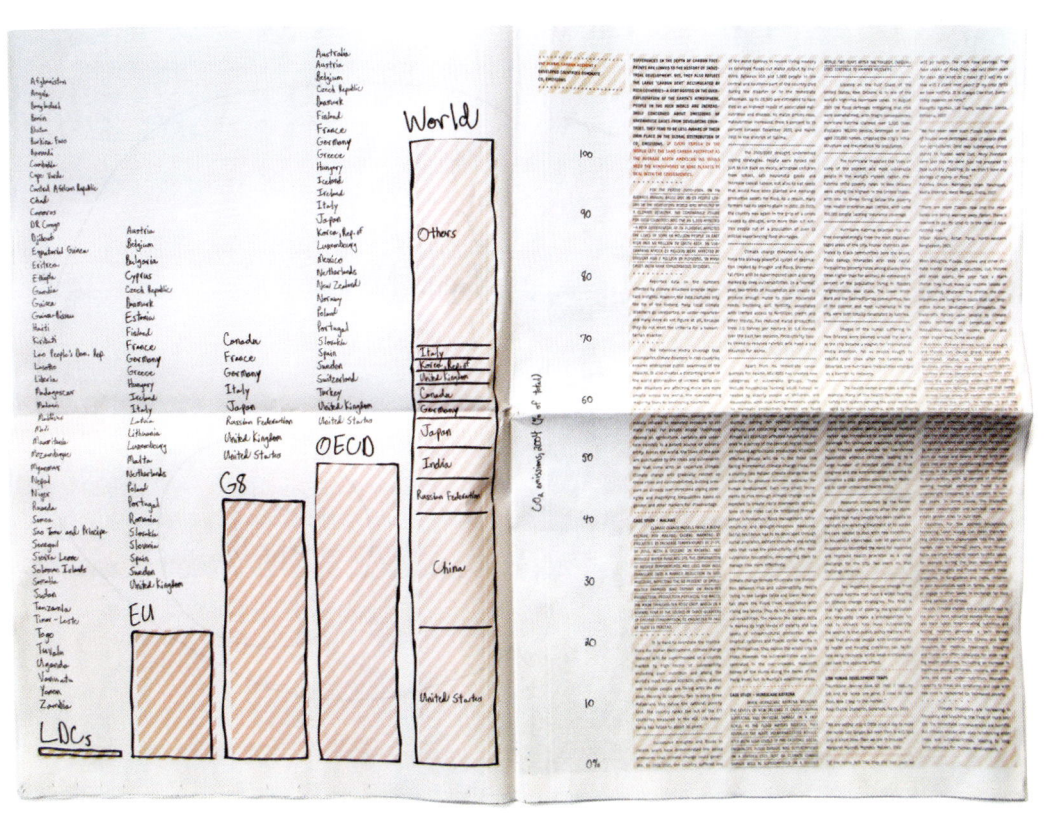

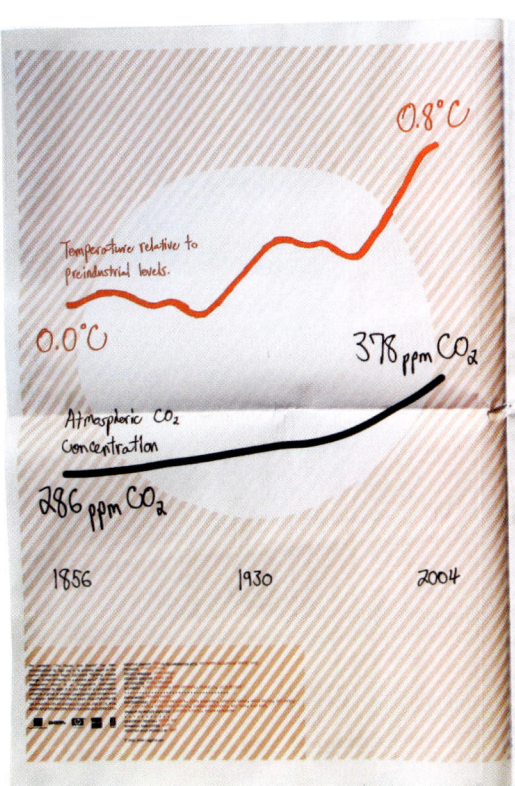

Climate change will not announce itself as an apocalyptic event

CLIMATE CHANGE WILL AFFECT RAINFALL, TEMPERATURE AND WATER AVAILABILITY FOR AGRICULTURE IN VULNERABLE AREAS. THE DANGER IS THAT EXTREME FOOD INSECURITY EPISODES WILL BECOME MORE COMMON. MAJOR KILLER DISEASES COULD EXPAND THEIR COVERAGE. RICH COUNTRIES ARE ALREADY PREPARING PUBLIC HEALTH TO DEAL WITH FUTURE CLIMATE SHOCKS. FOR POOR COUNTRIES IT IS MUCH HARDER; THEY NEED INTERNATIONAL SUPPORT TO ADAPT […]

Flocking Diplomats 01 ::
Catalogtree :: www.catalogtree.net ::

One day in 2006, information fell into the hands of the people at Catalogtree concerning parking fines that had not been paid by diplomats in New York. This was a Eureka moment that inspired them to create a series of award-winning posters. This, the first of such posters, shows all violations committed per hour (every hour from 1999 to 2002), plotted in relation to the position of the sun seen from Central Park.

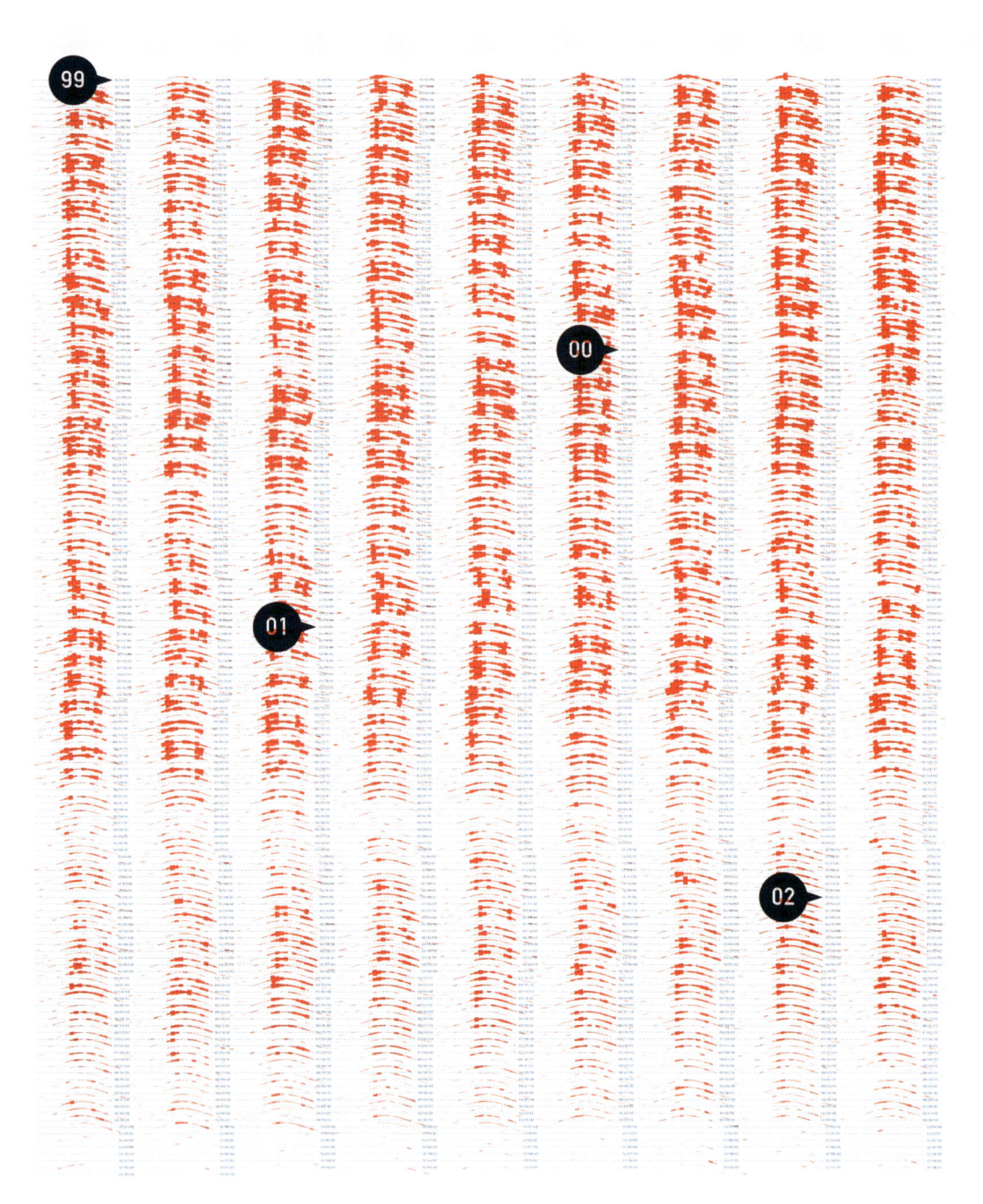

FLOCKING DIPLOMATS NYC 1999 – 2002

// VIOLATIONS/HOUR

Parking Violations by Diplomats / Hour in 1999 to 2002 in New York City. The violations are plotted in relation to the sun-position as seen from Central Park (LATITUDE 40° 47' N / LONGITUDE 73° 58' W).

ANNUAL TOTALS (YEAR: TOTAL (MAX / DATE))

1999: 42.542 (65 / 09-24) -- Security Council / Fifty-fourth Year, 4048th Meeting, Small Arms. Friday, 24 September 1999, 9.30 a.m.

2000: 38.338 (52 / 02-24) -- Security Council / Fifty-fifth Year, 4104th Meeting, The situation concerning the Democratic Republic of the Congo. Thursday, 24 February 2000, 11.30 a.m.

2001: 25.390 (56 / 02-12) -- Security Council / Fifty-sixth Year, 4276th Meeting, The situation along the borders of Guinea, Liberia, Sierra Leone. Monday, 12 February 2001, 3 p.m.

2002: 12.703 (33 / 04-23) -- Security Council / Fifty-seventh year, 4517th Meeting, The situation in Angola. Tuesday, 23 April 2002, 10.30 a.m.

SOURCES

- Based on data from: Ray Fisman and Edward Miguel, "Corruption, Norms and Legal Enforcement: Evidence from Diplomatic Parking Tickets", forthcoming, December 2007, Journal of Political Economy.
- Daylight Saving Time: http://sunearth.gsfc.nasa.gov/eclipse/SEhelp/daylightsaving.html
- Sun-position (method of calculation): http://answers.google.com/answers/threadview?id=782886 (L. Flores)
- Time of sunrise and dawn: http://aa.usno.navy.mil/data/docs/RS_OneYear.php
- New York City Department of Finance

DATA MINING / SCRIPTING / DESIGN

Catalogtree, january 2008

printed at Plaatsmaken, Arnhem

A Weird and Wonderful Guide to Amsterdam ::
Lava Amsterdam :: www.lava.nl ::

September is the month of love in Amsterdam. And in the months of love, there is nothing better than having company. For this reason, in this month's edition of this particular travel guide, *le cool* informs the singletons among its readership of the best places in the city to find a partner, according to the statistics. Data for which the Lava team found the perfect illustration in this beautiful romantic cake.

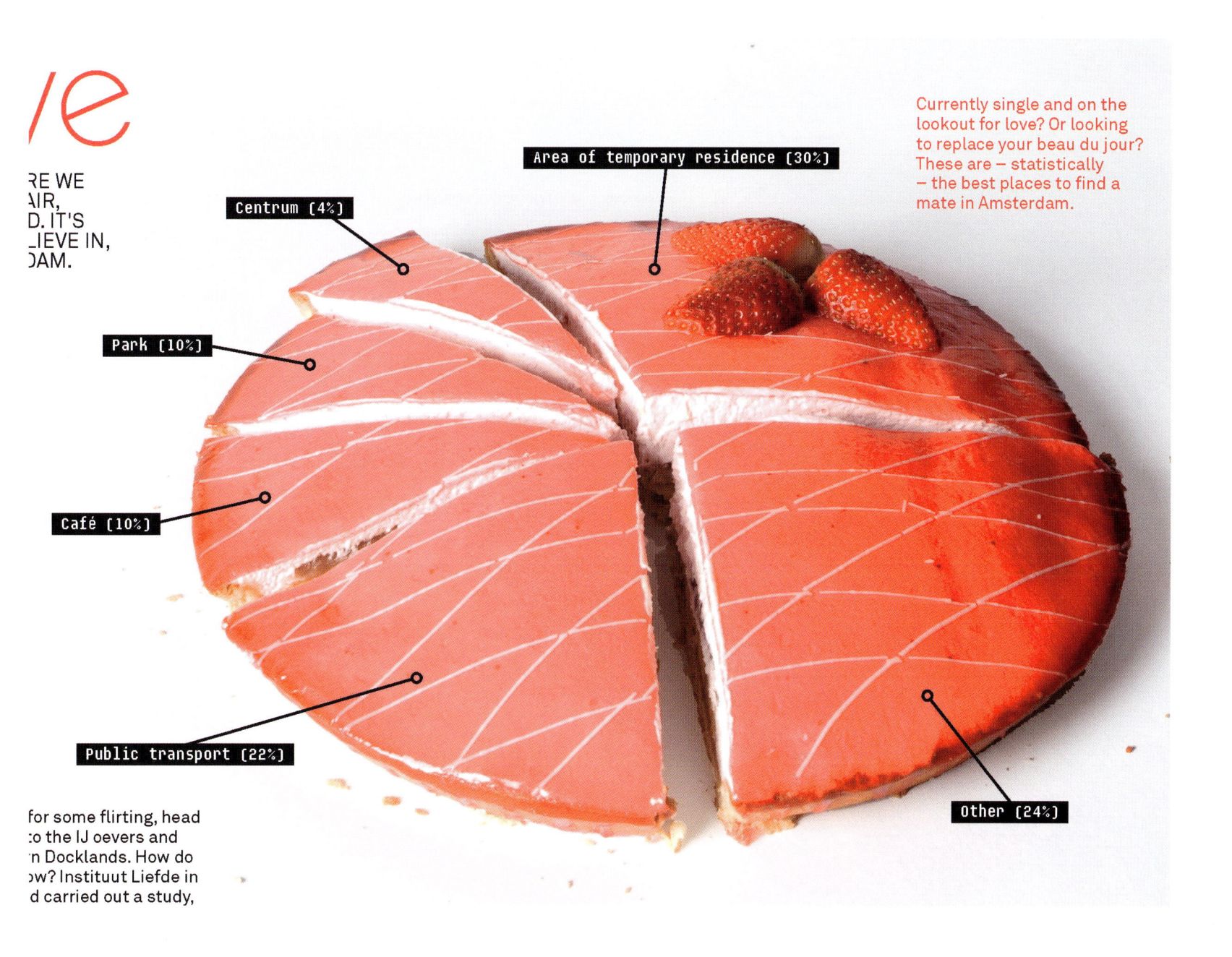

Currently single and on the lookout for love? Or looking to replace your beau du jour? These are — statistically — the best places to find a mate in Amsterdam.

- Area of temporary residence (30%)
- Centrum (4%)
- Park (10%)
- Café (10%)
- Public transport (22%)
- Other (24%)

Graphs 209

Interwined Histories ::
Abraham Ornelas, Aarón Gutiérrez, Julia Cerrud/Amorphica Design Research Office :: www.amorphica.com

The sense of disorientation experienced when going through a maze was used as a starting point to represent the responses collected for an urban study. Therefore a vertical axis has been incorporated into the graph to measure the time thanks to which positive and negative responses can be recorded, in keeping with historic trends. Thus, it is possible to see how the interrelationships successively come together, become entangled and then separate again.

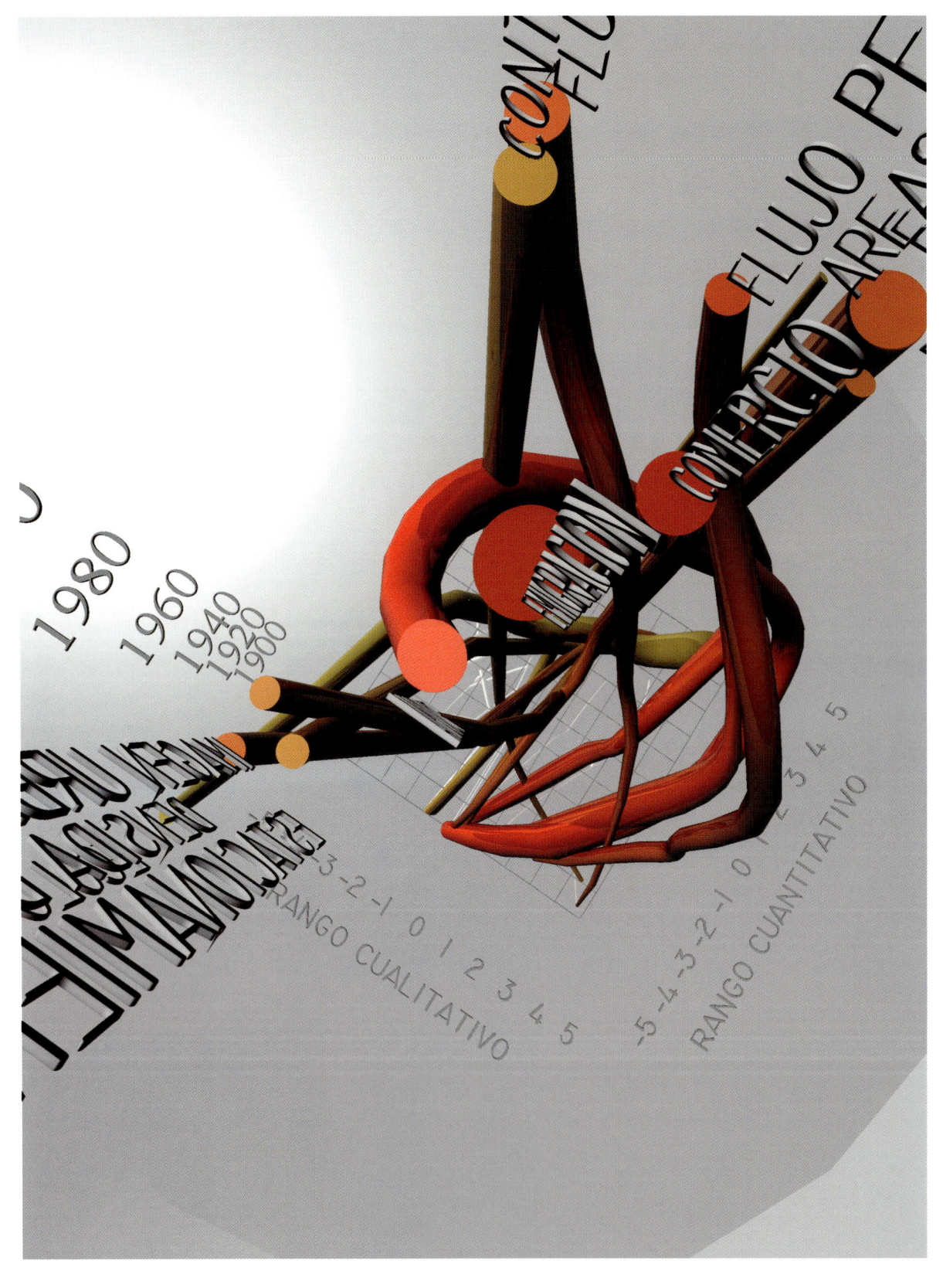

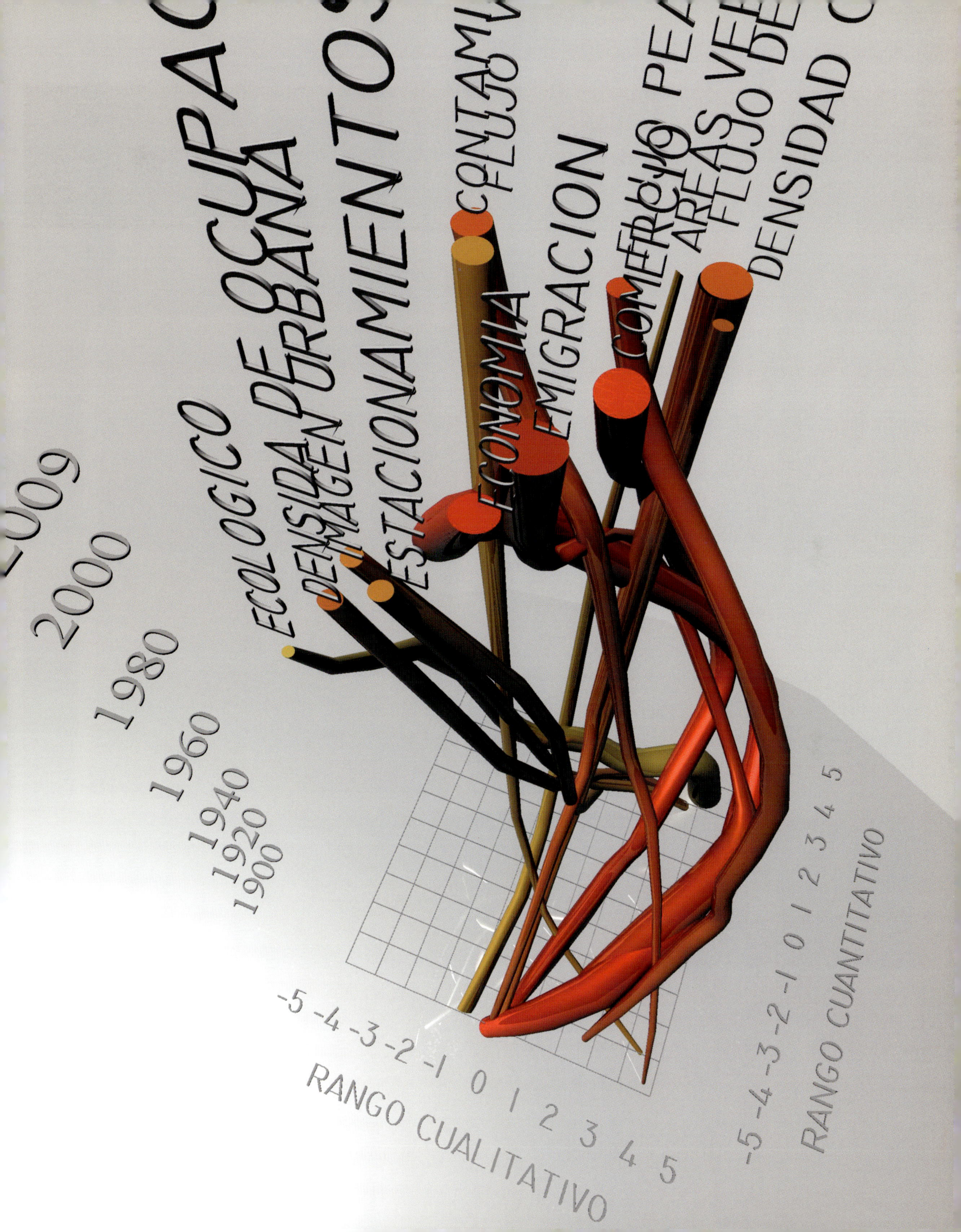

ECOLOGICO
IMAGEN URBANA
ESTACIONAMIENTOS
ECONOMIA
EMIGRACION
COMERCIO
DENSIDAD
2000
1980
1960
1940
1920
1900
-5 -4 -3 -2 -1 0 1 2 3 4 5
RANGO CUALITATIVO
-5 -4 -3 -2 -1 0 1 2 3 4 5
RANGO CUANTITATIVO

2003-2008 Kunsthaus Graz Annual Report ::
Lichtwitz – Büro für visuelle Kommunikation :: www.lichtwitz.com ::

The yearbook was edited on the occasion of the fifth anniversary of this space reserved for art exhibitions, which included all the projects exhibited to date—presented in the form of short reports— along with information about the place. To make it visually attractive, a bright color (fluorescent orange) was used, together with compelling graphics, like human figures instead of the typical bars of a chart.

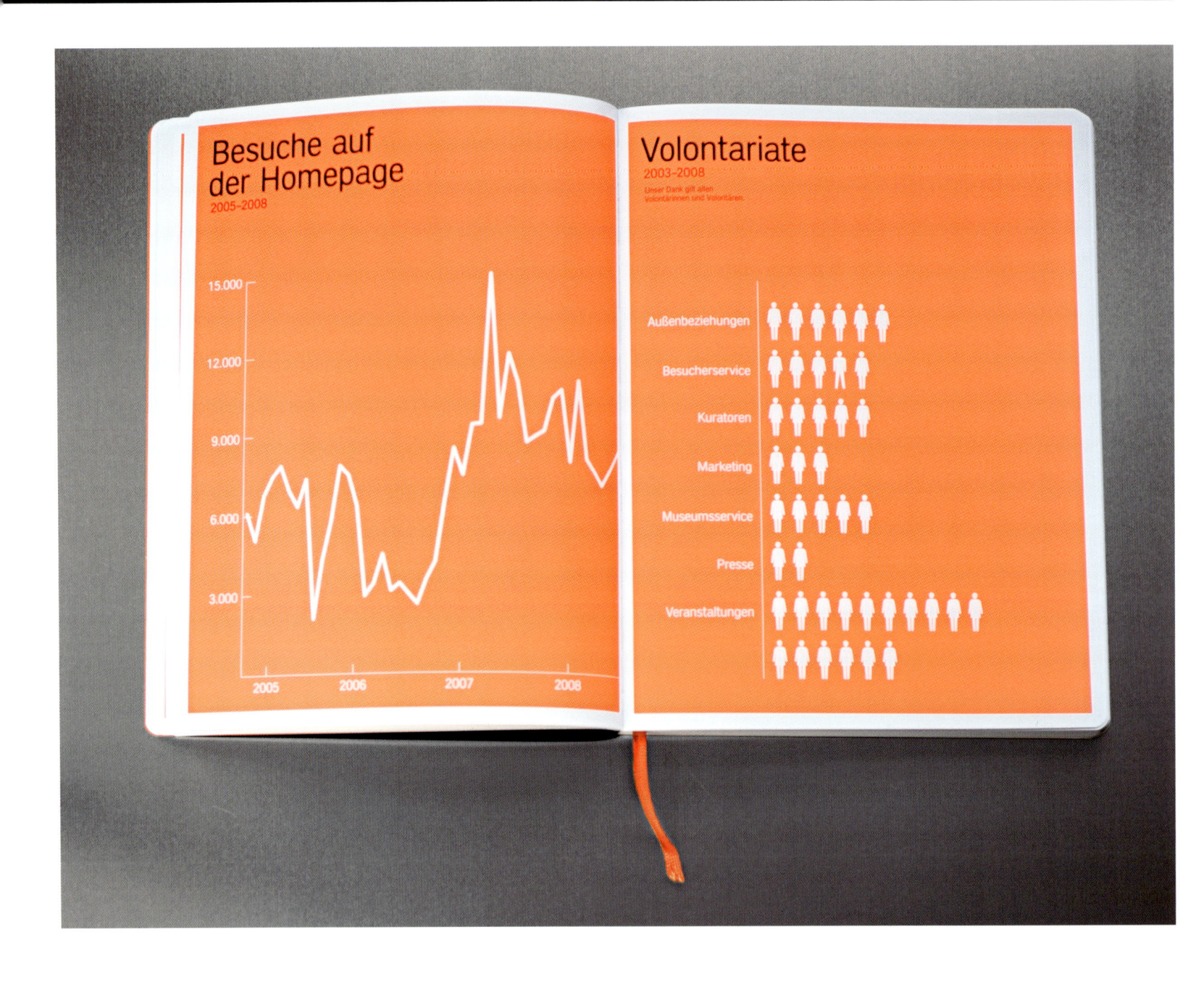

women'secret franchise book ::
Cla-se :: www.cla-se.com ::

These charts for women'secret form part of a book-object that summarizes all aspects of the company. The outside is completely white: it is only when the pages are opened that a world full of color is revealed reflecting the true spirit of the brand. The different colors help the designers distinguish the graph's variables and have the added benefit of making the chart easy to read.

Turnover: forecast 2005 – 2010

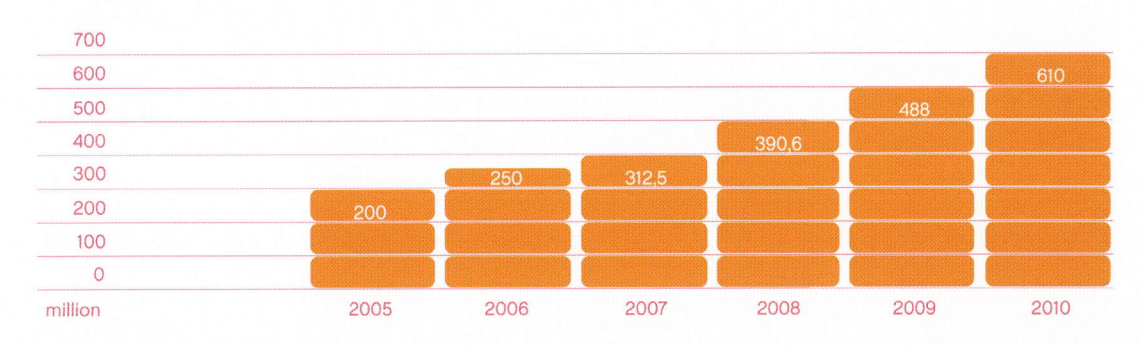

million	2005	2006	2007	2008	2009	2010
	200	250	312,5	390,6	488	610

Franchises: a unique model

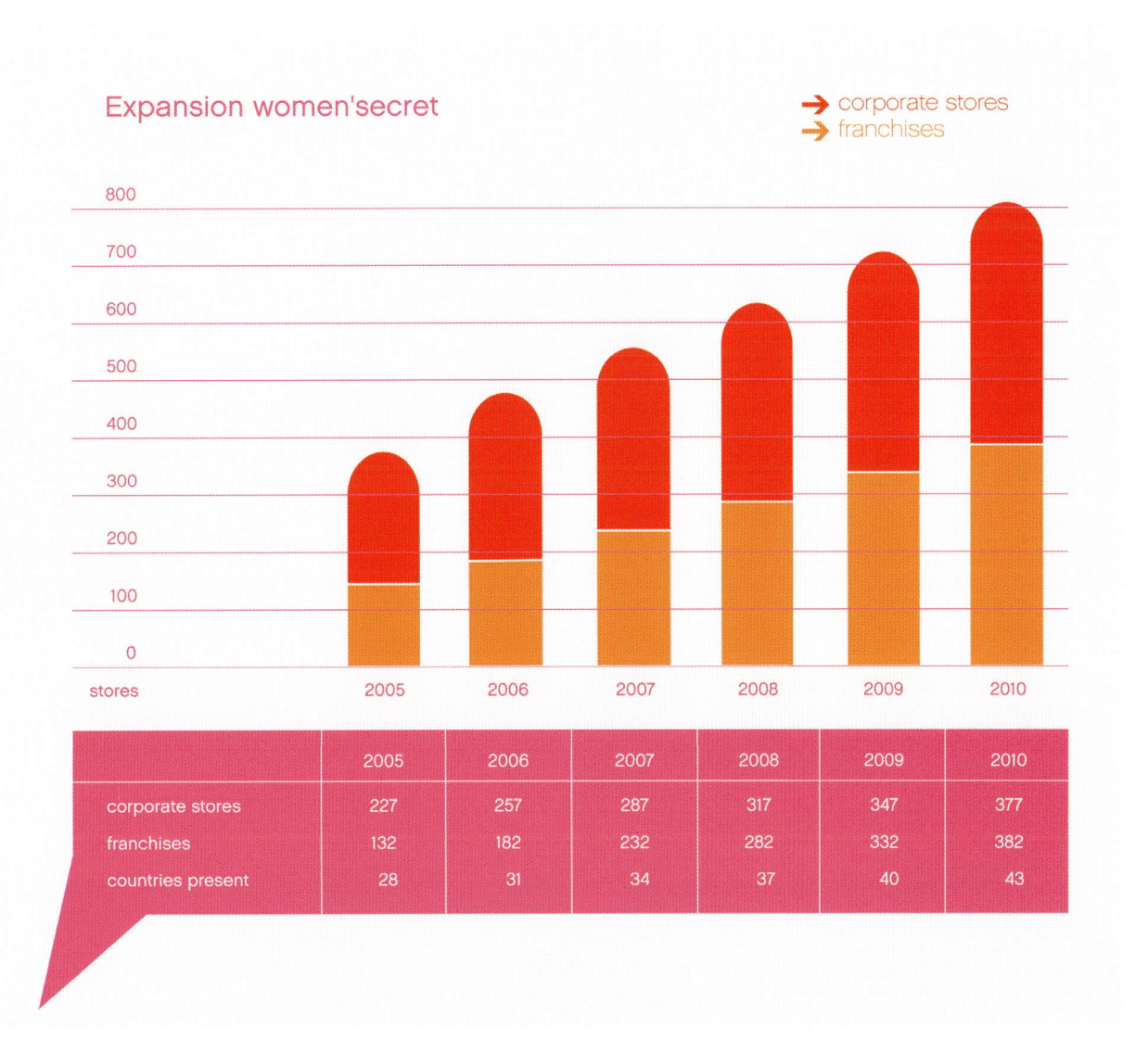

Expansion women'secret

→ corporate stores
→ franchises

	2005	2006	2007	2008	2009	2010
corporate stores	227	257	287	317	347	377
franchises	132	182	232	282	332	382
countries present	28	31	34	37	40	43

Graphs

Infographiti, Birthday Expectancy ::
Toko :: www.toko.nu ::

Under the name of Graphiti, this design studio, currently operating out of Sydney, Australia, explores the idea of the graph as an abstract work of art, in which the boundaries of art, science, research, and graphic design are constantly being challenged. This graph-installation shows the enormous difference that exists between countries with a greater or lesser life expectancy (Macao and Swaziland, respectively).

Graphs 215

Design Atlas for Global Shoes ::
LUST :: www.lust.nl ::

This is an experiment entailing the design of a brand using a different approach from the one usually found in marketing or communication strategies. The starting point was a shop window displaying sports shoes, in which each brand was assigned a different color. Various factors, such as country of manufacture or market share, were then examined, giving rise to a complex graphic analysis of the market strategies typical of this sector.

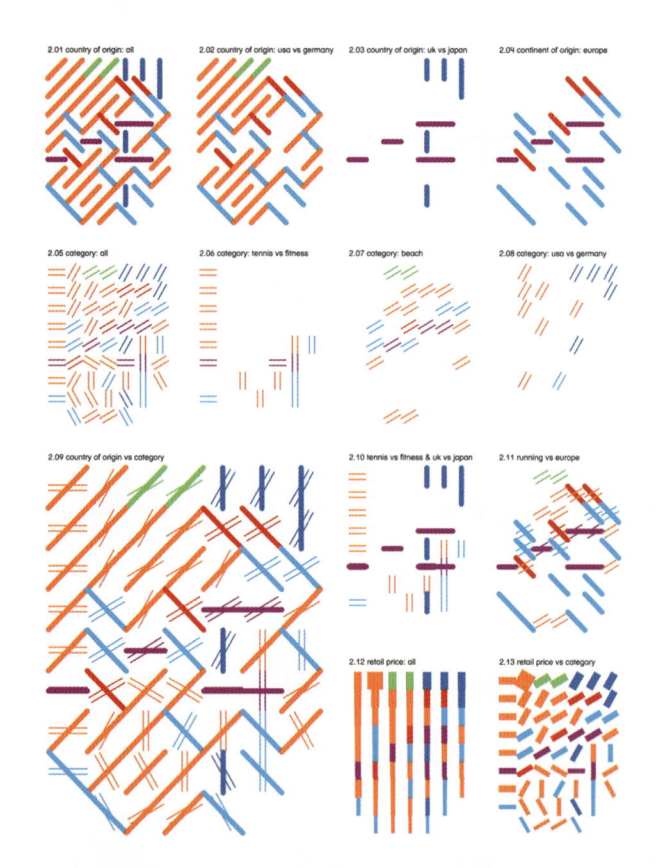

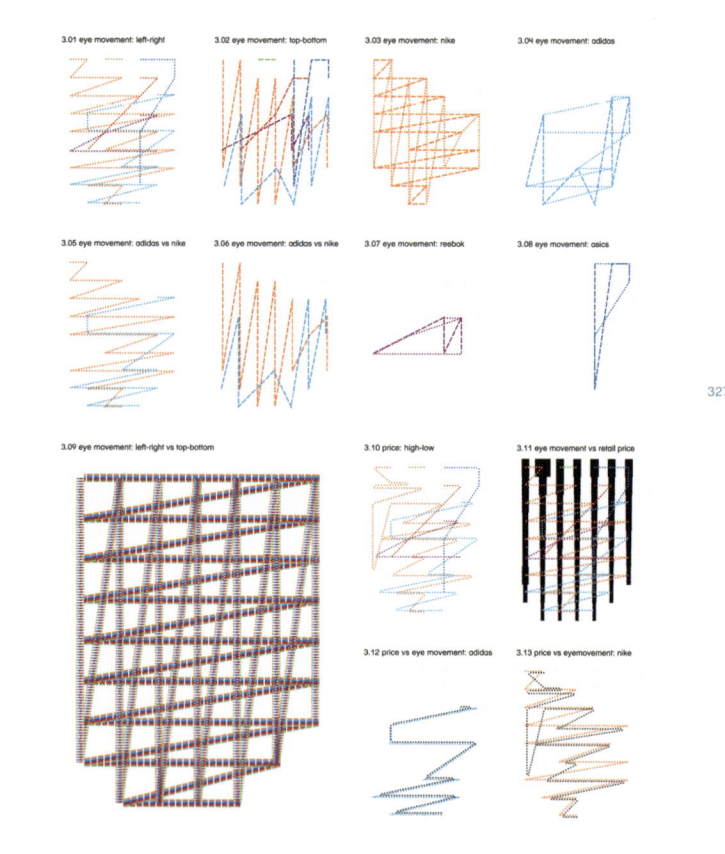

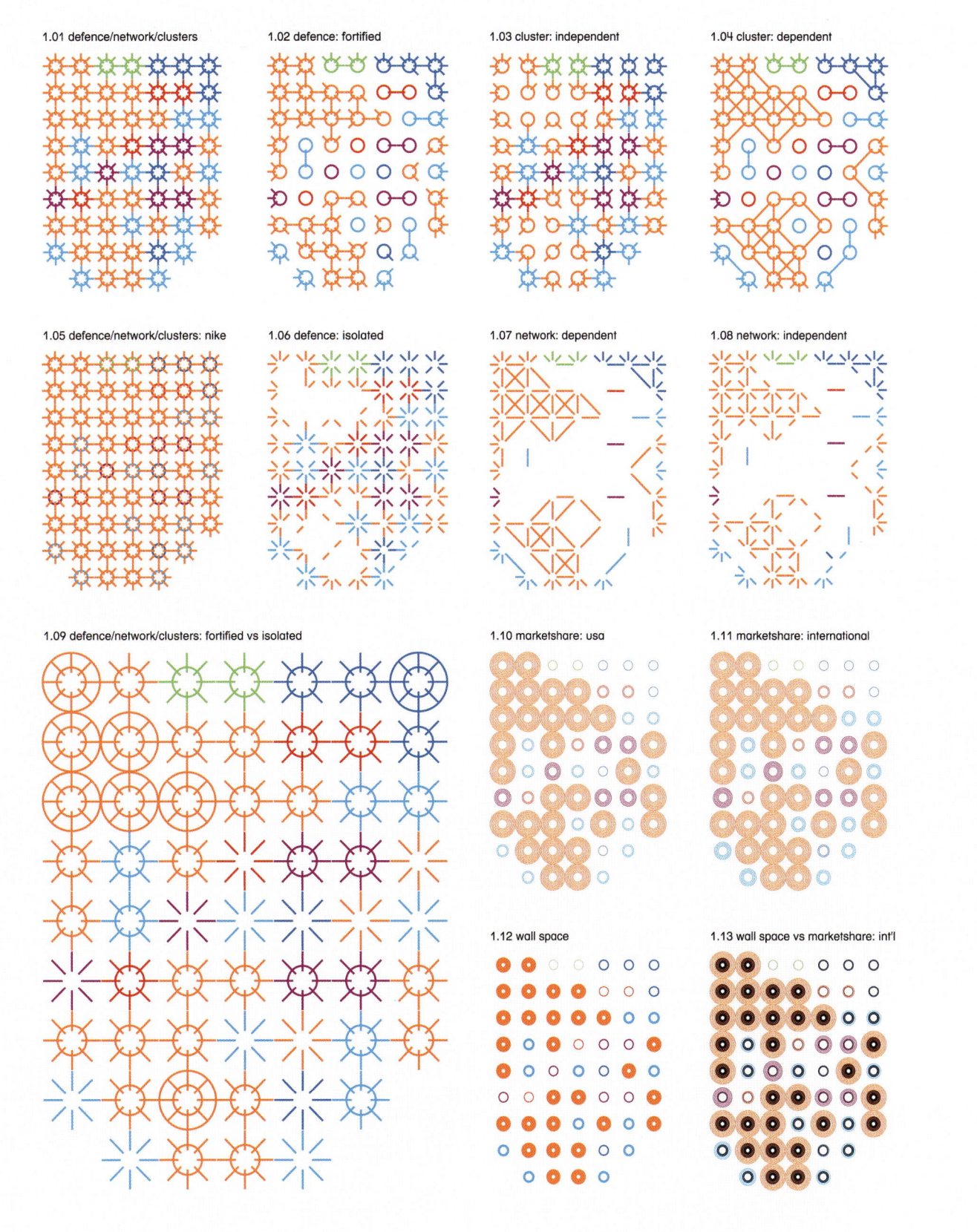

1.01 defence/network/clusters
1.02 defence: fortified
1.03 cluster: independent
1.04 cluster: dependent

1.05 defence/network/clusters: nike
1.06 defence: isolated
1.07 network: dependent
1.08 network: independent

325

1.09 defence/network/clusters: fortified vs isolated
1.10 marketshare: usa
1.11 marketshare: international

1.12 wall space
1.13 wall space vs marketshare: int'l

Graphs 217

Confluentialities ::
D. Luque, B. Jiménez, A. Gutiérrez, J. Cerrud/Amorphica Design Research Office :: www.amorphica.com

The great point of convergence between the United States and Mexico is the border that separates California from Baja California. The traffic of vehicles and pedestrians and, above all, social interaction in this particular intersection is reflected in this chart. The information that can be extracted is useful for examining these two cultures in depth.

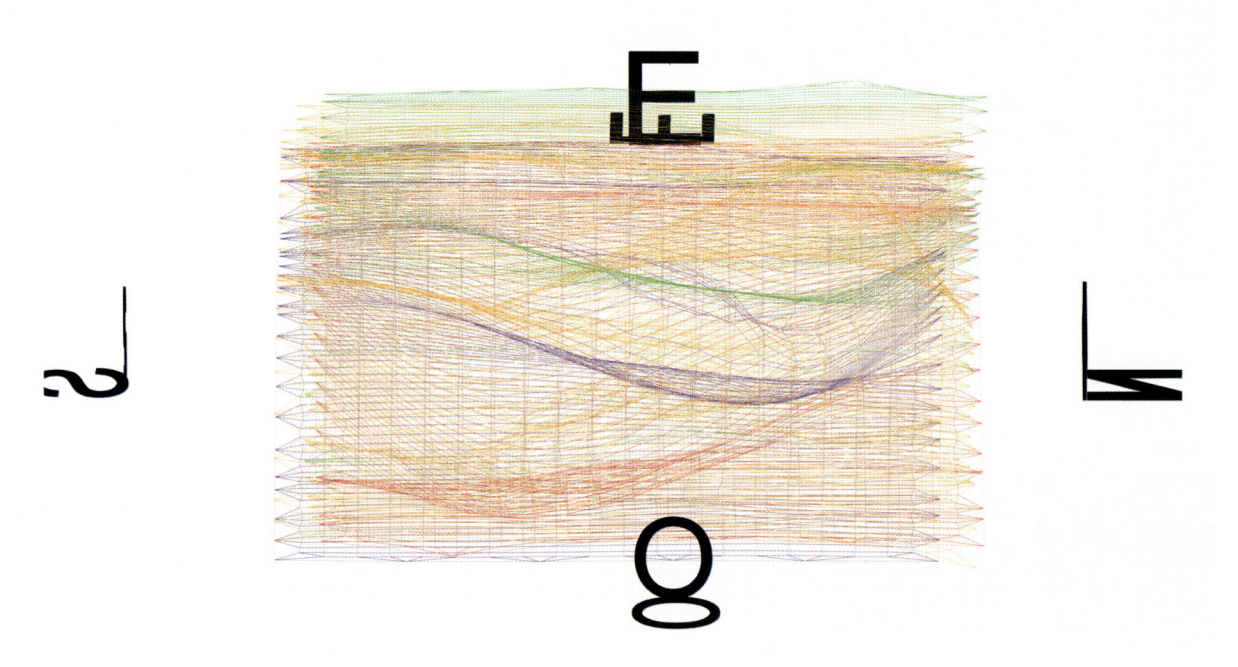

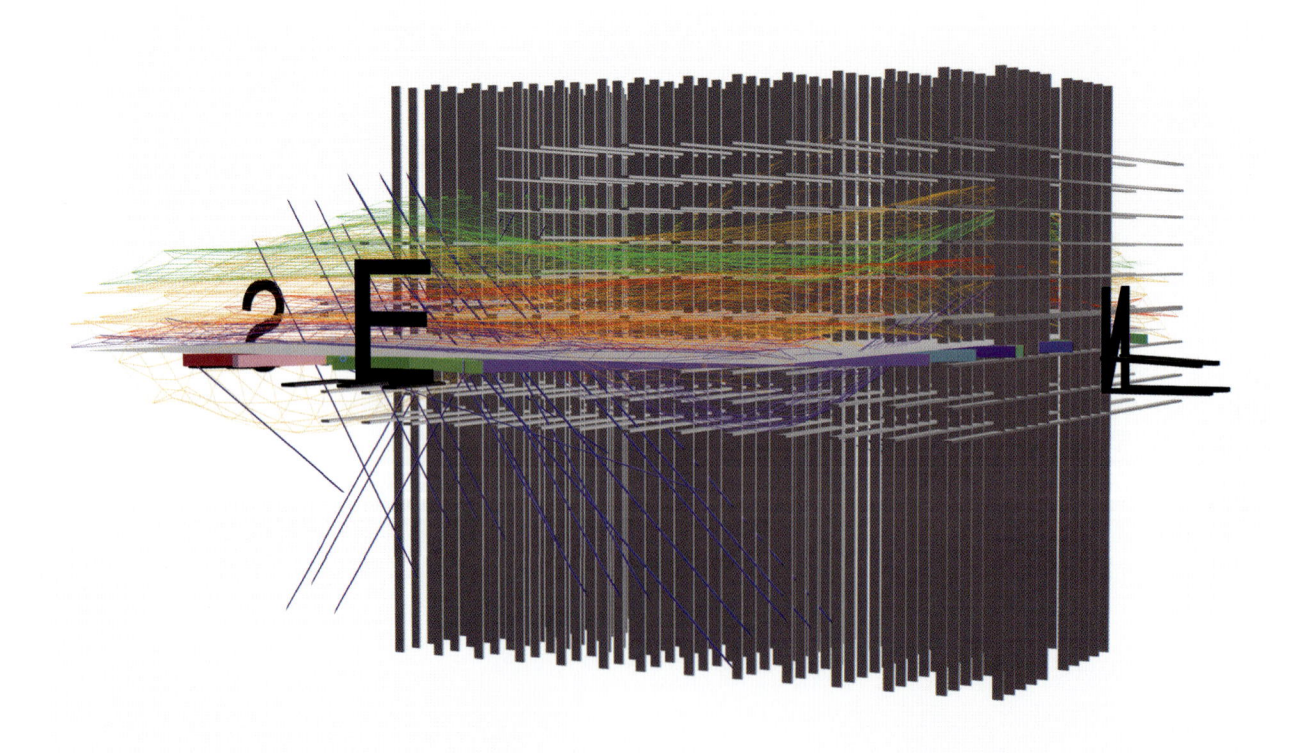

New York Times ::
Anna Filipova :: www.anfilip.com ::

During the Iraq War (2002–2005) there was a lot of censorship in the media, particularly the American media, and as proof of this, this poster shows censorship by *The New York Times*. The straight lines indicate factual information while the curves represent censored information. The upper part of the graph corresponds to the heading of the report, the lower part to its author and the color of the line to the year in which it was written.

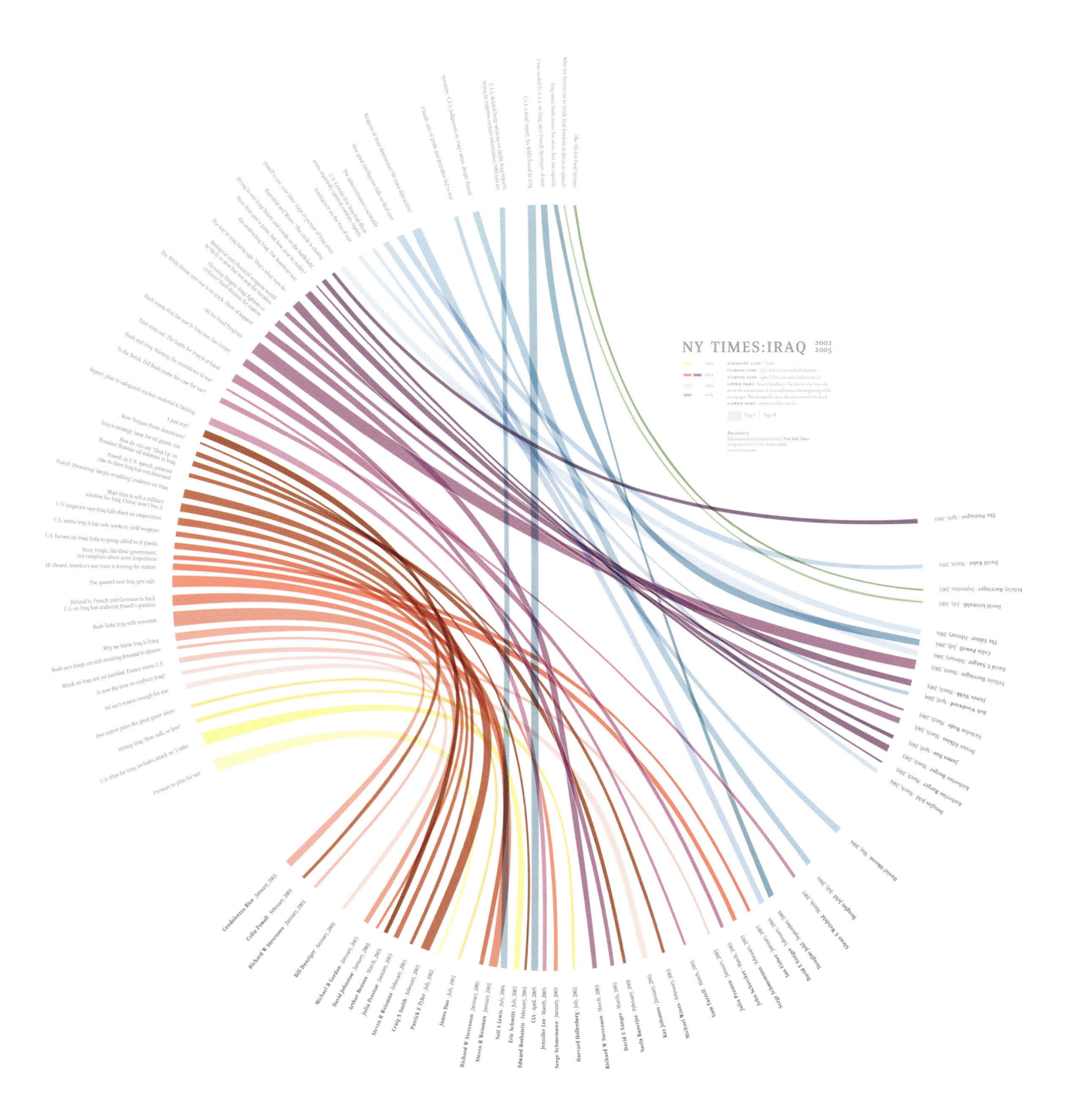

Graphs 219

Chronicles of Rock ::
Esam Lee, Heesun Seo :: www.hxx.kr ::

To make a graph relating to a specific theme, you only need to choose (at least) two variables and examine their relationship. In this case, the aim was to see whether there was any connection between the different types of rock and time. Thus, the y-axis corresponds to 350 outstanding artists and bands subscribing to 21 different genres, while the x-axis represents the years, from 1950–2008.

alternative rock / alternative metal | arena rock | blues rock | britpop | emo | folk rock

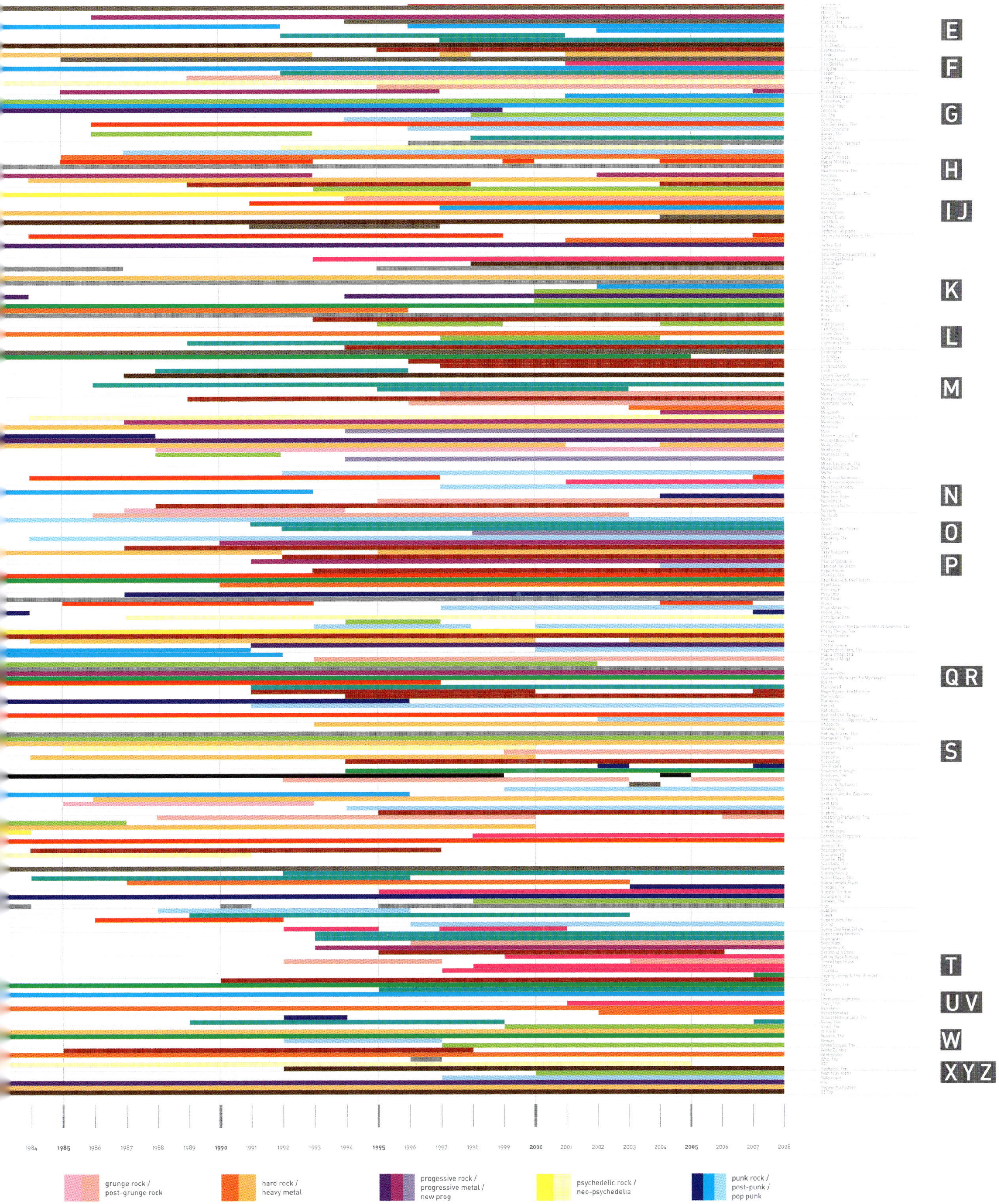
E
F
G
H
IJ
K
L
M
N
O
P
QR
S
T
UV
W
XYZ
1984
1985
1986
1987
1988
1989
1990
1991
1992
1993
1994
1995
1996
1997
1998
1999
2000
2001
2002
2003
2004
2005
2006
2007
2008
grunge rock / post-grunge rock
hard rock / heavy metal
progessive rock / progressive metal / new prog
psychedelic rock / neo-psychedelia
punk rock / post-punk / pop punk

La représentation des statistiques ::
Xavier Barrade :: www.xavierbarrade.com ::

This is a book about the visualization of statistical data that is divided into two parts. The first part explores the history and style of the graphs featured in PowerPoint (which are fairly standard) whereas the second part is more experimental and searches for alternative means to represent numerical data on various topics, from the growth of real estate to the sale of glazed doughnuts.

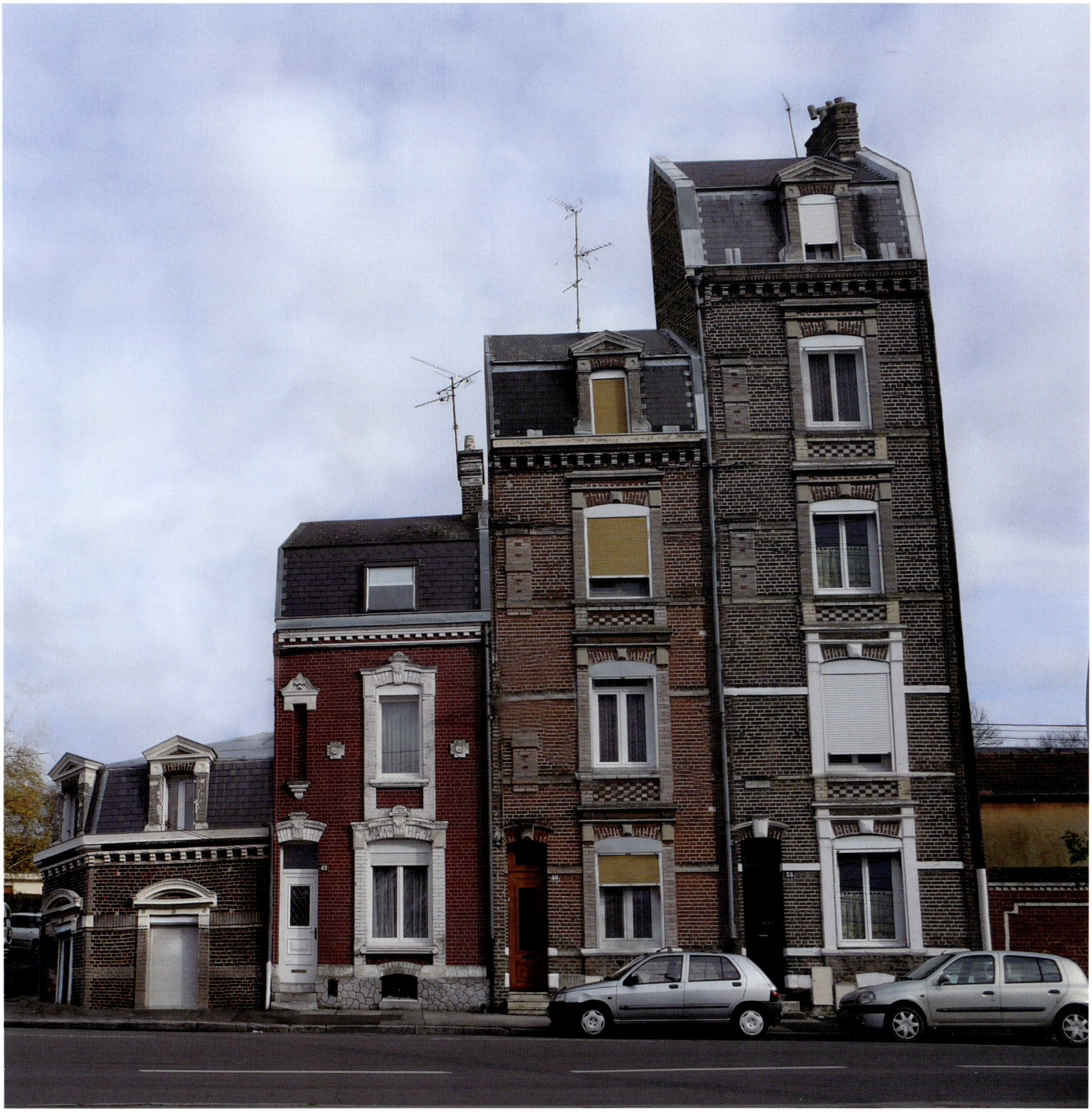

224 **Graphs**

Graphs 225

Ateneo Art Awards 2009: The Next Wave ::
Inksurge :: www.inksurge.com ::

Inksurge was asked to think up and develop a concept for applied graphics in posters, invitations, and forms for the 2009 Ateneo Art Awards and they went for infographics and charts. All those included were generated from information gathered from galleries and surveys conducted with artists about their exhibitions, types of work, techniques, and materials used.

226 **Graphs**

Graphs 227

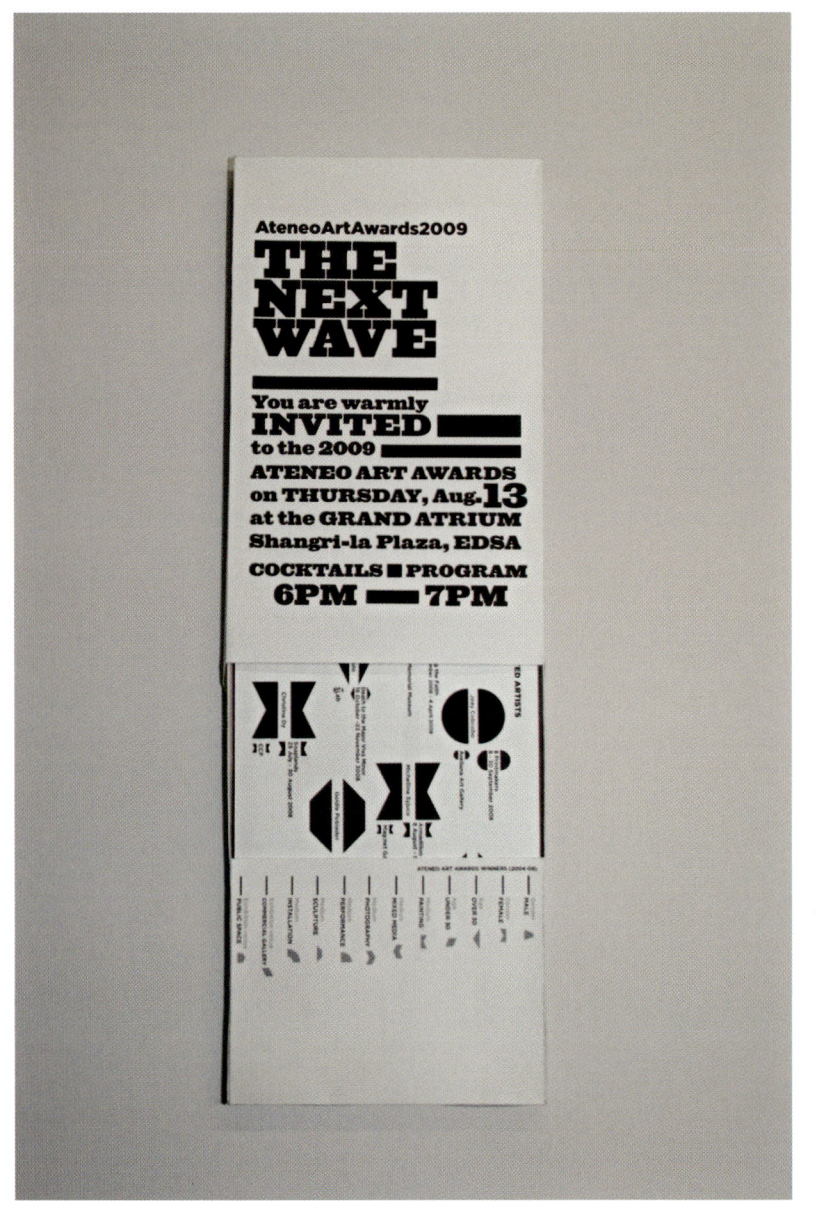

Research in the Visualization of Financial Data ::
Cybu Richli :: www.c2f.to ::

Morningstar is one of the major suppliers of financial data and analysis in the world, and over time has set certain standards for displaying information in this sector. For this reason, producing these graphics (collating various types of information) was a challenge that Cybu Richli met with great success, since investors are able to understand in a single glance.

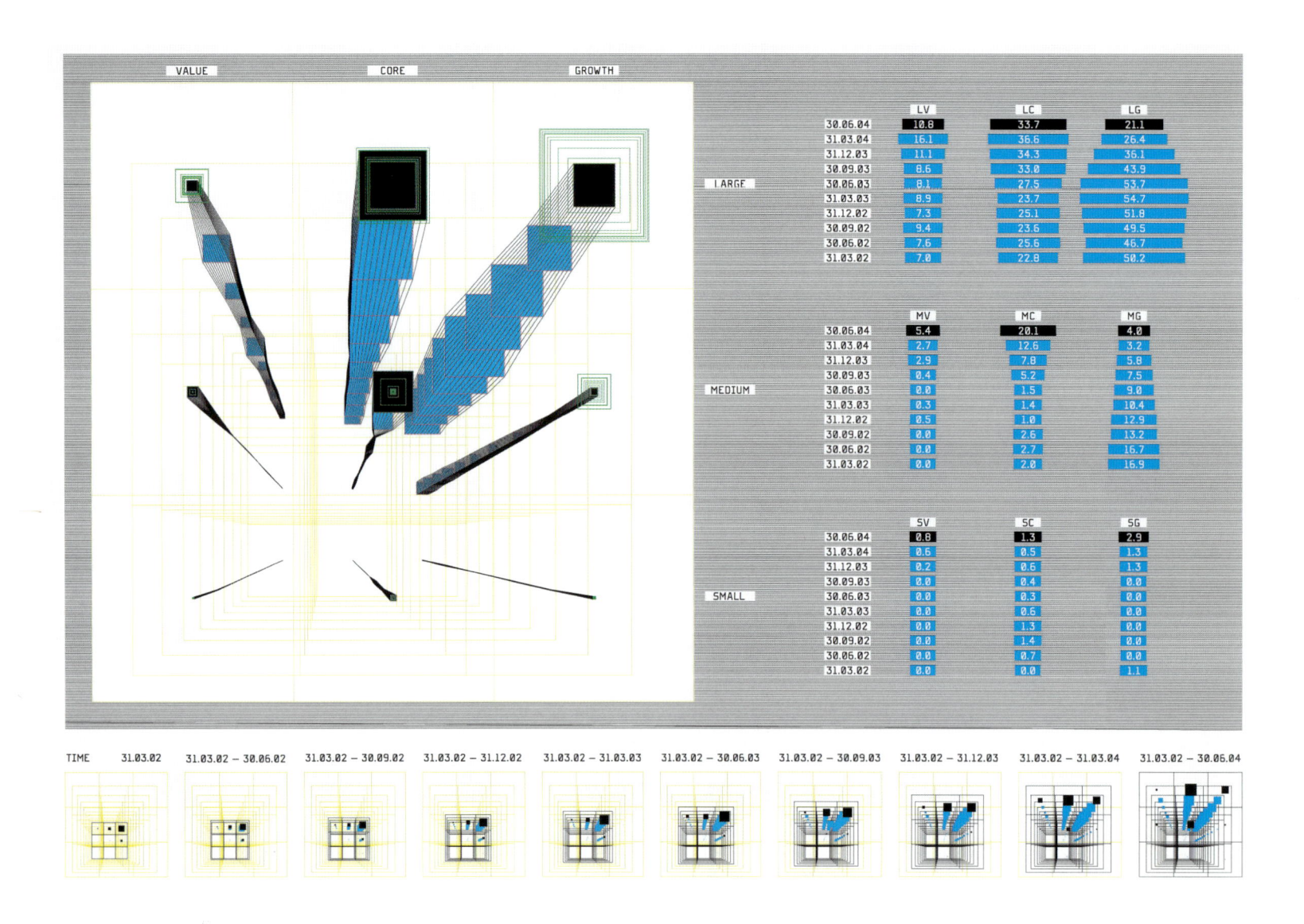

		LV	LC	LG
	30.06.04	10.8	33.7	21.1
	31.03.04	16.1	36.6	26.4
	31.12.03	11.1	34.3	36.1
	30.09.03	8.6	33.0	43.9
LARGE	30.06.03	8.1	27.5	53.7
	31.03.03	8.9	23.7	54.7
	31.12.02	7.3	25.1	51.8
	30.09.02	9.4	23.6	49.5
	30.06.02	7.6	25.6	46.7
	31.03.02	7.0	22.8	50.2

		MV	MC	MG
	30.06.04	5.4	20.1	4.0
	31.03.04	2.7	12.6	3.2
	31.12.03	2.9	7.8	5.8
	30.09.03	0.4	5.2	7.5
MEDIUM	30.06.03	0.0	1.5	9.0
	31.03.03	0.3	1.4	10.4
	31.12.02	0.5	1.0	12.9
	30.09.02	0.0	2.6	13.2
	30.06.02	0.0	2.7	16.7
	31.03.02	0.0	2.0	16.9

		SV	SC	SG
	30.06.04	0.8	1.3	2.9
	31.03.04	0.6	0.5	1.3
	31.12.03	0.2	0.6	1.3
	30.09.03	0.0	0.4	0.0
SMALL	30.06.03	0.0	0.3	0.0
	31.03.03	0.0	0.6	0.0
	31.12.02	0.0	1.3	0.0
	30.09.02	0.0	1.4	0.0
	30.06.02	0.0	0.7	0.0
	31.03.02	0.0	0.0	1.1

228 Graphs

STOCK SECTOR

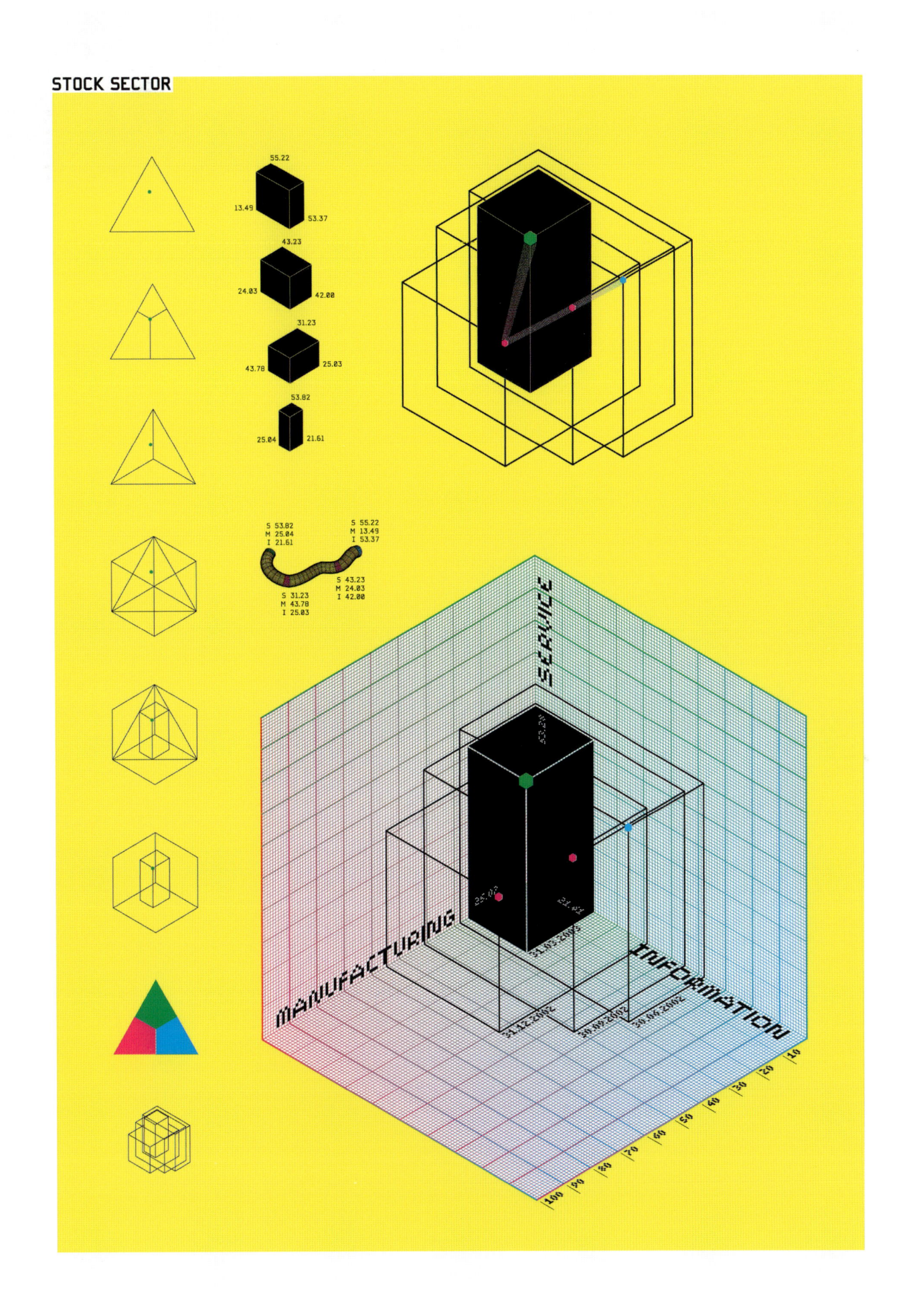

Graphs 229

2008 Boijmans Van Beuningen Annual Report ::
Thonik :: www.thonik.nl ::

The characteristic style of the Museum Boijmans Van Beuningen in Rotterdam, The Netherlands, is known for its lyrical graphic image composed of a font made up of three lines. The forms swirl and create colorful lines that interact visually with the art exhibited. In the annual report, these lines serve as inspiration for the graphs depicting data and help turn them into vivid illustrations.

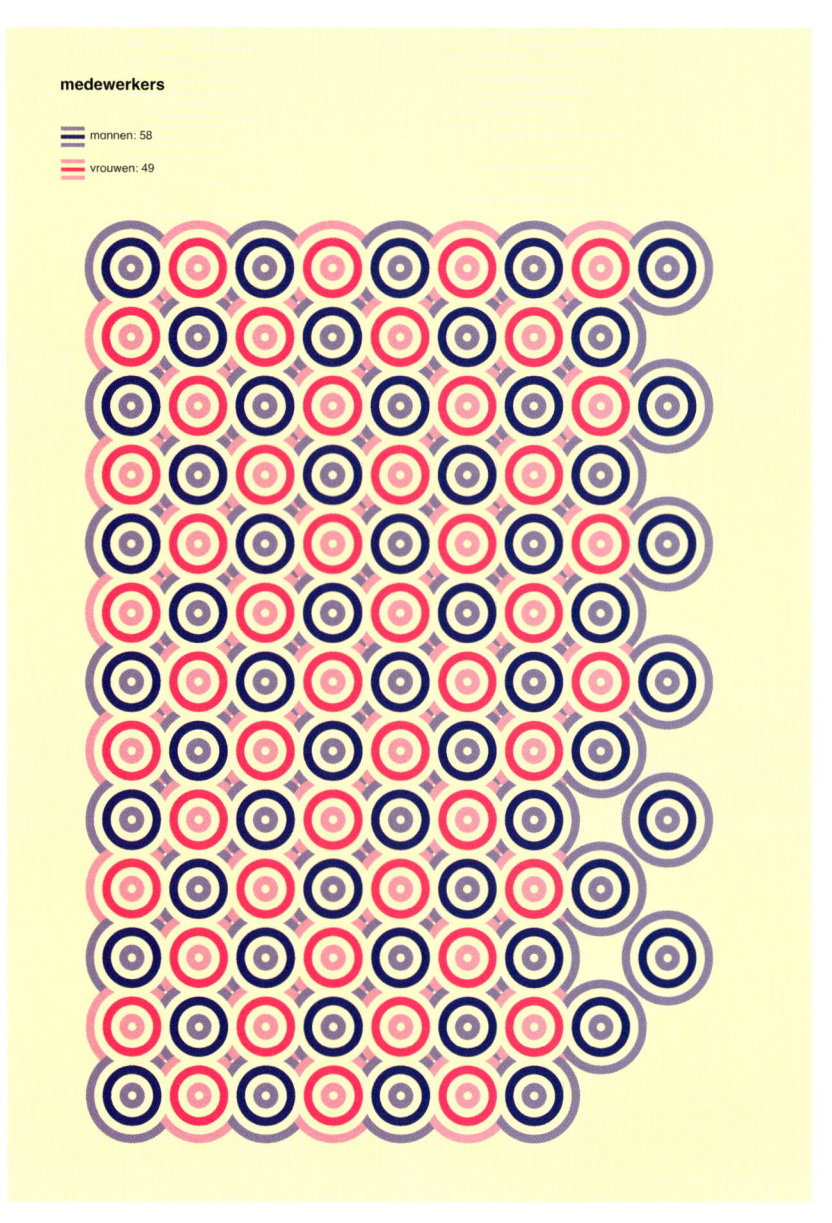

---

medewerkers

≡ mannen: 58
≡ vrouwen: 49

sector bedrijfsvoering

Onder de sector Bedrijfsvoering vallen niet alleen de afdelingen Financiën, automatisering en informatiebeheer, Personeel en organisatie, Huisvesting en onderhoud, Beveiliging en veiligheid, en Floormanagement, maar ook de winkel, het restaurant en de espressobar van Museum Boijmans Van Beuningen.
De sector Bedrijfsvoering biedt de facilitaire ondersteuning voor de kerntaken van het museum. Zo zorgt de sector onder andere voor het onderhoud van het gebouw, het klimaat, de veiligheid van de collectie en van de bezoeker, de financiële verslaglegging en controle en de ontvangst van gasten.
Bovendien draagt de sector in belangrijke mate bij aan de eigen inkomsten van het museum met de entreegelden en de opbrengst van winkel en restaurant.
Veel van de circa zeventig medewerkers van de sector zijn als beveiliger, kassier of garderobemedewerker een direct aanspreekpunt voor de bezoekers en vormen zo het gezicht van het museum. De overige medewerkers werken achter de schermen aan het goed functioneren van museum en museumorganisatie.
In 2008 is met name geïnvesteerd in het museumgebouw. De verbouwing van het entreegebied en de oplevering van het nieuwe depot voor prenten, tekeningen en kostbare uitgaven zijn daarvan zichtbare resultaten. Gelijktijdig wordt het complete glazen dak van het Bodon-gebouw vervangen, terwijl in de kelder een nieuwe werkplaats voor de technische dienst van het museum wordt gerealiseerd.
Ondertussen blijft het museum gewoon open en ontvangt het een recordaantal bezoekers.

Financiën, automatisering en informatiebeheer

Het jaar 2008 staat in het teken van het verder optimaliseren van de planning- en controle-cyclus. Risicobeheersing staat daarbij voorop. Om de vele ambities van het museum waar te maken is een adequate inschatting en beheersing van mogelijke risico's noodzakelijk; dit kan alleen als de museumorganisatie in staat is om (financiële) gegevens tijdig aan te leveren om deze in bruikbare managementinformatie om te zetten. Er is volop gewerkt aan de opzet van een managementinformatiesysteem, dat in 2009 verder wordt ingevoerd. Ook in 2008 is daartoe nauw samengewerkt met de auditcommissie van de Raad van Toezicht en is volop gebruik gemaakt van de expertise van KPMG-accountants.
Halverwege het jaar verschijnt het informatieplan dat bureau Reekx in opdracht van het museum heeft geschreven. In dit plan worden ict, het collectie-informatiesysteem en digitalisering als belangrijke speerpunten voor de komende jaren benoemd.
Op het gebied van automatisering maken we in 2008 een begin met het opstellen van een ict-beleidsplan. In dit plan worden de diverse eisen die de museumorganisatie stelt aan zijn ict-omgeving, omgezet in concrete acties en benodigde investeringen. De implementatie zal vooral in 2009 en daarna plaatsvinden en moet het museum in staat stellen om – naast de dagelijkse automatiseringsbehoefte – ambitieuze projecten als ALMA, ArtTube en de Collectie Online te realiseren. Voor het opstellen van het ict-beleidsplan maakt het museum gebruik van de expertise van een externe adviseur.
De postverwerking en het archiefbeheer zijn onderdeel van het informatiebeheer. Het museum heeft vroegtijdig erkend dat

**bezoekers per dag
2008 versus 2007**

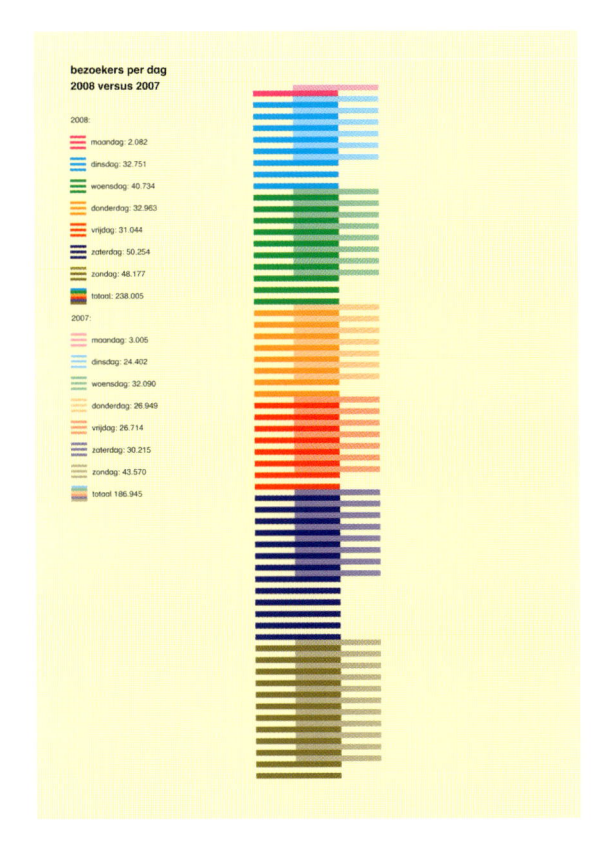

2008:
- maandag: 2.082
- dinsdag: 32.751
- woensdag: 40.734
- donderdag: 32.963
- vrijdag: 31.044
- zaterdag: 50.254
- zondag: 48.177
- totaal: 238.005

2007:
- maandag: 3.005
- dinsdag: 24.402
- woensdag: 32.090
- donderdag: 26.949
- vrijdag: 26.714
- zaterdag: 30.215
- zondag: 43.570
- totaal: 186.945

stafafdeling conservatoren

De conservatoren van Museum Boijmans Van Beuningen verrichten onderzoek naar de collectie, maken tentoonstellingen en representeren het museum. De conservatoren staan onder leiding van de directeur en worden bij het uitoefenen van hun werkzaamheden ondersteund door de sector Collectie en onderzoek en de sector Presentaties. Het aan de collectie gerelateerde werk bestaat onder meer uit het verrichten van wetenschappelijk onderzoek, het doen van restauratievoorstellen en het begeleiden van restauraties, het formuleren van aankoopvoorstellen en aankoopplannen, evenals het schrijven van bestandscatalogi en bijdragen voor de *Boijmans Studies*.
Op het terrein van presentaties doen de conservatoren voorstellen voor exposities. De conservator die het concept voor een tentoonstelling ontwikkelt, maakt deel uit van een projectgroep die in het museum verantwoordelijk is voor de realisatie van de tentoonstelling. Ook is de conservator verantwoordelijk voor de kwaliteit van de catalogus en de daarin te publiceren teksten. In onderstaande teksten beschrijven conservatoren, directeur en sectorhoofden hun werkzaamheden en projecten in 2008.

Peter van der Coelen (1961)
conservator prenten en tekeningen

Met genoegen stel ik de tentoonstelling *Erasmus in beeld* samen, die vanaf 8 november te zien is. Ik ben tevens verantwoordelijk voor de samenstelling van de bijbehorende catalogus – verschenen in een Nederlandse en een Engelse uitgave – met een zestal essays van mijn hand. In het kader van deze tentoonstelling geef ik diverse lezingen, inleidingen en rondleidingen.
Ondertussen is er het voorbereidende onderzoek voor toekomstige tentoonstellingen, onder meer op het terrein van de prentkunst en begeleid ik de verwerving van het vierde en laatste deel van de schenking van prenten en tekeningen uit een particuliere collectie.
Ik verzorg enkele colleges over de geschiedenis van de grafische technieken aan de Universiteit Utrecht, ben lid van de redactie van de vaktijdschriften *Delineavit et Sculpsit. Tijdschrift voor Nederlandse prent- en tekenkunst tot omstreeks 1850* en *Kroniek van het Rembrandthuis*, en treed op als adviseur van de Mondriaan Stichting in het kader van een aankoopvoorstel van het Persmuseum te Amsterdam voor een collectie politieke tekeningen van Fritz Behrendt.

Albert Elen (1955)
senior conservator tekeningen en prenten

Aan het eind van 2008 is een door mij opgestelde subsidieaanvraag voor museaal wetenschappelijk onderzoek gehonoreerd door de Mondriaan Stichting. Daarmee kunnen de komende drie jaar twee freelance onderzoekers werken aan de voorbereiding van de bestandscatalogus van onze vijftiende- en zestiende-eeuwse Nederlandse tekeningen. Zelf lever ik ook een inhoudelijke bijdrage, naast de voorbereiding, begeleiding en redactie.
In Dresden woon ik het tweejaarlijkse congres bij van The International Advisory Committee of Keepers of Public Collections of Graphic Art, beter bekend als de *50 Lux*

7

**verband herkomst en herhaalbezoeken
2008**

regio Rotterdam
- eerste bezoek: 12%
- tweede bezoek: 33%
- vaker: 54%

overig Nederland
- eerste bezoek: 22%
- tweede bezoek: 45%
- vaker: 33%

**verband bezoekdagen en herkomst
2008**

woensdag
- regio Rotterdam: 45%
- overig Nederland < 60 minuten reistijd: 24%
- overig Nederland > 60 minuten reistijd: 31%

weekend
- regio Rotterdam: 31%
- overig Nederland < 60 minuten reistijd: 23%
- overig Nederland > 60 minuten reistijd: 46%

Foreword

The economic crisis did not impact on Museum Boijmans Van Beuningen in 2008. The need for surprise, innovation, knowledge and pleasure seemed greater than ever. The public flocked to exhibitions like *Dutch Primitives, Surtout pas des principes! Charley Toorop* and *Images of Erasmus*, all supported by the museum's own art historical research and publications. Exhibitions of contemporary artists such as Yayoi Kusama and Roy Villevoye also attracted large numbers and gained international recognition. Last year's museum programme again included interventions by contemporary artists such as Geert Mul, Adam Colton, Karin van Dam and Olaf Nicolai, not forgetting presentations by Sarkis, Harmen Brethouwer, Olphaert den Otter and Ewoud van Rijn. All in all, the activities created numerous unforgettable, educational, visual and aesthetic experiences. The museum was well-visited throughout the year, and visitor numbers increased by almost 19 percent. This is a fantastic figure that will be analyzed in greater detail over the next few months. The proportion of visitors from other countries rose from 12 to 16 percent. Educationally the museum is in its element with a varied programme for young and old. We succeeded in completing an ambitious building programme: the new print room (with an ordering service), an updated entrance foyer and even a new roof on the Bodon Building – all this while the museum remained open. This does not, though, mean that the financial outlook is rosy. The fact that the subsidy has remained at the same level while costs continue to rise means that the museum is ever more dependent on its own earnings and also on considerable external financial support.

The Collection and Research Sector has gone from strength to strength. A huge amount of work went into *The Collection Two*, a new exhibition that was opened to the public on 17 January 2009. A great deal of care has gone into the conservation and management of the collection. The prints and drawings now have excellent new accommodation, and the plans for a new repository or a collection building look promising and will be evaluated by the local authority in early 2009. A conservation programme for the glass collection is going ahead. An important digitizing subsidy has been granted for the ALMA Project (Linking Image to Artefact). And requests for loans, especially abroad, are at their highest. Some splendid acquisitions have been added to the collection.
A heartfelt word of thanks on behalf of the Supervisory Board is due here to the people, the funds, the foundations and the companies that have enabled us to achieve so many ambitions. I would also particularly like to thank the staff and volunteers of Museum Boijmans Van Beuningen and the directors of the foundations for their dedication and for the pleasure they bring to their work. All the objectives of *Global & Local*, the long-term policy plan, come a step closer in 2008, or were achieved in full.

Sjarel Ex
Director, Museum Boijmans Van Beuningen

107

Graphs 231

2004 Mondriaan Foundation Annual Report ::
LUST :: www.lust.nl ::

All the graphs for this annual report have a basic pie chart with three rings, which are used in one way or another, depending on the variables and the data that need to be depicted. To prevent the result from looking static, the color of each segment of the chart has been chosen randomly (for example, red does not always represent art projects).

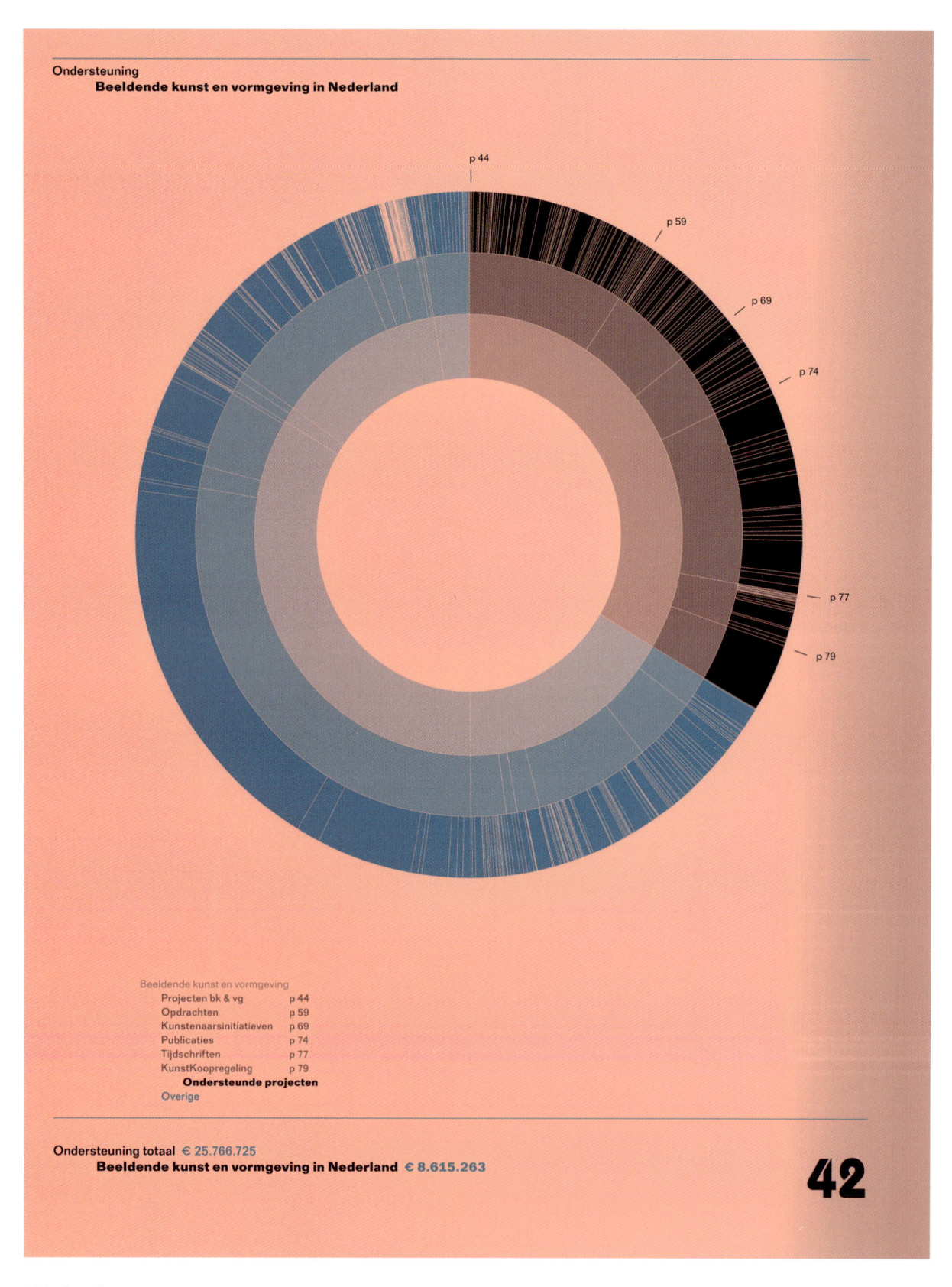

Ondersteuning
Beeldende kunst en vormgeving in Nederland

p 44
p 59
p 69
p 74
p 77
p 79

Beeldende kunst en vormgeving
  Projecten bk & vg   p 44
  Opdrachten   p 59
  Kunstenaarsinitiatieven p 69
  Publicaties   p 74
  Tijdschriften   p 77
  KunstKoopregeling   p 79
  Ondersteunde projecten
Overige

Ondersteuning totaal € 25.766.725
  Beeldende kunst en vormgeving in Nederland € 8.615.263

42

Graphs 233

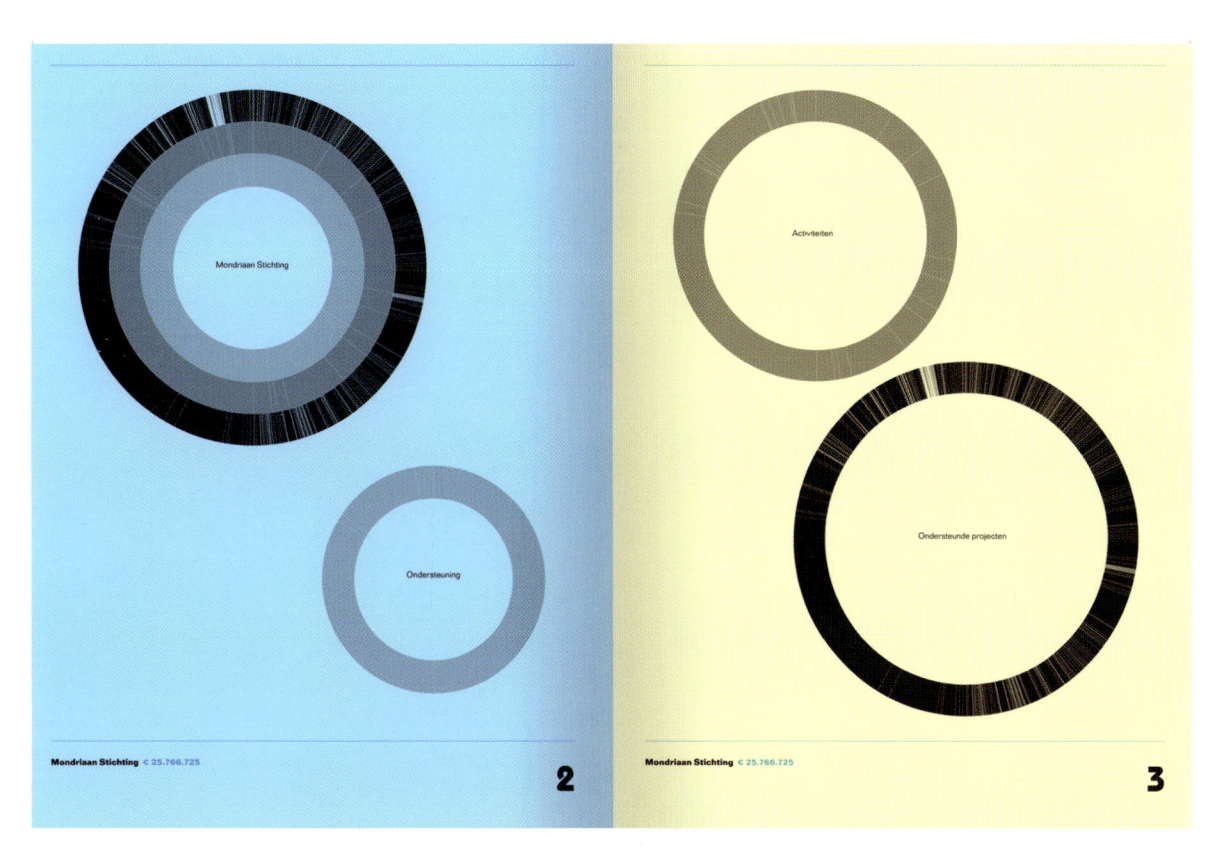

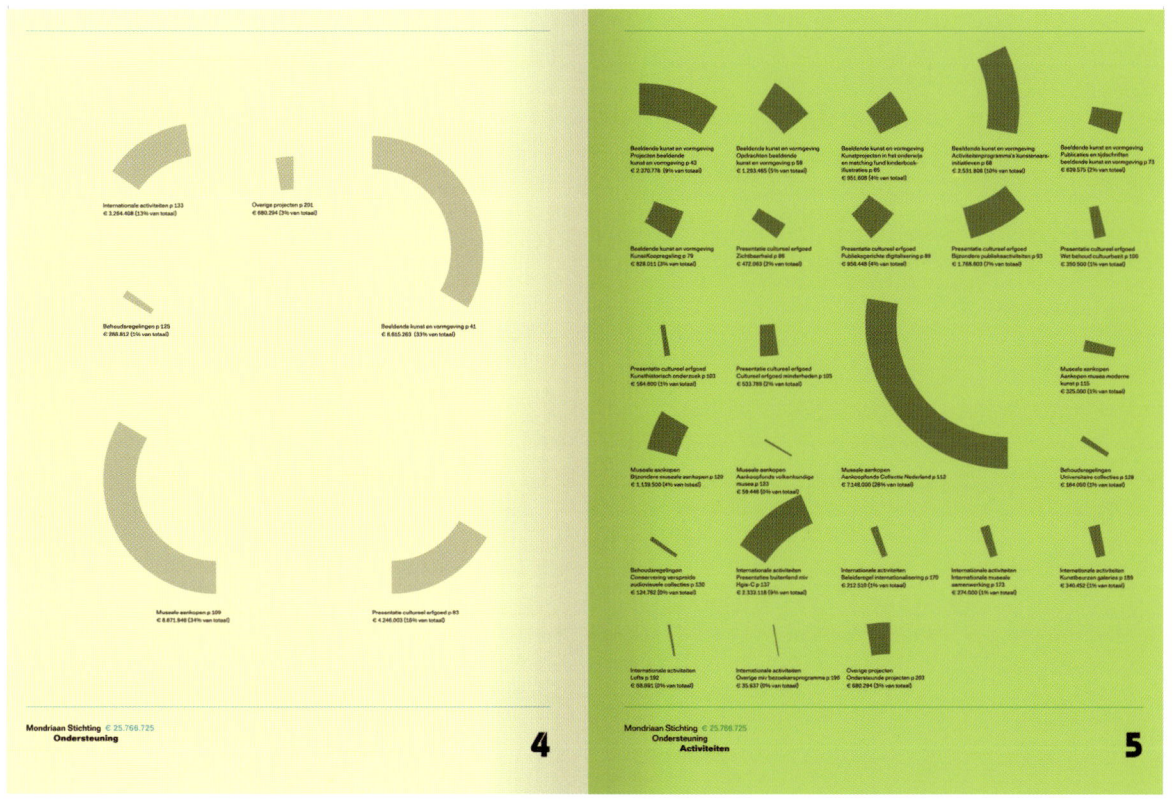

Vueling Business ::
***S,C,P,F... :: www.scpf.com ::**

Vueling is an airline that uses a style of communicative language that is immediate, modern, different, and fun. The brief for these posters was to keep this tone and come up with a product that was suitable for business people, the sole target of this particular campaign. A graphic code was designed that would convey the most prominent attributes of the service with an obvious allusion to Vueling.

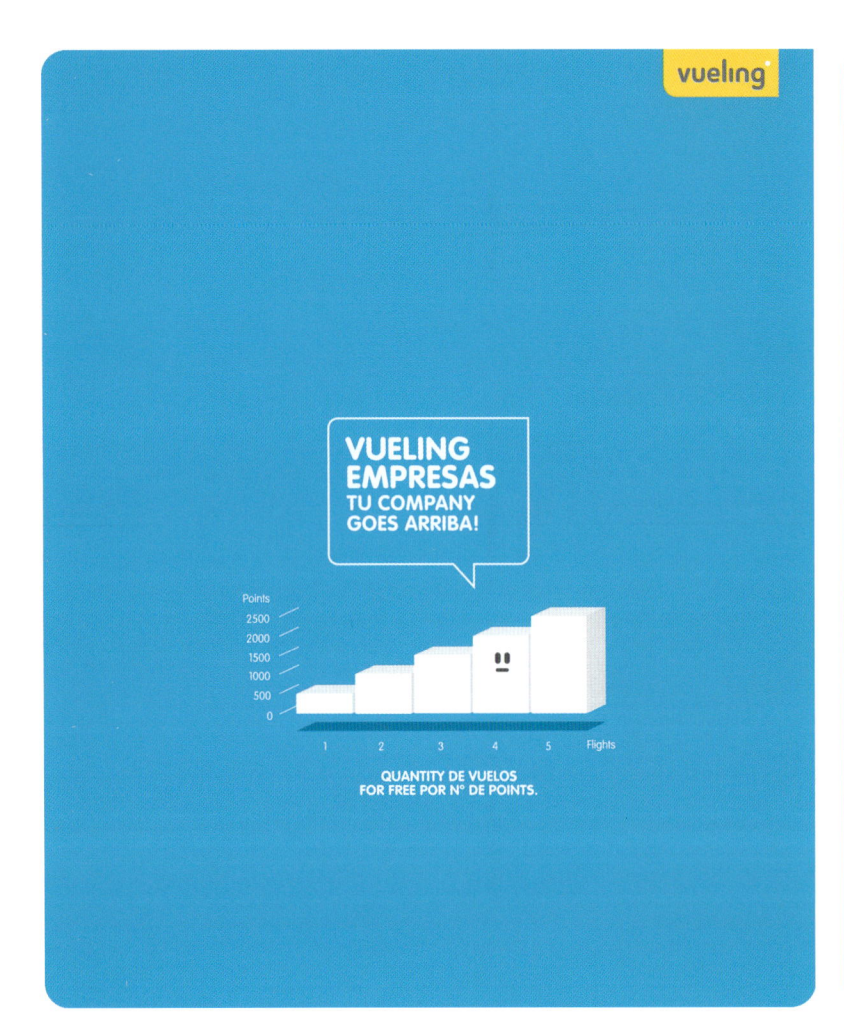

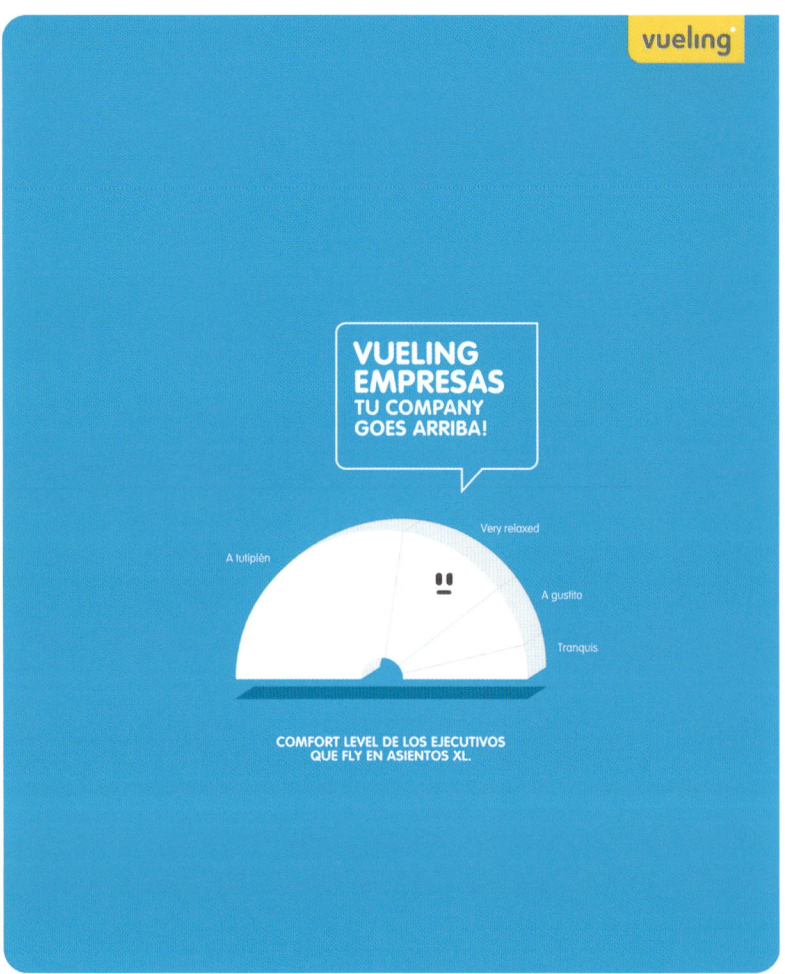

Executive art direction: Mauricio Alarcón. Art direction: Gaizka Sampedro. Editing: Jordi González

vueling

VUELING EMPRESAS
TU COMPANY GOES ARRIBA!

AHORRO WITH TARIFA FLEX. ●
AHORRO WITH OTHER TARIFAS. ●

Illinois: Visualizing Music/Word Usage Circles ::
Jax de León :: www.jaxdeleon.com ::

The album *Illinois* by Sufjan Stevens provides the inspiration for the whole of this project, which offers a visual representation of various aspects of music. This series of graphs measures the lyrics used in each song: each concentric circle corresponds to a word, with the outer thicker ones being the most common. This example in particular corresponds to the twentieth song on the album—*The Tallest Man, the Broadest Shoulders*.

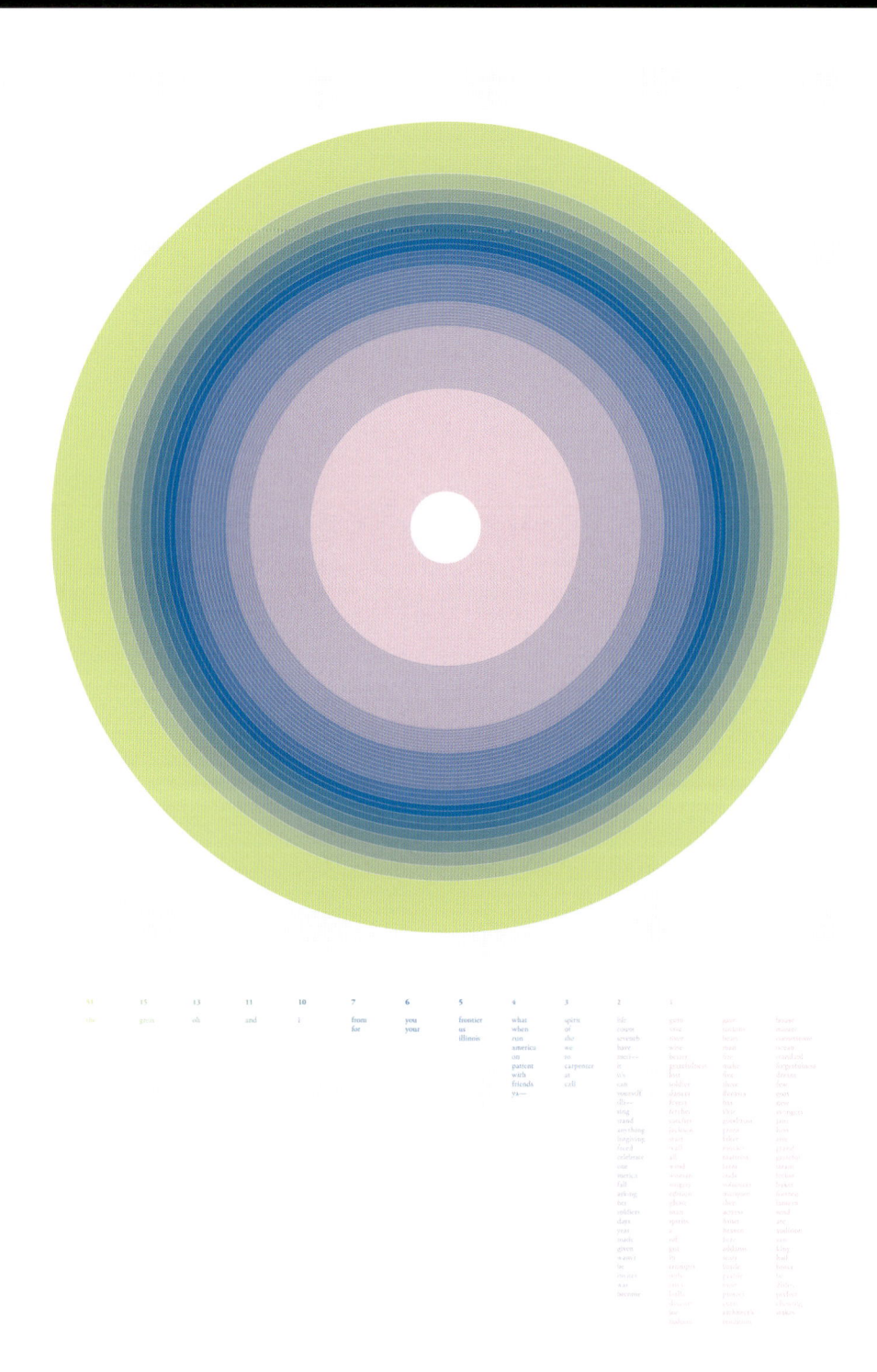

The Tallest Man, The Broadest Shoulders
  Part I: The Great Frontier
  Part II: Come to Me Only with Playthings Now

FD-3

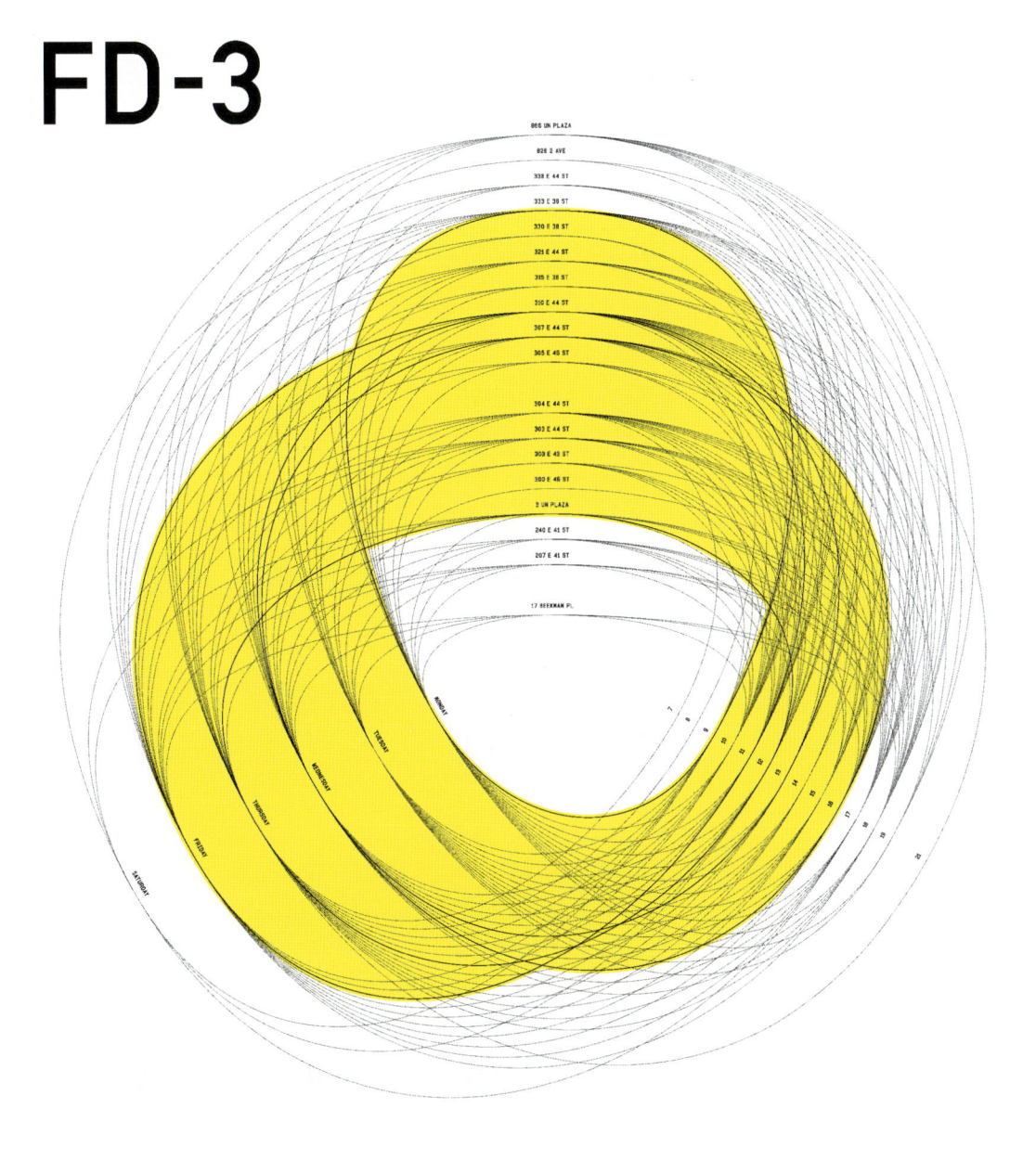

Flocking Diplomats 03 ::
Catalogtree :: www.catalogtree.net ::

The marks that can be left by individuals as they go about their routine is something that has always fascinated this Dutch duo, and it is in this series of posters that they have been able to capture this idea. In this specific polar chart, the vertical axis corresponds to the twenty addresses with most parking violations committed by New York diplomats and the other axes indicate the time and day of the week.

2008 Amsterdamse Hogeschool voor de Kunsten Annual Report ::
Thonik :: www.thonik.nl ::

The recognizable logo of this university consists of two perfect, slightly displaced circles. The one at the top on the right is black, with the yellow one below varying depending on the faculty. For the 2008 annual report, the logo was taken and duplicated to turn it into the figure eight, creating a basis for all the graphs contained within this book, which is accessible and easy to read.

94 Studenten

Totaal aantal studenten AHK peildatum 1 oktober 2008

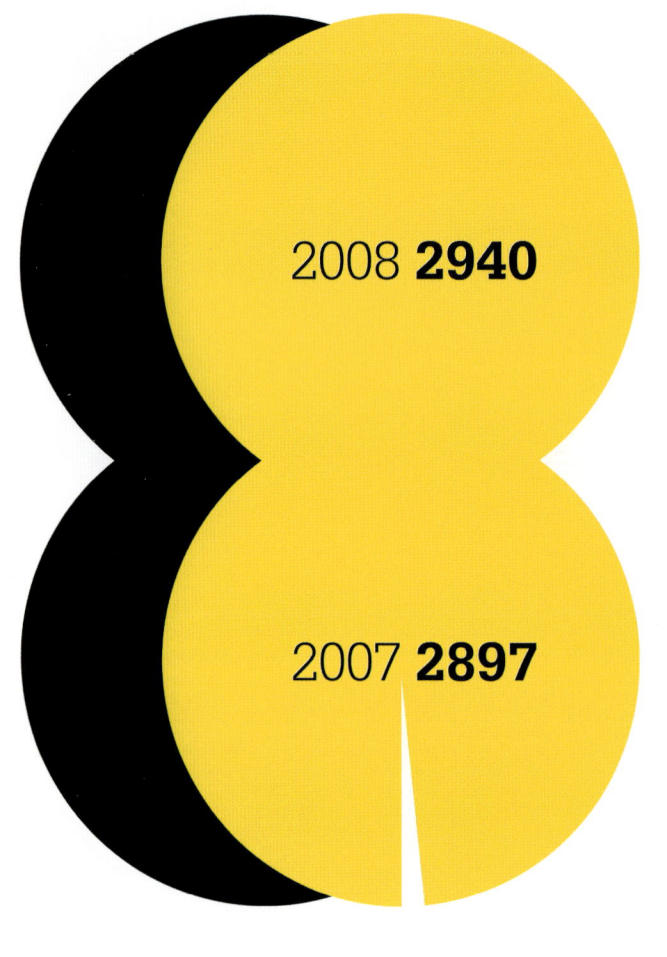

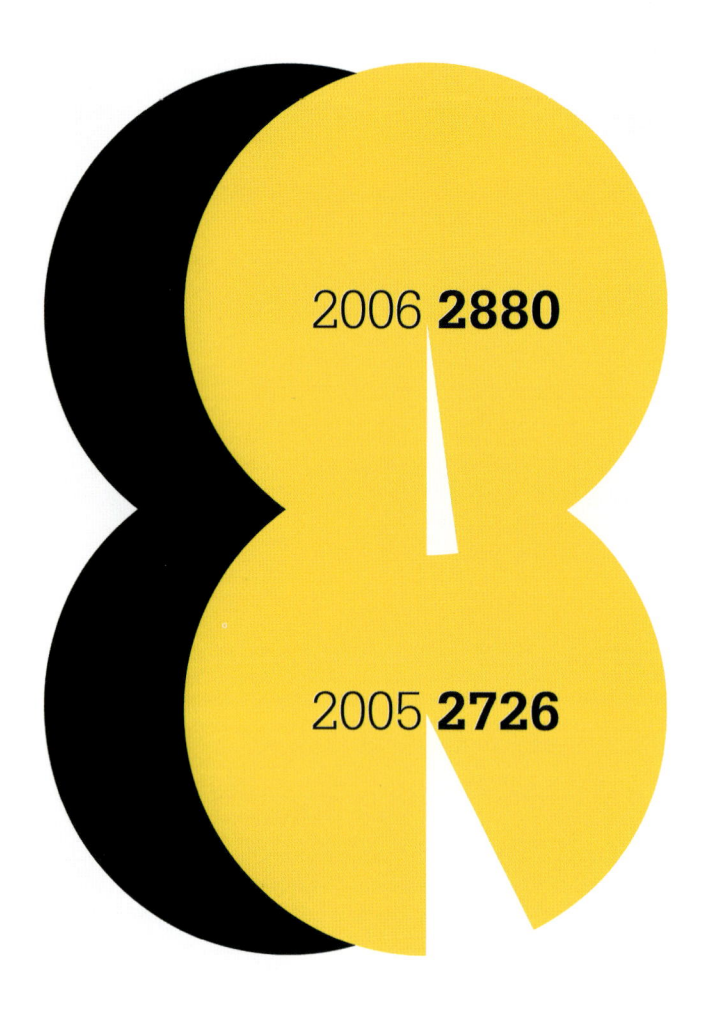

2008 **2940**

2007 **2897**

Studenten 95

2006 **2880**

2005 **2726**

238 **Graphs**

Leeftijdsverdeling totale personeelsbestand

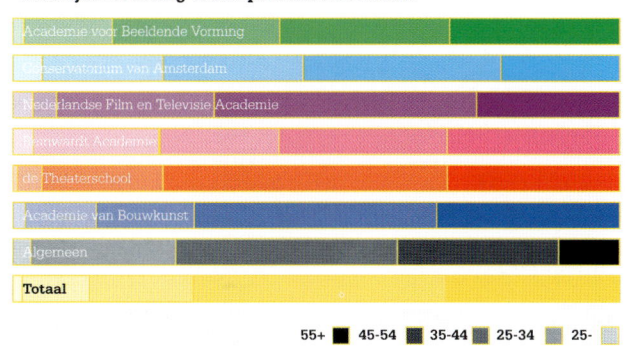

Academie voor Beeldende Vorming	
Conservatorium van Amsterdam	
Nederlandse Film en Televisie Academie	
Rietveld Academie	
de Theaterschool	
Academie van Bouwkunst	
Algemeen	
Totaal	

55+ ■ 45-54 ■ 35-44 ■ 25-34 ■ 25- ■

Net als vorig jaar is de leeftijdscategorie 55+ de snelst groeiende groep: inmiddels behoort ruim 25% van de hogeschoolmedewerkers tot deze groep. Zoals eerder aangegeven is dit deels een gevolg van het bewust aantrekken van ervaren kunstenaars. Daarnaast onttrekt ook de hogeschool zich niet aan de maatschappelijke trend dat langer doorwerken steeds normaler wordt. Overigens is ook het aandeel medewerkers jonger dan 25 en tussen 35 en 44 toegenomen. In de jongste categorie betreft dit alleen ondersteunend personeel.

Leeftijdsverdeling onderwijzend personeel

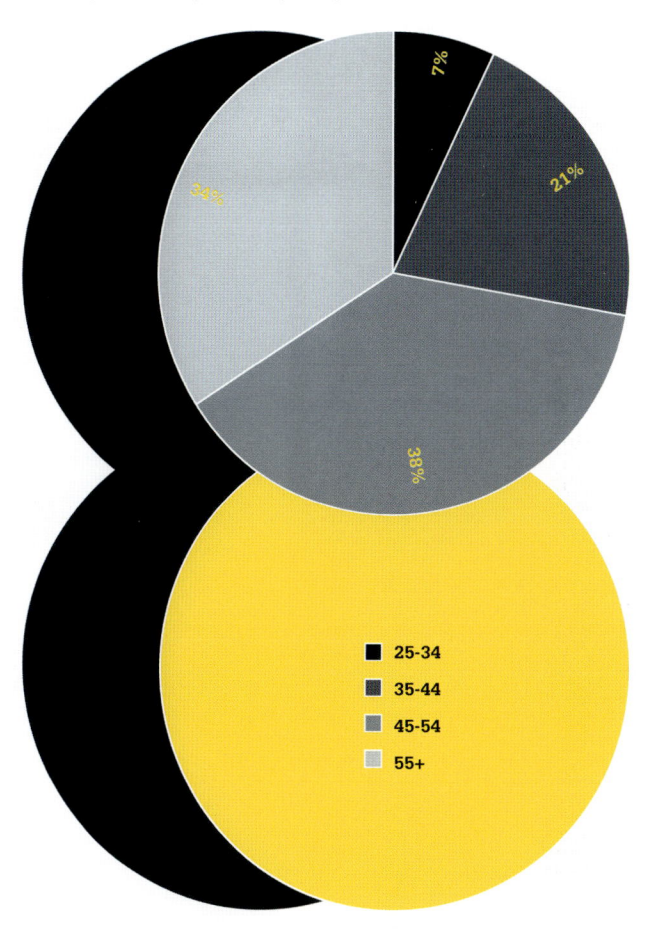

7%
21%
38%
24%

■ 25-34
■ 35-44
■ 45-54
■ 55+

Graphs 239

Everything is OK Poster ::
MINE™ :: www.minesf.com ::

The aim of this poster is to make a note of how people process, absorb, and address the information they receive throughout the course of their daily lives. It pairs objective with subjective information and qualitative with quantitative information and attempts to be formally attractive while at the same time maintaining a certain amount of crudeness in its content. In other words, the idea is to create something dark and somber, while at the same time revealing the idiosyncrasies of a gleaming banality.

Smart Moves ::
Lichtwitz – Büro für visuelle Kommunikation :: www.lichtwitz.com ::

The concept underlying Vienna City Council's presentation at the international public transport fair is based on the use of means of transport to get about the city, with this one being the most popular.

The result is a great pie chart drawn on the ground, which transforms the information in a closed loop of intertwined arrows, labeled with simple pictograms.

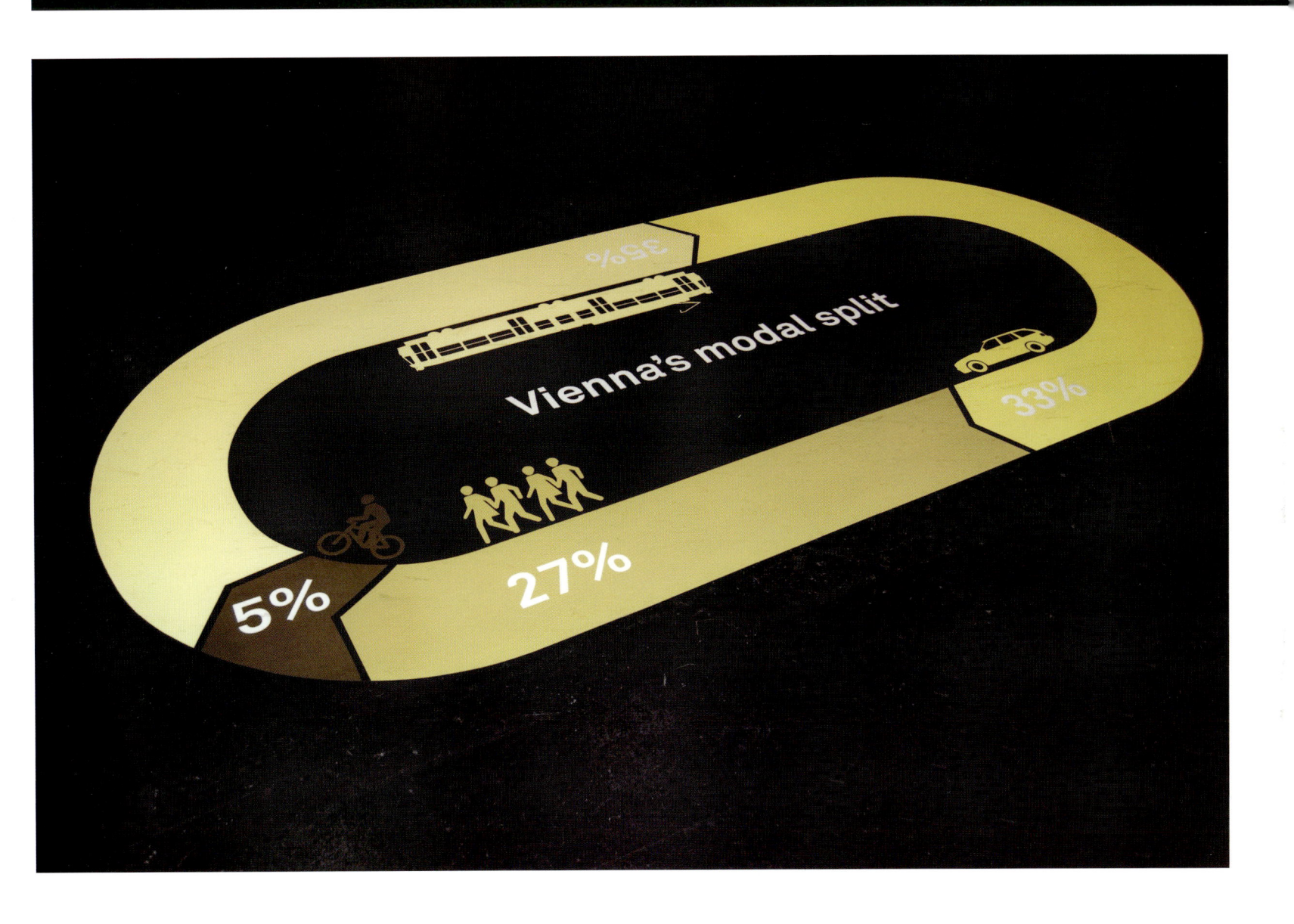

Infact ::
Lava Amsterdam :: www.lava.nl ::

There are several ways in which graphs can be represented, and originality is always appreciated, particularly when dealing with a project in which the comparison of data is the main feature. In this case, the Dutch agency decided to photograph the items in 3-D to obtain the images to represent the information in graph format. Thus, a bar chart, for instance, is composed of thousands of Post-Its.

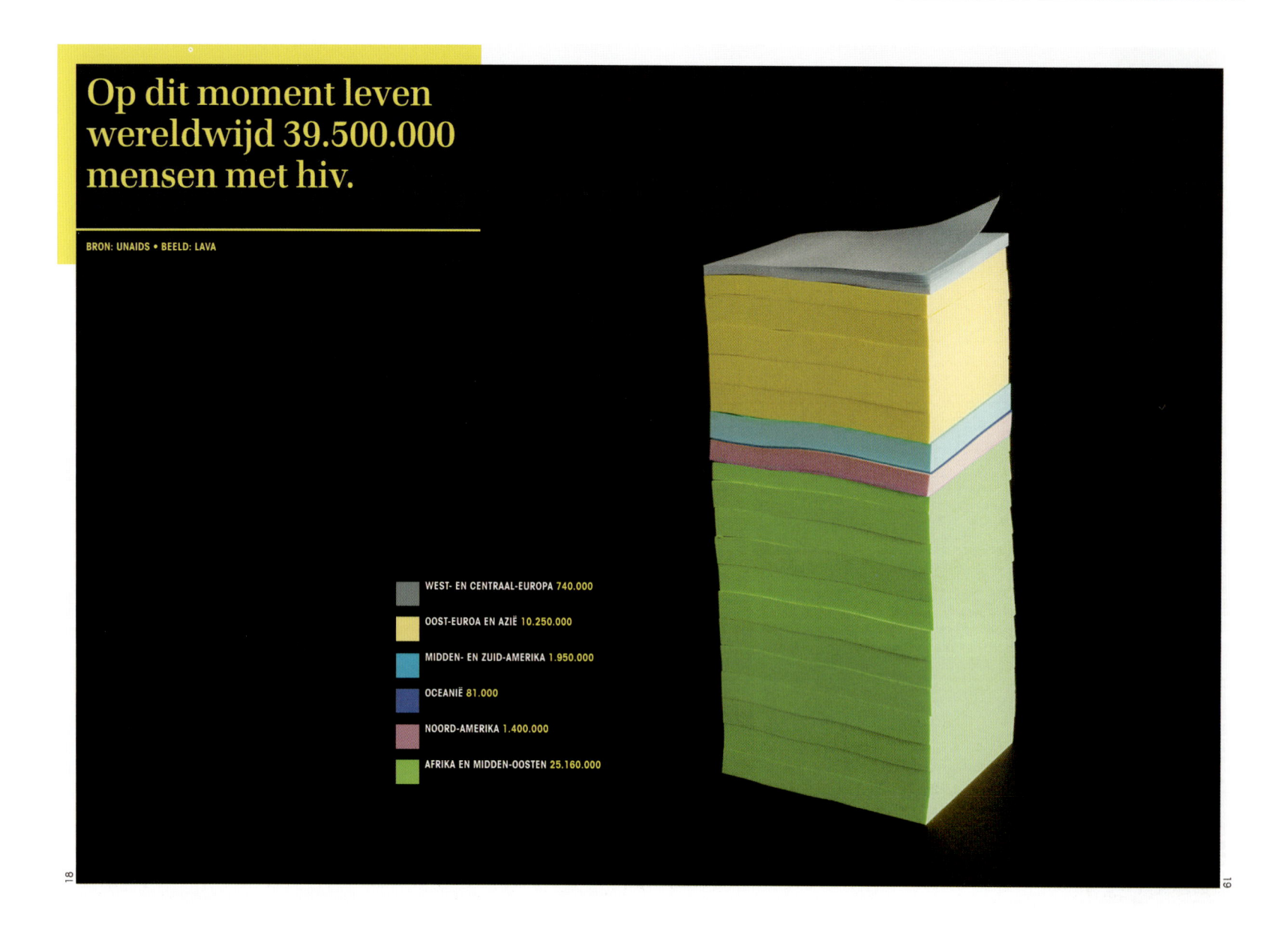

Op dit moment leven wereldwijd 39.500.000 mensen met hiv.

BRON: UNAIDS • BEELD: LAVA

- WEST- EN CENTRAAL-EUROPA 740.000
- OOST-EUROA EN AZIË 10.250.000
- MIDDEN- EN ZUID-AMERIKA 1.950.000
- OCEANIË 81.000
- NOORD-AMERIKA 1.400.000
- AFRIKA EN MIDDEN-OOSTEN 25.160.000

242 **Graphs**

De eerste hiv-infectie in Azië vond 25 jaar geleden plaats. Het was een 48-jarige Japanse hemofilie-patiënt.

BRON: TIME MAGAZINE • BEELDEN: LAVA

EERSTE BEKENDE GEVAL VAN HIV

JAPAN	1983
FILIPIJNEN	1984
THAILAND, HONG KONG	
CHINA, SINGAPORE, Z-KOREA	1985
INDIA, MALEISIË, TAIWAN	1986
PAKISTAN, INDONESIË	1987
NEPAL, MYANMAR	1988
BANGLADESH, LAOS, VIETNAM	1990
CAMBODJA	1991

Graphs 243

RJ Calendar ::
Equus Design :: www.equus-design.com ::

This poster is part of a calendar—created in collaboration with the stationer's RJ Paper and digital imaging specialists Colourscan, which was originally printed in A0 format—in which each month represents an instruction manual. This particular month—August—is a handbook for behavior, in which each letter has been created from a graph depicting information relating to good conduct.

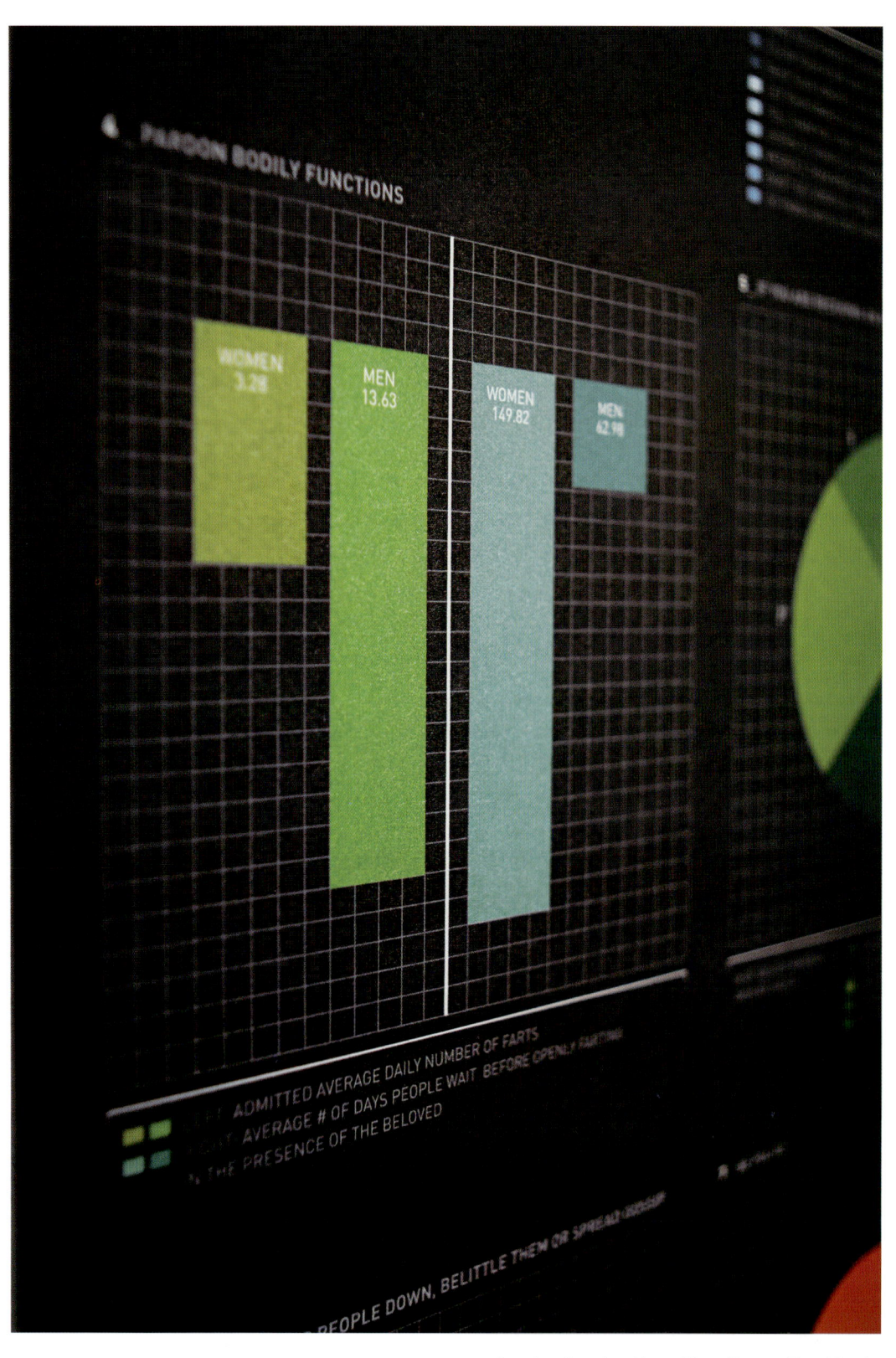

Creative direction: Fanny Khoo. Design: Tom Merckx

244 Graphs

AUGUST_HOW TO BEHAVE

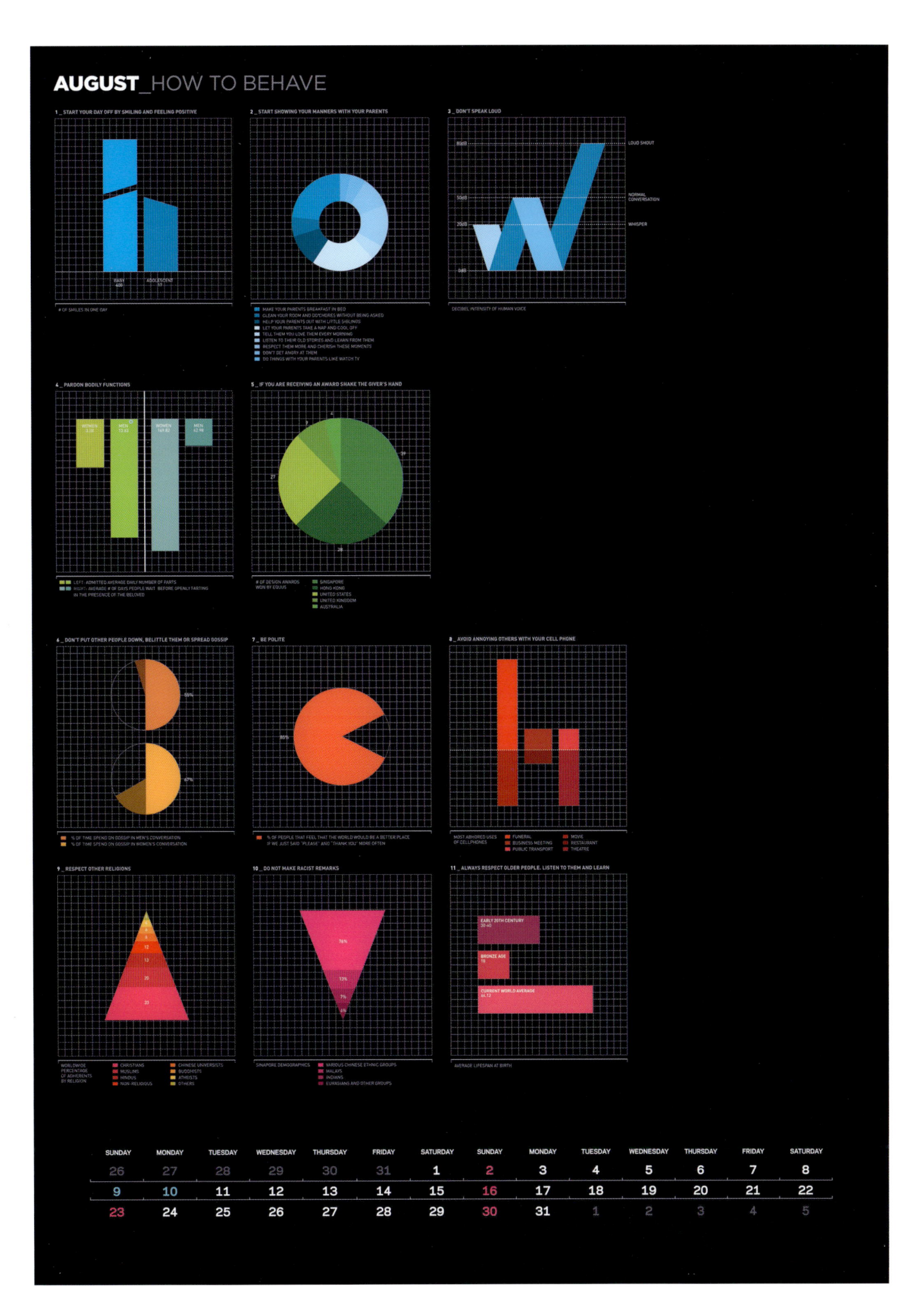

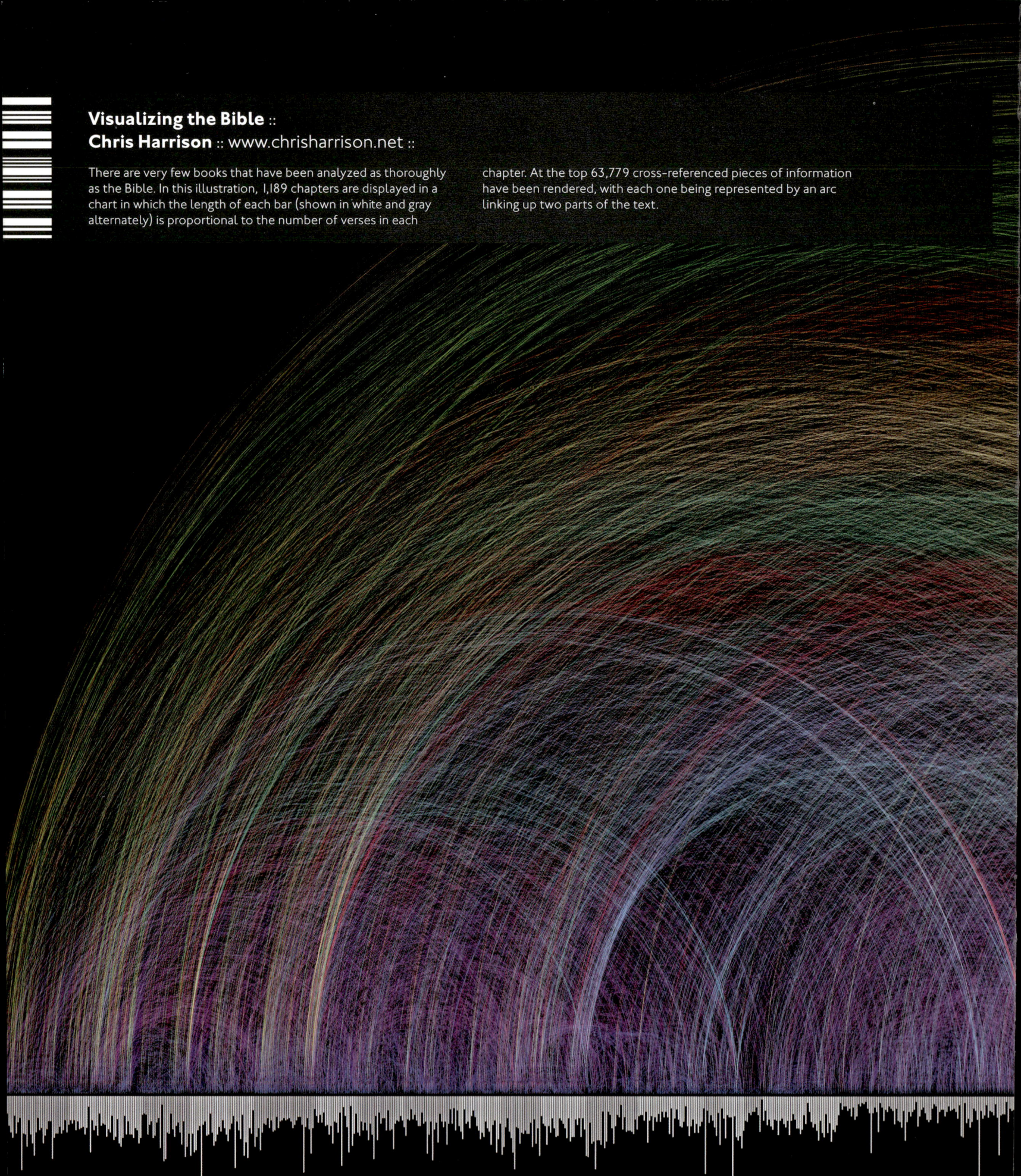

Visualizing the Bible ::
Chris Harrison :: www.chrisharrison.net ::

There are very few books that have been analyzed as thoroughly as the Bible. In this illustration, 1,189 chapters are displayed in a chart in which the length of each bar (shown in white and gray alternately) is proportional to the number of verses in each chapter. At the top 63,779 cross-referenced pieces of information have been rendered, with each one being represented by an arc linking up two parts of the text.

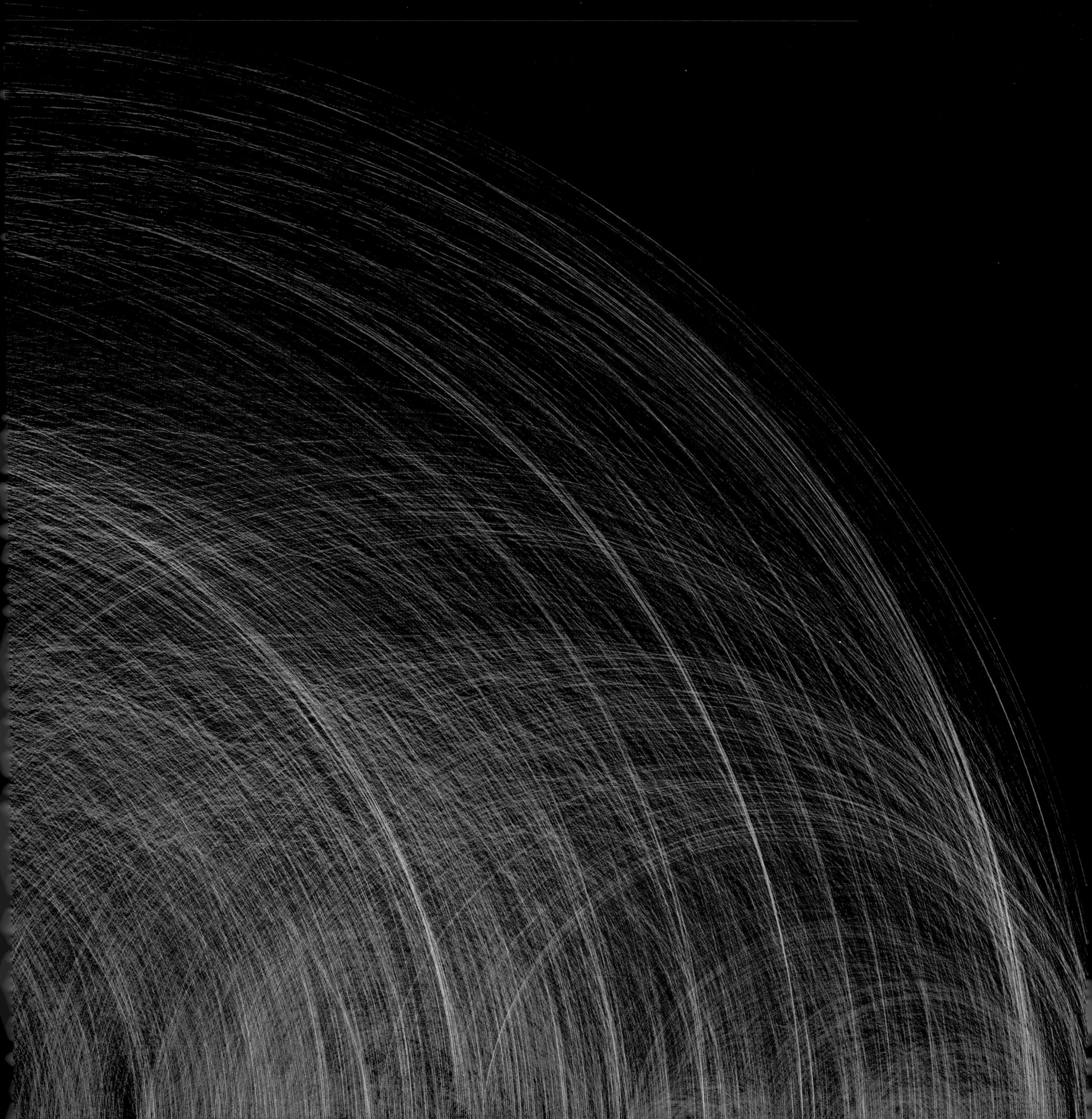

Design in the Creative Economy, a Summary ::
Mijksenaar :: www.mijksenaar.com ::

Many times design is seen as something that is purely artistic and esthetic, but we forget that it is also intrinsically functional. Thus, it is thanks to design that it is possible to organize complex information and present it in such a way that it is easy and pleasant to see. This is what happens in this attractive twenty-four-page public financial report, designed for the Premsela Foundation in Amsterdam.

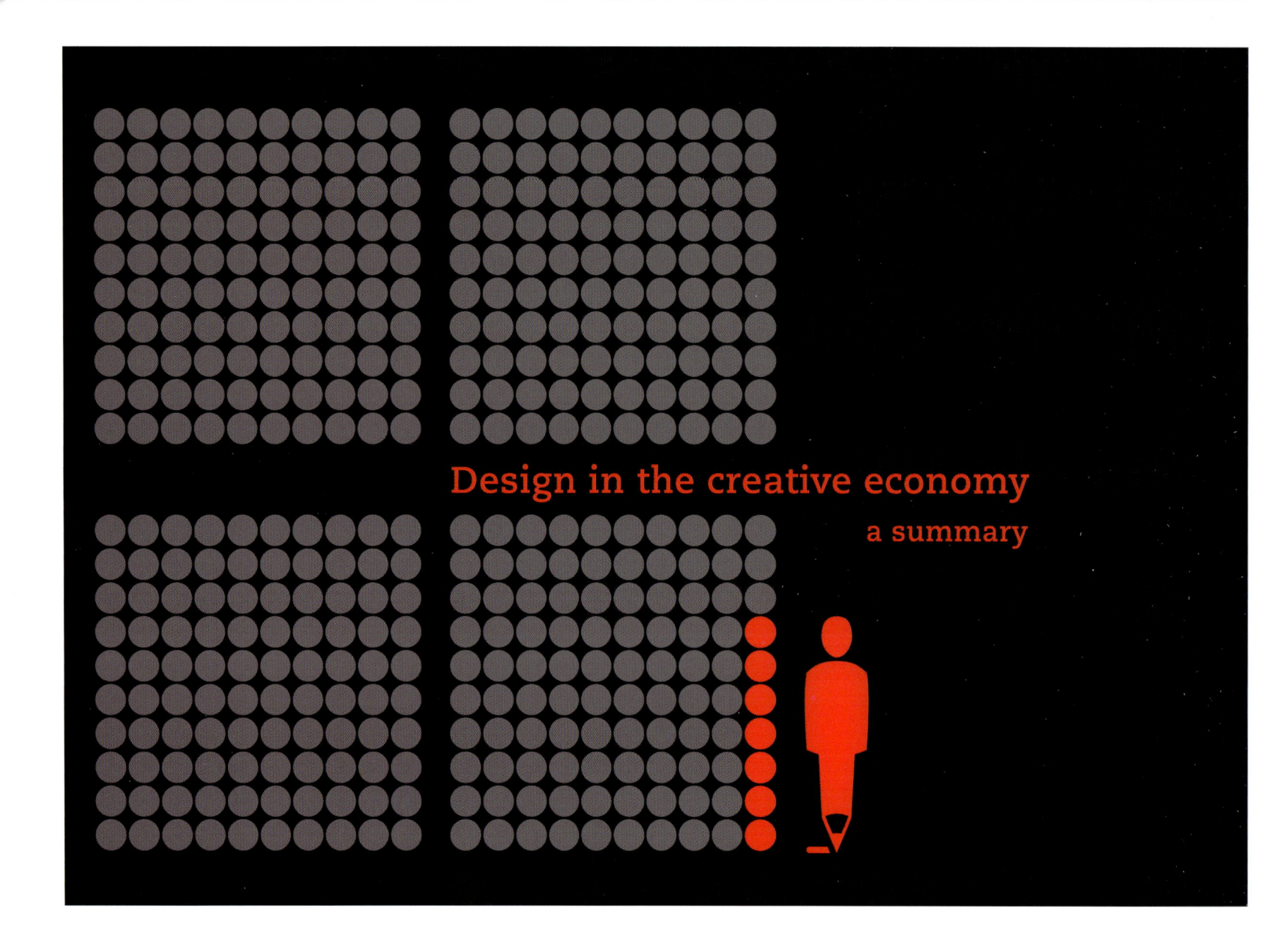

Design in the creative economy
a summary

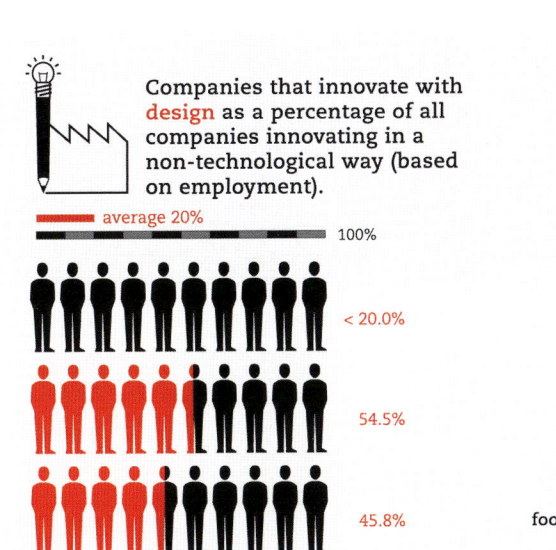

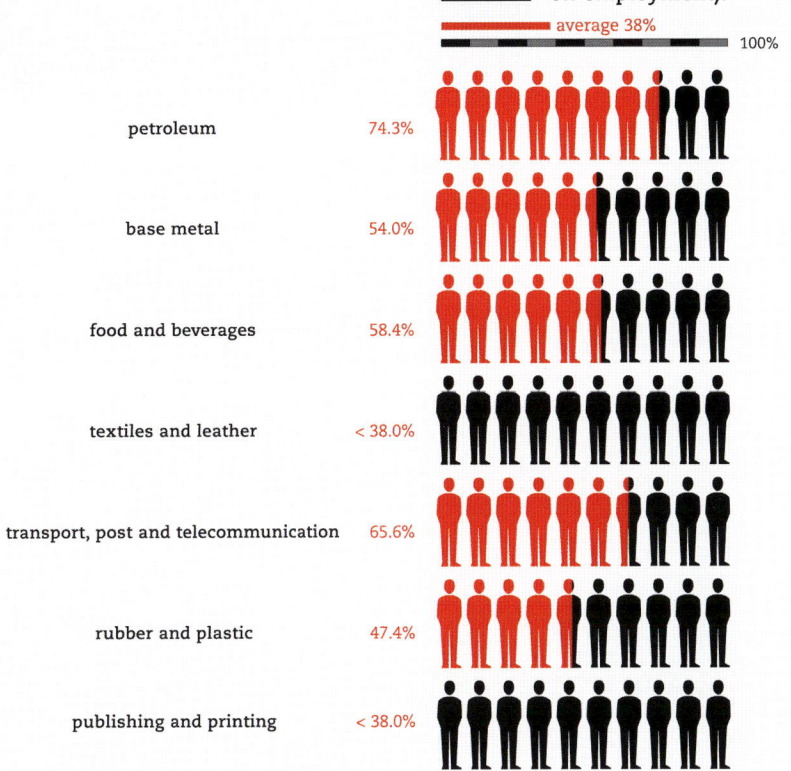

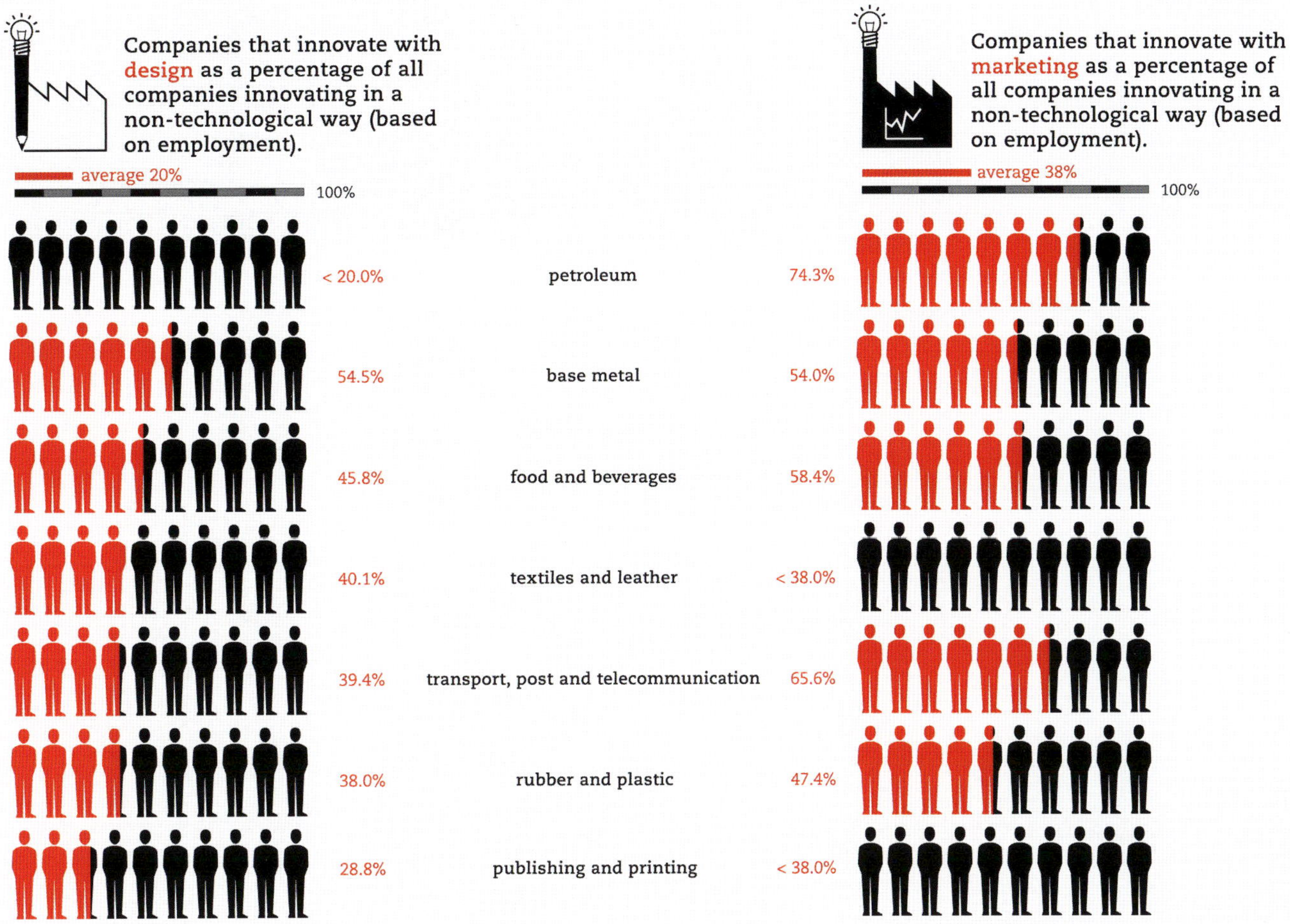

Companies that innovate with **design** as a percentage of all companies innovating in a non-technological way (based on employment).

average 20% — 100%

< 20.0%	petroleum	74.3%
54.5%	base metal	54.0%
45.8%	food and beverages	58.4%
40.1%	textiles and leather	< 38.0%
39.4%	transport, post and telecommunication	65.6%
38.0%	rubber and plastic	47.4%
28.8%	publishing and printing	< 38.0%

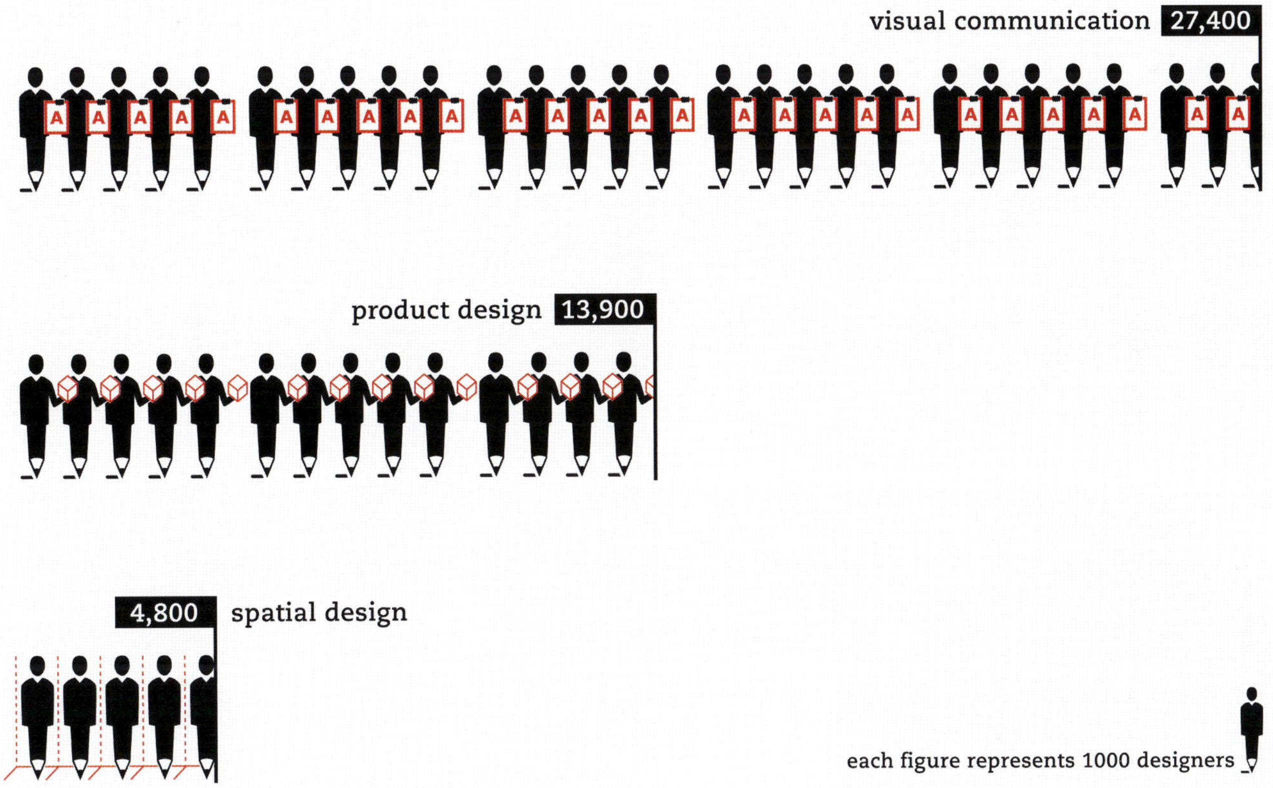

Companies that innovate with **marketing** as a percentage of all companies innovating in a non-technological way (based on employment).

average 38% — 100%

visual communication 27,400

product design 13,900

spatial design 4,800

each figure represents 1000 designers

Graphs 249

BALTIC Chronology ::
Blue River :: blueriver.co.uk ::

Ever since the BALTIC contemporary art center opened its doors in 1999, it has not stopped organizing exhibitions. To have a chronological record of these events, the Blue River team has designed a graph for each year, indicating (in months) the samples taken. They opted to just use white and black to create a visual impact and show the brand in its most minimalist version.

Love Will Tear Us Apart Again ::
The Luxury of Protest :: www.theluxuryofprotest.com ::

One of the songs that has most cover versions is *Love Will Tear Us Apart* by Joy Division, with over eighty-five different recordings. This graph shows the amount of time that has elapsed between these and the original version and provides details such as the name of the artist, and the length and year of the recording. This information has been put in order according to the basic principles of information design in such a way as to make it accessible and help it remain esthetically pleasing.

ADayInTheLife ::
Chris Ro :: www.adearfriend.com ::

This graph explores a different way of expressing a day in the life of a person, without any photographs or literal descriptions. Based on the activities conducted during the course of the day, excluding sleep, the diagram shows the high and low moments: the time is shown in hours on the horizontal axis, while the vertical axis shows the level of activity, divided into themes illustrated in different colors.

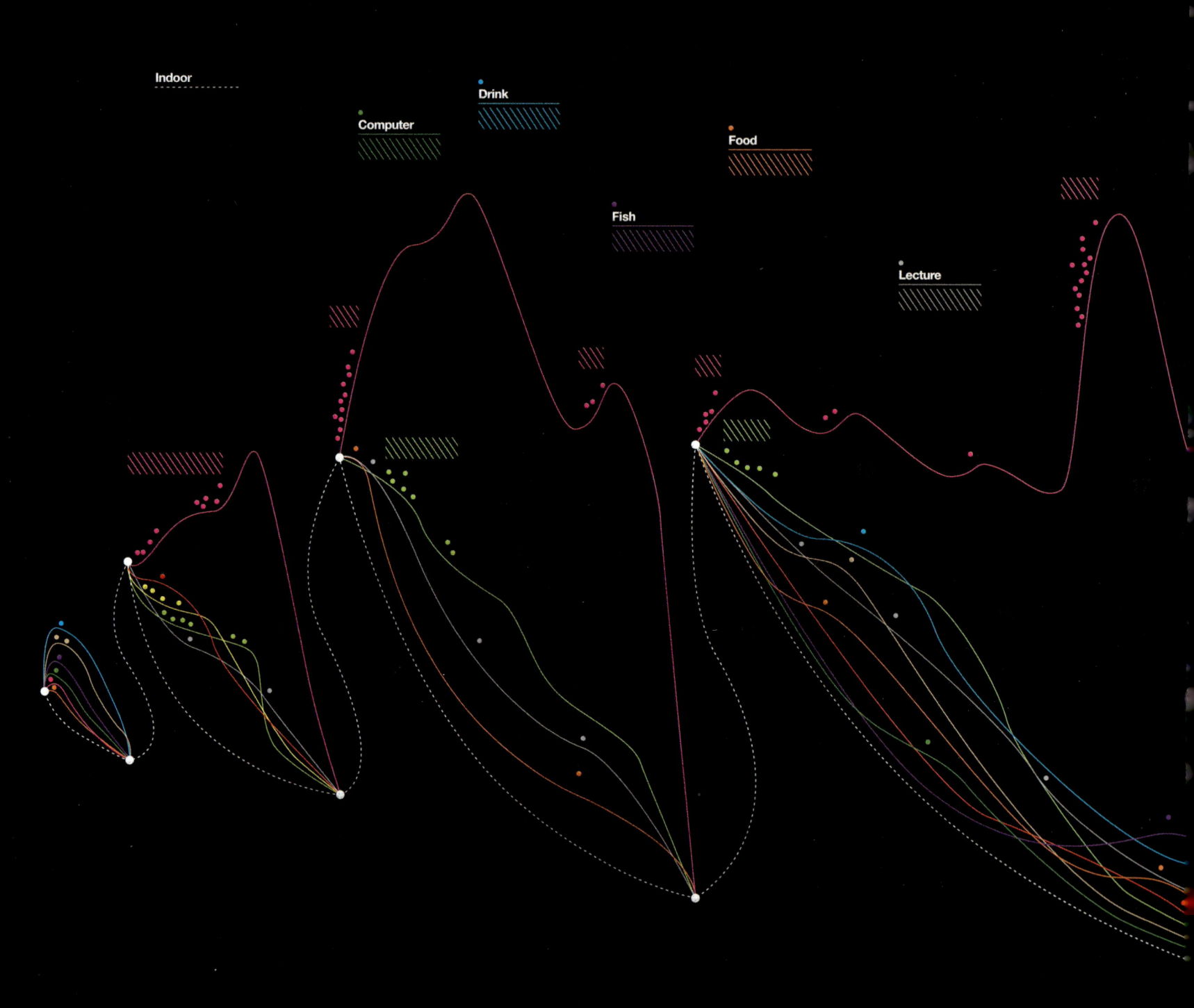

Indoor

Computer

Drink

Food

Fish

Lecture

Phone

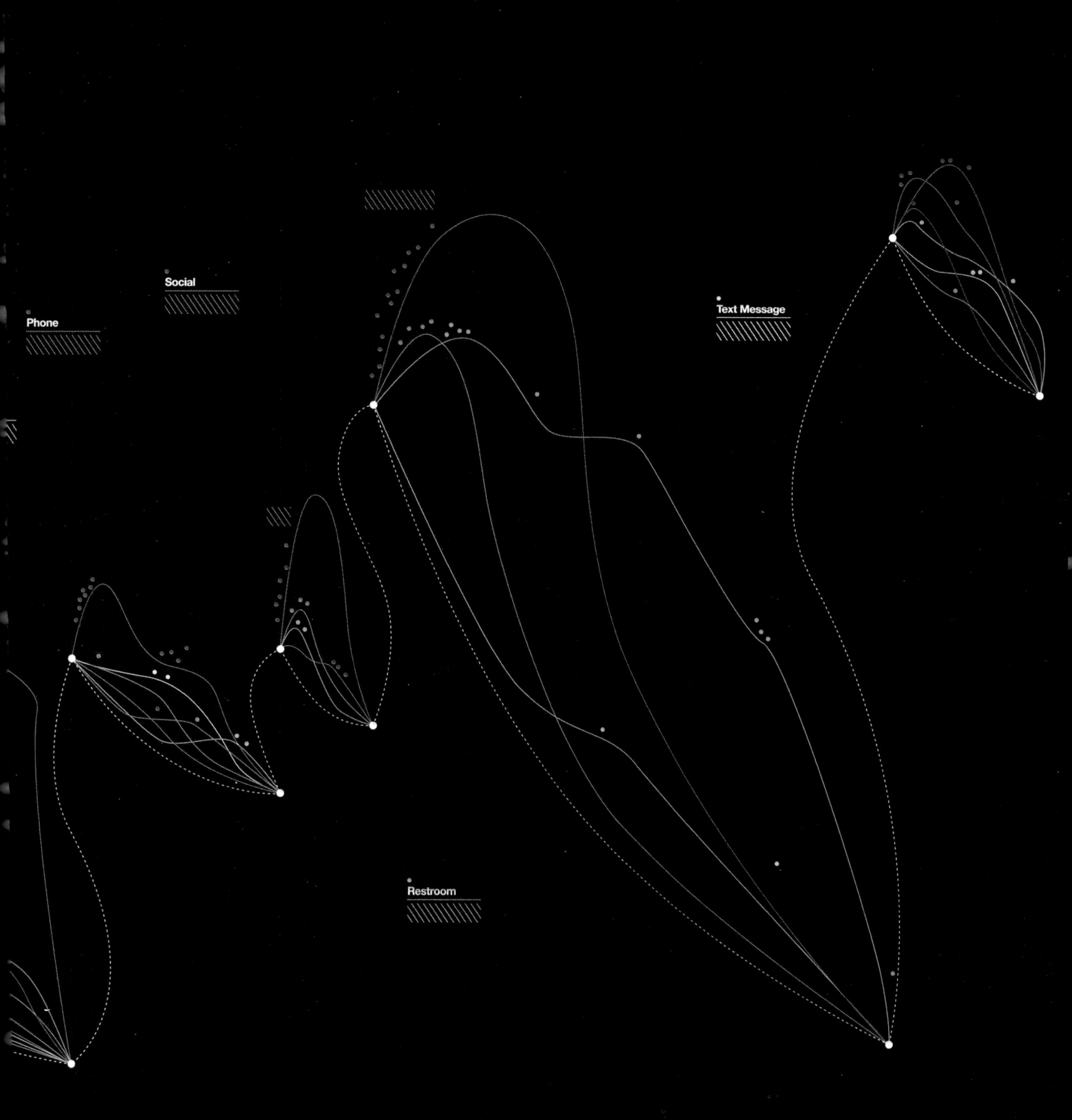

Social

Text Message

Restroom

Index

*S,C,P,F…	234
+ WONKSITE STUDIO +	156
Amorphica Design Research Office	210, 218
André Pahl	180
Andrej Filetin/Fiktiv	108
Andrio Abero	132
Anna Filipova	136, 182, 219
Annelys de Vet	24, 36, 64, 102
Apfel Zet	18, 45, 126
Ariane Spanier	22, 62, 148
Arlene Birt	116, 138
Artroom srl	107
Atelier Aquarium	10, 35, 86
Atelier Chévara etc	63, 184
Atelier for Typography and Graphic Design	44
Blok Design	143
Blue River	250
C2F	96, 103, 120, 128, 181
Catalogtree	110, 208, 237
Chris Harrison	246
Chris Ro	252
Cla-se	19, 213
Coup	34, 174
Cybu Richli	84, 125, 228, 168
Daniel A. Becker	200
Daniel Kaufmann	127
Enric Jardí	130, 204
Equus Design	244
Esam Lee, Heesun Seo	220
Espen Røyseland	22
häfelinger + wagner design	158
Inksurge	226
Jax de León	19, 236
Jennifer Daniel	101, 133
Jessica Scheurer	146
John Yunker	32
Jordi Boix 40Gurus	52, 66
José Manuel Hortelano	154
Julien Antonescu	112
JUNG + WENIG	48

Lava Amsterdam	13, 26, 49, 209, 242
Leftloft	38, 68, 111
Lesley Moore	40, 100, 164
Letterbox	197
Lichtwitz – Büro für visuelle Kommunikation	14, 16, 78, 88, 90, 190, 212, 241
LIGALUX	105, 114, 142
Lorenzo Geiger	54, 94
Lotie	124
LUST	28, 46, 58, 70, 73, 76, 80, 161, 178, 183, 192, 216, 232
Margus Tamm	106, 188
Martin Dominguez	85
me studio	152
Mijksenaar	248
MINE™	240
No Office	12
Øystein Rø	22
Patrick Maun	67
Pau de Riba, Guillem Cardona	172
Per Madsen/Scandinavian DesignLab	98
ps.2 arquitetura + design	198
Rose Zgodzinski	89, 194, 196
Shane Long	97
SLANG	140, 195
Stout/Kramer	162
Studio Laucke Siebein	118
Studio8 Design	160, 176
Supperstudio	170
Sweden Graphics	134
Tanja Bergquist	22
The Luxury of Protest	50, 150, 251
The Partners	27, 74
Thonik	230, 238
Toko	214
Topos Graphics	149
Toxic Design	104
TwoPoints.Net	72, 186
We Ain't Plastic	20
Xavier Barrade	92, 141, 222
Zago	206